Forecasting Examples for Business and Economics Using the SAS® System

SAS Institute Inc.
SAS Campus Drive
Cary, NC 27513

The correct bibliographic citation for this manual is as follows: SAS Institute Inc., *Forecasting Examples for Business and Economics Using the SAS® System*, Cary, NC: SAS Institute Inc., 1996. 404 pp.

Forecasting Examples for Business and Economics Using the SAS® System

ISBN 1-55544-763-5

SAS Institute Inc., SAS Campus Drive, Cary, North Carolina 27513.

1st printing, April 1996

Doc P8, 030796

Contents

Credits

Documentation

Design and Production	Design, Production, and Printing Services
Style Programming	Publications Technology Development
Technical Review	James J. Ashton, Gregory L. Brown, Donald J. Erdman, Anwar El-Jawhari, Minbo Kim, Tae Yoon Lee, Mark R. Little, Donna E. Woodward
Writing and Editing	Brent L. Cohen, Susan H. McCoy, Josephine P. Pope, James D. Seabolt, David A. Teal

Acknowledgments

David Dickey and Craig Newmark of North Carolina State University, Raleigh, NC, have been especially helpful in providing technical reviews of *Forecasting Examples for Business and Economics Using the SAS® System.*

The final responsibility for the SAS System lies with SAS Institute alone. We hope you will always let us know your opinions about the SAS System and its documentation. It is through your participation that the progress of SAS software has been accomplished.

The Staff of SAS Institute Inc.

Introduction: The Example Data Sets

Featured Tools:

- □ DATA step
- □ GPLOT procedure

This introduction describes the data sets used for the examples in this book. The examples in this chapter show how to create a SAS data set from the raw data. Some examples show how to plot the data.

The Almon Data Set

The Almon data set contains quarterly totals of capital expenditures (Y) and appropriations (X) for the U.S. for the period first quarter 1953 to fourth quarter 1966, as reported by the National Industrial Conference Board. The data on expenditures for 1967 are missing. You create a date variable and three indicator variables for the quarters in the DATA step. The data are taken from Maddala (1977).

Program

Create the ALMON data set. Use the INTNX function to create the DATE variable. Use Boolean operators to create the Q1, Q2, and Q3 indicator variables.

```
data almon;
   input y x @@;
   retain date '1oct52'd;
   date=intnx('qtr',date,1);
   format date yyq.;
   qtr = mod( _n_-1, 4 ) + 1;
   q1  = qtr=1;
   q2  = qtr=2;
   q3  = qtr=3;
   label y='Capital Expenditures'
         x='Appropriations';
   title 'National Industrial Conference Board Data';
   datalines;
2071 1660   2077 1926   2078 2181   2043 1897   2062 1695
2067 1705   1964 1731   1981 2151   1914 2556   1991 3152
2129 3763   2309 3903   2614 3912   2896 3571   3058 3199
3309 3262   3446 3476   3466 2993   3435 2262   3183 2011
2697 1511   2338 1631   2140 1990   2012 1993   2071 2520
2192 2804   2240 2919   2421 3024   2639 2725   2733 2321
2721 2131   2640 2552   2513 2234   2448 2282   2429 2533
2516 2517   2534 2772   2494 2380   2596 2568   2572 2944
2601 2629   2648 3133   2840 3449   2937 3764   3136 3983
3299 4381   3514 4786   3815 4094   4093 4870   4262 5344
4531 5433   4825 5911   5160 6109   5319 6542   5574 5785
5749 5707     .  5412     .  5465     .  5550     .  5465
;
```

The CES Production Function Data Set

The cross-sectional CES production function data set contains observations of the capital (K) and labor (L) inputs and the outputs (Q) of 25 firms. The data are found in Kmenta (1986).

Program

Create the CES data set.

```
data ces;
   input id k l q @@;
   label k ='Capital Input'
         l ='Labor Input'
         q ='Output';
   datalines;
01 8 23 106.00  02 9 14  81.08  03 4 38  72.80  04 2 97  57.34
05 6 11  66.79  06 6 43  98.23  07 3 93  82.68  08 6 49  99.77
09 8 36 110.00  10 8 43 118.93  11 4 61  95.05  12 8 31 112.83
13 3 57  64.54  14 6 97 137.22  15 4 93  86.17  16 2 72  56.25
17 3 61  81.10  18 3 97  65.23  19 9 89 149.56  20 3 25  65.43
21 1 81  36.06  22 4 11  56.92  23 2 64  49.59  24 3 10  43.21
25 6 71 121.24
;
```

The Construction Data Set

The Construction data are taken from the *Survey of Current Business* and *Business Statistics*. They are monthly data from January 1983 to October 1989 for three variables:

CONTRCTS is total U.S. construction contracts in millions of dollars.

INTRATE is the average new home mortgage rate.

HSTARTS is the number of private housing starts in thousands of units.

Program

Create the CONSTR data set.

```
data constr;
  input date:monyy5. contrcts intrate hstarts @@;
  format date monyy5.;
  title 'Construction Data';
  datalines;
```

```
JAN83 11358 13.00   91.3  FEB83 11355 12.62   96.3
MAR83 16100 12.97  134.6  APR83 16315 12.02  135.8
MAY83 19205 12.21  174.9  JUN83 20263 11.90  173.2
JUL83 16885 12.02  161.6  AUG83 19441 12.01  176.8
SEP83 17379 12.08  154.9  OCT83 16028 11.80  159.3
NOV83 15401 11.82  136.0  DEC83 13518 11.94  108.3
JAN84 14023 11.80  109.1  FEB84 14442 11.78  130.0
MAR84 17916 11.56  137.5  APR84 17655 11.55  172.7
MAY84 21990 11.68  180.7  JUN84 20036 11.61  184.0
JUL84 19224 11.91  162.1  AUG84 19367 11.89  147.4
SEP84 16923 12.03  148.5  OCT84 18413 12.27  152.3
NOV84 16616 12.27  126.2  DEC84 14220 12.05   98.9
JAN85 15154 11.77  105.4  FEB85 13652 11.74   95.8
MAR85 20004 11.42  145.2  APR85 20692 11.55  176.0
MAY85 22532 11.55  170.5  JUN85 20043 11.31  163.4
JUL85 22047 10.94  160.7  AUG85 21055 10.78  160.7
SEP85 20541 10.69  147.7  OCT85 21715 10.64  173.0
NOV85 17691 10.55  124.1  DEC85 16276 10.47  120.5
JAN86 15417 10.40  115.6  FEB86 16152 10.21  107.2
MAR86 19617 10.04  151.0  APR86 23754  9.87  188.2
MAY86 23050  9.84  186.6  JUN86 23740  9.74  183.6
JUL86 23621  9.89  172.0  AUG86 21884  9.84  163.8
SEP86 21763  9.74  154.0  OCT86 21862  9.57  154.8
NOV86 17998  9.45  115.6  DEC86 17982  9.28  113.0
JAN87 16694  9.14  105.1  FEB87 15729  8.87  102.8
MAR87 22622  8.77  141.2  APR87 23077  8.84  159.3
MAY87 22054  8.99  158.0  JUN87 25703  9.05  162.9
JUL87 24567  9.01  152.4  AUG87 23836  9.01  143.6
SEP87 22418  9.03  152.0  OCT87 23360  8.86  139.1
NOV87 18663  8.92  118.8  DEC87 19224  8.78   85.4
JAN88 15113  8.75   78.2  FEB88 17496  8.76   90.2
MAR88 22257  8.77  128.8  APR88 22344  8.76  153.2
MAY88 24138  8.59  140.2  JUN88 26940  8.90  150.2
JUL88 22309  8.80  137.0  AUG88 24826  8.68  136.8
SEP88 22670  8.90  131.1  OCT88 22223  8.77  135.1
NOV88 19767  9.05  113.0  DEC88 19125  9.04   94.2
JAN89 15776  9.20  100.1  FEB89 15086  9.46   85.8
MAR89 21080  9.63  117.8  APR89 21725  9.88  129.4
MAY89 23796  9.82  131.7  JUN89 24650 10.09  143.2
JUL89 22330 10.06  134.7  AUG89 24128  9.83  122.4
SEP89 23371  9.87  109.3  OCT89 22669  9.77  130.1
;
```

Plot the CONTRCTS variable.

```
goptions cback=white colors=(black) border reset=(axis symbol);

axis1 offset=(1 cm)
      label=('Year') minor=none
      order=('01jan83'd to '01jan90'd by year);
axis2 label=(angle=90 'Construction Contracts')
      order=(10000 to 30000 by 5000);

symbol1 i=join;

proc gplot data=constr;
   format date year4.;
   plot contrcts*date / haxis=axis1
                        vaxis=axis2
                        vminor=1;
   title2 'Construction Contracts';
run;
```

Output 1
Plot of CONTRCTS Variable

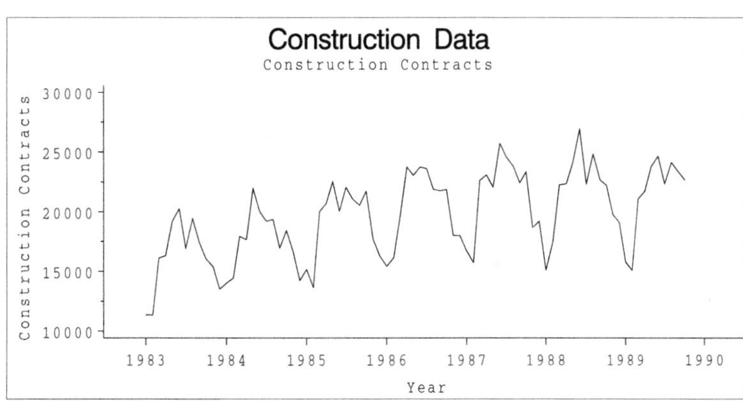

When you plot time series data with PROC GPLOT, the procedure prints a warning message to the log to indicate that the intervals on the axis are not evenly spaced. This message simply reflects the fact that there is a different number of days in each month. This warning message can be ignored.

Plot the INTRATE variable.

```
axis2 label=(angle=90 'Interest Rate')
      order=(8.0 to 14.0 by 1);
```

```
proc gplot data=constr;
   format date year4.;
   plot intrate*date / haxis=axis1
                       vaxis=axis2
                       vminor=1;
   title2 'Interest Rates';
run;
```

Output 2
Plot of INTRATE Variable

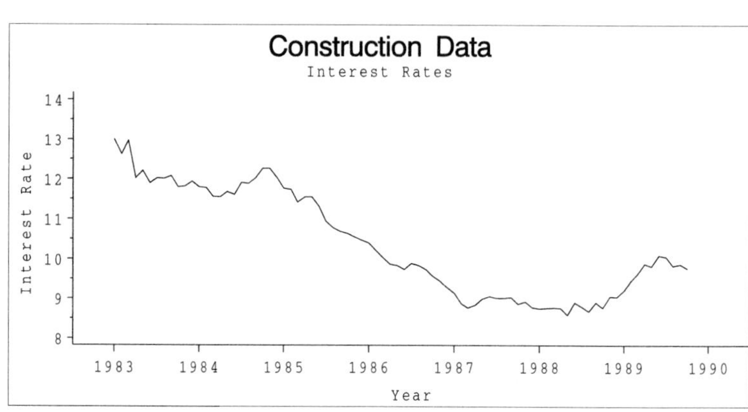

Plot the HSTARTS variable.

```
axis2 label=(angle=90 'Housing Starts')
      order=(75 to 200 by 25);

proc gplot data=constr;
   format date year4.;
   plot hstarts*date / haxis=axis1
                       vaxis=axis2
                       vminor=none;
   title2 'Housing Starts';
run;
```

Output 3
Plot of HSTARTS Variable

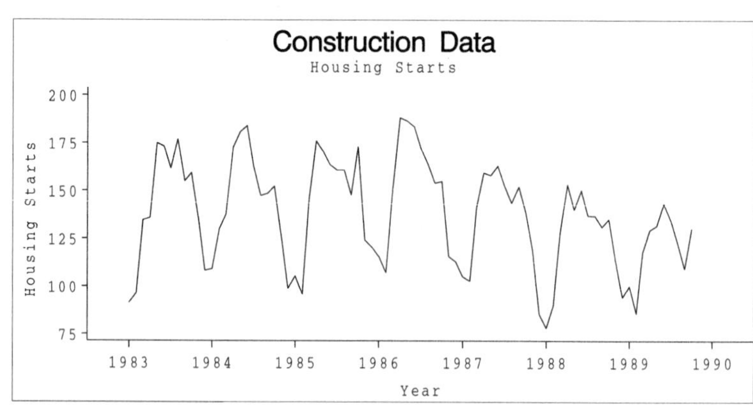

The Consumption Data Set

The consumption data are taken from the *Survey of Current Business*. These are monthly data for the period September 1982 to June 1990 for the following three variables:

C_N
: is total personal outlays (consumption) in billions of nominal U.S. dollars.

DI_N
: is disposable personal income in billions of nominal U.S. dollars.

CPI
: is US CPI 1982-84=100, all urban consumers U.S. city average (from the U.S. Department of Labor, Bureau of Labor Statistics).

You create the C and DI variables in the DATA step by dividing the nominal values by the value of CPI. These variables are consumption and disposable income expressed in constant dollars. Create the C_1 variable by taking the one-month lag of the C variable. The data for consumption in 1990 are missing.

Program

Create the CONSUME data set.

```
data consume;
   format date monyy.;
   input date:monyy5. di_n c_n cpi @@;
      c = c_n/cpi;
     di = di_n/cpi;
    c_1 = lag(c);
   label di='Real Disposable Income in Billions 1982$'
         c='Real Consumption in Billions of 1982$'
         c_1='1 Month Lagged Real C in Billions 1982$';
   title 'Consume Data';
   datalines;
SEP82 2283.2 2140.1  .979  OCT82 2299.8 2157.9  .982
NOV82 2321.7 2178.7  .980  DEC82 2332.7 2188.1  .976
JAN83 2344.3 2196.9  .978  FEB83 2339.2 2202.4  .979
MAR83 2353.7 2219.3  .979  APR83 2382.0 2249.9  .986
MAY83 2397.4 2276.9  .992  JUN83 2406.9 2296.3  .995
JUL83 2438.6 2318.1  .999  AUG83 2433.2 2329.8 1.002
SEP83 2457.7 2332.4 1.007  OCT83 2499.1 2366.2 1.010
NOV83 2528.7 2378.4 1.012  DEC83 2555.9 2402.9 1.013
JAN84 2585.2 2437.2 1.019  FEB84 2614.3 2414.2 1.024
MAR84 2635.9 2440.8 1.026  APR84 2637.8 2469.6 1.031
MAY84 2637.0 2489.7 1.034  JUN84 2653.5 2510.7 1.037
JUL84 2675.9 2508.1 1.041  AUG84 2688.0 2522.3 1.045
```

```
SEP84 2709.4 2547.3 1.050  OCT84 2710.9 2540.7 1.053
NOV84 2725.5 2585.2 1.053  DEC84 2749.5 2588.1 1.053
JAN85 2771.2 2620.3 1.055  FEB85 2764.6 2633.6 1.060
MAR85 2757.9 2653.6 1.064  APR85 2832.9 2654.0 1.069
MAY85 2890.2 2701.1 1.073  JUN85 2829.2 2693.7 1.076
JUL85 2835.1 2709.8 1.078  AUG85 2837.4 2742.1 1.080
SEP85 2847.5 2788.4 1.083  OCT85 2877.2 2764.0 1.087
NOV85 2887.5 2781.1 1.090  DEC85 2933.7 2818.2 1.093
JAN86 2944.9 2828.6 1.096  FEB86 2958.1 2819.2 1.093
MAR86 2974.6 2822.1 1.088  APR86 3010.6 2837.0 1.086
MAY86 3004.5 2859.1 1.089  JUN86 3004.2 2858.3 1.095
JUL86 3013.5 2882.5 1.095  AUG86 3022.2 2903.4 1.097
SEP86 3037.0 2967.1 1.102  OCT86 3047.4 2937.4 1.103
NOV86 3061.2 2944.5 1.104  DEC86 3081.4 3002.4 1.105
JAN87 3112.3 2965.1 1.112  FEB87 3149.5 3030.0 1.116
MAR87 3157.6 3039.5 1.121  APR87 3044.2 3065.0 1.127
MAY87 3163.6 3073.4 1.131  JUN87 3169.2 3101.3 1.135
JUL87 3192.5 3123.5 1.138  AUG87 3213.9 3158.9 1.144
SEP87 3227.0 3152.5 1.150  OCT87 3293.7 3158.5 1.153
NOV87 3281.6 3165.5 1.154  DEC87 3331.6 3193.7 1.154
JAN88 3341.9 3225.3 1.157  FEB88 3381.4 3235.1 1.160
MAR88 3412.6 3266.2 1.165  APR88 3399.3 3268.6 1.171
MAY88 3441.8 3295.5 1.175  JUN88 3477.0 3331.8 1.180
JUL88 3507.4 3345.2 1.185  AUG88 3516.8 3370.1 1.190
SEP88 3536.0 3374.3 1.198  OCT88 3585.0 3414.8 1.202
NOV88 3560.8 3427.8 1.203  DEC88 3590.8 3448.6 1.205
JAN89 3618.6 3460.8 1.211  FEB89 3669.1 3475.7 1.216
MAR89 3697.5 3479.4 1.223  APR89 3676.5 3518.9 1.231
MAY89 3696.2 3527.5 1.238  JUN89 3719.3 3539.0 1.241
JUL89 3740.1 3569.0 1.244  AUG89 3741.0 3597.8 1.246
SEP89 3749.0 3599.6 1.250  OCT89 3772.9 3605.0 1.256
NOV89 3802.1 3618.1 1.259  DEC89 3823.9 3653.4 1.261
JAN90 3861.2      .  1.274  FEB90 3886.1      .  1.280
MAR90 3915.9      .  1.287  APR90 3915.5      .  1.289
MAY90 3927.7      .  1.292  JUN90 3945.7      .  1.299
;
```

The Dow Jones Industrials Index Data Set

The Dow Jones Industrials Index data are taken from the *Survey of Current Business* and *Business Statistics.* The Dow Jones Industrials Index is an index of 30 industrial firms' stock prices. The values in this data set represent monthly averages of the end-of-day values for the index for the period January 1984 to February 1994.

Program

Create the DJM data set.

```
data djm;
   input date:monyy5. djiam @@;
   format date monyy5.;
   title 'Dow Jones Index Data';
   title2 'Monthly Average';
   datalines;
jan84 1258.89 feb84 1164.46 mar84 1161.97 apr84 1152.71
may84 1143.42 jun84 1121.14 jul84 1113.27 aug84 1212.82
sep84 1213.51 oct84 1199.30 nov84 1211.30 dec84 1188.96
jan85 1238.16 feb85 1283.23 mar85 1268.83 apr85 1266.36
may85 1279.40 jun85 1314.00 jul85 1343.17 aug85 1326.18
sep85 1317.95 oct85 1351.58 nov85 1432.88 dec85 1517.02
jan86 1534.86 feb86 1652.73 mar86 1757.35 apr86 1807.05
may86 1801.80 jun86 1867.70 jul86 1809.92 aug86 1843.45
sep86 1813.47 oct86 1817.04 nov86 1883.65 dec86 1924.07
jan87 2065.13 feb87 2202.34 mar87 2292.61 apr87 2302.64
may87 2291.11 jun87 2384.02 jul87 2481.72 aug87 2655.01
sep87 2570.80 oct87 2224.59 nov87 1931.86 dec87 1910.07
jan88 1947.35 feb88 1980.65 mar88 2044.31 apr88 2036.13
may88 1988.91 jun88 2104.94 jul88 2104.22 aug88 2051.29
sep88 2080.06 oct88 2144.31 nov88 2099.04 dec88 2148.58
jan89 2234.68 feb89 2304.30 mar89 2283.11 apr89 2348.91
may89 2439.55 jun89 2494.90 jul89 2554.03 aug89 2691.11
sep89 2693.41 oct89 2692.01 nov89 2642.49 dec89 2728.47
jan90 2679.24 feb90 2614.18 mar90 2700.13 apr90 2708.26
may90 2793.81 jun90 2894.82 jul90 2934.23 aug90 2681.89
sep90 2550.69 oct90 2460.54 nov90 2518.56 dec90 2610.92
jan91 2587.60 feb91 2863.04 mar91 2920.11 apr91 2925.53
may91 2928.42 jun91 2968.13 jul91 2978.18 aug91 3006.08
sep91 3010.35 oct91 3019.73 nov91 2986.12 dec91 2958.64
jan92 3227.06 feb92 3257.27 mar92 3247.41 apr92 3294.08
may92 3376.78 jun92 3337.79 jul92 3329.40 aug92 3307.45
sep92 3293.92 oct92 3198.69 nov92 3238.49 dec92 3303.15
jan93 3277.71 feb93 3367.26 mar93 3440.73 apr93 3423.62
may93 3478.17 jun93 3513.81 jul93 3529.43 aug93 3597.01
```

```
sep93 3592.28 oct93 3625.80 nov93 3674.69 dec93 3743.62
jan94 3868.36 feb94 3905.61
;
```

Plot the Dow Jones Index data.

```
goptions cback=white colors=(black) border reset=(axis symbol);

axis1 offset=(1 cm)
      label=('Year') minor=none
      order=('01jan84'd to '01jan95'd by year);
axis2 label=(angle=90 'Dow Jones Index')
      order=(1000 to 4000 by 500);

symbol1 i=join;

proc gplot data=djm;
   format date year4.;
   plot djiam*date / haxis=axis1
                     vaxis=axis2
                     vminor=1;
run;
```

Output 4
Plot of DJIAM Variable

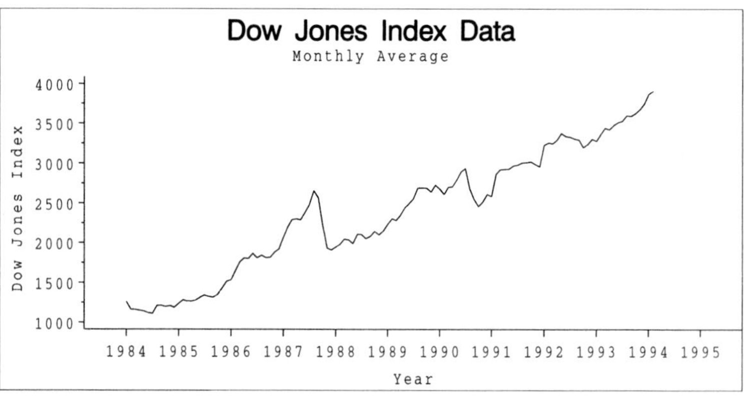

The Driver Casualties Data Set

The driver casualties data are taken from Harvey (1989). The INJURIES variable contains the number of deaths and serious injuries to car drivers on roads in Great Britain during the time period January 1980 to December 1984. Twelve missing values are added to the end of the data set for use in the example. In January 1983, a mandatory seatbelt law took effect. The BELTLAW variable takes on the value 0 before January 1, 1983, and it takes on the value 1 thereafter.

Program

Create the DRIVERS data set.

```
data drivers;
   format date monyy.;
   input date:monyy5. injuries @@;
   beltlaw = (date ge '01jan83'd);
   title 'Driver Casualties Data';
   title2 'monthly totals';
   datalines;
jan80  1665  feb80  1361  mar80  1506  apr80  1360
may80  1453  jun80  1522  jul80  1460  aug80  1552
sep80  1548  oct80  1827  nov80  1737  dec80  1941
jan81  1474  feb81  1458  mar81  1542  apr81  1404
may81  1522  jun81  1385  jul81  1641  aug81  1510
sep81  1681  oct81  1938  nov81  1868  dec81  1726
jan82  1456  feb82  1445  mar82  1456  apr82  1365
may82  1487  jun82  1558  jul82  1488  aug82  1684
sep82  1594  oct82  1850  nov82  1998  dec82  2079
jan83  1494  feb83  1057  mar83  1218  apr83  1168
may83  1236  jun83  1076  jul83  1174  aug83  1139
sep83  1427  oct83  1487  nov83  1483  dec83  1513
jan84  1357  feb84  1165  mar84  1282  apr84  1110
may84  1297  jun84  1185  jul84  1222  aug84  1284
sep84  1444  oct84  1575  nov84  1737  dec84  1763
jan85  .     feb85  .     mar85  .     apr85  .
may85  .     jun85  .     jul85  .     aug85  .
sep85  .     oct85  .     nov85  .     dec85  .
;
```

Plot the driver casualties data. Include a reference line to indicate the passage of the seatbelt law.

```
goptions cback=white colors=(black) border reset=(axis symbol);

axis1 offset=(1 cm) label=('Year')
      order=('01jan80'd to '01jan85'd by year);
```

```
axis2 label=(angle=90 'Casualties')
      order=(800 to 2200 by 200);

symbol1 i=join l=1 v=star;

proc gplot data=drivers;
   format date year4.;
   plot injuries*date=1 / haxis=axis1
                          vaxis=axis2
                          vminor=1
                          href='01jan83'd
                          lh=2;
run;
```

Output 5
Plot of INJURIES Variable

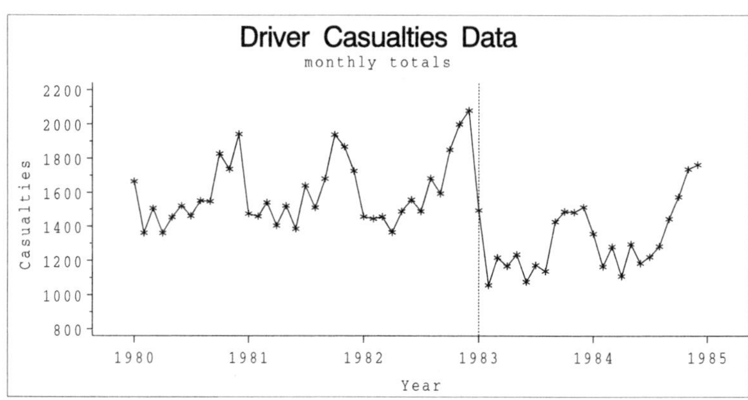

The Electricity Production Data Set

The electricity production data are taken from the *Survey of Current Business* and *Business Statistics.* The values represent total U.S. production of electricity, per month, in millions of kilowatt hours for the period January 1980 to November 1991.

Note: The *Survey of Current Business* no longer reports these data.

Program

Create the ELECTRIC data set.

```
data electric;
   input date:monyy5. elecprod @@;
   format date monyy5.;
   title 'Electricity Production Data';
```

```
   title2 '(millions of kilowatt hours)';
   datalines;
jan80 200005 feb80 188715 mar80 187464 apr80 168720
may80 175734 jun80 189430 jul80 216776 aug80 215393
sep80 191485 oct80 178555 nov80 178550 dec80 195613
jan81 206467 feb81 179613 mar81 185553 apr81 172545
may81 177806 jun81 202702 jul81 220373 aug81 210403
sep81 186838 oct81 181352 nov81 175570 dec81 195590
jan82 209403 feb82 180299 mar82 187687 apr82 172580
may82 177147 jun82 186128 jul82 210584 aug82 205656
sep82 180662 oct82 172966 nov82 173377 dec82 184722
jan83 195579 feb83 172479 mar83 182488 apr83 170372
may83 174392 jun83 191048 jul83 220165 aug83 229957
sep83 195604 oct83 182931 nov83 182949 dec83 212319
jan84 216632 feb84 189564 mar84 200107 apr84 181084
may84 192217 jun84 209649 jul84 221245 aug84 229296
sep84 195198 oct84 190936 nov84 190380 dec84 199996
jan85 227856 feb85 198242 mar85 194970 apr85 184877
may85 196790 jun85 205363 jul85 226722 aug85 226050
sep85 202499 oct85 194789 nov85 192427 dec85 219255
jan86 217470 feb86 192336 mar86 196834 apr86 186074
may86 197315 jun86 215015 jul86 242672 aug86 225166
sep86 206692 oct86 197754 nov86 196432 dec86 213551
jan87 222749 feb87 194034 mar87 201849 apr87 189496
may87 206074 jun87 225589 jul87 247915 aug87 247645
sep87 213008 oct87 203009 nov87 200258 dec87 220500
jan88 237600 feb88 216702 mar88 213838 apr88 195809
may88 208180 jun88 232507 jul88 257235 aug88 267408
sep88 220023 oct88 210377 nov88 209394 dec88 232550
jan89 231343 feb89 219066 mar89 226436 apr89 207749
may89 219803 jun89 235397 jul89 256744 aug89 258335
sep89 226848 oct89 219587 nov89 218980 dec89 258637
jan90 237339 feb90 212708 mar90 225254 apr90 211088
may90 222908 jun90 248935 jul90 266228 aug90 268483
sep90 237869 oct90 224794 nov90 213596 dec90 237257
jan91 247984 feb91 210496 mar91 221117 apr91 208936
may91 233991 jun91 248165 jul91 271492 aug91 267698
sep91 233897 oct91 223180 nov91 221029
;
```

Plot the electricity production data.

```
goptions cback=white colors=(black) border reset=(axis symbol);

axis1 offset=(1 cm)
      label=('Year') minor=none
      order=('01jan80'd to '01jan92'd by year);
```

```
axis2 label=(angle=90 'Electricity Production')
      order=(150000 to 300000 by 50000);

symbol1 i=join;

proc gplot data=electric;
   format date year4.;
   plot elecprod*date / haxis=axis1
                        vaxis=axis2
                        vminor=1;
run;
```

Output 6
Plot of ELECPROD Variable

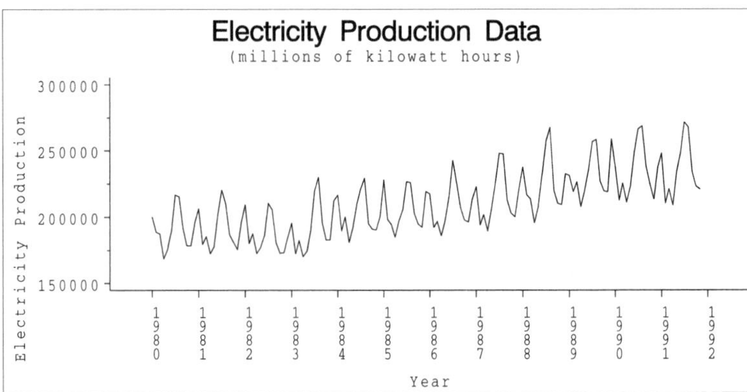

The Exchange Rate Data Set

The exchange rate data set consists of foreign exchange rates for the French franc, the German deutsche mark, and the Italian lira; that is, the exchange rate of foreign currency per U.S. dollar. These are annual data for the period 1977 to 1993. This data set also contains consumer price indices (CPI), money market (MM) rates, and industrial production indices (PROD) for the U.S., France, Germany, and Italy. Another set of variables contains the value of imports (IM) into the U.S. from France, Germany, and Italy. The nominal import values are divided by the U.S. CPI to convert them to constant 1984 U.S. dollar rates. Nine new variables to be used in analyses are computed from the original set of variables. The original variables and the computed variables are described in the list that follows.

The exchange rates, industrial production indices, and CPI data are from the *Economic Report of the President.* Money market rates and imports are from the Department of Commerce's *Statistical Abstract of the U.S.*

The INPUT statement reads the following variables into the EXCH1 data set:

YEAR
: is a date variable.

RATE_FR, RATE_WG, RATE_IT
: are exchange rates for France, Germany, and Italy, expressed as foreign currency per U.S. dollar.

CPI_US, CPI_FR, CPI_WG, CPI_IT
: are consumer price indices for the U.S., France, Germany, and Italy.

IMN_FR, IMN_WG, IMN_IT
: are nominal import values in U.S. dollars for France, Germany, and Italy.

MM_US, MM_FR, MM_WG, MM_IT
: are nominal money market rates for the U.S., France, Germany, and Italy.

PROD_US, PROD_FR, PROD_WG, PROD_IT
: are industrial production indices (1987=100) for the U.S., France, Germany, and Italy.

Use assignment statements to compute the following variables in the DATA step:

IUS, IFR, IWG, IIT
: are inflation rates (the percentage change in consumer price indices), for the U.S., France, Germany, and Italy, respectively. These are computational variables used only for other assignment statements.

IM_FR, IM_WG, IM_IT
: are the real values of imports from France, Germany, and Italy, respectively. The nominal import values are divided by the U.S. CPI to create real import values in constant 1984 dollars.

DI_FR, DI_WG, DI_IT
: are the differences in inflation rates between the U.S. and France, the U.S. and Germany, and the U.S. and Italy, respectively.

DR_FR, DR_WG, DR_IT
: are the differences in real money market rates between the U.S. and France, the U.S. and Germany, and the U.S. and Italy, respectively.

Program

Create the EXCH1 data set.

```
data exch1;
   input year rate_fr rate_wg rate_it cpi_us cpi_fr cpi_wg cpi_it
         imn_fr / imn_wg imn_it mm_us mm_fr mm_wg mm_it prod_us
         prod_fr prod_wg prod_it;
         ius = 100*dif(cpi_us)/lag(cpi_us);
         ifr = 100*dif(cpi_fr)/lag(cpi_fr);
         iwg = 100*dif(cpi_wg)/lag(cpi_wg);
         iit = 100*dif(cpi_it)/lag(cpi_it);
       im_fr = im_frn/cpi_us;
       im_wg = im_wgn/cpi_us;
       im_it = im_itn/cpi_us;
       di_fr = ius - ifr;
       di_wg = ius - iwg;
       di_it = ius - iit;
       dr_fr = (mm_fr-ifr)-(mm_us-ius);
       dr_wg = (mm_wg-iwg)-(mm_us-ius);
       dr_it = (mm_it-iit)-(mm_us-ius);
   label im_fr = 'Imports to US from France in 1984 $'
         im_wg = 'Imports to US from WG in 1984 $'
         im_it = 'Imports to US from Italy in 1984 $'
         di_fr = 'Difference in Inflation Rates US-France'
         di_wg = 'Difference in Inflation Rates US-WG'
         di_it = 'Difference in Inflation Rates US-Italy'
         dr_fr = 'Difference in Real MM Rates US-France'
         dr_wg = 'Difference in Real MM Rates US-WG'
         dr_it = 'Difference in Real MM Rates US-Italy';
   datalines;
1977 4.9161 2.3236  882.78 0.606 0.527 0.769 0.401  3032
   7238  3037   .     .     .     .    78.2  92    88.0  83.8
1978 4.5091 2.0096  849.13 0.652 0.575 0.790 0.451  4051
   9962  4102  7.93  8.16  3.70 11.49  82.6  94    90.4  85.4
1979 4.2567 1.8342  831.11 0.726 0.636 0.823 0.521  4768
  10955  4917 11.20  9.48  6.69 11.86  85.7  99    94.7  91.1
1980 4.2251 1.8175  856.21 0.824 0.723 0.868 0.635  5265
  11693  4325 13.36 12.20  9.10 17.17  84.1  98.9  95.0  96.2
1981 5.4397 2.2631 1138.58 0.909 0.820 0.922 0.753  5851
  11379  5189 16.38 15.26 12.11 19.60  85.7  98.3  93.2  94.7
1982 6.5794 2.4280 1354.00 0.965 0.916 0.970 0.877  5545
  11975  5301 12.26 14.73  8.88 20.18  81.9  97.3  90.3  91.7
1983 7.6204 2.5539 1519.32 0.996 1.005 1.003 1.008  6025
  12695  5455  9.09 12.63  5.78 18.44  84.9  96.5  90.9  88.9
1984 8.7356 2.8454 1756.11 1.039 1.079 1.027 1.115  8113
  16996  7935 10.23 11.88  5.55 17.27  92.8  97.1  93.5  91.8
```

```
1985 8.9800 2.9419 1908.88 1.076 1.142 1.048 1.211  9482
  20239  9674  8.10 10.08  5.20 15.25  94.4  97.2  97.7  92.9
1986 6.9257 2.1704 1491.16 1.096 1.172 1.047 1.285 10129
  25124 10607  6.81  7.74  4.60 13.41  95.3  98.0  99.6  96.2
1987 6.0122 1.7981 1297.03 1.136 1.209 1.049 1.344 10730
  27069 11040  6.66  7.98  3.70 11.51 100.0 100.0 100.0 100.0
1988 5.9595 1.7569 1302.39 1.183 1.242 1.063 1.411 12228
  26503 11611  7.61  7.52  4.00 11.29 104.4 104.6 103.9 105.9
1989 6.3802 1.8808 1372.28 1.240 1.286 1.092 1.504 13014
  24971 11933  9.22  9.07  6.59 12.69 106.0 108.9 108.8 109.2
1990 5.4467 1.6166 1198.27 1.307 1.330 1.121 1.595 13153
  28162 12751  8.10  9.85  7.92 12.38 106.0 111.0 114.5 109.4
1991 5.6468 1.6610 1241.28 1.362 1.372 1.160 1.698 13333
  26137 11764  5.70  9.49  8.84 12.18 104.3 111.0 117.9 108.4
1992  .      .       .    1.403 1.406 1.206 1.788 14797
  28829 12314  3.52 10.35  9.42 13.97 107.6 109.7 115.6 108.2
1993  .      .       .    1.445 1.435 1.256 1.863 15244
  28605 13223  3.02  8.75  7.49 10.20 112.0 105.6 107.2 105.4
;
```

The Finance Data Set

The finance data are taken from the *Survey of Current Business* and *Business Statistics* for the period January 1989 to February 1994. The finance data set contains the following variables:

DATE
: is a date variable.

DJIAM
: is the monthly average of the end-of-day values for the Dow Jones Index.

GOLD
: is the monthly average of the daily spot price (per troy ounce) for gold.

AAA
: is the monthly average of daily yields on Moody's AAA bonds.

The Dow Jones Index time series is plotted earlier in this section in Output 4. The plot in Output 4 includes more observations than are included in this data set. The GOLD and AAA variables are plotted in Output 7 and Output 8, respectively.

Program

Create the FINANCE data set.

```
data finance;
   format date date7.;
   input date : monyy5. djiam gold aaa @@;
   label djiam='DJIA Index Price'
         gold='Gold Price per Troy Ounce'
         aaa='Moody''s AAA Bond Yields';
   title 'Finance Data';
   datalines;
jan89 2234.68 404.014 9.62  feb89 2304.30 387.776 9.64
mar89 2283.11 390.143 9.80  apr89 2348.91 384.400 9.79
may89 2439.55 371.316 9.57  jun89 2494.90 367.598 9.10
jul89 2554.03 374.978 8.93  aug89 2691.11 364.928 8.96
sep89 2693.41 361.890 9.01  oct89 2692.01 366.884 8.92
nov89 2642.49 392.320 8.89  dec89 2728.47 409.150 8.86
jan90 2679.24 415.596 8.99  feb90 2614.18 416.826 9.22
mar90 2700.13 393.059 9.37  apr90 2708.26 374.265 9.46
may90 2793.81 369.191 9.47  jun90 2894.82 352.331 9.26
jul90 2934.23 362.531 9.24  aug90 2681.89 395.033 9.41
sep90 2550.69 389.458 9.56  oct90 2460.54 380.739 9.53
nov90 2518.56 381.718 9.30  dec90 2610.92 378.163 9.05
jan91 2587.60 383.640 9.04  feb91 2863.04 363.830 8.83
mar91 2920.11 363.340 8.93  apr91 2925.53 358.390 8.86
may91 2928.42 356.820 8.86  jun91 2968.13 366.720 9.01
jul91 2978.18 367.510 9.00  aug91 3006.08 356.230 8.75
sep91 3010.35 348.790 8.61  oct91 3019.73 358.680 8.55
nov91 2986.12 359.530 8.48  dec91 2958.64 361.060 8.31
jan92 3227.06 354.450 8.20  feb92 3257.27 353.890 8.29
mar92 3247.41 344.340 8.35  apr92 3294.08 338.500 8.33
may92 3376.78 337.240 8.28  jun92 3337.79 340.810 8.22
jul92 3329.40 353.050 8.07  aug92 3307.45 342.960 7.95
sep92 3293.92 345.550 7.92  oct92 3198.69 344.380 7.99
nov92 3238.49 335.080 8.10  dec92 3303.15 343.740 7.98
jan93 3277.71 329.010 7.91  feb93 3367.26 329.390 7.71
mar93 3440.73 329.010 7.58  apr93 3423.62 341.910 7.46
may93 3478.17 366.720 7.43  jun93 3513.81 371.890 7.33
jul93 3529.43 392.400 7.17  aug93 3597.01 378.460 6.85
sep93 3592.28 354.850 6.66  oct93 3625.80 364.180 6.67
nov93 3674.69 373.490 6.93  dec93 3743.62 383.690 6.93
jan94 3868.36 387.020 6.92  feb94 3905.61 382.010 7.08
;
```

Plot the GOLD time series.

```
goptions cback=white colors=(black) border reset=(axis symbol);

axis1 offset=(1 cm)
      label=('Year') minor=none
      order=('01jan89'd to '01jan95'd by year);
axis2 label=(angle=90 'Gold Price')
      order=(325 to 425 by 25);

symbol1 i=join;

proc gplot data=finance;
   format date year4.;
   plot gold*date / haxis=axis1
                    vaxis=axis2
                    vminor=0;
   title2 'Gold Prices';
run;
```

Output 7
Plot of GOLD Time Series

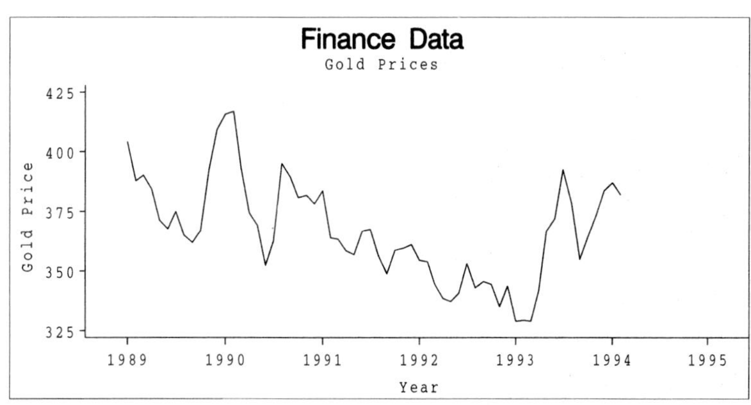

Plot the AAA time series.

```
axis2 label=(angle=90 'AAA Bond Yields')
      order=(6.5 to 10.0 by .5);

proc gplot data=finance;
   format date year4.;
   plot aaa*date / haxis=axis1
                   vaxis=axis2
                   vminor=0;
   title2 'AAA Bond Yields';
run;
```

Output 8
Plot of AAA Time Series

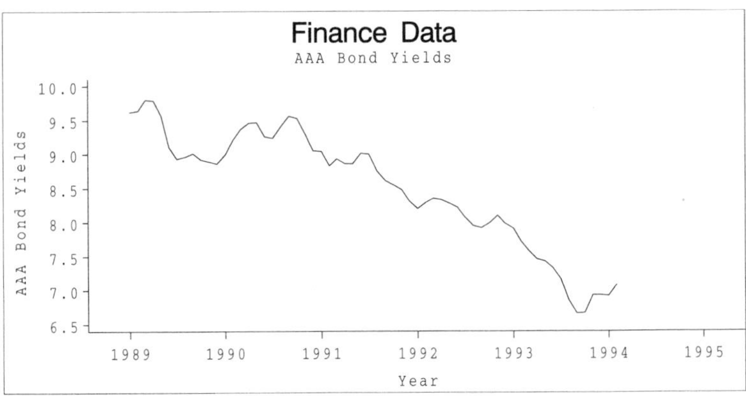

The Lead Production Data Set

The lead production data are taken from *Metal Statistics 1993* (Chilton Publications 1993). The values represent monthly totals of U.S. lead production, in tons, for the period January 1986 to September 1992.

Program

Create the LEADPRD data set.

```
data leadprd;
   input date:monyy5. leadprod @@;
   format date monyy5.;
   title 'Lead Production Data';
   title2 '(in tons)';
   datalines;
jan86 47400 feb86 41600 mar86 49400 apr86 40200 may86 40200 jun86 26500
jul86 16900 aug86 31300 sep86 27500 oct86 28600 nov86 28500 dec86 30100
jan87 38800 feb87 33600 mar87 36000 apr87 33200 may87 34200 jun87 29500
jul87 28800 aug87 30900 sep87 33400 oct87 37600 nov87 39500 dec87 36500
jan88 34300 feb88 35400 mar88 39100 apr88 34300 may88 36200 jun88 34800
jul88 31800 aug88 25300 sep88 32100 oct88 49600 nov88 40000 dec88 39300
jan89 41000 feb89 36000 mar89 39000 apr89 34000 may89 36200 jun89 35500
jul89 35700 aug89 38000 sep89 39300 oct89 34700 nov89 35300 dec89 32300
jan90 38500 feb90 37900 mar90 36900 apr90 38600 may90 36400 jun90 33300
jul90 34000 aug90 38000 sep90 37400 oct90 42300 nov90 36900 dec90 34800
jan91 33900 feb91 34000 mar91 37200 apr91 33300 may91 29800 jun91 24700
jul91 30800 aug91 31100 sep91 32400 oct91 32900 nov91 29100 dec91 31800
jan92 32100 feb92 30500 mar92 36800 apr92 30300 may92 29500 jun92 24700
jul92 27600 aug92 23800 sep92 21400
;
```

Plot the lead production data.

```
goptions cback=white colors=(black) border reset=(axis symbol);

axis1 offset=(1 cm)
      label=('Year') minor=none
      order=('01jan86'd to '01jan93'd by year);
axis2 label=(angle=90 'Lead Production')
      order=(15000 to 50000 by 5000);

symbol1 i=join;

proc gplot data=leadprd;
   format date year4.;
   plot leadprod*date / haxis=axis1
                        vaxis=axis2
                        vminor=1;
run;
```

Output 9
Plot of LEADPROD Variable

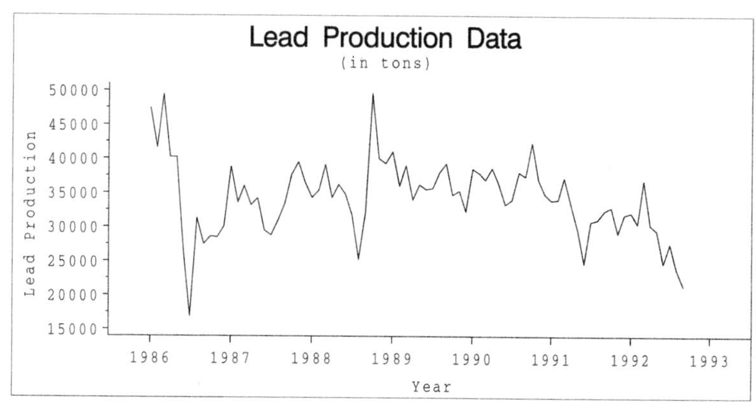

The Returns Data Set

The returns data set consists of monthly returns data for the period January 1978 to December 1987 from the Center for Research in Security Prices (CRSP). The following variables are input:

R_M contains returns for a broad market measure.

R_F contains returns for the risk-free asset.

R_IBM contains returns for the common stock of IBM Corporation.

R_WYR contains returns for the common stock of Weyerhauser Corporation.

The values of the R_IBM and R_WYR variables are missing for 1987. Risk premium variables MKT, IBM, and WYR are created in assignment statements.

Program

Create the RETURNS data set.

```
data returns;
   input date r_m r_f r_ibm r_wyr @@;
   format date monyy.;
   informat date monyy.;
   mkt = r_m - r_f;
   ibm = r_ibm - r_f;
   wyr = r_wyr - r_f;
   label mkt='Risk Premium for Market'
         r_f='Risk-Free Rate of Return'
         ibm='Risk Premium for IBM'
         wyr='Risk Premium for Weyerhauser';
   title 'Returns Data';
   datalines;
JAN78 -0.045 0.00487 -0.029 -0.116  FEB78  0.010 0.00494 -0.043 -0.135
MAR78  0.050 0.00526 -0.063  0.084  APR78  0.063 0.00491  0.130  0.144
MAY78  0.067 0.00513 -0.018 -0.031  JUN78  0.007 0.00527 -0.004  0.005
JUL78  0.071 0.00528  0.092  0.164  AUG78  0.079 0.00607  0.049  0.039
SEP78  0.002 0.00645 -0.051 -0.021  OCT78 -0.189 0.00685 -0.046 -0.090
NOV78  0.084 0.00719  0.031 -0.033  DEC78  0.015 0.00690  0.108 -0.034
JAN79  0.058 0.00761  0.034  0.203  FEB79  0.011 0.00761 -0.017 -0.038
MAR79  0.123 0.00769  0.052  0.097  APR79  0.026 0.00764 -0.004 -0.069
MAY79  0.014 0.00772 -0.022 -0.013  JUN79  0.075 0.00715 -0.035  0.053
JUL79 -0.013 0.00728 -0.049  0.000  AUG79  0.095 0.00789  0.016  0.165
SEP79  0.039 0.00802 -0.032 -0.015  OCT79 -0.097 0.00913 -0.079 -0.083
NOV79  0.116 0.00819  0.060 -0.065  DEC79  0.086 0.00747 -0.013  0.104
JAN80  0.124 0.00883  0.066  0.069  FEB80  0.112 0.01073 -0.062  0.033
MAR80 -0.243 0.01181 -0.122 -0.129  APR80  0.080 0.00753 -0.016  0.027
MAY80  0.062 0.00630  0.025  0.089  JUN80  0.086 0.00503  0.061 -0.026
JUL80  0.065 0.00602  0.111  0.140  AUG80  0.025 0.00731  0.017 -0.041
SEP80  0.015 0.00860 -0.021 -0.064  OCT80  0.006 0.00895  0.039  0.017
NOV80  0.092 0.01137  0.035  0.015  DEC80 -0.056 0.00977 -0.004  0.007
JAN81 -0.014 0.01092 -0.052  0.028  FEB81 -0.009 0.01096  0.011  0.025
MAR81  0.067 0.01025 -0.029  0.088  APR81 -0.008 0.01084 -0.060 -0.050
MAY81  0.064 0.01255  0.017 -0.031  JUN81 -0.003 0.01128 -0.015  0.021
JUL81 -0.033 0.01154 -0.030 -0.081  AUG81 -0.031 0.01169 -0.002 -0.061
SEP81 -0.164 0.01054 -0.018 -0.113  OCT81  0.062 0.01003 -0.048 -0.020
NOV81  0.069 0.00816  0.075  0.179  DEC81 -0.039 0.00740  0.044 -0.072
JAN82 -0.079 0.00949  0.119 -0.079  FEB82 -0.101 0.00946 -0.014  0.014
MAR82 -0.028 0.01067 -0.034 -0.009  APR82  0.041 0.00972  0.075  0.059
MAY82  0.003 0.00908 -0.029 -0.086  JUN82 -0.078 0.00914 -0.014 -0.015
```

```
JUL82 -0.006 0.00714  0.082 -0.012  AUG82  0.122 0.00503  0.087  0.221
SEP82  0.008 0.00563  0.041 -0.029  OCT82  0.136 0.00620  0.089  0.150
NOV82  0.049 0.00614  0.094  0.141  DEC82  0.014 0.00648  0.113 -0.040
JAN83  0.065 0.00646  0.027  0.023  FEB83  0.028 0.00599  0.010  0.065
MAR83  0.043 0.00686  0.028 -0.023  APR83  0.097 0.00652  0.150  0.091
MAY83  0.080 0.00649 -0.041 -0.067  JUN83  0.048 0.00673  0.081 -0.013
JUL83 -0.017 0.00714  0.001 -0.071  AUG83 -0.034 0.00668  0.001 -0.011
SEP83  0.000 0.00702  0.062 -0.033  OCT83 -0.082 0.00678 -0.001 -0.046
NOV83  0.066 0.00683 -0.066  0.151  DEC83 -0.012 0.00693  0.039 -0.069
JAN84 -0.029 0.00712 -0.065 -0.039  FEB84 -0.030 0.00672 -0.026 -0.093
MAR84  0.003 0.00763  0.034  0.094  APR84 -0.003 0.00741 -0.002 -0.088
MAY84 -0.058 0.00627 -0.044 -0.087  JUN84  0.005 0.00748 -0.019  0.019
JUL84 -0.058 0.00771  0.047  0.036  AUG84  0.146 0.00852  0.127  0.055
SEP84  0.000 0.00830  0.004 -0.069  OCT84 -0.035 0.00688  0.012  0.035
NOV84 -0.019 0.00602 -0.023  0.032  DEC84 -0.001 0.00612  0.011  0.026
JAN85  0.097 0.00606  0.108  0.084  FEB85  0.012 0.00586 -0.009 -0.016
MAR85  0.008 0.00650 -0.052 -0.081  APR85 -0.010 0.00601 -0.004  0.003
MAY85  0.019 0.00512  0.025  0.031  JUN85 -0.003 0.00536 -0.038 -0.004
JUL85  0.012 0.00562  0.062  0.020  AUG85  0.005 0.00545 -0.028 -0.013
SEP85 -0.055 0.00571 -0.022 -0.074  OCT85  0.026 0.00577  0.048  0.008
NOV85  0.059 0.00540  0.085  0.171  DEC85  0.013 0.00479  0.113 -0.004
JAN86 -0.009 0.00548 -0.026  0.072  FEB86  0.049 0.00523  0.003  0.123
MAR86  0.048 0.00508  0.004  0.051  APR86 -0.009 0.00444  0.031 -0.037
MAY86  0.049 0.00469 -0.018  0.010  JUN86  0.004 0.00478 -0.039 -0.061
JUL86 -0.076 0.00458 -0.096 -0.048  AUG86  0.049 0.00343  0.055  0.122
SEP86 -0.047 0.00416 -0.031 -0.058  OCT86  0.018 0.00418 -0.081  0.135
NOV86  0.000 0.00420  0.037  0.006  DEC86 -0.005 0.00382 -0.056 -0.041
JAN87  0.148 0.00454    .      .    FEB87  0.065 0.00437    .      .
MAR87  0.037 0.00423    .      .    APR87 -0.025 0.00207    .      .
MAY87  0.004 0.00438    .      .    JUN87  0.038 0.00402    .      .
JUL87  0.055 0.00455    .      .    AUG87  0.015 0.00460    .      .
SEP87 -0.015 0.00520    .      .    OCT87 -0.260 0.00358    .      .
NOV87 -0.070 0.00288    .      .    DEC87  0.073 0.00277    .      .
;
```

The Steel Shipments Data Set

The steel shipments data are taken from *Metal Statistics 1993* (Chilton Publications 1993). The values represent monthly totals of steel products shipped from U.S. steel mills, in thousands of net tons, for the period January 1984 to December 1991.

Program

Create the STEEL data set.

```
data steel;
   input date:monyy5. steelshp @@;
   format date monyy5.;
   title 'U.S. Steel Shipments Data';
   title2 '(thousands of net tons)';
   datalines;
JAN84 5980 FEB84 6150 MAR84 7240 APR84 6472 MAY84 6948 JUN84 6686
JUL84 5820 AUG84 6033 SEP84 5454 OCT84 6087 NOV84 5317 DEC84 4867
JAN85 6017 FEB85 5598 MAR85 6344 APR85 6425 MAY85 6519 JUN85 6125
JUL85 5710 AUG85 6064 SEP85 5848 OCT85 6308 NOV85 5654 DEC85 5821
JAN86 6437 FEB86 5799 MAR86 6142 APR86 6283 MAY86 6212 JUN86 6007
JUL86 5815 AUG86 5364 SEP86 5608 OCT86 5923 NOV86 4899 DEC86 5199
JAN87 5664 FEB87 5527 MAR87 6234 APR87 6312 MAY87 6247 JUN87 6656
JUL87 6295 AUG87 6364 SEP87 6726 OCT87 7077 NOV87 6606 DEC87 6977
JAN88 6608 FEB88 6848 MAR88 7693 APR88 7082 MAY88 7187 JUN88 7422
JUL88 6325 AUG88 7035 SEP88 6922 OCT88 6912 NOV88 6712 DEC88 6738
JAN89 7278 FEB89 6832 MAR89 7824 APR89 7164 MAY89 7446 JUN89 7331
JUL89 6387 AUG89 7224 SEP89 6779 OCT89 7174 NOV89 6652 DEC89 6053
JAN90 6863 FEB90 6502 MAR90 7569 APR90 7023 MAY90 7523 JUN90 7493
JUL90 6890 AUG90 7366 SEP90 6893 OCT90 7366 NOV90 6907 DEC90 6187
JAN91 6786 FEB91 6039 MAR91 5966 APR91 6450 MAY91 6762 JUN91 6623
JUL91 6420 AUG91 6954 SEP91 6747 OCT91 7499 NOV91 6427 DEC91 6118
;
```

Plot the steel shipments data.

```
goptions cback=white colors=(black) border reset=(axis symbol);

axis1 offset=(1 cm)
      label=('Year') minor=none
      order=('01jan84'd to '01jan92'd by year);
axis2 label=(angle=90 'Steel Shipments')
      order=(4500 to 8500 by 1000);

symbol1 i=join;
```

```
proc gplot data=steel;
   format date year4.;
   plot steelshp*date / haxis=axis1
                        vaxis=axis2
                        vminor=1;
run;
```

Output 10
Plot of STEELSHP Variable

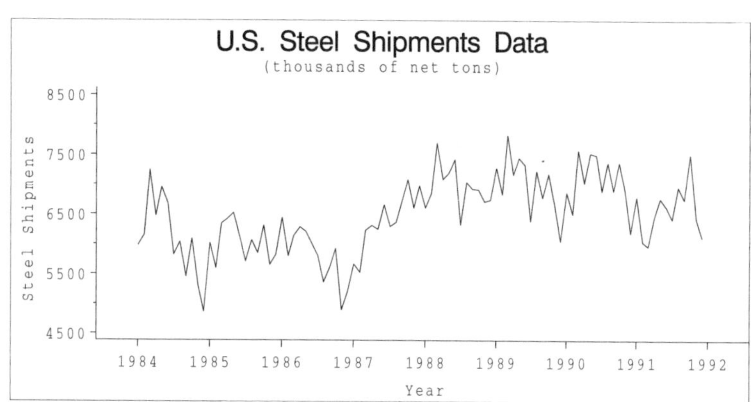

References

□ Chilton Publications (1993), *Metal Statistics 1993*, New York: Chilton Publications.

□ Harvey, A.C. (1989), *Forecasting, Structural Time Series Models and the Kalman Filter*, Cambridge: Cambridge University Press.

□ Kmenta, J. (1986), *Elements of Econometrics, Second Edition*, New York: Macmillan Publishing Co., Inc.

□ Maddala, G.S. (1977), *Econometrics*, New York: McGraw-Hill.

□ U.S. Department of Commerce, Bureau of Economic Analysis (1989), *Business Statistics, 1961-1988*, Washington, D.C.: U.S. Government Printing Office.

□ U.S. Department of Commerce, Bureau of Economic Analysis (1990-1995), *Survey of Current Business*, Washington, D.C.: U.S. Government Printing Office.

□ U.S. Department of Commerce (various years), *Statistical Abstract of the U.S.*, Washington, D.C.: U.S. Government Printing Office.

□ U.S. Department of Commerce (1995), *Economic Report of the President*, Washington, D.C.: U.S. Government Printing Office.

EXAMPLE 1

Forecasting an Autoregressive Process

Featured Tools:

- ARIMA procedure:

  IDENTIFY statement, NLAG= option

  ESTIMATE statement

  FORECAST statement

- FORECAST procedure

The most common type of time series models are autoregressive models, as described in Box and Jenkins (1976). The term *Box-Jenkins model* is often used to describe any of the models discussed in that text. These are models for the stochastic process that underlies a time series, where the time series values exhibit nonzero autocorrelation. The Durbin and Watson statistic (Durbin and Watson 1950, 1951; Pindyck and Rubinfeld 1991) provides a test of significance for autocorrelation in time series data.

Much of the probability theory of time series assumes that time series exhibit a constant mean and constant variance over time — a condition known as *stationarity.* Nonstationary components of time series can usually be removed to make the series stationary. For example, you can take differences of a time series to remove a trend or seasonal variations.

Consider the time series variable, Y_t. A first-order autoregressive model, called an AR(1) model, for this time series can be written as

$$Y_t - \mu = \phi_1 (Y_{t-1} - \mu) + \epsilon_t$$

where

μ	is the mean parameter.
ϕ_1	is the first-order autoregressive (AR) parameter.
Y_{t-1}	is the value of the time series in the previous time period.
ϵ_t	is the random error term uncorrelated over time, typically called *white noise.*

Another common way of writing this model is as follows:

$$Y_t = \theta_0 + \phi_1 Y_{t-1} + \epsilon_t$$

where θ_0 is called the constant parameter. Note that $\theta_0 = \mu(1 - \phi_1)$ for an AR(1) model.

In general, you express autoregressive models of order p (AR(p) models) as follows:

$$Y_t = \theta_0 + \phi_1 Y_{t-1} + \phi_2 Y_{t-2} + \dots + \phi_p Y_{t-p} + \epsilon_t$$

The forecast for one period into the future based on an AR(1) model can be written as follows:

$$\hat{Y}_{t+1} = \mu + \phi_1(Y_t - \mu)$$

In general, forecasts for *L* periods into the future for an AR(1) model can be written as follows:

$$\hat{Y}_{t+L} = \mu + \phi_1^L(Y_t - \mu)$$

If the time series is stationary, ϕ_1 raised to a high power will be close to 0, because stationarity implies that $\phi_1 < 1$. It follows that forecasts for all stationary series approach the mean of the series as you forecast further into the future. Thus, autoregressive models are best for short-term forecasting. Long-term forecasting with autoregressive models is not much better than using the mean for stationary time series.

PROC ARIMA performs analysis in three distinct phases and produces separate output for each phase.

1. The *identification phase* produces plots that you examine to identify the process that underlies a time series. After you identify an appropriate model for a time series, you can then attempt to fit that model to your data.
2. The *estimation phase* produces model parameter estimates and associated significance tests, goodness-of-fit statistics, and other estimation diagnostics. After you determine that a given model provides an adequate fit to your data, you can use that model to provide forecasted values for future time periods.
3. The *forecasting phase* produces forecasts, standard errors, and confidence limits for the specified number of time periods.

Program

Identifying the Time Series Process

Examine the plots and statistics that the identification phase of PROC ARIMA produces to determine a suitable candidate model to fit to your time series data.

Create the lead production data set. The complete lead production data set is in "Introduction: The Example Data Sets."

```
data leadprd;
   input date:monyy. leadprod @@;
   format date monyy.;
   title 'Lead Production Data';
   title2 '(in tons)';
   datalines;
jan86 47400  feb86 41600  mar86 49400  apr86 40200
more data lines
;
```

Identify the time series process. Abbreviate IDENTIFY as I. Use the NLAG= option to specify the number of lags to consider in computing the autocorrelations.

```
proc arima data=leadprd;
   i var=leadprod nlag=15;
run;
```

Output 1.1
Identifying the Lead Production Time Series Process

```
                         Lead Production Data                       1
                              (in tons)

                           ARIMA Procedure

                   ❶ Name of variable = LEADPROD.

                     Mean of working series = 34223.46
                     Standard deviation     = 5564.332
                     Number of observations =       81

                          ❷ Autocorrelations

Lag Covariance Correlation -1 9 8 7 6 5 4 3 2 1 0 1 2 3 4 5 6 7 8 9 1
  0   30961795    1.00000  |                    |********************|
  1   17092151    0.55204  |                  . |***********         |
  2   10490412    0.33882  |                 .  |*******             |
  3    4343266    0.14028  |                 .  |***  .              |
  4     238295    0.00770  |                 .  |     .              |
  5    -102076   -0.00330  |                 .  |     .              |
  6   -3257912   -0.10522  |                 . **|     .             |
  7    1441775    0.04657  |                 .  |*    .              |
  8     402326    0.01299  |                 .  |     .              |
  9     580512    0.01875  |                 .  |     .              |
 10    3579546    0.11561  |                 .  |**   .              |
 11    4864684    0.15712  |                 .  |***  .              |
 12    6680397    0.21576  |                 .  |**** .              |
 13    3553670    0.11478  |                 .  |**   .              |
 14    2240617    0.07237  |                 .  |*    .              |
 15   -1184298   -0.03825  |                 .  *|    .              |
                           "." marks two standard errors
```

```
                        Lead Production Data                            2
                             (in tons)

                          ARIMA Procedure

                  ❸ Inverse Autocorrelations

 Lag Correlation -1 9 8 7 6 5 4 3 2 1 0 1 2 3 4 5 6 7 8 9 1
   1   -0.41724  |            ********|   .                |
   2   -0.06514  |                .  *|   .                |
   3    0.04634  |                .   |*  .                |
   4    0.03883  |                .   |*  .                |
   5   -0.13760  |                .***|   .                |
   6    0.25334  |                .   |*****               |
   7   -0.19215  |                ****|   .                |
   8   -0.03391  |                .  *|   .                |
   9    0.13653  |                .   |***.                |
  10   -0.04267  |                .  *|   .                |
  11   -0.02496  |                .   |   .                |
  12   -0.03754  |                .  *|   .                |
  13    0.02024  |                .   |   .                |
  14   -0.05950  |                .  *|   .                |
  15    0.06899  |                .   |*  .                |
```

```
                        Lead Production Data                            3
                             (in tons)

                          ARIMA Procedure

                  ❹ Partial Autocorrelations

 Lag Correlation -1 9 8 7 6 5 4 3 2 1 0 1 2 3 4 5 6 7 8 9 1
   1    0.55204  |                .   |***********         |
   2    0.04900  |                .   |*  .                |
   3   -0.09321  |                . **|   .                |
   4   -0.07027  |                .  *|   .                |
   5    0.05224  |                .   |*  .                |
   6   -0.13405  |                .***|   .                |
   7    0.22031  |                .   |****                |
   8   -0.08853  |                . **|   .                |
   9   -0.00726  |                .   |   .                |
  10    0.15066  |                .   |***.                |
  11    0.09535  |                .   |** .                |
  12    0.03441  |                .   |*  .                |
  13   -0.04316  |                .  *|   .                |
  14   -0.02775  |                .  *|   .                |
  15   -0.10420  |                . **|   .                |
```

```
                        Lead Production Data                            4
                             (in tons)

                          ARIMA Procedure

            ❺ Autocorrelation Check for White Noise

 To    Chi                          Autocorrelations
Lag  Square DF   Prob
  6   38.07  6  0.000  0.552  0.339  0.140  0.008 -0.003 -0.105
 12   46.49 12  0.000  0.047  0.013  0.019  0.116  0.157  0.216
```

Explanation

The identification phase output helps you determine what type of process underlies the time series you analyze with PROC ARIMA.

❶ The name of the time series variable, the mean and standard deviation of the variable, and the number of observations are all printed at the top of the output when you request the identification of a time series variable.

❷ The `Autocorrelations` plot displays the sample autocorrelation function (ACF) for lags up to and including the NLAG= option value. The autocorrelation is the correlation between Y_t and Y_{t-p}, where *p* is known as the *lag*. Standard errors of the autocorrelations also appear to the right of the autocorrelation plot if the line size is sufficiently large. Dots mark two standard errors for the sample autocorrelation at each lag *p*, based on a null hypothesis that all correlations at or beyond lag *p* are 0.

❸ The `Inverse Autocorrelations` plot displays the sample inverse autocorrelation function (IACF). Dots mark the bounds of an approximate 95% confidence interval for the null hypothesis that the series is from a white noise process.

❹ The `Partial Autocorrelations` plot displays the sample partial autocorrelation function (PACF). Dots mark two standard errors for the partial autocorrelation at each lag *p*, based on a null hypothesis that all partial correlations at or beyond lag *p* are 0.

❺ The `Autocorrelation Check for White Noise` table contains test statistics, called *Q*-statistics, that test whether the time series is white noise. Each row of the table contains the value of the *Q*-statistic, the corresponding degrees of freedom, the *p*-value associated with the *Q*-statistic under a null hypothesis of white noise, and up to six sample autocorrelation values.

Interpretation

From the identification phase output, you can see the following items:

□ The sample ACF tails off exponentially. This indicates that the process is stationary. The plot has a slight sine wave pattern, which indicates that the time series may have more than one autoregressive coefficient.

□ The sample IACF and sample PACF have large spikes at lag 1 and drop to 0 after that, although there are some smaller spikes at lags 6 and 7. This indicates that the process is most likely autoregressive of order 1, but it might be a higher order process.

- The autocorrelation check for white noise has significant *Q*-statistics, which indicates that the time series is not simply white noise.

From these results, you can tentatively identify an AR(1) model as a suitable candidate model for the lead production time series.

Estimating an AR(1) Model

Use the estimation phase output of PROC ARIMA to assess the adequacy of a given model's fit to your time series data. PROC ARIMA is an interactive procedure, so you do not need to repeat the PROC ARIMA statement after you first invoke it.

Estimate an AR(1) model. Abbreviate ESTIMATE as E. Use the P= option to specify the number of autoregressive parameters to estimate.

```
   e p=1;
run;
```

Output 1.2
Estimating a Model for the Lead Production Time Series

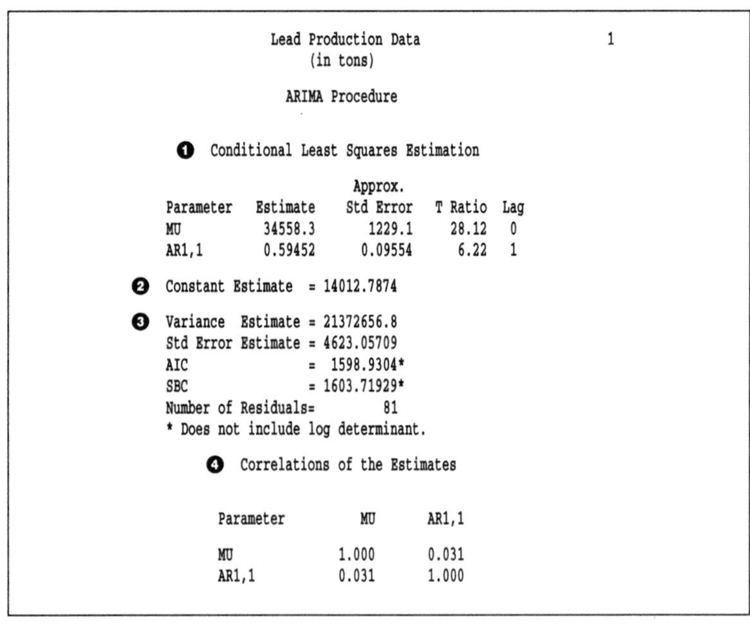

```
                    Lead Production Data                        1
                         (in tons)

                      ARIMA Procedure

         ❶ Conditional Least Squares Estimation

                                Approx.
     Parameter   Estimate    Std Error   T Ratio  Lag
     MU           34558.3       1229.1     28.12   0
     AR1,1        0.59452      0.09554      6.22   1

   ❷ Constant Estimate  = 14012.7874

   ❸ Variance  Estimate = 21372656.8
     Std Error Estimate = 4623.05709
     AIC                =  1598.9304*
     SBC                = 1603.71929*
     Number of Residuals=         81
     * Does not include log determinant.

         ❹ Correlations of the Estimates

         Parameter          MU       AR1,1

         MU              1.000       0.031
         AR1,1           0.031       1.000
```

```
                         Lead Production Data                        2
                              (in tons)

                           ARIMA Procedure

            ❺ Autocorrelation Check of Residuals

 To    Chi                    Autocorrelations
Lag  Square DF   Prob
  6    6.71  5  0.243 -0.040  0.100 -0.016 -0.073  0.094 -0.223
 12   13.68 11  0.251  0.153 -0.019 -0.073  0.074  0.042  0.193
 18   15.43 17  0.565 -0.024  0.082 -0.046 -0.058 -0.060 -0.026
 24   18.15 23  0.749  0.038 -0.103  0.072  0.046 -0.056  0.043


            ❻ Model for variable LEADPROD

              Estimated Mean = 34558.2874

              Autoregressive Factors
              Factor 1: 1 - 0.59452 B**(1)
```

Explanation

❶ The parameter estimates, approximate standard errors, *t*-ratios, and lags for the model you specify in the ESTIMATE statement are printed at the top of the output.

❷ The estimate of the constant term is printed unless you specify the NOCONSTANT option in the ESTIMATE statement. The constant estimate is $\mu(1 - \phi_1 - \phi_2 - \ldots - \phi_p)$ when the model includes an AR(p) component. For this example, the constant estimate of 14012.787 is equal to $34558.3(1 - .59452)$.

❸ Several measures of goodness of fit are printed. The output shows a variance estimate, a standard-error estimate, Akaike's Information Criterion (AIC) (Akaike 1974), Schwarz's Bayesian Criterion (SBC) (Schwarz 1978). In some references, SBC is called BIC. The better the fit of the model, the smaller these values will be. The output also lists the number of residuals used in the calculations.

❹ The correlation matrix of the parameter estimates is printed. Highly correlated parameter estimates may reduce the accuracy of the calculations in PROC ARIMA.

❺ The **Autocorrelation Check of Residuals** table contains Q-statistics that test whether the residuals of the model are white noise. This table is similar to the **Autocorrelation Check for White Noise** table in the identification phase output, but it tests the residuals of the model rather than the original time series values.

❻ A summary of the estimated model is shown, which lists the estimated mean and the estimated autoregressive parameters in backshift notation. The B**(1) notation is actually B^1, which represents a first-order backshift operator.

Interpretation

The **Autocorrelation Check of Residuals** table shows no significant Q-statistics, which indicates that the residuals of the model are simply white noise. From this result you conclude that an AR(1) model provides an adequate fit to the lead production time series process. The final model can be written as follows:

$$Y_t - 34558 = .59452\left(Y_{t-1} - 34558\right) + \epsilon_t$$

Forecasting the Time Series

The forecasting phase output from PROC ARIMA prints the estimated model and the desired number of forecasted values. However, the estimated model is not printed if it is printed in the estimation phase output.

The last observation in the original lead production time series is 21400. Thus, the one-step-ahead forecast $\hat{Y}_{t+L}$ for L future periods is

$$\hat{Y}_{t+L} = 34558 + (.59452)^L(21400 - 34558)$$

Forecast the AR(1) model.
Abbreviate FORECAST as F. Use the LEAD= option to specify the number of future periods for which forecasts are desired.

```
   f lead=12;
run;
```

Output 1.3
Printing Forecasts for the Lead Production Time Series

```
                         Lead Production Data
                              (in tons)

                           ARIMA Procedure

Forecasts for variable LEADPROD

 Obs    Forecast Std Error   Lower 95%   Upper 95%
  82  26735.4578 4623.0571  17674.4324  35796.4832
  83  29907.4798 5378.3678  19366.0726  40448.8870
  84  31793.3018 5621.1095  20776.1295  42810.4741
  85  32914.4556 5704.4367  21733.9652  44094.9460
  86  33581.0010 5733.5991  22343.3533  44818.6486
  87  33977.2737 5743.8711  22719.4932  45235.0542
  88  34212.8647 5747.4974  22947.9768  45477.7526
  89  34352.9276 5748.7785  23085.5287  45620.3265
  90  34436.1975 5749.2313  23167.9112  45704.4838
  91  34485.7028 5749.3913  23217.1029  45754.3028
  92  34515.1346 5749.4479  23246.4238  45783.8454
  93  34532.6323 5749.4679  23263.8824  45801.3823
```

Explanation

The forecast phase output prints a table of forecasts that contains the following items:

Obs — is the observation number.

Forecast — is the forecast value.

Std Error — is the forecast standard error.

Lower 95% — is the lower limit of the approximate 95% confidence interval.

Upper 95% — is the upper limit of the approximate 95% confidence interval.

A Closer Look

Backshift Notation

Autoregressive integrated moving average (ARIMA) models can be expressed in terms of the backshift operator B. For example, BY_t means Y_{t-1} and B^2Y_t means Y_{t-2}. In SAS output, B raised to the power of x is written as B**(x).

Variations

Using Other Estimation Methods

The default estimation method in PROC ARIMA is the conditional least squares (CLS) method. You can also use the unconditional least squares (ULS) method or the maximum likelihood (ML) method. Specify METHOD=ULS or METHOD=ML in the ESTIMATE statement to use the ULS method or ML method, respectively.

Forecasts are generated with forecasting equations consistent with the method used to estimate the model parameters. Thus, the estimation method specified in the ESTIMATE statement also controls the way the FORECAST statement produces forecasts.

Using the FORECAST Procedure

The FORECAST procedure provides a way of forecasting one or more time series automatically. It does not enable you to identify models or test for model adequacy. It is most efficient when you want to generate forecasts for multiple univariate time series. This example shows how to use PROC FORECAST to generate forecasts for the lead production data.

Note: PROC FORECAST produces no printed output. It writes forecast values and other information to output data sets.

Forecast the lead production data using PROC FORECAST. Specify the desired options for the model and forecasts in the PROC FORECAST statement.

```
proc forecast data=leadprd
              ar=1            /* number of AR parameters to estimate  */
              interval=month  /* frequency of input time series       */
              trend=1         /* fit a constant trend model           */
              method=stepar   /* use stepwise autoregressive method   */
              out=leadout1    /* create output data set for forecasts */
              lead=12         /* number of forecast periods           */
```

Write one-step-ahead forecasts, confidence limits, and standard errors of forecasts to the output data set. Use the OUTLIMIT and OUTSTD options to write these values to the data set.

```
      outlimit
      outstd;
```

Forecast the variable or variables listed in the VAR statement.

```
   var leadprod;

   id date;                          /* identification variable          */
run;
```

Print the OUT= data set that contains the forecasts.

```
proc print data=leadout1;
run;
```

Output 1.4
Output Data Set Created with PROC FORECAST

Lead Production Data
(in tons)

OBS	DATE	_TYPE_	_LEAD_	LEADPROD
1	OCT92	FORECAST	1	27144.39
2	OCT92	L95	1	17855.09
3	OCT92	STD	1	4739.53
4	OCT92	U95	1	36433.70
5	NOV92	FORECAST	2	30315.53
6	NOV92	L95	2	19726.41
7	NOV92	STD	2	5402.71
8	NOV92	U95	2	40904.65
9	DEC92	FORECAST	3	32066.13
10	DEC92	L95	3	21111.51
11	DEC92	STD	3	5589.19
12	DEC92	U95	3	43020.74
13	JAN93	FORECAST	4	33032.52
14	JAN93	L95	4	21968.92
15	JAN93	STD	4	5644.80
16	JAN93	U95	4	44096.13
17	FEB93	FORECAST	5	33566.01
18	FEB93	L95	5	22469.41
19	FEB93	STD	5	5661.64
20	FEB93	U95	5	44662.62
21	MAR93	FORECAST	6	33860.52
22	MAR93	L95	6	22753.88
23	MAR93	STD	6	5666.76
24	MAR93	U95	6	44967.16
25	APR93	FORECAST	7	34023.10
26	APR93	L95	7	22913.41
27	APR93	STD	7	5668.32
28	APR93	U95	7	45132.80
29	MAY93	FORECAST	8	34112.85
30	MAY93	L95	8	23002.23
31	MAY93	STD	8	5668.79
32	MAY93	U95	8	45223.48
33	JUN93	FORECAST	9	34162.40
34	JUN93	L95	9	23051.49
35	JUN93	STD	9	5668.94
36	JUN93	U95	9	45273.31
37	JUL93	FORECAST	10	34189.75
38	JUL93	L95	10	23078.75
39	JUL93	STD	10	5668.98
40	JUL93	U95	10	45300.75

```
41  AUG93  FORECAST  11  34204.85
42  AUG93  L95       11  23093.83
43  AUG93  STD       11   5668.99
44  AUG93  U95       11  45315.87
45  SEP93  FORECAST  12  34213.18
46  SEP93  L95       12  23102.15
47  SEP93  STD       12   5669.00
48  SEP93  U95       12  45324.22
```

Explanation

For each forecast of future periods there are four types of observations in this example:

FORECAST	is the forecast value.
L95	is the lower 95% confidence limit for the forecast.
STD	is the standard error of the forecast.
U95	is the upper 95% confidence limit for the forecast.

Godfrey's Test for White Noise

Maddala (1992) suggests that *Q*-statistics are not appropriate for autoregressive models. He recommends Godfrey's Lagrange multiplier tests of model adequacy. The GODFREY option (available with Release 6.11) in the AUTOREG procedure or the MODEL procedure of SAS/ETS software enables you to perform these tests.

The example code for PROC AUTOREG is shown here. No output is shown. Example 10 shows the output from the GODFREY option and provides more information about it.

```
proc autoreg data=leadprd;
   model leadprod = / nlag=1 godfrey;
run;
```

Further Reading

For more information on PROC ARIMA, PROC AUTOREG, PROC FORECAST, and PROC MODEL, see the *SAS/ETS User's Guide, Version 6, Second Edition.*

References

- Akaike, H. (1974), "A New Look at the Statistical Model Identification," *IEEE Transaction on Automatic Control*, AC-19, 716-723.
- Box, G.E.P. and Jenkins, G.M. (1976), *Time Series Analysis: Forecasting and Control*, San Francisco: Holden-Day.
- Durbin, J. and Watson, G.S. (1950), "Testing for Serial Correlation in Least Squares Regression I," *Biometrika*, 37, 409-428.
- Durbin, J. and Watson, G.S. (1951), "Testing for Serial Correlation in Least Squares Regression II," *Biometrika*, 38, 159-178.
- Maddala, G.S. (1992), *Introduction to Econometrics, Second Edition*, New York: Macmillan Publishing Company.
- Pindyck, R.S. and Rubinfeld, D.L. (1991), *Econometric Models and Economic Forecasts, Third Edition*, New York: McGraw-Hill, Inc.
- Schwarz, G. (1978), "Estimating the Dimension of a Model," *Annals of Statistics*, 6, 461-464.

EXAMPLE 2

Forecasting a Moving Average Process

Featured Tools and Tasks:

- ARIMA procedure:
  - CENTER option
  - NOCONSTANT option
  - differencing
- FORECAST procedure

Moving average models form another subset of the class of Box-Jenkins models for a time series. In a moving average process, the current time series value is related to the random errors from some of the previous time periods. Contrast this with autoregressive models (described in Example 1), where the current time series value is related to the actual time series values from some of the previous time periods.

Consider the time series variable, Y_t. A first-order moving average model, called an MA(1) model, for this time series can be written as

$$Y_t = \theta_0 + \epsilon_t - \theta_1 \epsilon_{t-1}$$

where

θ_0	is the constant parameter.
ϵ_t	is the random error for the current time period.
θ_1	is the first-order moving average (MA) parameter.
ϵ_{t-1}	is the random error for the previous time period.

In general, you express moving average models of order q (MA(q) models) as follows:

$$Y_t = \theta_0 + \epsilon_t - \theta_1 \epsilon_{t-1} - \theta_2 \epsilon_{t-2} - \ldots - \theta_q \epsilon_{t-q}$$

The forecast for one period into the future based on an MA(1) model can be written as follows:

$$\hat{Y}_{t+1} = \theta_0 - \theta_1 \epsilon_t$$

Forecasts for the MA(1) model for L periods into the future, $L > 1$, are simply equal to θ_0, the series mean. In general, forecasts for MA(q) models for L periods into the future, $L > q$, are equal to the series mean. If a series has a deterministic trend, however, forecasts for future periods follow that trend. For example, if a series steadily increases according to a linear trend, forecasts based on the trend plus an MA model for that series follow the pattern of steady increase according to the linear trend.

This example uses the ARIMA procedure to produce forecasts for a moving average process of a differenced time series. Often, a differenced time series can be fit with an MA model. To speed up computations, you can use the CENTER and NOCONSTANT options to subtract the mean from all observations and fit a model without a mean parameter. However, this may reduce the accuracy of the estimation.

See Example 1 for more details on the three phases of output that PROC ARIMA generates for identifying, estimating, and forecasting time series.

Program

Preliminary Identification of the Time Series Process

Create the Dow Jones Index data set. The complete Dow Jones Index data set is in "Introduction: the Example Data Sets."

```
data djm;
   input date:monyy5. djiam @@;
   format date monyy5.;
   title 'Dow Jones Index Data';
   title2 'Monthly Average';
   datalines;
jan84 1258.89 feb84 1164.46 mar84 1161.97 apr84 1152.71
more data lines
;
```

Invoke PROC ARIMA and attempt to identify the time series process.

```
proc arima data=djm;
   i var=djiam;
run;
```

Output 2.1
Identifying the Dow Jones Index Time Series Process (Partial Output)

```
                       Dow Jones Index Data
                         Monthly Average

                         ARIMA Procedure


                  Name of variable = DJIAM.

                  Mean of working series = 2381.074
                  Standard deviation     = 772.4888
                  Number of observations =      122

                         Autocorrelations

Lag Covariance Correlation -1 9 8 7 6 5 4 3 2 1 0 1 2 3 4 5 6 7 8 9 1
  0     596739     1.00000 |                    |********************|
  1     578547     0.96951 |                  . |*******************  |
  2     557449     0.93416 |                 .  |*******************  |
  3     537611     0.90092 |                .   |******************   |
  4     518674     0.86918 |               .    |*****************    |
  5     500626     0.83894 |               .    |*****************    |
  6     483171     0.80969 |              .     |****************     |
  7     465384     0.77988 |             .      |****************     |
  8     448773     0.75204 |             .      |***************      |
  9     432649     0.72502 |            .       |***************      |
 10     417192     0.69912 |            .       |**************       |
 11     401879     0.67346 |           .        |*************.       |
 12     384770     0.64479 |           .        |*************.       |
 13     369178     0.61866 |          .         |************  .      |
 14     354548     0.59414 |          .         |************  .      |
 15     338543     0.56732 |          .         |***********   .      |
 16     323456     0.54204 |         .          |***********     .    |
 17     309078     0.51794 |         .          |**********      .    |
 18     294007     0.49269 |         .          |**********      .    |
 19     278698     0.46703 |         .          |*********       .    |
```

```
    20    263224    0.44110  |    .              |*********      .  |
    21    248311    0.41611  |   .               |********       .  |
    22    233269    0.39091  |   .               |********       .  |
    23    219661    0.36810  |   .               |*******        .  |
    24    207382    0.34753  |   .               |*******        .  |
                             "." marks two standard errors
```

Interpretation

From the partial identification phase output, note that the sample ACF tails off very slowly. This indicates that the process is not stationary. That is, the mean or the variance of the time series are not constant over time. You cannot use the Box-Jenkins ARIMA methodology to identify any model for this type of nonstationary process, nor are the usual test statistics valid for a nonstationary process. One approach to modeling a nonstationary process is to take first differences of the series and run the identification phase again.

Differencing, Identifying, Estimating, and Forecasting the Time Series

Take first differences of the Dow Jones Index time series. Specify the desired degree of differencing inside the parentheses that follow the variable name in the IDENTIFY statement. Use the CENTER option to subtract the mean from all observations.

```
   i var=djiam(1) center;
run;
```

Estimate an MA(1) model. Use the Q= option to specify the number of moving average parameters to estimate. Use the NOCONSTANT option to fit a model without a mean parameter. NOCONSTANT is typically used in conjunction with the CENTER option or with differenced data.

```
   e q=1 noconstant;
run;
```

Produce forecasts for 12 future periods. The FORECAST statement forecasts the differences for the differenced series and automatically sums the differences back to produce the final forecasts with appropriate standard errors.

```
   f lead=12;
run;
```

Output 2.2
Identifying the Differenced Dow Jones Index Time Series

```
                         Dow Jones Index Data                    1
                           Monthly Average

                           ARIMA Procedure


                 Name of variable = DJIAM.

             ❶  Period(s) of Differencing = 1.
                 Mean of working series = 21.87372
                 Standard deviation     = 81.18672
                 Number of observations =      121
                 NOTE: The first observation was eliminated by
                       differencing.

                      ❷ Autocorrelations

Lag Covariance Correlation -1 9 8 7 6 5 4 3 2 1 0 1 2 3 4 5 6 7 8 9 1
  0   6591.284    1.00000  |                    |********************|
  1   2030.074    0.30799  |                  . |****** ❸            |
  2   -196.681   -0.02984  |                  .*|  .                 |
  3   -592.709   -0.08992  |                 .**|  .                 |
  4   -831.381   -0.12613  |                .***|  .                 |
  5   -848.580   -0.12874  |                .***|  .                 |
  6   -270.315   -0.04101  |                  .*|  .                 |
  7    141.561    0.02148  |                  . |  .                 |
  8   -734.798   -0.11148  |                 .**|  .                 |
  9   -801.911   -0.12166  |                 .**|  .                 |
 10    212.541    0.03225  |                  . |* .                 |
 11    938.667    0.14241  |                  . |***.                |
 12   -580.823   -0.08812  |                 .**|  .                 |
 13    164.689    0.02499  |                  . |  .                 |
 14    509.608    0.07732  |                  . |** .                |
 15   -549.975   -0.08344  |                 .**|  .                 |
 16   -502.865   -0.07629  |                 .**|  .                 |
 17   -605.287   -0.09183  |                 .**|  .                 |
 18 -86.271660   -0.01309  |                  . |  .                 |
 19   -704.905   -0.10695  |                 .**|  .                 |
 20  -1192.666   -0.18095  |                ****|  .                 |
 21   -496.859   -0.07538  |               .  **|   .                |
 22 -74.696413   -0.01133  |               .    |   .                |
 23   -374.542   -0.05682  |               .   *|   .                |
 24    947.819    0.14380  |               .    |*** .               |
                           "." marks two standard errors
```

```
                    Dow Jones Index Data                  2
                      Monthly Average

                      ARIMA Procedure


                 Inverse Autocorrelations

Lag Correlation -1 9 8 7 6 5 4 3 2 1 0 1 2 3 4 5 6 7 8 9 1
  1    -0.29768 |          ❸  ******|   .               |
  2     0.06513 |               .   |*  .               |
  3     0.13522 |               .   |***.               |
  4     0.06487 |               .   |*  .               |
  5     0.11176 |               .   |** .               |
  6     0.00047 |               .   |   .               |
  7    -0.04887 |               .  *|   .               |
  8     0.18707 |               .   |****               |
  9     0.04200 |               .   |*  .               |
 10    -0.00067 |               .   |   .               |
 11    -0.09236 |               . **|   .               |
 12     0.23633 |               .   |*****   ❹          |
 13    -0.02164 |               .   |   .               |
 14    -0.06471 |               .  *|   .               |
 15     0.16586 |               .   |***.               |
 16    -0.05539 |               .  *|   .               |
 17     0.15419 |               .   |***.               |
 18    -0.01536 |               .   |   .               |
 19    -0.02036 |               .   |   .               |
 20     0.14321 |               .   |***.               |
 21     0.04197 |               .   |*  .               |
 22    -0.06300 |               .  *|   .               |
 23     0.10793 |               .   |** .               |
 24    -0.04573 |               .  *|   .               |
```

```
                    Dow Jones Index Data                  3
                      Monthly Average

                      ARIMA Procedure


                 Partial Autocorrelations

Lag Correlation -1 9 8 7 6 5 4 3 2 1 0 1 2 3 4 5 6 7 8 9 1
  1     0.30799 |               .   |******  ❸          |
  2    -0.13777 |               .***|   .               |
  3    -0.04171 |               .  *|   .               |
  4    -0.09698 |               . **|   .               |
  5    -0.07779 |               . **|   .               |
  6     0.00563 |               .   |   .               |
  7     0.00572 |               .   |   .               |
  8    -0.16507 |               .***|   .               |
  9    -0.06192 |               .  *|   .               |
 10     0.07096 |               .   |*  .               |
 11     0.09529 |               .   |** .               |
 12    -0.22195 |          ❹    ****|   .               |
 13     0.12195 |               .   |** .               |
 14     0.02227 |               .   |   .               |
 15    -0.11899 |               . **|   .               |
 16    -0.01424 |               .   |   .               |
 17    -0.12878 |               .***|   .               |
 18     0.05260 |               .   |*  .               |
 19    -0.11561 |               . **|   .               |
 20    -0.22261 |               ****|   .               |
 21    -0.03616 |               .  *|   .               |
 22    -0.00977 |               .   |   .               |
 23    -0.10907 |               . **|   .               |
 24     0.06551 |               .   |*  .               |
```

```
    ❺ Autocorrelation Check for White Noise

 To   Chi                     Autocorrelations
Lag  Square DF   Prob
 6    17.26  6  0.008  0.308 -0.030 -0.090 -0.126 -0.129 -0.041
12    24.87 12  0.015  0.021 -0.111 -0.122  0.032  0.142 -0.088
18    28.82 18  0.051  0.025  0.077 -0.083 -0.076 -0.092 -0.013
24    39.85 24  0.022 -0.107 -0.181 -0.075 -0.011 -0.057  0.144
```

Interpretation

From the identification phase output for the differenced series, note the following items:

❶ The output lists the periods of differencing.

❷ The sample ACF drops to 0 after lag 1, which indicates an MA(1) process; however, see ❹. Because the sample ACF does not tail off slowly as it did in Output 2.1, it indicates that the process is now stationary.

❸ The sample ACF, sample IACF, and sample PACF all have spikes at lag 1. This indicates that the time series may be an AR(1) process.

❹ The sample IACF and sample PACF have modest spikes at lag 12. This may be evidence of some degree of seasonality in the process.

❺ The Autocorrelation Check for White Noise has significant Q-statistics. This indicates that the differenced series is not simply white noise.

Output 2.3
Estimating the Dow Jones Index Time Series

```
                Dow Jones Index Data
                  Monthly Average

                  ARIMA Procedure

     ❶ Conditional Least Squares Estimation

                             Approx.
Parameter   Estimate   Std Error   T Ratio  Lag
MA1,1       -0.34789     0.08572     -4.06   1

Variance  Estimate = 5923.79073
Std Error Estimate = 76.9661662
AIC                = 1395.47352*
SBC                = 1398.26931*
Number of Residuals=        121
* Does not include log determinant.
```

```
❷ Autocorrelation Check of Residuals

 To    Chi                    Autocorrelations
Lag  Square DF   Prob
  6    2.56  5  0.767  0.001 -0.012 -0.063 -0.077 -0.095 -0.031
 12   14.19 11  0.223  0.063 -0.103 -0.090 -0.000  0.193 -0.162
 18   19.26 17  0.314  0.044  0.098 -0.111 -0.011 -0.101  0.042
 24   29.86 23  0.154 -0.075 -0.145 -0.042  0.038 -0.119  0.163


❸ Model for variable DJIAM

  Data have been centered by subtracting the value 21.873719008.
  No mean term in this model.
  Period(s) of Differencing = 1.

  Moving Average Factors
  Factor 1: 1 + 0.34789 B**(1)
```

Explanation

Because you specified the NOCONSTANT option in the ESTIMATE statement, the parameter estimates list only the MA(1) parameter ❶. That is, no mean parameter is estimated for this model. Also, the estimate of the constant term is not printed. After you center the observations, the constant term should be 0, so there is no need to compute its value.

Interpretation

The Autocorrelation Check of Residuals table shows that none of the *Q*-statistics are significant ❷. Thus, the residuals of the model are simply white noise. You conclude that an MA(1) model provides an adequate fit to the differenced Dow Jones Index time series process.

The model information at the bottom of the output ❸ shows that you have performed the following actions:

- subtracted the mean (of the differenced data) of 21.87 from all observations (the CENTER option)
- fit a model with no mean term (the NOCONSTANT option)
- taken first differences of the time series.

Output 2.4
Forecasting the Dow Jones Index Time Series

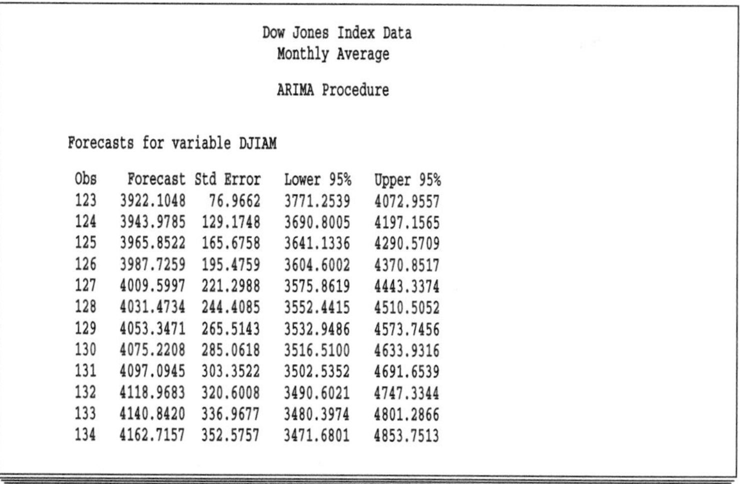

Dow Jones Index Data
Monthly Average

ARIMA Procedure

Forecasts for variable DJIAM

Obs	Forecast	Std Error	Lower 95%	Upper 95%
123	3922.1048	76.9662	3771.2539	4072.9557
124	3943.9785	129.1748	3690.8005	4197.1565
125	3965.8522	165.6758	3641.1336	4290.5709
126	3987.7259	195.4759	3604.6002	4370.8517
127	4009.5997	221.2988	3575.8619	4443.3374
128	4031.4734	244.4085	3552.4415	4510.5052
129	4053.3471	265.5143	3532.9486	4573.7456
130	4075.2208	285.0618	3516.5100	4633.9316
131	4097.0945	303.3522	3502.5352	4691.6539
132	4118.9683	320.6008	3490.6021	4747.3344
133	4140.8420	336.9677	3480.3974	4801.2866
134	4162.7157	352.5757	3471.6801	4853.7513

Interpretation

The forecasts for the Dow Jones Index data begin at 3922.48 for the first future period. They increase by a constant amount of 21.87 points each period, and reach a value of 4162.72 in the twelfth future period.

Variation

Using the FORECAST Procedure

The FORECAST procedure produces forecasts for exponential smoothing models, which are virtually equivalent to MA models. These models are also known as *exponentially weighted moving average* (EWMA) models (Roberts 1959), and they are often used as a quality control tool (Chow 1965; Crowder 1987; Hunter 1986). PROC FORECAST requires less user input than does PROC ARIMA, so it may be more efficient to use PROC FORECAST if you want to produce quick forecasts for several time series.

In this example, you specify a linear trend model and you use the default exponential smoothing weight. For a linear trend model, the default weight is .10557. You also use the default number of beginning values of the series to compute starting values for the trend parameters. For the exponential smoothing method, the default number is 8. You can change this value with the NSTART= option.

Forecast the Dow Jones Index data using PROC FORECAST. Specify the desired options for the model and forecasts in the PROC FORECAST statement.

```
proc forecast data=djm
              interval=month
              trend=2          /* fit a linear trend model              */
              method=expo      /* use exponential smoothing method  */
              out=djmout1
              lead=12
              outstd;
```

Produce forecasts for the DJIAM variable listed in the VAR statement.

```
   var djiam;
   id date;
run;
```

Print the OUT= data set that contains the forecasts.

```
proc print data=djmout1;
run;
```

Output 2.5
Output Data Set Created with PROC FORECAST

Dow Jones Index Data
Monthly Average

OBS	DATE	_TYPE_	_LEAD_	DJIAM
1	MAR94	FORECAST	1	3817.14
2	MAR94	STD	1	171.81
3	APR94	FORECAST	2	3845.39
4	APR94	STD	2	173.64
5	MAY94	FORECAST	3	3873.64
6	MAY94	STD	3	175.63
7	JUN94	FORECAST	4	3901.89
8	JUN94	STD	4	177.78
9	JUL94	FORECAST	5	3930.14
10	JUL94	STD	5	180.08
11	AUG94	FORECAST	6	3958.38
12	AUG94	STD	6	182.53
13	SEP94	FORECAST	7	3986.63
14	SEP94	STD	7	185.11
15	OCT94	FORECAST	8	4014.88
16	OCT94	STD	8	187.83
17	NOV94	FORECAST	9	4043.13
18	NOV94	STD	9	190.68
19	DEC94	FORECAST	10	4071.38
20	DEC94	STD	10	193.65
21	JAN95	FORECAST	11	4099.63
22	JAN95	STD	11	196.73
23	FEB95	FORECAST	12	4127.87
24	FEB95	STD	12	199.93

Interpretation

The forecasts of the Dow Jones Index data that PROC FORECAST produces with the exponential smoothing method begin with a value of 3817.14 for the first future period. The forecasts increase linearly by the constant amount of about 28.25 each period, until they reach a value of 4127.87 in the twelfth future period.

Further Reading

- For more information on PROC ARIMA and PROC FORECAST, see the *SAS/ETS User's Guide, Version 6, Second Edition.*
- For more information on using EWMA models in statistical quality control, see Part 5, "The MACONTROL Procedure," in *SAS/QC Software: Usage and Reference, Version 6, First Edition.*

References

- Chow, W.M. (1965), "Adaptive Control of the Exponential Smoothing Constant," *Journal of Industrial Engineering*, 16, 314-317.
- Crowder, S.V. (1987), "A Simple Method for Studying Run-Length Distributions of Exponentially Weighted Moving Average Charts," *Technometrics*, 29, 401-408.
- Hunter, J.S. (1986), "The Exponentially Weighted Moving Average," *Journal of Quality Technology*, 18, 203-210.
- Roberts, S.W. (1959), "Control Chart Tests Based on Geometric Moving Averages," *Technometrics*, 1, 239-250.

EXAMPLE 3

Forecasting a Seasonal Process

Featured Tools and Tasks:

- ARIMA procedure:
  - ARMA modeling
  - estimation process options
  - modeling seasonal data
- FORECAST procedure
- GPLOT procedure

Many economic and business variables are affected by seasonal factors. For example, power usage is highest in the months when temperatures are most extreme. The most common type of seasonality is variation due to the time of year, but other types of seasonality are also found in time series data.

Seasonal models are often multiplicative rather than additive. A multiplicative model includes the product of one or more nonseasonal parameters with one or more seasonal parameters. For example, a multiplicative model with both autoregressive and moving average terms (an ARMA model) and yearly seasonality for a time series, Y_t, can be written as follows:

$$Y_t = \theta_0 + \left(\phi_1 Y_{t-1} + \phi_{12} Y_{t-12} - \phi_1 \phi_{12} Y_{t-13}\right) - \left(\theta_1 \epsilon_{t-1} + \theta_{12} \epsilon_{t-12} - \theta_1 \theta_{12} \epsilon_{t-13}\right) + \epsilon_t$$

where

θ_0 is the intercept parameter.

ϕ_1 is the nonseasonal first-order autoregressive parameter.

ϕ_{12} is the seasonal autoregressive parameter.

θ_1 is the nonseasonal first-order moving average parameter.

θ_{12} is the seasonal moving average parameter.

To identify a seasonal model, you need to examine the ACF and IACF plots. For multiplicative MA processes, there are small spikes in the ACF plot q lags before and after the seasonal lag, where q is the number of nonseasonal MA parameters necessary to model the data. These small spikes are usually in the opposite direction of the seasonal spike. For example, a multiplicative MA(1, 12) process will typically have small spikes at lags 11 and 13 on either side of, and in the opposite direction of, a large spike at lag 12.

An additive MA process typically has small spikes q lags before the spike at the seasonal lag, where q is the number of nonseasonal MA parameters necessary to model the data. For example, an additive MA(1, 12) process will typically have a small spike at lag 11 and a larger spike at lag 12.

To identify an AR process, look for the patterns described previously in the IACF plot rather than in the ACF plot. If a process contains both AR and MA components, the patterns may appear in both the ACF and IACF plots.

The seasonal component, the nonseasonal component, or both components of the model can be nonstationary. In such cases, the data may require differencing to achieve stationarity before you fit a model. See Dickey, Hasza, and Fuller (1984) for more information on tests for seasonal nonstationarity.

Program

Identifying the Time Series Process

Create the steel shipments data set. The complete steel shipments data set is in "Introduction: The Example Data Sets."

```
data steel;
   format date monyy.;
   input date:monyy. steelshp @@;
   title 'U.S. Steel Shipments Data';
   title2 '(thousands of net tons)';
   datalines;
jan84 5980  feb84 6150  mar84 7240  apr84 6472
more data lines
;
```

Invoke PROC ARIMA and identify the time series process.

```
proc arima data=steel;
   i var=steelshp;
run;
```

Output 3.1
Identifying the Steel Shipments Time Series Process

```
                        U.S. Steel Shipments Data                      1
                         (thousands of net tons)

                            ARIMA Procedure


                   Name of variable = STEELSHP.

                   Mean of working series = 6488.135
                   Standard deviation     = 637.5279
                   Number of observations =       96

                            Autocorrelations

 Lag Covariance Correlation -1 9 8 7 6 5 4 3 2 1 0 1 2 3 4 5 6 7 8 9 1
   0     406442     1.00000  |                    |********************|
   1     262630     0.64617  |                  . |*************       |
   2     261597     0.64363  |                 .  |*************       |
   3     235909     0.58042  |                .   |************        |
   4     168515     0.41461  |                .   |********            |
   5     201896     0.49674  |               .    |**********          |
   6     129000     0.31739  |               .    |****** .            |
   7     152701     0.37570  |              .     |********.           |
   8     113117     0.27831  |              .     |******  .           |
   9     127532     0.31378  |              .     |******  .           |
  10     137000     0.33707  |              .     |*******  .          |
  11     130723     0.32163  |              .     |******   .          |
  12     200408     0.49308  |             .      |**********    ❶     |
  13     112496     0.27678  |             .      |******     .        |
  14     135119     0.33244  |             .      |*******    .        |
  15     103295     0.25414  |             .      |*****      .        |
  16  62982.090     0.15496  |             .      |***        .        |
  17     108381     0.26666  |             .      |*****      .        |
  18  42836.479     0.10539  |            .       |**          .       |
  19  65840.039     0.16199  |            .       |***         .       |
  20  37765.859     0.09292  |            .       |**          .       |
```

```
21  27790.106     0.06837  |          .          |*         .          |
22  40303.846     0.09916  |          .          |**        .          |
23  46097.710     0.11342  |          .          |**        .          |
24  76317.464     0.18777  |          .          |****      .   ❷      |
                             "." marks two standard errors
```

```
                         U.S. Steel Shipments Data                        2
                          (thousands of net tons)

                              ARIMA Procedure


                         Inverse Autocorrelations

         Lag Correlation -1 9 8 7 6 5 4 3 2 1 0 1 2 3 4 5 6 7 8 9 1
           1   -0.37291   |             *******|   .                  |
           2    0.08136   |        ❸         . |** .                  |
           3   -0.31032   |              ******|   .                  |
           4    0.16197   |                 .  |***.                  |
           5   -0.20750   |                ****|   .                  |
           6    0.16115   |                 .  |***.                  |
           7   -0.02341   |                 .  |   .                  |
           8    0.06910   |                 .  |*  .                  |
           9    0.00628   |                 .  |   .                  |
          10    0.02046   |                 .  |   .                  |
          11    0.02875   |                 .  |*  .                  |
          12   -0.23279   |               *****|   .                  |
          13    0.03755   |                 .  |*  .                  |
          14    0.04050   |                 .  |*  .                  |
          15    0.03498   |                 .  |*  .                  |
          16    0.09969   |                 .  |** .                  |
          17   -0.10703   |                 . **|  .                  |
          18    0.04901   |                 .  |*  .                  |
          19   -0.08634   |                 . **|  .                  |
          20    0.02281   |                 .  |   .                  |
          21    0.00844   |                 .  |   .                  |
          22    0.10510   |                 .  |** .                  |
          23   -0.10923   |                 . **|  .                  |
          24    0.02676   |                 .  |*  .                  |
```

```
                         U.S. Steel Shipments Data                        3
                          (thousands of net tons)

                              ARIMA Procedure


                         Partial Autocorrelations

         Lag Correlation -1 9 8 7 6 5 4 3 2 1 0 1 2 3 4 5 6 7 8 9 1
           1    0.64617   |                 .  |*************         |
           2    0.38816   |                 .  |********              |
           3    0.15190   |                 .  |***.                  |
           4   -0.18616   |                ****|   .                  |
           5    0.21835   |                 .  |****                  |
           6   -0.16003   |                .***|   .                  |
           7    0.15783   |                 .  |***.                  |
           8   -0.14831   |                .***|   .                  |
           9    0.26920   |                 .  |*****                 |
          10   -0.05397   |                 . *|   .                  |
          11    0.24830   |                 .  |*****                 |
          12    0.17869   |                 .  |****                  |
```

```
13  -0.29738 |            ******|  .              |
14  -0.07949 |              . **|  .              |
15  -0.11524 |              . **|  .              |
16   0.00960 |              .   |  .              |
17   0.09426 |              .   |** .             |
18   0.01714 |              .   |  .              |
19  -0.03146 |              .  *|  .              |
20  -0.01588 |              .   |  .              |
21  -0.07355 |              .  *|  .              |
22  -0.03907 |              .  *|  .              |
23   0.15518 |              .   |***.             |
24  -0.05162 |              .  *|  .              |


         Autocorrelation Check for White Noise

 To   Chi                 Autocorrelations
Lag  Square DF  Prob
  6  170.51  6  0.000  0.646  0.644  0.580  0.415  0.497  0.317
 12  255.47 12  0.000  0.376  0.278  0.314  0.337  0.322  0.493
 18  296.96 18  0.000  0.277  0.332  0.254  0.155  0.267  0.105
 24  309.34 24  0.000  0.162  0.093  0.068  0.099  0.113  0.188
```

Interpretation

❶ The large spike at lag 12 in the ACF plot provides evidence that the steel shipments time series has a seasonal autoregressive component.

❷ The lack of a large spike at lag 24 indicates that the series is stationary at the seasonal level.

❸ The spikes at lags 1 and 3 in the IACF plot indicate that other components are necessary to fit an adequate model.

You may need to try several candidate models before you find one that provides an appropriate fit to the data.

Estimating a Seasonal Model

Fit a seasonal ARMA model to the time series. In the syntax of the ESTIMATE statement, the two multiplicative AR terms are enclosed in separate parentheses. The two additive MA terms are separated by a space within a single set of parentheses.

```
   e p=(2)(12) q=(1 3);
run;
```

Output 3.2
Estimating a Seasonal Model for the Steel Shipments Time Series

```
                        U.S. Steel Shipments Data
                         (thousands of net tons)

                             ARIMA Procedure


                  Conditional Least Squares Estimation

                                    Approx.  ❷
              Parameter   Estimate   Std Error  T Ratio  Lag
              MU            6057.1   232.96713    26.00    0
              MA1,1       -0.55505     0.08021    -6.92    1
              MA1,2       -0.43689     0.07936    -5.51    3
              AR1,1        0.54234     0.09903     5.48    2
              AR2,1        0.64802     0.09392     6.90   12

              Constant Estimate  = 975.739084

              Variance  Estimate = 126334.132
              Std Error Estimate =  355.43513
              AIC                = 1404.98309*
              SBC                = 1417.80484*
              Number of Residuals=         96
              * Does not include log determinant.


                     Correlations of the Estimates

    Parameter          MU       MA1,1       MA1,2       AR1,1       AR2,1

    MU              1.000      -0.012      -0.022      -0.243      -0.128
    MA1,1          -0.012       1.000      -0.922      -0.329       0.069
    MA1,2          -0.022      -0.922       1.000       0.253      -0.153
    AR1,1          -0.243      -0.329       0.253       1.000       0.005
    AR2,1          -0.128       0.069      -0.153       0.005       1.000

               ❶ Autocorrelation Check of Residuals

      To   Chi                      Autocorrelations
     Lag  Square DF   Prob
       6    2.42  2  0.298 -0.009 -0.051  0.071  0.070  0.104  0.018
      12    3.63  8  0.889 -0.084  0.032 -0.024  0.013 -0.033 -0.035
      18   11.86 14  0.618 -0.082  0.168  0.014 -0.137  0.107  0.073
      24   16.16 20  0.707  0.023  0.019 -0.010 -0.047  0.174 -0.000


              Model for variable STEELSHP

              Estimated Mean = 6057.12204

              Autoregressive Factors
              Factor 1: 1 - 0.54234 B**(2)
              Factor 2: 1 - 0.64802 B**(12)


              Moving Average Factors
              Factor 1: 1 + 0.55505 B**(1) + 0.43689 B**(3)
```

Interpretation

❶ The **Autocorrelation Check of Residuals** shows that none of the *Q*-statistics are statistically significant. This indicates that the model provides an adequate fit to the data.

❷ All of the estimated parameters have relatively large *t*-statistics, which indicates that these parameters cannot be omitted from the model.

Forecasting the Time Series

Produce forecasts for 12 future periods.

```
   f lead=12;
run;
```

Output 3.3
Printing Forecasts for the Steel Shipments Time Series

U.S. Steel Shipments Data
(thousands of net tons)

ARIMA Procedure

Forecasts for variable STEELSHP

Obs	Forecast	Std Error	Lower 95%	Upper 95%
97	6563.4472	355.4351	5866.8072	7260.0873
98	5781.9412	406.5156	4985.1853	6578.6971
99	5958.3743	449.9041	5076.5785	6840.1701
100	6168.8410	520.7739	5148.1430	7189.5390
101	6492.3639	531.1638	5451.3020	7533.4258
102	6346.3350	549.8806	5268.5887	7424.0812
103	6280.5960	552.7960	5197.1358	7364.0563
104	6596.2903	558.1530	5502.3304	7690.2501
105	6497.8413	558.9994	5402.2226	7593.4600
106	6968.6914	560.5630	5870.0082	8067.3746
107	6293.3744	560.8110	5194.2051	7392.5437
108	6084.2116	561.2698	4984.1430	7184.2803

Interpretation

Because the model fit to the steel shipments data includes a seasonal component, the forecasts do not follow a simple linear trend. Instead, the forecasts show variability due to the season (month of the year).

Plotting the Forecasts

Create an output data set that contains the forecasts. Rerun the FORECAST statement with additional options.

```
   f lead=12
     out=steel2
     id=date
     interval=month
     noprint;
run;
```

Prepare the output data set for plotting. Change the values for the forecasts and confidence limits to missing for all dates prior to the future forecast periods.

```
data steel3;
   set steel2;
   if date lt '01jan92'd then do;
      forecast=.;
      l95=.;
      u95=.;
   end;
run;
```

Set graphics options.

```
goptions cback=white colors=(black) border reset=(axis symbol);
```

Specify details for the axes of the plot. When you plot time series data with PROC GPLOT, the procedure prints a warning message to the log to indicate that the intervals on the axis are not evenly spaced. This message simply reflects the fact that there is a different number of days in each month. You can ignore this warning message.

```
axis1 offset=(1 cm)
      label=('Year') minor=none
      order=('01jan84'd to '01jan93'd by year);
axis2 label=(angle=90 'Steel Shipments')
      order=(4500 to 8500 by 1000);
```

Specify details of the plot symbols.

```
symbol1 i=join l=1 h=2 pct v=star;
symbol2 i=join l=1 h=3 pct v=F;
symbol3 i=join l=20;
```

Plot the original data as well as the forecasts and 95% confidence limits for the future periods.

```
proc gplot data=steel3;
   format date year4.;
   plot steelshp*date=1
        forecast*date=2
        l95*date=3
        u95*date=3 / overlay
                     haxis=axis1
                     vaxis=axis2
                     vminor=1;
run;
```

Output 3.4
Plot of Original Steel Shipments Time Series, Forecasts, and 95% Confidence Limits

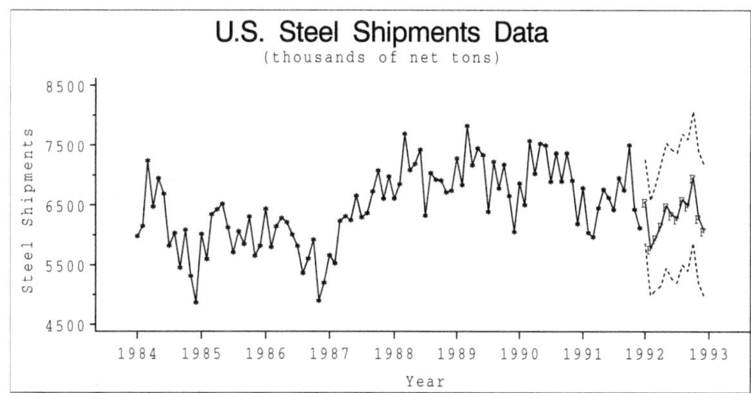

Interpretation

The values of the original steel shipments time series are plotted with the star symbol. The forecasts are plotted with the F symbol, and the upper and lower 95% confidence limits for the forecasts are plotted with dashed lines. To reduce the clutter in the plot and to focus on the forecasts for future time periods, the forecasts and confidence limits for time periods prior to the future forecast periods have been removed from the data.

A Closer Look

Syntax of the ESTIMATE Statement

The syntax of the P= and Q= options in the ESTIMATE statement enables you to specify several different types of models. You can fit a model with *n* lags or a model that includes only a subset of *n* lags. You can fit additive or multiplicative models and models that include AR components, MA components, or both. You perform differencing, if necessary, in the IDENTIFY statement of PROC ARIMA before you attempt to fit a model with the ESTIMATE statement.

Some examples of various model specifications follow:

ESTIMATE P=4;	estimates AR parameters for lags 1, 2, 3, and 4.
ESTIMATE Q=(4);	estimates one MA parameter at lag 4.
ESTIMATE P=(1 4);	estimates an AR parameter at lag 1 and an AR parameter at lag 4. The AR parameter estimates for lags 2 and 3 are constrained to 0. Use a space or a comma to separate the lags within the parentheses.
ESTIMATE P=(2) Q=2;	estimates an AR parameter at lag 2 and MA parameters at lags 1 and 2. This is a subset ARMA(2,2) model or an ARIMA(2,*d*,2) model (if you apply a difference of order *d*).
ESTIMATE P=(1)(12);	estimates a multiplicative AR model with one factor at lag 1 and another factor at lag 12.
ESTIMATE P=(1 12 13);	estimates an additive AR model with estimates for lags 1, 12, and 13.

Variations

Using the FORECAST Procedure

You can use PROC FORECAST to fit an additive or multiplicative seasonal model to time series data. Specify the WINTERS method in the METHOD= option to fit a multiplicative model; specify ADDWINTERS to fit an additive model. The WINTERS method is a variation on exponential smoothing.

Use the SEASONS= option to specify the type of seasonality to model. Specify QTR or MONTH for yearly seasonal cycles; specify DAY for weekly seasonal cycles; specify HOUR for daily seasonal cycles. In this example, you specify SEASONS=MONTH to have PROC FORECAST estimate a seasonal parameter for each month.

Invoke PROC FORECAST and specify modeling and forecasting options.

```
proc forecast data=steel
              interval=month
              method=winters   /* use Winters seasonal method  */
              seasons=month    /* specify seasonality          */
              out=steelout
              lead=12
              outstd;
   var steelshp;
   id date;
run;
```

Print the OUT= data set that contains the forecasts.

```
proc print data=steelout;
run;
```

Output 3.5
Forecasts and Standard Errors from a Seasonal Model fit Using PROC FORECAST

U.S. Steel Shipments Data
(thousands of net tons)

OBS	DATE	_TYPE_	_LEAD_	STEELSHP
1	JAN92	FORECAST	1	6497.83
2	JAN92	STD	1	474.07
3	FEB92	FORECAST	2	6141.38
4	FEB92	STD	2	452.31
5	MAR92	FORECAST	3	6797.15
6	MAR92	STD	3	505.97
7	APR92	FORECAST	4	6635.05
8	APR92	STD	4	499.85
9	MAY92	FORECAST	5	6888.97
10	MAY92	STD	5	525.93
11	JUN92	FORECAST	6	6811.29
12	JUN92	STD	6	527.69
13	JUL92	FORECAST	7	6246.94
14	JUL92	STD	7	491.81
15	AUG92	FORECAST	8	6636.62
16	AUG92	STD	8	531.67
17	SEP92	FORECAST	9	6374.49

```
18    SEP92    STD          9     520.35
19    OCT92    FORECAST    10    6800.63
20    OCT92    STD         10     566.40
21    NOV92    FORECAST    11    6096.12
22    NOV92    STD         11     518.68
23    DEC92    FORECAST    12    5826.47
24    DEC92    STD         12     507.03
```

When the Estimation Process Does Not Converge

In some cases, the estimation algorithm in PROC ARIMA fails to converge. When this occurs, a message is printed in the Output window. Output 3.6 shows an example of such a message.

Output 3.6
Message Printed When PROC ARIMA Fails to Converge

```
                              ARIMA Procedure

ERROR: The estimation algorithm did not converge after 50 iterations.

                  ARIMA Estimation Optimization Summary

     Estimation Method:                       Conditional Least Squares
     Parameters Estimated:                                            6
     Termination Criteria:        Maximum Relative Change in Estimates
     Iteration Stopping Value:                                    0.001
     Criteria Value:                                          0.0151252
     Alternate Criteria:         Relative Change in Objective Function
     Alternate Criteria Value:                               2.61934E-6
     Maximum Absolute Value of Gradient:                     7644.81165
     R-Square (Relative Change in Regression SSE) from Last Iteration
        Step:                                                 0.0012818
     Objective Function:                         Sum of Squared Residuals
     Objective Function Value:                               13437928.1
     Marquardt's Lambda Coefficient:                              1E-12
     Numerical Derivative Perturbation Delta:                     0.001
     Iterations:                                                     50
     Warning Message:       The estimation algorithm did not converge.
```

There are several steps you can take to achieve convergence, all of which involve the ESTIMATE statement in PROC ARIMA.

- □ Attempt to fit a different set of parameters; that is, reconsider your identification. Nonconvergence is more likely when you include too many AR and MA parameters.
- □ Increase the number of iterations. Use the MAXITER= option.

- Use a different estimation method. Use the METHOD= option. The choices are:

CLS (default)	specifies conditional least squares estimation.
ML	specifies maximum likelihood estimation.
ULS	specifies unconditional least squares estimation.

- Center the data and drop the constant parameter. Use the CENTER option in the IDENTIFY statement and the NOCONSTANT option in the ESTIMATE statement to reduce by one the number of parameters to estimate.

- Set a different convergence criterion. Use the CONVERGE= option. Convergence is assumed when the largest change in the estimate for any parameter is less than the CONVERGE= option value. If the absolute value of the parameter estimate is greater than 0.01, the relative change is used; otherwise the absolute change in the estimate is used. The default is CONVERGE=.001.

- Supply initial estimates for the parameters. Use the AR= option to supply starting values for the autoregressive parameter estimates. Use the MA= option to supply starting values for the moving average parameter estimates. Use the MU= option to supply a starting value for the mean parameter estimate. The number of values given must agree with the model specification. Parameter estimates for the AR and MA parts of the model must always remain within the stationary and invertible regions, respectively, throughout the iteration process. You can specify the NOSTABLE option to remove this restriction, however.

- Suppress the estimation process. The NOEST option causes PROC ARIMA to use the values specified in the AR= and MA= options as final parameter estimates. Only the residual variance is estimated. Use this step to circumvent convergence, not to achieve it. The NOEST option is useful, for example, when you want to generate forecasts based on a published model.

Other options are available to provide information or control parts of the estimation process in PROC ARIMA. See the *SAS/ETS User's Guide, Version 6, Second Edition* for more information.

Further Reading

- For more information on PROC ARIMA and PROC FORECAST, see the *SAS/ETS User's Guide, Version 6, Second Edition.*
- For complete reference information on PROC GPLOT and other features available in SAS/GRAPH software, see *SAS/GRAPH Software: Reference, Version 6, First Edition, Volumes 1 and 2.*

Reference

Dickey, D.A., Hasza, D.P., and Fuller, W.A. (1984), "Testing for Unit Roots in Seasonal Time Series," *Journal of the American Statistical Association*, 79, 355-367.

EXAMPLE 4

Seasonal Adjustment and Forecasting

Featured Tools and Tasks:

- X11 procedure:
  - seasonal adjustment
  - SSPAN statement
  - ARIMA statement

One approach to modeling and forecasting seasonal data is to take seasonal differences and model the differenced time series. Another approach is to fit a model with parameters for the seasons (see Example 3, "Forecasting a Seasonal Process"). This example shows a third approach, which is to remove the seasonality from the time series with a seasonal adjustment process. You can fit a model and generate forecasts for the seasonally adjusted time series as if it were nonseasonal.

The X11 procedure, an adaptation of the U.S. Bureau of the Census X-11 Seasonal Adjustment program, seasonally adjusts monthly or quarterly time series. If you use non-seasonally adjusted data in conjunction with data from government sources or other data that have been seasonally adjusted, then you may want to use PROC X11 to seasonally adjust your data.

Seasonal adjustment is based on the assumption that the original time series, Y_t, $t = 1, \ldots, n$, is made up of seasonal (S_t), trend cycle (C_t), trading day (TD_t), and irregular (I_t) components. These components are usually related multiplicatively:

$$Y_t = \left(S_t \times C_t \times TD_t \times I_t\right)$$

However, these components are sometimes related additively:

$$Y_t = \left(S_t + C_t + TD_t + I_t\right)$$

A seasonally adjusted time series consists of only the trend cycle and irregular components. The following list describes the four components:

seasonal components
: are regular seasonal fluctuations, such as power usage peaks in months where the temperatures are most extreme.

trend cycle components
: are variations due to long-term trend, the business cycle, and other cyclical factors.

trading day components
: are variations due to calendar composition. That is, some months have more working days than others, and this difference can account for some of the variations in a time series. The trading day component is not estimated for quarterly data.

irregular components
: are residual variations not accounted for by the other components.

PROC X11 produces a large number of tables and charts, which are classified into several groups. Tables in groups A, B, and C contain intermediate calculations. Tables in group D contain the final estimates of the components and the seasonally adjusted time series. Group E contains analytical tables, and group F contains summary measures. Charts are in group G. Tables in group S contain output from the sliding spans analysis, which is new in Release 6.11. See "Variations" later in this example for more details and an example.

This example shows how to use PROC X11 to seasonally adjust the electricity production time series. See the plot of the electricity production time series (Output 6 in "Introduction: The Example Data Sets") and note that it shows strong evidence of seasonality, with peaks in the summer and winter months.

In addition to the seasonal adjustment methods available in PROC X11, you may also use some SAS/IML software subroutines for seasonal adjustment. These are part of the Time Series Analysis and Control (TIMSAC) package developed by the Institute of Statistical Mathematics in Japan. The TSBAYSEA and TSDECOMP subroutines, based on Bayesian modeling, are alternatives to PROC X11.

Program

Create the electricity production data set. The complete electricity production data set is in "Introduction: The Example Data Sets."

```
data electric;
   format date monyy.;
   input date:monyy. elecprod @@;
   title 'Electricity Production Data';
   title2 '(millions of kilowatt hours)';
   datalines;
jan80 200005 feb80 188715 mar80 187464 apr80 168720
more data lines
;
```

Invoke PROC X11. Specify the input data set with the DATA= option.

```
proc x11 data=electric;
```

Specify the name of the date variable in the MONTHLY statement (if you have monthly data). Use the QUARTERLY statement if you have quarterly data.

```
   monthly date=date;
```

Specify exactly which tables to print.

```
   tables d10      /* final seasonal factors          */
          d11      /* final seasonally adjusted series */
          d12      /* final trend cycle                */
          d13;     /* final irregular series           */
```

Create an output data set. Specify a variable name for each table that you write to the output data set.

```
   output out=adjelec b1=original
                      d10=seasonal
                      d11=adjusted
                      d12=trend
                      d13=irreg;
```

Specify the variable or variables to be seasonally adjusted.

```
   var elecprod;
run;
```

Print part of the output data set from PROC X11.

```
proc print data=adjelec(obs=15);
run;
```

Output 4.1
Final Estimates of Seasonal Components from PROC X11

```
                        Electricity Production Data                        1
                        (millions of kilowatt hours)

                               X11 Procedure

                      X-11 Seasonal Adjustment Program
                         U. S. Bureau of the Census
                    Economic Research and Analysis Division
                             November 1, 1968

            The X-11 program is divided into seven major parts.
              Part         Description
               A.  Prior adjustments, if any
               B.  Preliminary estimates of irregular component weights
                       and regression trading day factors
               C.  Final estimates of above
               D.  Final estimates of seasonal, trend-cycle and
                       irregular components
               E.  Analytical tables
               F.  Summary measures
               G.  Charts

              Series - ELECPROD
                 Period covered - 1/1980 to 11/1991

                 Type of run multiplicative seasonal adjustment.
                  No printout.   No charts.
            Sigma limits for graduating extreme values are 1.5 and 2.5
             Irregular values outside of 2.5-sigma limits are excluded
               from trading day regression
```

D10 Final Seasonal Factors

Year	JAN	FEB	MAR	APR	MAY	JUN	JUL	AUG	SEP	OCT	NOV	DEC	Avg
1980	108.353	94.380	98.534	90.597	93.444	100.249	114.412	111.860	98.903	94.034	93.110	102.012	99.991
1981	108.314	94.378	98.601	90.571	93.493	100.451	114.249	112.025	98.795	94.025	93.106	102.093	100.008
1982	108.145	94.440	98.345	90.584	93.758	100.722	113.962	112.132	98.700	94.215	93.217	102.308	100.044
1983	107.799	94.389	97.867	90.448	94.151	101.132	113.629	112.281	98.518	94.313	93.409	102.338	100.023
1984	107.446	94.365	97.277	90.339	94.628	101.676	113.489	112.502	98.481	94.331	93.399	102.376	100.026
1985	107.204	94.215	96.828	89.963	94.942	102.416	113.557	112.826	98.360	94.205	93.343	102.284	100.012
1986	107.020	94.177	96.456	89.685	95.215	102.984	113.676	112.959	98.345	94.153	93.169	102.172	100.001
1987	106.993	94.092	96.326	89.486	95.204	103.485	113.756	113.035	98.414	94.183	93.008	102.007	99.999
1988	106.951	94.029	96.296	89.439	95.119	103.803	113.694	113.041	98.569	94.158	92.771	101.941	99.984
1989	107.079	94.044	96.397	89.367	94.871	104.145	113.607	113.091	98.743	94.291	92.690	101.801	100.010
1990	107.029	94.128	96.338	89.360	94.823	104.214	113.370	112.968	98.855	94.408	92.720	101.821	100.003
1991	106.983	94.228	96.336	89.415	94.774	104.170	113.171	112.835	98.927	94.499	92.743	.	99.826
Avg	107.443	94.239	97.133	89.938	94.535	102.454	113.714	112.630	98.634	94.235	93.057	102.105	

Electricity Production Data
(millions of kilowatt hours)

2

D11 Final Seasonally Adjusted Series

Year	JAN	FEB	MAR	APR	MAY	JUN	JUL	AUG	SEP	OCT	NOV	DEC	Total
1980	184587	199953	190253	186231	188063	188959	189470	192556	193608	189883	191761	191755	2287078
1981	190619	190313	188185	190508	190182	201792	192888	187819	189117	192876	188570	191580	2294450
1982	193631	190914	190845	190520	188940	184793	184785	183404	183042	183586	185993	180555	2241008
1983	181429	182731	186465	188364	185226	188909	193757	204805	198547	193961	195859	207469	2307522
1984	201619	200883	205708	200449	203129	206193	194949	203815	198209	202410	203836	195355	2416555
1985	212545	210414	201357	205504	207274	200518	199655	200354	205875	206771	206150	214359	2470776
1986	203205	204229	204066	207474	207230	208785	213477	199334	210170	210034	210835	209012	2487852
1987	208191	206218	209548	211761	216455	217992	217935	219087	216440	215548	215313	216162	2570649
1988	222159	230463	222064	218931	218863	223988	226252	236557	223217	223429	225711	228121	2699755
1989	216049	232940	234899	232468	231685	226027	225993	228432	229735	232883	236251	254062	2781425
1990	221752	225978	233817	236221	235078	238870	234831	237662	240624	238109	230368	233014	2806323
1991	231797	223391	229526	233669	246892	238232	239896	237247	236434	236171	238325	.	2591580
Avg	205632	208202	208061	208508	209918	210422	209491	210923	210418	210472	210748	211040	

Total: 29954974 Mean: 209475 S.D.: 18065

D12 Final Trend Cycle - Henderson Curve
13-term Moving Average Applied I/C Ratio is 2.447

Year	JAN	FEB	MAR	APR	MAY	JUN	JUL	AUG	SEP	OCT	NOV	DEC	Total
1980	189068	188718	188499	188414	188672	189281	190159	191069	191742	191928	191632	191083	2280264
1981	190457	190086	190064	190162	190344	190540	190545	190425	190376	190528	190915	191428	2285868
1982	191787	191654	190901	189645	187965	186273	184988	184101	183452	182980	182731	182720	2239198
1983	182958	183549	184565	186184	188321	190569	192613	194475	196022	197339	198478	199526	2294599
1984	200737	201934	202911	203384	203288	202859	202327	201820	201808	202392	203327	204517	2431304
1985	205563	206025	205677	204597	203361	202416	202223	202826	203879	204838	205464	205477	2452346
1986	205043	204825	205258	206344	207698	208988	209954	210487	210556	210157	209407	208622	2497340
1987	208315	208807	210223	212421	214842	216791	217674	217569	216995	216693	217043	217910	2575282
1988	218888	219774	220538	221217	221897	222605	223332	223942	224375	224982	226099	227964	2675614
1989	230170	231848	232380	231704	230239	228784	228136	228690	230273	232178	233746	234576	2772723
1990	234815	234852	234912	235219	236007	236967	237639	237743	237204	235988	234305	232573	2828225
1991	231352	231121	232100	233829	235593	236945	237699	237840	237650	237428	237177	.	2588734
Avg	207429	207766	208169	208593	209019	209418	209774	210082	210361	210619	210860	208763	

Total: 29921497 Mean: 209241 S.D.: 17692

Electricity Production Data 3
(millions of kilowatt hours)

D13 Final Irregular Series

Year	JAN	FEB	MAR	APR	MAY	JUN	JUL	AUG	SEP	OCT	NOV	DEC	S.D.
1980	97.630	105.954	100.930	98.841	99.677	99.830	99.637	100.778	100.973	98.935	100.067	100.352	1.965
1981	100.085	100.119	99.011	100.182	99.915	105.905	101.230	98.632	99.339	101.233	98.772	100.079	1.888
1982	100.962	99.614	99.971	100.461	100.519	99.206	99.890	99.621	99.776	100.331	101.785	98.815	0.769
1983	99.164	99.555	101.029	101.171	98.356	99.129	100.594	105.311	101.288	98.288	98.680	103.981	2.190
1984	100.439	99.479	101.378	98.557	99.922	101.644	96.353	100.988	98.217	100.009	100.250	95.520	1.931
1985	103.397	102.130	97.900	100.443	101.924	99.063	98.731	98.781	100.979	100.944	100.334	104.322	2.021
1986	99.104	99.709	99.419	100.548	99.775	99.903	101.678	94.701	99.816	99.941	100.682	100.186	1.659
1987	99.940	98.760	99.679	99.690	100.751	100.554	100.120	100.698	99.744	99.472	99.203	99.198	0.628
1988	101.494	104.864	100.692	98.967	98.633	100.621	101.308	105.633	99.484	99.310	99.828	100.069	2.308
1989	93.865	100.471	101.084	100.330	100.628	98.795	99.061	99.887	99.766	100.304	101.072	108.307	3.058
1990	94.437	96.222	99.534	100.426	99.606	100.803	98.818	99.966	101.442	100.898	98.320	100.189	2.113
1991	100.193	96.655	98.891	99.932	104.796	100.543	100.924	99.751	99.488	99.471	100.484	.	1.845
S.D.	2.748	2.763	1.031	0.764	1.654	1.892	1.432	2.794	0.913	0.843	0.998	3.382	

Total: 14317 Mean: 100.12 S.D.: 1.9618

Explanation

The first page in Output 4.1 describes the general structure of PROC X11 output, prints the name of the analysis variable and the dates for which it is analyzed, and lists details about print options and analysis options that you may have specified.

The other pages in Output 4.1 list the four tables that you specified in the TABLES statement. At the bottom of each table is an average value for each month and a total. Some of the tables also list an overall mean and a standard deviation.

Output 4.2
The First 15 Observations of the Output Data Set from PROC X11

Electricity Production Data
(millions of kilowatt hours)

OBS	DATE	ORIGINAL	SEASONAL	❶ ADJUSTED	TREND	IRREG
1	JAN80	200005	108.353	184586.78	189067.65	97.630
2	FEB80	188715	94.380	199953.19	188717.56	105.954
3	MAR80	187464	98.534	190252.53	188499.08	100.930
4	APR80	168720	90.597	186230.85	188413.69	98.841
5	MAY80	175734	93.444	188063.11	188671.63	99.677
6	JUN80	189430	100.249	188958.70	189280.98	99.830
7	JUL80	216776	114.412	189469.72	190159.35	99.637
8	AUG80	215393	111.860	192556.09	191069.09	100.778
9	SEP80	191485	98.903	193608.34	191742.44	100.973
10	OCT80	178555	94.034	189882.73	191927.58	98.935
11	NOV80	178550	93.110	191761.47	191632.30	100.067
12	DEC80	195613	102.012	191754.74	191082.93	100.352
13	JAN81	206467	108.314	190619.42	190456.78	100.085
14	FEB81	179613	94.378	190313.24	190086.18	100.119
15	MAR81	185553	98.601	188184.94	190063.80	99.011

Explanation

Output 4.2 shows the output data set from PROC X11. It contains a date variable that identifies each observation, and one variable for each of the tables that you write to the data set. In this case, you have five variables that correspond to five tables. You can use the ADJUSTED variable ❶ as an input series to the ARIMA procedure (or the FORECAST procedure) to generate forecasts for these data. If you attempt to fit a model that uses the ADJUSTED variable, you do not need to estimate a parameter for the seasonal factor because the series has already been seasonally adjusted. Bell and Hillmer (1984) have documented some problems that you may encounter when you attempt to analyze the seasonally adjusted data as a time series process.

A Closer Look

Specifying Tables to Print

Use the TABLES statement to specify exactly which tables to print in the output. The tables you specify in the TABLES statement will print in addition to any tables that print automatically based on your specification for the PRINTOUT= option or the CHARTS= option in the MONTHLY or QUARTERLY statement.

The PRINTOUT= option has four possible specifications:

STANDARD (default)
: prints between 17 and 27 tables, depending on the other options that you specify.

LONG
: prints between 27 and 39 tables.

FULL
: prints between 44 and 59 tables.

NONE
: suppresses the automatic printing of all tables.

The CHARTS= option has three possible specifications:

STANDARD (default)
: prints 12 seasonal charts and a trend cycle chart for monthly data; it prints 4 seasonal charts and a trend cycle chart for quarterly data.

FULL | ALL
: prints charts of irregular and seasonal factors, in addition to the standard charts.

NONE
: suppresses the automatic printing of all charts.

Variations

Performing Sliding Spans Analysis

Use sliding spans analysis to determine if the time series is suitable for seasonal adjustment. *Sliding spans analysis* takes an initial span of data, typically eight years in length, and performs a seasonal adjustment on this span of data. Next, one year of data is deleted from the beginning and one year is added to the end of the initial span. This new span is seasonally adjusted, and the process continues until the end of the data is reached. If the difference in the seasonal factors between spans for a given month is excessive (greater than 3%), and if many (more than 25%) of these factors have excessive differences, then the series is judged unstable and, thus, unsuitable for seasonal adjustment. For marginally stable series, between 15% and 25% of the factors have excessive differences. These are not exact significance levels; they are empirical thresholds established by the examination of over 500 economic series (Findley et al. 1990; Findley and Monsell 1986). You can specify your own percentage values to determine an excessive difference within a span. Use the CUTOFF= option in the SSPAN statement to specify a new percentage.

CAUTION!

If you change the CUTOFF= value from its default value of 3%, then the empirical threshold ranges no longer apply. ■

Perform a sliding spans analysis. Specify the SSPAN statement with no other options. Suppress the printing of all tables and charts other than the sliding spans tables.

```
proc x11 data=electric;
   monthly date=date printout=none charts=none;
   var elecprod;
   sspan;
run;
```

Output 4.3
Sliding Spans Tables Created with PROC X11 (Partial Output)

```
                              Electricity Production Data                            1
                              (millions of kilowatt hours)

                                     X11 Procedure

                           ❶ S 0.A Sliding Spans Analysis
                             for variable ELECPROD: Number,
                               Length, and Dates of Spans

                           Number of Spans              4
                           Length of Spans (Months)   107

                               Span   Begin     End

                                  1   JAN1980   NOV1988
                                  2   JAN1981   NOV1989
                                  3   JAN1982   NOV1990
                                  4   JAN1983   NOV1991

                        ❷ S 0.B Summary of F-tests for Stable
                          and Moving Seasonality for each Span

               Seasonality Type              Span 1     Span 2     Span 3     Span 4

               Stable Seasonality            134.11     129.97     112.55     112.51
               Moving Seasonality              0.89       0.89       0.74       0.55
               Identifiable Seasonality?        Yes        Yes        Yes        Yes

               ❸ S 1.A  Range Analysis of Seasonal Factors: Means of Seasonal Factors
                    for Each Month (Movements Within a Month Should be Small)

      Month        Span 1           Span 2           Span 3           Span 4           MPD   Average

      January      107.54           107.37           106.69           106.93           0.80   107.13
      February      94.20            94.36            94.18            94.11           0.26    94.21
      March         97.26            97.19            96.97            96.49           0.80    96.98
      April         90.06    MIN     90.09    MIN     89.89    MIN     89.62    MIN    0.52    89.91    MIN
      May           94.43            94.78            94.89            95.00           0.61    94.77
      June         101.86           102.47           102.82           103.21           1.33   102.59
      July         114.15    MAX    113.89    MAX    113.50    MAX    113.12    MAX    0.91   113.66    MAX
      August       112.62           112.74           112.86           112.93           0.27   112.79
      September     98.62            98.32            98.45            98.54           0.31    98.48
      October       94.22            94.11            94.08            94.20           0.15    94.15
      November      93.30            93.05            93.02            92.94           0.38    93.08
      December     101.95           101.75           102.73           102.94           1.17   102.34

         MPD = Maximum Percent Difference = 100*(max-min)/min ;   Average = average taken over all 4 spans
```

Electricity Production Data
(millions of kilowatt hours) 2

S 1.B Summary of Range Measures

	Range Means	R-R Means	Min SF	Max SF	Range SF	R-R SF
Span 1	24.09	1.27	89.22	114.69	25.46	1.29
Span 2	23.81	1.26	89.37	114.31	24.94	1.28
Span 3	23.60	1.26	89.51	113.77	24.27	1.27
Span 4	23.50	1.26	89.34	113.60	24.25	1.27
Ave. Spans	23.75	1.26	89.22	114.69	25.46	1.29

R-R = Range Ratio = Max / Min, SF = Seasonal Factors

❹ S 4.A.1 Breakdown of 3.00% or
Greater Differences in the Seasonally
Adjusted Data by Month

Month	Exceed Count	Total Count	Average Maximum Percentage Difference
January	0	10	0.60
February	0	10	0.37
March	0	10	0.50
April	0	10	0.31
May	0	10	0.38
June	0	10	0.26
July	0	10	0.74
August	0	10	0.27
September	0	10	0.31
October	0	10	0.37
November	0	10	0.36
December	0	9	1.20

S 4.A.2 Breakdown of 3.00% or
Greater Differences in the Seasonally
Adjusted Data by Year

Year	Exceed Count	Total Count	Average Maximum Percentage Difference
1981	0	12	0.21
1982	0	12	0.55
1983	0	12	0.81
1984	0	12	0.57
1985	0	12	0.41
1986	0	12	0.38
1987	0	12	0.44
1988	0	12	0.52
1989	0	12	0.45
1990	0	11	0.31

```
                    Electricity Production Data                              3
                    (millions of kilowatt hours)

          S 4.A.3 Breakdown Summary of Flagged Observations
          Based on 3.00% Cutoff for Seasonally Adjusted Data

                                     Number      Total
Type                                  Found     Tested       Percentage

Flagged MPD                               0        119             0.00
Sign Change                               0        119             0.00
Turning Point                             0         95             0.00
Flagged Sign Change                       0          0             0.00
Flagged Turning Point                     0          0             0.00

                For Flagged MPD, usually, 15% is too
                  high, and 25% is much too high.)

            ❺  S 4.C  Statistics for Maximum
                 Percentage Difference of the
                   Seasonally Adjusted Data

                 Minimum                0.0021
                 25th Percentile        0.2284
                 median                 0.3563
              -> 65th percentile        0.4498 <-
                 75th percentile        0.5496
              -> 85th percentile        0.7694 <-
                 maximum                2.4598
```

Explanation

Note: To conserve space, some of the standard output generated by the SSPAN statement is omitted from Output 4.3.

Most of the tables in the sliding spans output contain footnotes that explain the abbreviations and calculations in the tables. For more information, see *SAS/ETS Software: Changes and Enhancements, Release 6.11.*

❶ Table `S 0.A` lists the number, length, and dates of the spans.

❷ Table `S 0.B` summarizes the *F*-tests for stable seasonality. If the **`Identifiable Seasonality?`** row has a value of 'YES' then that span is judged suitable for seasonal adjustment. The **`Moving Seasonality`** test listed in this table is an *F*-test from a two-way analysis of variance. The two factors are seasons (months or quarters) and years. The years effect is tested separately; the null hypothesis is that there is no effect due to years, after accounting for variation due to months or quarters.

❸ Tables `S 1.A` and `S 1.B` display the range analysis and the summary of the range analysis of seasonal factors, respectively, for each span.

❹ Tables `S 4.A.1` through `S 4.A.3` contain the breakdown of excessive differences and changes in trend across spans for the seasonally adjusted data.

❺ Table `S 4.C` displays selected percentiles of the Maximum Percent Difference (MPD) for the seasonally adjusted data.

❻ (not shown) Tables `S 5.A.1` through `S 5.A.3` and Table `S 5.C` follow the same format as Tables `S 4.A.1` through `S 4.A.3` and Table `S 4.C`, respectively, except that they follow the month-to-month changes in the seasonally adjusted series.

❼ (not shown) Tables `S 6.A.1` through `S 6.A.3` and Table `S 6.C` follow the same format as Tables `S 4.A.1` through `S 4.A.3` and Table `S 4.C`, respectively, except that they follow the year-to-year changes in the seasonally adjusted series.

Fitting an ARIMA Model with PROC X11

The ARIMA statement in PROC X11 applies the X-11-ARIMA method to the series specified in the VAR statement. This method uses an ARIMA model estimated from the original time series to generate forecasts that extend the series one (default) or more years.

Use the MODEL= option in the ARIMA statement to specify exactly the type of model to fit to the time series. Much of the functionality of the ARIMA procedure is available in the ARIMA statement. However, the syntax of the ARIMA statement is different from that of PROC ARIMA. The syntax of the ARIMA statement is as follows:

ARIMA <MODEL=(*options*)> <TRANSFORM=*operation*>;

Specify the following options inside the parentheses of the MODEL= option to estimate ARIMA model parameters:

P= specifies the number of nonseasonal AR parameter estimates.

Q= specifies the number of nonseasonal MA parameter estimates.

SP= specifies the number of seasonal AR parameter estimates.

SQ= specifies the number of seasonal MA parameter estimates.

DIF= specifies the degree of nonseasonal differencing.

SDIF= specifies the degree of seasonal differencing.

Use the TRANSFORM= option to perform log transformations or other mathematical transformations described within parentheses.

Other options available in the ARIMA statement include the following:

METHOD=	specifies the estimation method.
NOPRINT	suppresses the normal printout generated by the ARIMA statement.
FORECAST=	specifies the number of years to forecast the series. The default is 1.
NOINT	suppresses the intercept parameter in the ARIMA model. This option is new for Release 6.11.
CENTER	centers the data for a time series by subtracting the mean from each observation. This option is new for Release 6.11.

If you specify the ARIMA statement without any options, PROC X11 attempts to fit the best-fitting model out of five predefined model types. If no ARIMA model provides an adequate fit to the data, then no ARIMA processing is performed on the data. However, PROC X11 still performs any requested seasonal adjustment on the unextended time series. The five predefined models are described in the following list, in which the first pair of parentheses in each item contains the nonseasonal ARIMA(p,d,q) parameters and the second pair of parentheses in each item contains the seasonal ARIMA (p,d,q) parameters:

- (0,1,1)(0,1,1)s log transform for multiplicative
- (0,1,2)(0,1,1)s log transform for multiplicative
- (2,1,0)(0,1,1)s log transform for multiplicative
- (0,2,2)(0,1,1)s log transform for multiplicative
- (2,1,2)(0,1,1)s no transform.

Invoke PROC X11. Use the OUTEXTRAP option to add extra observations used in ARIMA processing to the output data set. Use the NOPRINT option to suppress all printed output.

```
proc x11 data=electric
         outextrap
         noprint;
   monthly date=date;
   var elecprod;
   output out=adjelec2 b1=original
                       d10=seasonal
                       d11=adjusted
                       d12=trend
                       d13=irreg;
```

Fit a predefined ARIMA model and generate forecasts to extend the data by one year.

```
   arima;
run;
```

Print the last part of the output data set from PROC X11.

```
proc print data=adjelec2(firstobs=132);
run;
```

Output 4.4
ARIMA Forecasts Created with PROC X11

Electricity Production Data
(millions of kilowatt hours)

OBS	DATE	ORIGINAL	SEASONAL	ADJUSTED	TREND	IRREG
132	DEC90	237257.00	102.464	231552.39	232133.28	99.750
133	JAN91	247984.00	106.233	233434.84	230927.10	101.086
134	FEB91	210496.00	92.179	228354.65	230682.00	98.991
135	MAR91	221117.00	96.140	229994.60	231620.95	99.298
136	APR91	208936.00	89.521	233392.51	233274.87	100.050
137	MAY91	233991.00	95.312	245501.01	234914.86	104.506
138	JUN91	248165.00	104.499	237480.68	236090.07	100.589
139	JUL91	271492.00	113.637	238912.41	236801.82	100.891
140	AUG91	267698.00	113.385	236097.34	236968.57	99.632
141	SEP91	233897.00	99.338	235456.52	236907.10	99.388
142	OCT91	223180.00	94.728	235600.69	237143.19	99.350
143	NOV91	221029.00	92.756	238291.17	237807.05	100.204
144	DEC91	247370.50	102.594	241116.73	238806.08	100.968
145	JAN92	251394.44	106.061	237027.81	239846.42	98.825
146	FEB92	223338.81	91.945	242903.98	240627.64	100.946
147	MAR92	231168.21	95.983	240842.10	241070.09	99.905
148	APR92	215459.39	89.574	240538.68	241315.66	99.678
149	MAY92	231397.84	95.403	242547.69	241465.94	100.448
150	JUN92	251161.16	104.580	240162.01	241590.87	99.409
151	JUL92	275162.61	113.558	242309.22	241712.35	100.247
152	AUG92	274969.96	113.355	242573.70	241932.88	100.265
153	SEP92	240075.80	99.417	241483.43	242191.02	99.708
154	OCT92	229202.07	94.755	241888.23	242447.63	99.769
155	NOV92	225670.59	92.637	243607.75	242640.14	100.399

Explanation

The original electricity production time series ends in November, 1991. The OUTEXTRAP option writes the extrapolated values — based on the ARIMA forecasts — to the output data set. The extended data end with an observation for November, 1992.

The output data set listed in Output 4.4 is similar to the one shown in Output 4.2. However, the estimates of the components listed in Output 4.4 are based on the extended series rather than just the original series. At the beginning of the series, the ARIMA forecasts have little effect on the estimates of the components. As you get closer to the end of the time series, however, the effect of the ARIMA forecasts on the estimates of the components is larger.

Further Reading

- □ For more information on PROC ARIMA and PROC X11, see the *SAS/ETS User's Guide, Version 6, Second Edition*, and *SAS/ETS Software: Changes and Enhancements, Release 6.11.*
- □ For more information on the TIMSAC subroutines, see *SAS/IML Software: Changes and Enhancements through Release 6.11.*

References

- □ Bell, W.R. and Hillmer, S.C (1984), "Issues Involved with the Seasonal Adjustment of Economic Time Series," *Journal of Business and Economic Statistics*, 2, 291-320.
- □ Findley, D.F. and Monsell, B.C. (1986), "New Techniques for Determining if a Time Series Can be Seasonally Adjusted Reliably, and Their Application to U.S. Foreign Trade Series," in *Regional Econometric Modeling*, eds. M.R. Perryman and J.R. Schmidt, Amsterdam: Kluwer-Nijhoff, 195-228.
- □ Findley, D.F., Monsell, B.C., Shulman, H.B., Pugh, M.G. (1990), "Sliding Spans Diagnostics for Seasonal and Related Adjustments," *Journal of the American Statistical Association*, 85, 345-355.

EXAMPLE 5

Forecasting with Transfer Function Models

Featured Tools:

- ARIMA procedure:
  CROSSCORR= option
  INPUT= option

Transfer function models use forecasted values of explanatory variables to produce forecasts of the dependent variable. The variability in the forecasts of the explanatory variables is incorporated into the forecasts of the dependent variable.

Simple transfer function models assume a contemporaneous relationship between the explanatory variables and the dependent variable. That is, forecasts of the explanatory variables at time $t + 1$ explain the behavior of the dependent variable at time $t + 1$. General transfer function models extend simple transfer function models to include previous, or lagged, values of the explanatory variables in the model. For example, a general transfer function model could use forecasts of the explanatory variables at time $t + 1$ to explain the behavior of the dependent variable at time $t + 2$. General transfer function models often involve a time lag, called *pure delay,* before the explanatory variables have an effect on the dependent variable. You can use multiple explanatory variables in transfer function models, but the explanatory variables must be linearly independent of each other to produce valid forecasts.

Transfer function models are sometimes referred to as *dynamic regression models* (Pankratz 1991) or ARIMAX models.

A general transfer function model with one explanatory variable and k lags is expressed as follows:

$$Y_t = \mu + \beta_0 X_t + \beta_1 X_{t-1} + \beta_2 X_{t-2} + \ldots + \beta_k X_{t-k} + Z_t$$

where

Y_t	is the dependent time series variable.
μ	is the constant term.
β_0	is the parameter associated with the current value of the explanatory variable.
X_t	is the current value of the explanatory variable.

$\beta_1, \beta_2, \ldots, \beta_k$ — are the parameters associated with lagged values of the explanatory variable. These parameters, along with β_0, are called *impulse-response weights* or *transfer function weights.*

$X_{t-1}, X_{t-2}, \ldots, X_{t-k}$ — are the lagged values of the explanatory variable up to period k.

Z_t — is a time series of autocorrelated errors.

A general transfer function model is also called a *rational transfer function* model. You can express a rational transfer function model with one explanatory variable as follows:

$$Y_t = \mu + \Sigma_{k=0}^{\infty} \Phi_k X_{t-k} + Z_t$$

where Φ_k represents the transfer function weights for the input variable X_{t-k}, expressed as a ratio of polynomials in the backshift operator. The numerator of the ratio is analogous to moving average (MA) terms and the denominator of the ratio is analogous to autoregressive (AR) terms in ARIMA models.

To completely fit a transfer function model to a set of data, you must fit two components of the model:

- the transfer function component (the Φ_k's)
- the error, or noise, component, which is the ARIMA model for Z_t.

You first fit a preliminary transfer function component. Then, you fit an error component to the residuals from the preliminary transfer function part of the model.

The Crosscorrelation Function Plot and Prewhitening

To identify the appropriate transfer function model for a set of data, you examine the plot of the *sample crosscorrelation function.* For the sample crosscorrelation function to be meaningful, the input and response series must be *prewhitened.*

To prewhiten the input and response series and to analyze the appropriate crosscorrelation, follow this procedure:

1. Fit an ARIMA model to the input series so that the residuals of the model are white noise.
2. Filter the response series with the same model that you use on the input series.

3. Cross correlate the filtered response series with the filtered input series to determine the relationship between the series.
4. Interpret the crosscorrelation plot as you would an autocorrelation function plot. Autoregressive indicators indicate denominator terms, and moving average indicators indicate numerator terms.

The ARIMA procedure prewhitens automatically when you include the appropriate statements in the SAS code. The example in this chapter shows how to do this.

The prewhitening method assumes that the input variables do not depend on past values of the response variable; that is, it assumes no *feedback*. PROC ARIMA cannot estimate feedback models. To model a feedback relationship, use the STATESPACE procedure.

Backshift Notation and Transfer Functions

Recall that ARIMA models can be expressed in terms of the backshift operator B. For example, BY_t means Y_{t-1} and B^2Y_t means Y_{t-2}. In SAS output, B raised to the power of x is written as B**(x).

A transfer function applies a ratio of backshift polynomials to one or more observable explanatory variables, X_t. For example,

$$Y_t - \mu = \frac{(1 - \theta_1 B)}{(1 - \phi_1 B)}(X_{t-s} - \mu) + Z_t$$

After a pure delay of s periods, this model has a leading coefficient followed by one arbitrary dropoff, then exponentially decaying coefficients for X_{t-j}.

The prewhitened crosscorrelation plot of a transfer function with q numerator terms and p denominator terms displays the same pattern, after s lags, as the autocorrelation function plot of an ARMA (p,q) process. This is the key to transfer function identification. Such behavior is not guaranteed without prewhitening, however.

Program

Identify All the Time Series Processes

Create the construction data set. The complete construction data set is in "Introduction: The Example Data Sets." In this example, you use construction contracts (CONTRCTS) and home mortgage interest rates (INTRATE) as explanatory variables. The dependent variable is housing starts (HSTARTS).

```
data constr;
  input date:monyy5. contrcts intrate hstarts;
  format date monyy5.;
  title 'Construction Data';
  datalines;
JAN83     11358    13.00   91.3
more data lines
;
```

Invoke PROC ARIMA and attempt to identify the three time series.

```
proc arima data=constr;
   i var=hstarts nlag=15;
   i var=contrcts nlag=15;
   i var=intrate nlag=15;
run;
```

Output 5.1
Identifying the Time Series Processes (Partial Output)

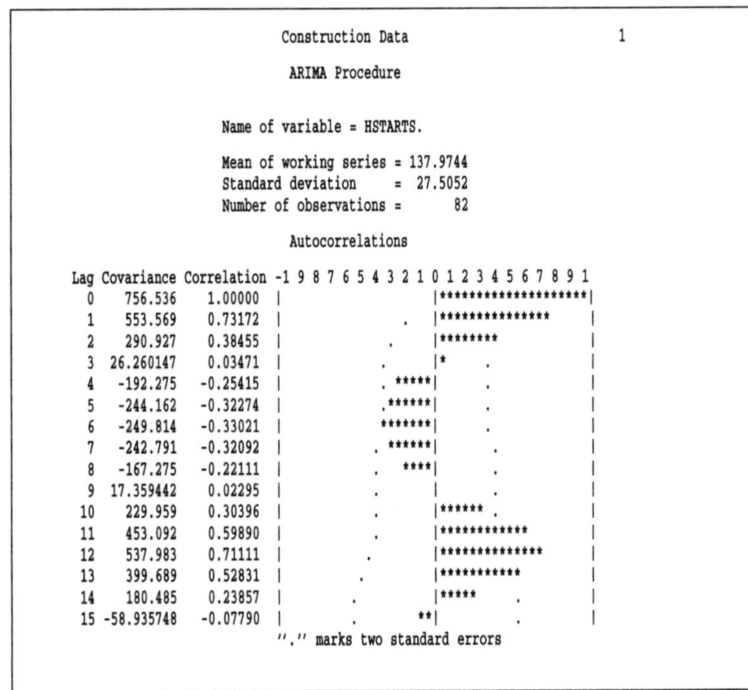

```
                                 Construction Data                              1

                                  ARIMA Procedure

                           Name of variable = HSTARTS.

                           Mean of working series = 137.9744
                           Standard deviation     =  27.5052
                           Number of observations =       82

                                  Autocorrelations

Lag Covariance Correlation -1 9 8 7 6 5 4 3 2 1 0 1 2 3 4 5 6 7 8 9 1
  0     756.536     1.00000 |                    |********************|
  1     553.569     0.73172 |                .   |***************     |
  2     290.927     0.38455 |              .     |********            |
  3   26.260147     0.03471 |             .      |*     .             |
  4    -192.275    -0.25415 |             . *****|      .             |
  5    -244.162    -0.32274 |             .******|      .             |
  6    -249.814    -0.33021 |             *******|      .             |
  7    -242.791    -0.32092 |            . ******|       .            |
  8    -167.275    -0.22111 |            .   ****|       .            |
  9   17.359442     0.02295 |            .       |       .            |
 10     229.959     0.30396 |            .       |****** .            |
 11     453.092     0.59890 |            .       |************        |
 12     537.983     0.71111 |           .        |**************      |
 13     399.689     0.52831 |          .         |***********         |
 14     180.485     0.23857 |         .          |*****     .         |
 15  -58.935748    -0.07790 |         .        **|          .         |
                            "." marks two standard errors
```

```
                              Construction Data                          2

                               ARIMA Procedure

                      Name of variable = CONTRCTS.

                      Mean of working series = 19683.91
                      Standard deviation     = 3519.801
                      Number of observations =       82

                               Autocorrelations

Lag Covariance Correlation -1 9 8 7 6 5 4 3 2 1 0 1 2 3 4 5 6 7 8 9 1
  0   12388999    1.00000  |                    |********************|
  1    8920254    0.72001  |                 .  |**************      |
  2    6172135    0.49819  |                .   |**********          |
  3    3008811    0.24286  |               .    |***** .             |
  4    -303132   -0.02447  |               .    |      .             |
  5   -1369606   -0.11055  |               .  **|      .             |
  6   -1741779   -0.14059  |               . ***|      .             |
  7   -1826824   -0.14746  |               . ***|      .             |
  8    -313305   -0.02529  |               .   *|      .             |
  9    2483366    0.20045  |               .    |****  .             |
 10    4940220    0.39876  |               .    |********            |
 11    7471969    0.60311  |              .     |************        |
 12    8869096    0.71588  |             .      |**************      |
 13    6606305    0.53324  |            .       |***********         |
 14    4778284    0.38569  |            .       |******** .          |
 15    1677947    0.13544  |           .        |***       .         |
                          "." marks two standard errors
```

```
                              Construction Data                          3

                               ARIMA Procedure

                      Name of variable = INTRATE.

                      Mean of working series = 10.37463
                      Standard deviation     = 1.315968
                      Number of observations =       82

                               Autocorrelations

Lag Covariance Correlation -1 9 8 7 6 5 4 3 2 1 0 1 2 3 4 5 6 7 8 9 1
  0   1.731771    1.00000  |                    |********************|
  1   1.668065    0.96321  |                 .  |******************* |
  2   1.622606    0.93696  |                .   |******************* |
  3   1.550141    0.89512  |              .     |******************  |
  4   1.509165    0.87146  |             .      |*****************   |
  5   1.459070    0.84253  |            .       |*****************   |
  6   1.413819    0.81640  |           .        |****************    |
  7   1.363428    0.78730  |           .        |****************    |
  8   1.307693    0.75512  |          .         |***************     |
  9   1.248799    0.72111  |         .          |************** .    |
 10   1.192364    0.68852  |         .          |************** .    |
 11   1.130432    0.65276  |        .           |*************    .  |
 12   1.063379    0.61404  |  .                 |************      . |
 13   0.995038    0.57458  |  .                 |***********       . |
 14   0.930451    0.53728  |  .                 |***********       . |
 15   0.867234    0.50078  | .                  |**********        . |
                          "." marks two standard errors
```

Interpretation

From the partial identification phase output, note that the sample ACF for the HSTARTS and CONTRCTS time series have large spikes at the seasonal lag (lag 12). This may indicate that these processes have seasonal nonstationarity. The sample ACF for the INTRATE time series tails off very slowly, which indicates that it has month-to-month nonstationarity. To perform a statistical test for stationarity, you can use the %DFTEST macro. (See Example 9, "Using Macros for Forecasting Tasks.")

Estimating Models for the Explanatory Variables

In practice, you would probably need to fit several models before you found one that provided an adequate fit to the data. To conserve space and to focus on the transfer function model, the process of finding an adequate model is assumed to be complete at this stage. For this example, the identification and estimation phase outputs for the explanatory variables are omitted. See Examples 1, 2, and 3 for details on identifying and estimating basic ARIMA models.

Estimate models for the explanatory variables CONTRCTS and INTRATE.

```
   i var=contrcts(12) /* Take a span-12 difference of the CONTRCTS variable */
     noprint;         /* Suppress printing the identification phase output  */
   e p=(2,3)          /* Fit a subset AR(3) model with two parameters       */
     method=ml        /* Use the maximum likelihood method                  */
     noprint;         /* Suppress printing the estimation phase output      */

   i var=intrate(1)   /* Take first differences of the INTRATE variable     */
     noprint;
   e q=(2)            /* Fit a subset MA(2) model with one parameter        */
     method=ml
     noprint;
run;
```

Print the crosscorrelation plot. Use the CROSSCOR= option. The ESTIMATE statements submitted previously prewhiten the explanatory variables and automatically prewhiten the dependent variable.

```
   i var=hstarts(12) crosscor=(contrcts(12) intrate(1)) nlag=12;
run;
```

Output 5.2
Crosscorrelation Plots from PROC ARIMA (Partial Output)

```
                         Construction Data                      1

                          ARIMA Procedure

                 Correlation of HSTARTS and CONTRCTS
                 Variable CONTRCTS has been differenced.
                 Period(s) of Differencing = 12.
                 Both series have been prewhitened.
                 Variance of transformed series = 189.0796 and  1751098
                 Number of observations =      70
                 NOTE: The first 12 observations were eliminated by
                       differencing.

                   ❶  Crosscorrelations

Lag Covariance Correlation -1 9 8 7 6 5 4 3 2 1 0 1 2 3 4 5 6 7 8 9 1
-12  -3094.081   -0.17004  |                 . ***|    .              |
-11  28.128489    0.00155  |                 .    |    .              |
-10   -529.327   -0.02909  |                 .   *|    .              |
 -9   3386.855    0.18613  |                 .    |****.              |
 -8   -626.520   -0.03443  |                 .   *|    .              |
 -7   -724.793   -0.03983  |                 .   *|    .              |
 -6   3349.865    0.18410  |                 .    |****.              |
 -5  -1913.996   -0.10519  |                 .  **|    .              |
 -4  -1071.629   -0.05889  |                 .   *|    .              |
 -3  -2455.556   -0.13495  |                 . ***|    .              |
 -2  -3464.828   -0.19042  |                 .****|    .              |
 -1   2753.642    0.15133  |                 .    |*** .              |
  0   8005.908    0.43998  |                 .    |*********          |
  1   4240.914    0.23307  |                 .    |*****              |
  2   2254.783    0.12392  |                 .    |**  .              |
  3    337.621    0.01855  |                 .    |    .              |
  4  -1019.200   -0.05601  |                 .   *|    .              |
  5  58.640144    0.00322  |                 .    |    .              |
  6   -881.982   -0.04847  |                 .   *|    .              |
  7   -290.529   -0.01597  |                 .    |    .              |
  8   4188.837    0.23021  |                 .    |*****              |
  9   2453.580    0.13484  |                 .    |*** .              |
 10 -82.320303   -0.00452  |                 .    |    .              |
 11  -2362.428   -0.12983  |                 . ***|    .              |
 12  -3153.920   -0.17333  |                 . ***|    .              |
                           "." marks two standard errors
```

```
                         Construction Data                      2

                          ARIMA Procedure

             ❷  Crosscorrelation Check Between Series

     To   Chi                     Crosscorrelations
     Lag  Square DF   Prob
      5    18.67  6  0.005  0.440  0.233  0.124  0.019 -0.056  0.003
     11    25.02 12  0.015 -0.048 -0.016  0.230  0.135 -0.005 -0.130

     Both variables have been prewhitened by the following filter:

 ❸   Prewhitening Filter


     Autoregressive Factors
     Factor 1: 1 - 0.26672 B**(2) - 0.30236 B**(3)
```

```
                           Construction Data                             3

                            ARIMA Procedure


                 Correlation of HSTARTS and INTRATE
                 Variable INTRATE has been differenced.
                 Period(s) of Differencing = 1.
                 Both series have been prewhitened.
                 Variance of transformed series = 206.6222 and 0.023068
                 Number of observations =       70
                 NOTE: The first observation was eliminated by
                       differencing.

                    ❹ Crosscorrelations

Lag Covariance Correlation -1 9 8 7 6 5 4 3 2 1 0 1 2 3 4 5 6 7 8 9 1
-12   0.030838    0.01413  |                    .   |   .                |
-11  -0.201114   -0.09212  |                    . **|   .                |
-10  -0.257636   -0.11801  |                    . **|   .                |
 -9  -0.299813   -0.13733  |                    .***|   .                |
 -8  -0.355440   -0.16281  |                    .***|   .                |
 -7  -0.158032   -0.07239  |                    .  *|   .                |
 -6  -0.057915   -0.02653  |                    .  *|   .                |
 -5   0.298548    0.13675  |                    .   |***.                |
 -4   0.154535    0.07078  |                    .   |*  .                |
 -3  0.0098795    0.00453  |                    .   |   .                |
 -2  -0.200092   -0.09165  |                    . **|   .                |
 -1   0.150587    0.06898  |                    .   |*  .                |
  0  -0.148275   -0.06792  |                    .  *|   .                |
  1  -0.391168   -0.17917  |                    ****|   .                |
  2  -0.223301   -0.10228  |                    . **|   .                |
  3  -0.402513   -0.18437  |                    ****|   .                |
  4  -0.298002   -0.13650  |                    .***|   .                |
  5  -0.113600   -0.05203  |                    .  *|   .                |
  6   0.123125    0.05640  |                    .   |*  .                |
  7  -0.243946   -0.11174  |                    . **|   .                |
  8  -0.226083   -0.10356  |                    . **|   .                |
  9  -0.365709   -0.16751  |                    .***|   .                |
 10  -0.158274   -0.07250  |                    .  *|   .                |
 11   0.051716    0.02369  |                    .   |   .                |
 12  -0.112505   -0.05153  |                    .  *|   .                |
                           "." marks two standard errors
```

```
                           Construction Data                             4

                            ARIMA Procedure

             ❺ Crosscorrelation Check Between Series

     To    Chi                   Crosscorrelations
    Lag  Square DF   Prob
      5    7.18  6  0.305 -0.068 -0.179 -0.102 -0.184 -0.136 -0.052
     11   11.39 12  0.495  0.056 -0.112 -0.104 -0.168 -0.072  0.024


     Both variables have been prewhitened by the following filter:

   ❻ Prewhitening Filter

     Moving Average Factors
     Factor 1: 1 - 0.11063 B**(1) + 0.40612 B**(2)
```

Interpretation

Output 5.2 shows only the crosscorrelation plots from the PROC ARIMA identification phase output. The sample ACF, IACF, and PACF are not shown because they are not relevant at this stage of the analysis. You use the crosscorrelation plots to identify the transfer function component of the model.

Transfer function models can be difficult to identify. The first step is to examine the negative lags in the crosscorrelation plot. For valid forecasts from transfer function models, none of the negative lags should have spikes. If the negative lags do have significant spikes, then you have a model with feedback, which PROC ARIMA cannot model adequately. Use the STATESPACE procedure for feedback models.

Next, check for the amount of delay in the model. A model has an n-period delay if there are no spikes in the crosscorrelation plot at lag 0 and for $n - 1$ lags after lag 0. After the period of delay, there will be a spike in the crosscorrelation plot. The number of spikes after the first spike corresponds to the number of numerator parameters in the transfer function part of the model. If there are no spikes after the first spike, then the process is probably white noise.

Following the spikes, the crosscorrelation plot can have one of the following patterns. It can

- □ tail off exponentially, which indicates the need for one denominator parameter in the transfer function part of the model
- □ tail off exponentially in a sine-wave pattern, which indicates the need for two or more denominator parameters in the transfer function part of the model
- □ drop immediately to 0, which indicates the need for no denominator parameters in the model.

❶ The first plot in Output 5.2 shows the sample crosscorrelation between HSTARTS and CONTRCTS.

  - □ None of the negative lags have significant spikes.
  - □ There is a spike at lag 0, which indicates that there is no delay in this model.
  - □ After the spike at lag 0, the crosscorrelations tail off exponentially, which indicates that one denominator parameter is needed for the transfer function part of the model.

❷ The **Crosscorrelation Check Between Series** lists *S*-statistics for the crosscorrelations. The *S*-statistic is based on the chi-square approximation suggested by Box and Jenkins (1976, pp. 395-396). If there is a sufficiently large correlation between the prewhitened inputs and the residuals, then the transfer function model is judged to be inadequate. In this case, the significant *S*-statistics indicate that the relationship between HSTARTS and CONTRCTS is not simply white noise.

❸ Both HSTARTS and CONTRCTS have been prewhitened by the filter described in the output. These are the estimated parameters of the model you fit to the CONTRCTS time series.

❹ The second plot in Output 5.2 shows the sample crosscorrelation between HSTARTS and INTRATE. In this plot, none of the lags have significant spikes. You can conclude that the relationship between HSTARTS and INTRATE is simply white noise.

❺ The **Crosscorrelation Check Between Series** confirms this conclusion because all of the *S*-statistics are nonsignificant.

❻ The filter used to prewhiten both HSTARTS and INTRATE is listed at the bottom of the output. These are the estimated parameters of the model you fit to the INTRATE time series.

Estimating a Preliminary Transfer Function Model

Estimate a preliminary transfer function model. Include the CONTRCTS explanatory variable in the INPUT= option and specify one denominator term. Specify the PLOT option to plot the ACF, IACF, and PACF for the residuals from the preliminary transfer function model.

```
   e input=(/(1) contrcts)
     method=ml
     plot;
run;
```

Output 5.3
Results of Preliminary Transfer Function Model

```
                         Construction Data                         1

                           ARIMA Procedure

                ❶ Maximum Likelihood Estimation

                            Approx.                  ❷
Parameter    Estimate     Std Error   T Ratio  Lag  Variable Shift
MU          -12.22599      2.41731     -5.06    0   HSTARTS     0
NUM1        0.0032886    0.0011995      2.74    0   CONTRCTS    0
DEN1,1        0.61948      0.14891      4.16    1   CONTRCTS    0

Constant Estimate  = -12.225986

Variance  Estimate = 168.797949
Std Error Estimate = 12.9922265
AIC                = 552.626814
SBC                = 559.329133
Number of Residuals=         69

                  Correlations of the Estimates

                               HSTARTS    CONTRCTS    CONTRCTS
   Variable     Parameter           MU        NUM1      DEN1,1

   HSTARTS      MU               1.000       0.027      -0.432
   CONTRCTS     NUM1             0.027       1.000      -0.843
   CONTRCTS     DEN1,1          -0.432      -0.843       1.000

               ❸ Autocorrelation Check of Residuals

 To   Chi                     Autocorrelations
Lag  Square DF   Prob
  6   32.05  6  0.000  0.274  0.403  0.224  0.210  0.289  0.130
 12   46.37 12  0.000  0.100 -0.060  0.116 -0.174 -0.076 -0.326
 18   74.66 18  0.000 -0.188 -0.178 -0.216 -0.192 -0.341 -0.199
 24   97.54 24  0.000 -0.347 -0.130 -0.210 -0.137  0.021 -0.163
```

```
                         Construction Data                         2

                           ARIMA Procedure

               ❹ Autocorrelation Plot of Residuals

Lag Covariance Correlation -1 9 8 7 6 5 4 3 2 1 0 1 2 3 4 5 6 7 8 9 1
  0    168.798    1.00000  |                    |********************|
  1  46.207624    0.27375  |                 .  |*****               |
  2  68.063854    0.40323  |                 .  |********            |
  3  37.868622    0.22434  |                .   |**** .              |
  4  35.514015    0.21039  |                .   |**** .              |
  5  48.725125    0.28866  |                .   |******              |
  6  21.910722    0.12980  |               .    |***   .             |
  7  16.886983    0.10004  |               .    |**    .             |
  8 -10.100721   -0.05984  |               .   *|      .             |
  9  19.601456    0.11612  |               .    |**    .             |
 10 -29.364972   -0.17397  |               .  ***|     .             |
 11 -12.884432   -0.07633  |               .   **|     .             |
 12 -55.044559   -0.32610  |               *******|     .             |
 13 -31.694254   -0.18776  |               .  ****|     .             |
 14 -30.039555   -0.17796  |               .  ****|     .             |
 15 -36.454703   -0.21597  |               .  ****|     .             |
 16 -32.441306   -0.19219  |              .   ****|      .            |
 17 -57.501383   -0.34065  |              .*******|      .            |
                           "." marks two standard errors
```

```
                    ❺ Inverse Autocorrelations

Lag Correlation -1 9 8 7 6 5 4 3 2 1 0 1 2 3 4 5 6 7 8 9 1
  1   -0.09125  |                 .  **|    .                |
  2   -0.21896  |                 .****|    .                |
  3   -0.03765  |                 .   *|    .                |
  4    0.15084  |                 .    |*** .                |
  5   -0.19652  |                 .****|    .                |
  6   -0.08240  |                 .  **|    .                |
  7    0.03568  |                 .    |*   .                |
  8    0.08521  |                 .    |**  .                |
  9   -0.18033  |                 .****|    .                |
 10    0.05546  |                 .    |*   .                |
 11    0.02484  |                 .    |    .                |
 12    0.17402  |                 .    |*** .                |
 13   -0.01770  |                 .    |    .                |
 14   -0.02742  |                 .   *|    .                |
 15   -0.03154  |                 .   *|    .                |
 16    0.01362  |                 .    |    .                |
 17    0.06516  |                 .    |*   .                |
```

```
                         Construction Data                          3

                          ARIMA Procedure

                    ❻ Partial Autocorrelations

Lag Correlation -1 9 8 7 6 5 4 3 2 1 0 1 2 3 4 5 6 7 8 9 1
  1    0.27375  |                 .    |*****                |
  2    0.35488  |                 .    |*******              |
  3    0.06924  |                 .    |*   .                |
  4    0.02382  |                 .    |    .                |
  5    0.18527  |                 .    |****.                |
  6   -0.03870  |                 .   *|    .                |
  7   -0.10563  |                 .  **|    .                |
  8   -0.17588  |                 .****|    .                |
  9    0.14204  |                 .    |*** .                |
 10   -0.24092  |                 *****|    .                |
 11   -0.11248  |                 .  **|    .                |
 12   -0.24409  |                 *****|    .                |
 13    0.03538  |                 .    |*   .                |
 14    0.00701  |                 .    |    .                |
 15   -0.01557  |                 .    |    .                |
 16   -0.04168  |                 .   *|    .                |
 17   -0.08482  |                 .  **|    .                |
```

```
❼ Crosscorrelation Check of Residuals with Input CONTRCTS

 To   Chi                    Crosscorrelations
Lag  Square DF   Prob
  5    1.07  5  0.957 -0.000 -0.033  0.074 -0.057 -0.075  0.003
 11    6.15 11  0.863 -0.116 -0.013  0.203  0.031  0.018 -0.133
 17    8.95 17  0.942 -0.142  0.002 -0.023 -0.020 -0.065  0.124
 23   15.47 23  0.877 -0.187 -0.015 -0.201 -0.134 -0.008 -0.028


              Model for variable HSTARTS

              Estimated Intercept = -12.225986
              Period(s) of Differencing = 12.

              Input Number 1 is CONTRCTS.
              Period(s) of Differencing = 12.
              Overall Regression Factor  = 0.003289

              The Denominator Factors are
              Factor 1: 1 - 0.61948 B**(1)
```

Interpretation

Output 5.3 shows the results from the preliminary transfer function model.

❶ The parameter estimates all have significant *t*-statistics, but because this model does not have parameter estimates for the error process, these statistics cannot be used as evidence for or against the model.

- □ MU is the estimated model intercept parameter for the dependent variable, HSTARTS.
- □ NUM1 is the lag 0 numerator parameter for the variable listed first in the INPUT= option in the ESTIMATE statement. In this case, only the CONTRCTS variable is listed in the INPUT= option.
- □ DEN1,1 is the denominator parameter for the first variable.

❷ The `Variable` column helps you identify how the parameter estimates are associated with the variables in the model.

❸ The `Autocorrelation Check of Residuals` has significant *Q*-statistics, which indicates that the residuals from this preliminary transfer function model are not white noise. That is, you still need to estimate parameters for the error process of this model.

❹ The ACF plot of the residuals tails off quickly, which indicates an AR process.

❺ The IACF plot has small spikes at lags 2, 5, and 9.

❻ The PACF plot has moderate spikes at lags 1, 2, 10, and 12.

❼ The **Crosscorrelation Check of Residuals with Input CONTRCTS** has no significant *S*-statistics, which is evidence that the transfer function model provides an adequate fit to the data.

Use the analysis of the residual plots to fit an appropriate error process to the data.

Estimating a Final Transfer Function Model

Estimate a final transfer function model. Fit an AR error process with the P= option in the ESTIMATE statement.

```
   e p=2 input=(/(1) contrcts) method=ml;
run;
```

Produce forecasts based on the final transfer function model.

```
   forecast lead=12;
run;
```

Output 5.4
Results from Final Transfer Function Model

```
                          Construction Data                          1

                           ARIMA Procedure

               ❶ Maximum Likelihood Estimation

                              Approx.
 Parameter   Estimate       Std Error   T Ratio  Lag  Variable Shift
 MU         -12.40801       4.17683     -2.97    0   HSTARTS      0
 AR1,1        0.16598       0.11617      1.43    1   HSTARTS      0
 AR1,2        0.37256       0.12093      3.08    2   HSTARTS      0
 NUM1       0.0038052     0.0011203      3.40    0   CONTRCTS     0
 DEN1,1       0.58797       0.15350      3.83    1   CONTRCTS     0

 Constant Estimate  = -5.7257548

 Variance  Estimate = 139.089762
 Std Error Estimate = 11.7936322
 AIC                = 541.517757
 SBC                =  552.68829
 Number of Residuals=         69
```

```
                       Correlations of the Estimates


                          HSTARTS    HSTARTS    HSTARTS   CONTRCTS   CONTRCTS
Variable    Parameter          MU      AR1,1      AR1,2       NUM1      DEN1,1

HSTARTS     MU              1.000      0.028     -0.012     -0.141     -0.494
HSTARTS     AR1,1           0.028      1.000     -0.326     -0.210      0.106
HSTARTS     AR1,2          -0.012     -0.326      1.000      0.278     -0.189
CONTRCTS    NUM1           -0.141     -0.210      0.278      1.000     -0.551
CONTRCTS    DEN1,1         -0.494      0.106     -0.189     -0.551      1.000

                ❷ Autocorrelation Check of Residuals

     To   Chi                      Autocorrelations
    Lag   Square DF   Prob
      6     5.19  4  0.269 -0.030 -0.035 -0.003 -0.001  0.244  0.077
     12    15.41 10  0.118 -0.055 -0.103  0.182 -0.078  0.008 -0.263
     18    20.04 16  0.218 -0.080  0.038 -0.028 -0.023 -0.195 -0.052
     24    32.69 22  0.066 -0.209  0.047 -0.113 -0.046  0.160 -0.189


          Crosscorrelation Check of Residuals with Input CONTRCTS

     To   Chi                      Crosscorrelations
    Lag   Square DF   Prob
      5     2.43  5  0.787  0.027 -0.091  0.097 -0.066 -0.102  0.046
     11    11.12 11  0.433 -0.113  0.009  0.278 -0.009 -0.076 -0.173
     17    14.54 17  0.629 -0.133  0.096  0.018 -0.024 -0.052  0.139
     23    20.66 23  0.602 -0.207 -0.017 -0.147 -0.110  0.108  0.012
```

```
                              Construction Data                            2

                               ARIMA Procedure


             ❸ Model for variable HSTARTS

                Estimated Intercept = -12.408013
                Period(s) of Differencing = 12.

                Autoregressive Factors
                Factor 1: 1 - 0.16598 B**(1) - 0.37256 B**(2)


                Input Number 1 is CONTRCTS.
                Period(s) of Differencing = 12.
                Overall Regression Factor  = 0.003805

                The Denominator Factors are
                Factor 1: 1 - 0.58797 B**(1)
```

Interpretation

Output 5.4 lists the results of the final transfer function model with AR parameter estimates for lags 1 and 2.

Note the following items from this output:

❶ The parameter estimate for the AR(1) coefficient is not significant. All of the other parameter estimates are significant. Even though the lag 1 parameter estimate is not significant, it may be reasonable to include it in the model.

❷ The **`Autocorrelation Check of Residuals`** has no significant *Q*-statistics, which indicates that the model provides an adequate fit to the data. However, the last *Q*-statistic, with a value of 32.69, has a probability value of .066, which is nearly significant.

❸ The final transfer function model is listed at the bottom of the output.

Other models may provide more significant parameter estimates or a better result in the **`Autocorrelation Check of Residuals`**. For example, an AR(2,5) error process model produces better estimation results than does the current AR(2) error process model. However, the AR(2) model fit in this example provides an adequate fit to the data. It is more sensible than an AR(2,5) model, which skips lags 1, 3, and 4, while it includes the nonseasonal lag 5.

Output 5.5
Forecasts from Final Transfer Function Model

Construction Data

ARIMA Procedure

Forecasts for variable HSTARTS

Obs	Forecast	Std Error	Lower 95%	Upper 95%
83	100.6116	12.8473	75.4314	125.7919
84	87.7942	13.3365	61.6553	113.9332
85	92.0062	14.4868	63.6126	120.3997
86	79.5281	14.9515	50.2237	108.8325
87	111.5294	15.2674	81.6059	141.4529
88	123.8088	15.4514	93.5246	154.0931
89	126.2786	15.5885	95.7258	156.8315
90	138.1636	15.6605	107.4695	168.8577
91	129.8085	15.7146	99.0086	160.6085
92	117.7222	15.7472	86.8582	148.5862
93	104.7486	15.7680	73.8440	135.6533
94	125.6675	15.7819	94.7356	156.5993

Interpretation

The FORECAST statement with the LEAD=12 specification produces 12 monthly forecasts for the HSTARTS variable. The forecasts start with the forecast for November 1989. The standard errors and 95% confidence limits are also listed in Output 5.5.

A Closer Look

Syntax of the INPUT= Option

Specify the names and transfer function forms of the explanatory variables for transfer function models in the INPUT= option of the ESTIMATE statement in PROC ARIMA. These variables must be named in the CROSSCORR= option in the previous IDENTIFY statement. The syntax for transfer functions is as follows:

INPUT = (<*form-1*> *variable-1* ... <, <*form-n*> *variable-n*>)

where the optional *form* specification describes the structure of the transfer function for the corresponding variable. The specification for form is as follows:

$$S \$ \left(L_{1,1}, L_{1,2}, \ldots\right)\left(L_{2,1}, \ldots\right) \ldots / \left(L_{j,1} \ldots\right) \ldots$$

where

S	is the number of time periods of pure delay.
$L_{1,1}, L_{2,1}$ ...	represent lag numbers for the parameters of the transfer function model. You can use these terms to represent additive or multiplicative models of any complexity. Terms before the slash are numerator factors, analogous to MA parameters. Terms after the slash are denominator factors, analogous to AR parameters.

Naming of Model Parameters

In the PROC ARIMA estimation phase output, the model parameters are named as follows:

NUM1 ... NUM*k*	are the lag 0 numerator parameter estimates, which are computed for all transfer function models. The value of *k* corresponds to the position of the input variable in the INPUT= option variable list.

NUM1,1 ... NUM*i,j*	are numerator terms. The values of *i* and *j* correspond to the *j*th term in the *i*th factor.
DEN1,1 ... DEN*i,j*	are denominator terms. The values of *i* and *j* correspond to the *j*th term in the *i*th factor.

Further Reading

For more information on transfer functions and PROC ARIMA, see the *SAS/ETS User's Guide, Version 6, Second Edition.*

References

□ Box, G.E.P. and Jenkins, G.M. (1976), *Time Series Analysis: Forecasting and Control,* San Francisco: Holden-Day.

□ Pankratz, A. (1991), *Forecasting with Dynamic Regression Models*, New York: John Wiley & Sons, Inc.

EXAMPLE 6

Forecasting with Intervention Models

Featured Tools:

- ☐ ARIMA procedure
- ☐ GPLOT procedure

Intervention models are transfer function models in which the explanatory variables are indicator, or dummy, variables. That is, the explanatory variables take on the values of 0 or 1. Intervention models usually represent abrupt changes in a time series process.

You can express a simple intervention model as follows:

$$Y_t = \mu + \beta X_t + \epsilon_t$$

where

Y_t is the dependent time series variable.

μ is a constant value.

β is the parameter associated with the explanatory variable.

X_t is an explanatory indicator variable that represents the intervention.

ϵ_t is an error term.

In a more general intervention model, β is replaced in the previous equation by a general transfer function — a ratio of polynomials in the backshift operator. The methods you use to fit intervention models are similar to the ones you use to fit transfer function models (see Example 5, "Forecasting with Transfer Function Models").

- ☐ Estimate a preliminary intervention model with an appropriate input form for the intervention variable.
- ☐ Identify the error process for the model from plots of the autocorrelation function (ACF), inverse autocorrelation function (IACF), and partial autocorrelation function (PACF).
- ☐ Estimate a final intervention model that includes autoregressive and moving average parameters for the error process.

Intervention models are different from transfer function models in that you cannot use the crosscorrelation plot to identify the transfer lag term of the input component for an intervention model. Because the intervention variable is not an ARIMA process, the intervention variable and the dependent variable cannot be prewhitened. Without prewhitening, crosscorrelations are meaningless. The only way to identify the appropriate input form for the intervention variable is to compare a plot of the dependent time series to theoretical plots for several different input processes. For example, one arbitrary drop-off and then exponential decay to a new level indicate one numerator and one denominator lag, respectively. Straight exponential decay indicates one denominator lag. Also, if you want to produce forecasts based on an intervention model, you must include values for the intervention variable for all future periods for which you want forecasts.

Interventions can create either abrupt or gradual changes in the values of a time series. For example, the arrival of a new company president may lead to a gradual improvement in the stock price for the firm. For another example, the installation of a new computer system may cause a sudden drop in the time it takes to process daily transactions. Both of these examples represent interventions that continue for a relatively long time. Intervention variables of this type are called *step functions.* Interventions can also be short-term events. For example, a temporary change in a factory's machine configuration may temporarily increase or decrease the production from the factory. Intervention variables of this type are known as *impulse functions* or *pulse functions.*

The example in this chapter uses data on driver casualties (deaths and serious injuries) in road accidents in Great Britain. The intervention variable is the passage of a mandatory seatbelt law in January, 1983. Enforcement of the law began on January 31, 1983, but seatbelt usage increased dramatically during the month of January in anticipation of the law's passage. Thus, the intervention is treated as if it began on January 1, 1983.

Program

Inputting the Data and Testing it for Stationarity

Create the driver casualties data set. The complete driver casualties data set is in "Introduction: The Example Data Sets." Add 12 missing observations for the INJURIES variable to the end of the data set, which enables you to use the intervention model to produce forecasts for those 12 time periods.

```
data drivers;
   format date monyy.;
   input date:monyy5. injuries @@;
   beltlaw = (date ge '01jan83'd);
   title 'Driver Casualties Data';
   title2 'monthly totals';
   datalines;
jan80  1665  feb80  1361  mar80  1506  apr80  1360

more data lines

jan85  .     feb85  .     mar85  .     apr85  .
may85  .     jun85  .     jul85  .     aug85  .
sep85  .     oct85  .     nov85  .     dec85  .
;
```

Test the data for seasonal nonstationarity. See Example 9, "Using Macros for Forecasting Tasks," for details on the %DFTEST macro. The %PUT macro program statement writes the probability value of the test statistic to the SAS log.

```
%dftest(drivers,injuries,dlag=12)
%put &dfpvalue;
```

The probability value of the test statistic is .001, which indicates that the time series is stationary. No differencing is required. The plot of the original data (see Output 6.4 in this example or Output 5 in "Introduction: The Example Data Sets") seems to indicate an immediate drop-off to the new level after the intervention. Thus, the preliminary intervention model uses just a single coefficient for BELTLAW.

Fitting a Preliminary Intervention Model

Include the intervention variable in the model and identify the residuals from the preliminary model. Use the PLOT option in the ESTIMATE statement to display the residual autocorrelation functions. Suppress printing the identification phase output.

```
proc arima data=drivers;
   i var=injuries crosscorr=beltlaw noprint;
   e input=beltlaw plot;
run;
```

Output 6.1
Identifying the Residuals from the Preliminary Intervention Model

```
                        Driver Casualties Data                           1
                            monthly totals

                           ARIMA Procedure


                  Conditional Least Squares Estimation

                               Approx.
Parameter   Estimate      Std Error   T Ratio  Lag  Variable Shift
MU            1598.4       32.65279     48.95   0   INJURIES     0
NUM1      -269.48611       51.62859     -5.22   0   BELTLAW      0

Constant Estimate  = 1598.36111

Variance  Estimate = 38383.3609
Std Error Estimate = 195.916719
AIC                = 805.561291*
SBC                =  809.74998*
Number of Residuals=         60
* Does not include log determinant.

                    Correlations of the Estimates


                                       INJURIES      BELTLAW
         Variable    Parameter               MU         NUM1

         INJURIES    MU                   1.000       -0.632
         BELTLAW     NUM1                -0.632        1.000


                ❶  Autocorrelation Check of Residuals

 To   Chi                         Autocorrelations
Lag  Square DF   Prob
  6   54.89  6  0.000  0.577  0.302 -0.080 -0.268 -0.346 -0.463
 12  116.97 12  0.000 -0.398 -0.394 -0.117  0.126  0.425  0.556
 18  163.47 18  0.000  0.443  0.233 -0.069 -0.259 -0.316 -0.367
 24  230.26 24  0.000 -0.363 -0.310 -0.143  0.114  0.364  0.533
```

```
                    Driver Casualties Data                    2
                        monthly totals

                       ARIMA Procedure

             ❷ Autocorrelation Plot of Residuals

Lag Covariance Correlation -1 9 8 7 6 5 4 3 2 1 0 1 2 3 4 5 6 7 8 9 1
  0  38383.361    1.00000  |                    |********************|
  1  22157.160    0.57726  |                 .  |************        |
  2  11577.969    0.30164  |                .   |******.             |
  3  -3052.509   -0.07953  |                . **|      .             |
  4 -10298.236   -0.26830  |                .*****|     .             |
  5 -13263.442   -0.34555  |              *******|      .             |
  6 -17776.713   -0.46314  |            *********|       .            |
  7 -15271.233   -0.39786  |             ********|       .            |
  8 -15128.015   -0.39413  |             .********|       .           |
  9  -4495.770   -0.11713  |              .    **|        .           |
 10   4825.532    0.12572  |              .     |***      .           |
 11  16312.744    0.42500  |              .     |********.            |
 12  21342.204    0.55603  |             .      |***********          |
 13  17015.802    0.44331  |            .       |*********  .         |
 14   8925.542    0.23254  |            .       |*****      .         |
 15  -2630.148   -0.06852  |            .      *|           .         |
                           "." marks two standard errors

                   Inverse Autocorrelations

       Lag Correlation -1 9 8 7 6 5 4 3 2 1 0 1 2 3 4 5 6 7 8 9 1
         1   -0.27368  |               *****|    .               |
         2   -0.14001  |               . ***|    .               |
         3    0.13112  |               .    |*** .               |
         4    0.00362  |               .    |    .               |
         5   -0.11387  |               .  **|    .               |
         6    0.11564  |               .    |**  .               |
         7   -0.03470  |               .   *|    .               |
         8    0.16267  |               .    |*** .               |
         9   -0.03255  |               .   *|    .               |
        10    0.05257  |               .    |*   .               |
        11   -0.01974  |               .    |    .               |
        12   -0.08621  |               .  **|    .               |
        13   -0.05497  |               .   *|    .               |
        14    0.01410  |               .    |    .               |
        15    0.09432  |               .    |**  .               |
```

```
                    Driver Casualties Data                    3
                        monthly totals

                       ARIMA Procedure

               ❸ Partial Autocorrelations

       Lag Correlation -1 9 8 7 6 5 4 3 2 1 0 1 2 3 4 5 6 7 8 9 1
         1    0.57726  |               .    |************        |
         2   -0.04737  |               .   *|    .               |
         3   -0.35257  |             *******|    .               |
         4   -0.11678  |               .  **|    .               |
         5   -0.05410  |               .   *|    .               |
         6   -0.34050  |             *******|    .               |
         7   -0.10102  |               .  **|    .               |
         8   -0.23602  |               *****|    .               |
         9    0.09027  |               .    |**  .               |
        10    0.09700  |               .    |**  .               |
```

```
  11    0.21397 |               .    |****.               |
  12    0.14916 |               .    |***  .              |
  13   -0.04315 |               .   *|     .              |
  14   -0.12885 |               . ***|     .              |
  15   -0.13127 |               . ***|     .              |


          Model for variable INJURIES

          Estimated Intercept = 1598.36111

          Input Number 1 is BELTLAW.
          Overall Regression Factor  = -269.486
```

Interpretation

The circled numbers in Output 6.1 correspond to the numbered items in the following list:

1. The **`Autocorrelation Check of Residuals`** has significant *Q*-statistics, which indicates that the residuals are not white noise.
2. The **`Autocorrelation Plot of Residuals`** follows a sine-wave pattern, with large spikes at lags 6 and 12.
3. The **`Partial Autocorrelations`** plot has spikes at lags 1, 3, and 6.

These results are not easy to interpret. It is reasonable to assume that the model requires a seasonal parameter, but it may also require additional parameters. Your best strategy is to fit some reasonable candidate models until you find a model that fits the data adequately.

Estimating an Error Process

After some trial and error, the following model is found to provide an adequate fit to the time series data.

Estimate a seasonal error process for the intervention model.

```
   e input=beltlaw p=(1)(2 12);
run;
```

Output 6.2
Fitting an Error Process to the Residuals from the Intervention Model

```
                         Driver Casualties Data
                             monthly totals

                            ARIMA Procedure

               ❶ Conditional Least Squares Estimation

                                Approx.
      Parameter    Estimate    Std Error   T Ratio  Lag  Variable Shift
      MU             1652.2     75.50144     21.88    0  INJURIES     0
      AR1,1         0.40301      0.15095      2.67    1  INJURIES     0
      AR2,1         0.27567      0.12785      2.16    2  INJURIES     0
      AR2,2         0.53024      0.13728      3.86   12  INJURIES     0
      NUM1       -354.46226     84.10861     -4.21    0  BELTLAW      0

      Constant Estimate  = 191.444765

      Variance  Estimate = 19313.8668
      Std Error Estimate = 138.974339
      AIC                = 767.166658*
      SBC                = 777.638381*
      Number of Residuals=         60
      * Does not include log determinant.

                        Correlations of the Estimates

                          INJURIES   INJURIES   INJURIES   INJURIES     BELTLAW
Variable   Parameter            MU      AR1,1      AR2,1      AR2,2        NUM1

INJURIES   MU                1.000      0.136      0.144     -0.034      -0.278
INJURIES   AR1,1             0.136      1.000     -0.263     -0.362      -0.302
INJURIES   AR2,1             0.144     -0.263      1.000     -0.023      -0.086
INJURIES   AR2,2            -0.034     -0.362     -0.023      1.000       0.203
BELTLAW    NUM1             -0.278     -0.302     -0.086      0.203       1.000

                 ❷ Autocorrelation Check of Residuals

       To   Chi                  Autocorrelations
      Lag  Square DF   Prob
        6    2.08  3  0.556 -0.001  0.040 -0.110  0.038  0.071 -0.104
       12   12.09  9  0.208 -0.023 -0.223  0.033 -0.034  0.221 -0.181
       18   16.83 15  0.329  0.175  0.051 -0.040 -0.080 -0.100  0.079
       24   29.64 21  0.099 -0.139  0.075 -0.092  0.074  0.070  0.290


              Model for variable INJURIES

              Estimated Intercept = 1652.21569

              Autoregressive Factors
              Factor 1: 1 - 0.40301 B**(1)
              Factor 2: 1 - 0.27567 B**(2) - 0.53024 B**(12)

              Input Number 1 is BELTLAW.
              Overall Regression Factor  = -354.462
```

Interpretation

The following items from Output 6.2 provide evidence that the model provides an adequate fit to the data:

❶ The parameter estimates all have *t*-ratios with absolute values of 2.16 or greater. This indicates that all of the parameter estimates are significant.

❷ In the `Autocorrelation Check of Residuals`, none of the *Q*-statistics are significant at the .05 level. This is evidence that the residuals from this model are white noise. The lag 24 autocorrelation is .290, which is relatively high. This may account for the marginally significant probability value (.099) of the last *Q*-statistic.

This is not the only model that provides an adequate fit to these data. You can use the values of Akaike's Information Criterion (AIC) and Schwarz's Bayesian Criterion (SBC) to compare models for a given set of time series data. The smaller these values are, the better the model. Finally, you must use your judgment and experience to decide which model provides the most reasonable explanation for your data.

Forecasting Using the Intervention Model

Produce 12 forecasts based on the final intervention model. Create an output data set to contain the forecasts and confidence limits.

```
   f lead=12 out=fore2
             id=date
             interval=month;
run;
```

Output 6.3
Forecasts from the Intervention Model

```
                         Driver Casualties Data
                             monthly totals

                            ARIMA Procedure

   Forecasts for variable INJURIES
```

Obs	Forecast	Std Error	Lower 95%	Upper 95%
61	1560.9542	138.9743	1288.5695	1833.3389
62	1400.2279	149.8356	1106.5556	1693.9002
63	1379.9352	161.7322	1062.9460	1696.9245
64	1233.6933	163.5827	913.0771	1554.3095
65	1322.9288	164.8559	999.8172	1646.0404
66	1221.4844	165.0617	897.9693	1544.9995
67	1265.0001	165.1794	941.2545	1588.7457
68	1269.6271	165.1985	945.8440	1593.4101
69	1366.3474	165.2084	1042.5449	1690.1500
70	1437.0386	165.2101	1113.2328	1760.8444
71	1549.5818	165.2109	1225.7745	1873.3892
72	1582.8479	165.2110	1259.0403	1906.6555

Interpretation

Output 6.3 lists the forecasts, standard errors, and 95% confidence limits for 12 forecasts of the INJURIES time series. The forecasts indicate the seasonality in the data, with January, November, and December having the highest numbers of driver injuries (1561, 1550, and 1583, respectively). Perhaps winter weather conditions contribute to these results.

Plotting the Forecasts

Plot the original data, the forecasts, and the confidence limits.

```
goptions cback=white colors=(black) border reset=(axis symbol);

axis1 offset=(1 cm) label=('Year')
      order=('01jan80'd to '01jan86'd by year);
axis2 label=(angle=90 'Casualties')
      order=(750 to 2250 by 500);

symbol1 i=join l=1;
symbol2 h=2 pct v=F;
symbol3 l=20 i=join;

proc gplot data=fore2;
   format date year4.;
   plot injuries*date=1
        forecast*date=2
        l95*date     =3
        u95*date     =3 / overlay
                          haxis=axis1
                          vaxis=axis2
                          vminor=4
                          href='01jan83'd
                          lh=2;
run;
```

Output 6.4
Plot of Original Series, Forecasts, and 95% Confidence Limits

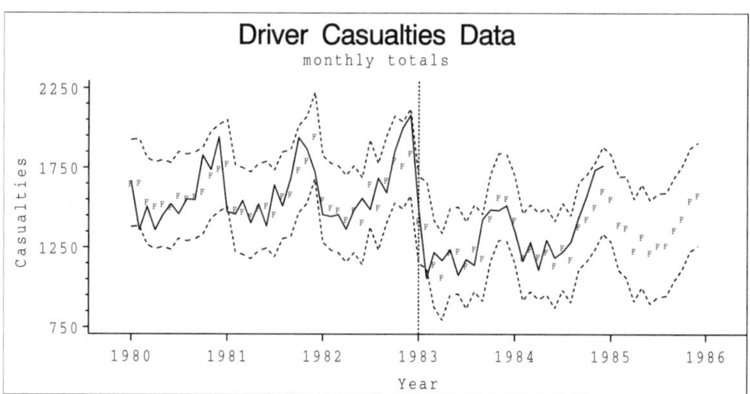

Interpretation

The values of the original INJURIES time series are plotted with the solid line. The forecasts are plotted with the F symbol, and the upper and lower 95% confidence limits for the forecasts are plotted with dashed lines. The reference line indicates when the seatbelt law was passed.

A Closer Look

Testing for Nonstationarity

The %DFTEST macro performs the Dickey-Fuller test for unit roots. The Phillips-Perron test for unit roots is available for Release 6.11 in the AUTOREG procedure. Specify STATIONARITY=(PHILLIPS) after a slash in the MODEL statement in PROC AUTOREG to use the default version of the Phillips-Perron test for stationarity.

Further Reading

- For more information on PROC ARIMA, see the *SAS/ETS User's Guide, Version 6, Second Edition.*
- For complete reference information on PROC GPLOT and other features available in SAS/GRAPH software, see *SAS/GRAPH Software: Reference, Version 6, First Edition, Volumes 1 and 2.*

EXAMPLE 7

Forecasting Multivariate Time Series

Featured Tool:

- STATESPACE procedure

The *state space model*, first introduced by Kalman (1960) and Kalman and Bucy (1961), is appropriate for jointly modeling and forecasting several related time series that have dynamic interactions. By taking into account the autocorrelations among the whole set of variables, the state space model may give better forecasts than methods that model each series separately. For a summary of state space modeling of time series, see Akaike (1976).

The state space model represents time series through auxiliary variables (a *state vector*), some of which may not be directly observable. The state vector summarizes all information from the present and past values of the time series relevant to the prediction of future values of the series.

The SAS/ETS STATESPACE procedure automatically selects the best state space model for forecasting the series. Alternatively, you can specify the state space model to fit to your data and you can specify restrictions on the model. PROC STATESPACE prints out the estimation results and writes forecasts to an output data set.

PROC STATESPACE is based on Akaike's method of estimating state space models, which uses canonical correlations. It is not a general purpose state space modeling procedure.

CAUTION!

PROC STATESPACE should be used only with stationary time series, because with nonstationary series the convergence process may fail or an inappropriate state space model may be selected. Nonstationary series must be made stationary by some preliminary transformation, usually by differencing. ■

The State Space Model

The model is defined by the following state transition equation:

$$\mathbf{z}_{t+1} = \mathbf{F}\,\mathbf{z}_t + \mathbf{G}\,\mathbf{e}_{t+1}$$

The vectors and matrices are defined as follows:

$\mathbf{z}_t$ is the state vector of dimension s. The first r elements of $\mathbf{z}_t$ consist of $\mathbf{x}_t$, the vector of observed variables. The last $s - r$ elements consist of the conditional prediction of future $\mathbf{x}_t$.

$\mathbf{F}$ is the $s \times s$ transition matrix, which determines the dynamic properties of the model.

G is the $s \times r$ input matrix, which determines the variance structure of the transition equation. This controls how random shocks are incorporated in $\mathbf{z}_t$.

$\mathbf{e}_t$ is a sequence of independent normally distributed random vectors of dimension r with mean $\mathbf{0}$ and covariance matrix Σ_{ee}. The random error is sometimes called the *innovation* or *shock vector*.

State Space Modeling

Closely following the modeling strategy proposed by Akaike (1976), PROC STATESPACE performs the following steps:

1. fits a sequence of unrestricted vector autoregressive (VAR) models for lags 0 through 10, and computes Akaike's information criterion (AIC) for each model. The order of the VAR model that produces the smallest AIC is chosen as the order to use in the canonical correlation analysis.
2. determines the elements of the state vector through a sequence of canonical correlation analyses of the sample autocovariance matrices through the selected order. The sample canonical correlations of the past are computed with an increasing number of steps into the future. Variables with significant correlations are added to the state vector; variables with insignificant correlations are excluded from further consideration. If you specify the state vector explicitly, these model identification steps are omitted.
3. fits the state space model to the data by approximate maximum likelihood. Optionally, you can fit the model with conditional least squares estimation. You can also impose restrictions on elements of the **F** and **G** matrices.

In this example, you fit a state space model to the finance data, which includes time series for the monthly average Dow Jones Index, the monthly average Moody's AAA bond yield, and the monthly average spot price for gold. These are time series for which you might expect dynamic interactions. See Outputs 4, 7, and 8 in "Introduction: The Example Data Sets," for plots of the three time series. All three series exhibit evidence of linear trends and are, therefore, nonstationary in the mean. After you take first differences of all three series to make them stationary, fit a state space model to the data and write 12 forecasts to an output data set.

Program

Creating the Data Set and Testing for Stationarity

Create the finance data set. The complete finance data set is in "Introduction: The Example Data Sets."

```
data finance;
   format date date7.;
   input date : monyy5. djiam gold aaa @@;
   label djiam='DJIA Index Price'
         gold='Gold Price per Troy Ounce'
         aaa='Moody''s AAA Bond Yields';
   title 'Multivariate Financial Data';
   datalines;
jan89 2234.68 404.014 9.62  feb89 2304.30 387.776 9.64
more data lines
;
```

Test the time series for stationarity. PROC STATESPACE requires that the series be stationary. This example uses the Dickey-Fuller test for unit roots. The Phillips-Perron test for unit roots is also available in Release 6.11. (See Example 6, "Forecasting with Intervention Models.")

```
%dftest(finance,djiam)
%put &dfpvalue;
%dftest(finance,gold)
%put &dfpvalue;
%dftest(finance,aaa)
%put &dfpvalue;
```

The probability values for all three of these tests exceed .05, which indicates that these time series are nonstationary. The unrejected null hypothesis is that there is a unit root. Retest the series with first differences.

Retest the time series for stationarity after taking first differences.

```
%dftest(finance,djiam,dif=(1))
%put &dfpvalue;
%dftest(finance,gold,dif=(1))
%put &dfpvalue;
%dftest(finance,aaa,dif=(1))
%put &dfpvalue;
```

All of these tests are significant, which indicates that the first differences remove the unit roots and make the time series stationary.

Fitting a State Space Model and Producing Forecasts

Invoke PROC STATESPACE. Specify the input data set with the DATA= option.

```
proc statespace data=finance
                lead=12          /* number of forecasts to produce      */
                interval=month   /* time interval between observations */
```

Write forecasts, forecast standard errors, actual values, and residuals to a SAS data set. Rename the variables that contain the forecasts. By default, the variable named FOR*i* contains forecasts for the *i*th variable in the VAR statement list.

```
                out=finout1(rename=(for1=djiaa_f1
                                    for2=gold_f1
                                    for3=aaa_f1));
```

Specify the variables in the input data set to model and forecast. Take differences of each variable by specifying the desired degree of differencing within the parentheses that follow each variable name.

```
   var djiam(1) gold(1) aaa(1);
```

Specify a variable in the input data set to identify observations.

```
   id date;
run;
```

Print the output data set that contains the forecasts. The FIRSTOBS= option specifies the first observation to be printed.

```
proc print data=finout1(firstobs=60);
   var date djiam djia_f1 gold gold_f1 aaa aaa_f1;
   title2 'State Space Model Forecasts';
run;
```

Output 7.1
State Space Model for the Finance Data

```
                    Multivariate Financial Data                    1

                        STATESPACE Procedure

                     ❶     Nobs = 61

                    Variable      Mean       Std
                    DJIAM      27.3923  78.88165
                    Has been differenced.
                    With period(s) = 1.
                    GOLD      -0.36072  11.61921
                    Has been differenced.
                    With period(s) = 1.
                    AAA       -0.04164  0.140821
                    Has been differenced.
                    With period(s) = 1.

        ❷  Information Criterion for Autoregressive Models

       Lag=0         Lag=1         Lag=2         Lag=3         Lag=4
  577.427739    574.066512    581.628217    595.553758    599.252070

       Lag=5         Lag=6         Lag=7         Lag=8         Lag=9
  593.794264    602.338882    605.976534    612.294057    622.734003

      Lag=10
  632.087505

            ❸  Schematic Representation of Correlations

  Name/Lag   0    1    2    3    4    5    6    7    8    9    10
  DJIAM     +--  ...  ...  ...  ...  ...  .+.  ...  ...  ...  ...
  GOLD      -+.  ...  ...  ...  .-.  ...  ...  ...  ...  ...  ...
  AAA       -.+  ..+  ...  ..-  ...  ...  ...  ...  ...  ...  ...

       + is > 2*std error,  - is < -2*std error,  . is between

        ❹  Schematic Representation of Partial Autocorrelations

     Name/Lag   1    2    3    4    5    6    7    8    9    10
     DJIAM     ...  ...  ...  ...  ...  ...  ...  ...  ...  ...
     GOLD      ...  ...  ...  ...  ...  ...  ...  ...  ...  ...
     AAA       ..+  ..-  ...  ...  ...  ...  ...  ...  ...  ...

       + is > 2*std error,  - is < -2*std error,  . is between
```

```
                    Multivariate Financial Data                    2

                        STATESPACE Procedure

             ❺ Yule-Walker Estimates for the Min AIC


                        Lag=1
                        DJIAM         GOLD          AAA
           DJIAM        0.06956    -0.59273    -42.29647

           GOLD         0.00816     0.22687    -12.00271

           AAA          0.00034     0.00098      0.47296

     NOTE: Some variable(s) with positive Infor. are not selected in the model
           because of singularity of the covariance matrix. The variable(s) may
           be contained in the model by increasing PASTMIN value.
```

```
                    Multivariate Financial Data                    3

                        STATESPACE Procedure

            Selected Statespace Form and Preliminary Estimates

                          ❻ State Vector

           DJIAM(T;T)        GOLD(T;T)         AAA(T;T)

               ❼ Estimate of the Transition Matrix

                          0.070  -0.593 -42.296

                          0.008   0.227 -12.003

                          0.000   0.001   0.473


               ❽ Input Matrix for the Innovation

                              1       0       0

                              0       1       0

                              0       0       1


               ❾ Variance Matrix for the Innovation

                     6046.88922 -310.90681 -3.3658967

                     -310.90681 126.726266  0.3438631

                     -3.3658967  0.3438631 0.01572395
```

```
                 Multivariate Financial Data                        4

                    STATESPACE Procedure

          Selected Statespace Form and Fitted Model

                     ❿ State Vector

     DJIAM(T;T)        GOLD(T;T)         AAA(T;T)

          ⓫ Estimate of the Transition Matrix

                     0.070  -0.593 -42.296

                     0.008   0.227 -12.003

                     0.000   0.001   0.473

           ⓬ Input Matrix for the Innovation

                        1       0       0

                        0       1       0

                        0       0       1

          ⓭ Variance Matrix for the Innovation

               6046.88922 -310.90681 -3.3658967

               -310.90681 126.726266  0.3438631

               -3.3658967  0.3438631 0.01572395

                 ⓮ Parameter Estimates

            Parameter Estimate  Std. Err.  T value

            F(1,1)    0.069558  0.133846   0.51969
            F(1,2)    -0.59273  0.889256  -0.66654
            F(1,3)    -42.2965  4.042321  -10.4634
            F(2,1)    0.008161  0.019552  0.417401
            F(2,2)    0.226873  0.131541  1.724731
            F(2,3)    -12.0027  3.763246  -3.18946
            F(3,1)     0.00034  0.000226  1.502862
            F(3,2)    0.000977  0.001468  0.665263
            F(3,3)    0.472961  0.113085   4.18233
```

Explanation

The numbered items in Output 7.1 correspond to the numbered items in the following list:

❶ descriptive statistics, which list the number of observations used for analysis (labeled **Nobs**), the mean (after any differencing), the standard deviation, and the specified order of differencing.

❷ the Akaike Information Criterion (AIC) for the vector autoregressive models (orders 0 through 10). The model with the minimum AIC is used for further analysis. For this example, the AR(1) model is selected.

❸ schematic representations of the autocorrelation functions (ACFs). Statistically significant autocorrelations are noted.

❹ schematic representations of the partial autocorrelation functions (PACFs). Statistically significant partial autocorrelations are noted.

❺ the Yule-Walker parameter estimates for the autoregressive model with the minimum AIC.

❻ the state vector, $\mathbf{z}_t$. In this example, it consists of the current values of the variables because, with an AR(1) model, only the current value is necessary to forecast the series (in addition to the autoregressive parameters).

❼ the preliminary estimate of the transition matrix, **F**.

❽ the preliminary estimate of the input matrix, **G** (an identity matrix).

❾ the preliminary estimate of the variance matrix for innovations, Σ_{ee}.

❿ the state vector, $\mathbf{z}_t$, printed again.

⓫ the final estimate of the transition matrix, **F**, which is identical to the preliminary estimate in this example.

⓬ the final estimate of the input matrix, **G**. It is an identity matrix, which indicates that the preliminary AR(1) model could not be improved by the addition of MA terms.

⓭ the final estimate of the variance matrix for innovations, Σ_{ee}, which is also identical to its preliminary estimate in this example.

⓮ the parameter estimates, standard errors, and *t*-values of the **F** transition matrix. At the .05 level of significance only the **F**(1,3), **F**(2,3), and **F**(3,3) elements are significantly different from 0.

Only lagged changes in the AAA variable seem helpful in forecasting changes in the three series.

Output 7.2
Forecasts from the State Space Model

Multivariate Financial Data
State Space Model Forecasts

OBS	DATE	DJIAM	DJIA_F1	GOLD	GOLD_F1	AAA	AAA_F1
60	01DEC93	3743.62	3685.09	383.69	371.878	6.93	7.04777
61	01JAN94	3868.36	3765.88	387.02	385.564	6.92	6.93248
62	01FEB94	3905.61	3899.00	382.01	387.911	7.08	6.93000
63	01MAR94	.	3927.92	.	378.255	.	7.13254
64	01APR94	.	3952.98	.	375.952	.	7.13039
65	01MAY94	.	3979.69	.	374.658	.	7.10475
66	01JUN94	.	4006.92	.	373.888	.	7.06953
67	01JUL94	.	4034.27	.	373.356	.	7.03047
68	01AUG94	.	4061.65	.	372.925	.	6.98987
69	01SEP94	.	4089.04	.	372.535	.	6.94865
70	01OCT94	.	4116.43	.	372.163	.	6.90718
71	01NOV94	.	4143.82	.	371.798	.	6.86561
72	01DEC94	.	4171.21	.	371.435	.	6.82400
73	01JAN95	.	4198.61	.	371.074	.	6.78237
74	01FEB95	.	4226.00	.	370.713	.	6.74073

Explanation

Output 7.2 lists the last three observations of the original data and the 12 forecasts. Even though the time series are differenced, PROC STATESPACE automatically integrates forecasts of the differenced series to produce forecasts of the original series. The forecasts for the time series follow linear trends of steady increase for the Dow Jones Index and steady decreases for gold prices and AAA bond yields.

A Closer Look

Estimating the State Space Model

To interpret the preliminary results of the state space model before you estimate a final model, use the NOEST option in the PROC STATESPACE statement. The NOEST option suppresses the final estimation phase and prints out only the preliminary results for the state space model. The final estimation phase can be time-consuming and expensive in some cases.

Differencing Time Series Variables

To take differences of time series variables before you analyze them in PROC STATESPACE, specify the desired degree of differencing within the parentheses that follow each variable name in the VAR statement. For example, this statement specifies first differencing of the X variable, second differencing of the Y variable, and span-12 differencing of the Z variable:.

```
var x(1) y(1,1) z(12);
```

By default, the sample mean is subtracted from the input series after differencing. You can prevent the subtraction of the sample means by specifying the NOCENTER option in the PROC STATESPACE statement.

Variations

Specifying the Form of the State Vector

Although the form of the state vector, $\mathbf{z}_t$, is automatically determined for you by PROC STATESPACE, you can specify its form with the FORM statement. There may be theoretical or empirical reasons for you to specify explicitly the form of the state vector.

For example, the following FORM statement specifies that the state vector contain Y_t, $Y_{t+1|t}$, and $Y_{t+2|t}$, and it may possibly contain other variables:

```
form y 3;
```

The notation $Y_{t+1|t}$ indicates the conditional expectation of Y_{t+1} given the information available at time t. The state vector consists of current values and conditional expectations of future values of the variables that are analyzed. If the FORM statement includes specifications for all the variables listed in the VAR statement, the state vector is completely defined and automatic selection of the state space model is not performed.

The following example specifies that the state vector contain $DJIA_{t|t}$ (the current DJIA value), $AAA_{t|t}$ (the current AAA value), and $AAA_{t+1|t}$ (the next period AAA value). No form is specified for the GOLD time series. The state space model parameters are estimated and the series are forecast 12 periods ahead. Only the final matrix estimates and parameter estimates are shown in Output 7.3.

```
proc statespace data=finance
                lead=12
                interval=month
                out=finout2(rename=(for1=djia_f2
                                    for2=gold_f2
                                    for3=aaa_f2));
   var djiam(1) gold(1) aaa(1);
   form djiam 1 aaa 2;
   id date;
run;
```

Output 7.3
State Space Model Matrices and Parameters Based on a Specified State Vector (Partial Output)

```
                    Multivariate Financial Data

                       STATESPACE Procedure

            Selected Statespace Form and Fitted Model

                           State Vector

DJIAM(T;T)        GOLD(T;T)        AAA(T;T)          AAA(T+1;T)

                 Estimate of the Transition Matrix

                     0.070  -0.593 -42.296       0

                     0.008   0.227 -12.003       0

                         0       0       0       1

                    -0.000  -0.000  -0.394   0.732


                  Input Matrix for the Innovation

                             1       0       0

                             0       1       0

                             0       0       1

                         0.000   0.000   0.611


                 Variance Matrix for the Innovation

                   6046.88922 -310.90681 -3.2773862

                   -310.90681 126.726266 0.28869912

                   -3.2773862 0.28869912 0.01408264


                        Parameter Estimates

               Parameter Estimate  Std. Err.  T value

               F(1,1)    0.069558  0.141257  0.492425
               F(1,2)    -0.59273  0.914141   -0.6484
               F(1,3)    -42.2965  75.40804   -0.5609
               F(2,1)    0.008161  0.020449  0.399084
               F(2,2)    0.226873  0.132337  1.714361
               F(2,3)    -12.0027  10.91654   -1.0995
               F(4,1)    -0.00021  0.000235  -0.88541
               F(4,2)    -0.00047  0.001341  -0.34976
               F(4,3)    -0.39448  0.196232  -2.01026
               F(4,4)    0.731986  0.367029  1.994352
               G(4,1)    0.000344  0.000219  1.570264
               G(4,2)    0.000236  0.001451  0.162709
               G(4,3)    0.611332  0.134731  4.537418
```

Interpretation

Compare Output 7.3 to the last page of Output 7.1. Note that the state vector in Output 7.3 represents the new form of the model that you specified in the FORM statement. The **F**, **G**, and Σ_{ee} matrices have changed slightly to reflect the new model.

Restricting Parameters in State Space Modeling

Use the RESTRICT statement in PROC STATESPACE to restrict state space model parameters estimates of the **F** and **G** matrices. The following PROC STATESPACE statements refit the state space model for the finance data with the **F**(1,1) parameter restricted to a value of 0. Then forecasts are produced for the series 12 periods ahead. Only the parameter estimates are shown in Output 7.4.

Note: Restrict or remove parameters from state space models one at a time. Then, re-examine the model and parameter estimates after each change. If you misspecify the form of one series in the transition or innovation matrices, then you might obtain poor parameter estimates for all series because of the dynamic interactions of the state space model. This is analogous to multiple equation regression models, in which misspecifying one equation often results in poor fits for all equations.

```
proc statespace data=finance
                lead=12
                interval=month
                out=finout3(rename=(for1=djia_f3
                                    for2=gold_f3
                                    for3=aaa_f3));
   var djiam(1) gold(1) aaa(1);
   id date;
   restrict f(1,1)=0;
run;
```

Output 7.4
Parameter Estimates from a Restricted State Space Model (Partial Output)

```
                 Multivariate Financial Data

                    STATESPACE Procedure

                    Parameter Estimates

          Parameter Estimate  Std. Err.  T value

          F(1,2)    -0.73147  0.871363  -0.83945
          F(1,3)    -53.7149  71.88547  -0.74723
          F(2,1)    0.011737  0.019116  0.614008
          F(2,2)    0.234006  0.131572  1.778547
          F(2,3)    -11.4156   10.8535  -1.05179
          F(3,1)    0.000378  0.000214  1.770111
          F(3,2)    0.001054  0.001466  0.718917
          F(3,3)    0.479316  0.120937  3.963361
```

Interpretation

In Output 7.4, the **F**(1,1) parameter element is not listed because you have restricted it to 0. The remaining parameter estimates have changed somewhat from the unrestricted estimates shown at the bottom of Output 7.1.

Further Reading

For more information on state space models and PROC STATESPACE, see the *SAS/ETS User's Guide, Version 6, Second Edition.*

References

- Akaike, H. (1976), "Canonical Correlations Analysis of Time Series and the Use of an Information Criterion," in *Advances and Case Studies in System Identification*, eds. R. Mehra and D.G. Lainiotis, New York: Academic Press.
- Kalman, R.E. (1960), "A New Approach to Linear Filtering and Prediction Problems," *Transactions ASME Journal of Basic Engineering*, 82, 35-45.
- Kalman, R.E. and Bucy, R.S. (1961), "New Results in Linear Filtering and Prediction Theory," *Transactions ASME Journal of Basic Engineering*, 83, 95-108.

EXAMPLE 8

Preparing Time Series Data for Forecasting

Featured Tool:

- EXPAND procedure

Most time series analysis and forecasting procedures assume that the time series data observations are taken at equally spaced time intervals or periods. Furthermore, many methods require that there be no missing values for the time series data. If your data are not equally spaced in time or if you have missing values, then your analysis may fail or your results may be invalid.

To avoid misleading or incorrect forecasts from your time series data, it is important to know exactly how your data have been measured. These are the *characteristics* of the observations:

Point-in-time data
: are measured at one moment during a time interval. For example, stock prices are typically measured at the end of each trading day. Data can be measured at the beginning of the time period, the end of the time period, or at the midpoint of the time period.

Total data
: consist of the sum of all measurements during the time period. For example, sales for a retailer can be totaled over the course of a week or a month.

Average data
: are average measurements for a specified time unit. For example, the total weekly sales for a retailer can be divided by the number of working days in a week to get the average daily sales for a given week. Similarly, you can average the daily point-in-time stock price data over the number of trading days in a month to produce monthly average data (on a per day basis).

The SAS/ETS EXPAND procedure can interpolate missing data values, change the observation characteristics, and change the frequency of time series data.

Transformations and differences can also be applied to time series data in PROC EXPAND. You can apply a transformation, such as the log transformation, to your data, along with differencing to deal with nonstationary data. Other types of transformations, such as square root or reciprocal transformations, may also be useful in some situations. Time series with a nonconstant mean can sometimes be made stationary by taking differences.

Program

Interpolating Missing Values

Use part of the steel shipments data set and change four values to missing. The complete steel shipments data set is in "Introduction: The Example Data Sets."

```
data steel1;
   input date:monyy. steelshp @@;
   format date monyy.;
   title 'U.S. Steel Shipments Data';
   title2 '(with missing values)';
   datalines;
JAN89 7278 FEB89 6832 MAR89 7824 APR89 7164
MAY89 7446 JUN89 7331 JUL89 6387 AUG89 7224
SEP89 .    OCT89 7174 NOV89 6652 DEC89 6053
JAN90 6863 FEB90 6502 MAR90 7569 APR90 7023
MAY90 7523 JUN90 7493 JUL90 6890 AUG90 .
SEP90 6893 OCT90 .    NOV90 6907 DEC90 6187
JAN91 6786 FEB91 6039 MAR91 .    APR91 6450
MAY91 6762 JUN91 6623 JUL91 6420 AUG91 6954
SEP91 6747 OCT91 7499 NOV91 6427 DEC91 6118
;
```

Invoke PROC EXPAND and specify the input and output data sets.

```
proc expand data=steel1
            out=steel2
```

Specify the time interval between observations in the input data set.

```
            from=month;
```

Use the cubic spline curve method to interpolate the four missing values for the variable named in the CONVERT statement. Specify a new name for each variable listed in the CONVERT statement. Specify the observation characteristic with the OBSERVED= option.

```
   convert steelshp=steelcon / observed=total;
```

Specify an identification variable.

```
   id date;
run;
```

Round off the interpolated values. If you do not round the interpolated values, they will be printed with decimal places.

```
data steel2;
   set steel2;
   steelcon=round(steelcon);
run;
```

Print the output data set from PROC EXPAND.

```
proc print data=steel2;
run;
```

Output 8.1
Interpolating Missing Values with PROC EXPAND

U.S. Steel Shipments Data
(with missing values)

OBS	DATE	STEELCON	STEELSHP
1	JAN89	7278	7278
2	FEB89	6832	6832
3	MAR89	7824	7824
4	APR89	7164	7164
5	MAY89	7446	7446
6	JUN89	7331	7331
7	JUL89	6387	6387
8	AUG89	7224	7224
9	SEP89	7283	.
10	OCT89	7174	7174
11	NOV89	6652	6652
12	DEC89	6053	6053
13	JAN90	6863	6863
14	FEB90	6502	6502
15	MAR90	7569	7569
16	APR90	7023	7023
17	MAY90	7523	7523
18	JUN90	7493	7493
19	JUL90	6890	6890
20	AUG90	6630	.
21	SEP90	6893	6893
22	OCT90	7585	.
23	NOV90	6907	6907
24	DEC90	6187	6187
25	JAN91	6786	6786
26	FEB91	6039	6039
27	MAR91	6566	.
28	APR91	6450	6450
29	MAY91	6762	6762
30	JUN91	6623	6623
31	JUL91	6420	6420
32	AUG91	6954	6954
33	SEP91	6747	6747
34	OCT91	7499	7499
35	NOV91	6427	6427
36	DEC91	6118	6118

Explanation

Output 8.1, the output data set from PROC EXPAND, contains these three variables:

DATE — is the date variable specified in the ID statement.

STEELSHP — is the original time series with the four missing values.

STEELCON — is the new time series, for which the missing values are interpolated and rounded to the nearest integer.

Changing the Frequency from Monthly to Quarterly

Aggregate the original time series to a lower frequency and simultaneously interpolate the missing values. Use the TO= option to specify that the output series is to be quarterly data.

```
proc expand data=steel1
            out=steel3
            from=month
            to=qtr;
   convert steelshp=steelqtr / observed=total
```

Use the linear spline method to interpolate the missing values.

```
                               method=join;
```

```
   id date;
run;
```

Round off the interpolated values and print the output data set.

```
data steel3;
   set steel3;
   steelqtr=round(steelqtr);
run;

proc print data=steel3;
run;
```

Output 8.2
Aggregating Time Series Data to a Lower Frequency

```
              U.S. Steel Shipments Data
               (with missing values)

              OBS      DATE     STEELQTR

                1    1989:1      21934
                2    1989:2      21941
                3    1989:3      20677
                4    1989:4      19879
                5    1990:1      20934
                6    1990:2      22039
                7    1990:3      20706
                8    1990:4      20327
                9    1991:1      19476
               10    1991:2      19835
               11    1991:3      20121
               12    1991:4      20044
```

Explanation

For the data set shown in Output 8.2, the missing values are interpolated with the linear spline method and the monthly data are aggregated into quarterly data. The observation characteristics are unchanged, so the time series values still represent totals.

Changing the Frequency from Quarterly to Monthly and Changing the Characteristics from Totals to Averages

Convert the quarterly time series data to a higher frequency (monthly). Use the STEEL3 data set, which contains quarterly totals, as the input data set.

```
proc expand data=steel3
            out=steel4
            from=qtr
            to=month;
   convert steelqtr=steelmon /
```

Convert the observation characteristics of the data from totals to averages.

```
                           observed=(total,average);
```

```
   id date;
run;
```

Round off the values to the nearest tenth and print the output data set.

```
data steel4;
   set steel4;
   steelmon=round(steelmon, .1);
run;

proc print data=steel4;
   title2 'Daily Averages';
run;
```

Output 8.3
Converting Time Series Data to a Higher Frequency and Changing the Characteristics

U.S. Steel Shipments Data
Daily Averages

OBS	DATE	STEELMON
1	JAN1989	240.1
2	FEB1989	244.8
3	MAR1989	246.3
4	APR1989	245.0
5	MAY1989	241.6
6	JUN1989	236.6
7	JUL1989	230.7
8	AUG1989	224.5
9	SEP1989	218.8
10	OCT1989	215.1
11	NOV1989	214.7
12	DEC1989	218.4
13	JAN1990	225.3
14	FEB1990	232.9
15	MAR1990	239.7
16	APR1990	244.1
17	MAY1990	243.9
18	JUN1990	238.4
19	JUL1990	230.4
20	AUG1990	223.6
21	SEP1990	221.1
22	OCT1990	221.3
23	NOV1990	221.5
24	DEC1990	220.1
25	JAN1991	217.6
26	FEB1991	215.8
27	MAR1991	215.7
28	APR1991	216.8
29	MAY1991	218.2
30	JUN1991	218.9
31	JUL1991	219.0
32	AUG1991	218.8
33	SEP1991	218.3
34	OCT1991	217.9
35	NOV1991	217.7
36	DEC1991	218.0

Explanation

The output data set shown in Output 8.3 shows that the quarterly totals are converted to monthly averages. Each observation of the STEELMON variable represents an average daily value for steel shipments for each month.

Transforming the Data

Invoke PROC EXPAND to perform transformations on the monthly time series data.

```
proc expand data=steel1
            out=steel5
            from=month
```

Specify METHOD=NONE to perform no interpolation.

```
            method=none;
```

Use the TRANSFORMOUT= option to perform various transformations of the original time series.

```
   convert steelshp=stllag1 / transformout=(lag 1);
   convert steelshp=stllead1 / transformout=(lead 1);
   convert steelshp=stldif2 / transformout=(dif 2);
   convert steelshp=stllog / transformout=(log);
   convert steelshp=stlma3 / transformout=(movave 3);
   id date;
run;

proc print data=steel5;
   title2 'Transformed Series';
run;
```

Output 8.4
Transforming Time Series Data in PROC EXPAND

U.S. Steel Shipments Data
Transformed Series

OBS	DATE	STLLAG1	STLLEAD1	STLDIF2	STLLOG	STLMA3	STEELSHP
1	JAN89	.	6832	.	8.89261	.	7278
2	FEB89	7278	7824	.	8.82937	7311.33	6832
3	MAR89	6832	7164	546	8.96495	7273.33	7824
4	APR89	7824	7446	332	8.87682	7478.00	7164
5	MAY89	7164	7331	-378	8.91543	7313.67	7446
6	JUN89	7446	6387	167	8.89987	7054.67	7331
7	JUL89	7331	7224	-1059	8.76202	6980.67	6387
8	AUG89	6387	.	-107	8.88516	.	7224
9	SEP89	7224	7174	.	.	.	.
10	OCT89	.	6652	-50	8.87822	.	7174
11	NOV89	7174	6053	.	8.80267	6626.33	6652
12	DEC89	6652	6863	-1121	8.70831	6522.67	6053
13	JAN90	6053	6502	211	8.83390	6472.67	6863
14	FEB90	6863	7569	449	8.77987	6978.00	6502
15	MAR90	6502	7023	706	8.93182	7031.33	7569
16	APR90	7569	7523	521	8.85695	7371.67	7023
17	MAY90	7023	7493	-46	8.92572	7346.33	7523

18	JUN90	7523	6890	470	8.92172	7302.00	7493
19	JUL90	7493	.	-633	8.83783	.	6890
20	AUG90	6890	6893	.	.	.	.
21	SEP90	.	.	3	8.83826	.	6893
22	OCT90	6893	6907	.	.	.	.
23	NOV90	.	6187	14	8.84029	.	6907
24	DEC90	6907	6786	.	8.73021	6626.67	6187
25	JAN91	6187	6039	-121	8.82262	6337.33	6786
26	FEB91	6786	.	-148	8.70599	.	6039
27	MAR91	6039	6450	.	.	.	.
28	APR91	.	6762	411	8.77184	.	6450
29	MAY91	6450	6623	.	8.81907	6611.67	6762
30	JUN91	6762	6420	173	8.79830	6601.67	6623
31	JUL91	6623	6954	-342	8.76717	6665.67	6420
32	AUG91	6420	6747	331	8.84707	6707.00	6954
33	SEP91	6954	7499	327	8.81685	7066.67	6747
34	OCT91	6747	6427	545	8.92252	6891.00	7499
35	NOV91	7499	6118	-320	8.76826	6681.33	6427
36	DEC91	6427	.	-1381	8.71899	.	6118

Explanation

Output 8.4 lists the output data set from PROC EXPAND that contains the five transformations applied to the original steel shipments time series.

STLLAG1 contains the lagged value of the time series, that is, the value of the time series one time period earlier.

STLLEAD1 contains the value of the time series one time period later.

STLDIF2 contains the span-2 differences of the time series values. The span-2 difference is the difference between the current time series value and the time series value from two time periods earlier.

STLLOG contains the natural log of the time series values.

STLMA3 contains the three-period moving average of the time series.

The original time series, STEELSHP, is listed as the last variable in the output data set.

A Closer Look

Interpolation Methods

You can specify one of three different methods to interpolate missing values in PROC EXPAND.

cubic spline interpolation
: joins segments of third-degree (cubic) polynomial curves to the nonmissing input values, so that the whole curve and its first and second derivatives are continuous. This is the default method, so you can omit the METHOD= option in the CONVERT statement, or you can specify METHOD=SPLINE to request this method.

linear spline interpolation
: fits a continuous curve by connecting successive straight line segments to the nonmissing input values. Specify METHOD=JOIN in the CONVERT statement to use the linear spline interpolation method.

step function interpolation
: fits a discontinuous piecewise constant curve to the nonmissing input values. Specify METHOD=STEP in the CONVERT statement to use this method.

You can also specify METHOD=NONE to request that no interpolation be performed. This option is typically used in conjunction with the TRANSFORMIN= and TRANSFORMOUT= options.

Changing Observation Characteristics

Use the OBSERVED= option in the CONVERT statement to change the observation characteristics for time series data. Specify any of the following values in the OBSERVED= option to convert observation characteristics from one type to another:

BEGINNING (default)	indicates that the data are beginning-of-period values.
MIDDLE	indicates that the data are midpoint values.
END	indicates that the data are end-of-period values.
TOTAL	indicates that the data are totals for the time period.
AVERAGE	indicates that the data are average values for the time period.

The syntax for changing observation characteristics is as follows:

OBSERVED=(*from-characteristic, to-characteristic*);

If you specify only one value in the OBSERVED= option, that value applies to both the input and output series. For example, OBSERVED=MIDDLE is the same as OBSERVED=(MIDDLE, MIDDLE). However, the specification OBSERVED=(BEGINNING, END) indicates that the input series represents beginning-of-period values and that the output series should be converted to represent end-of-period values.

Performing Transformations

The TRANSFORMIN= (or TIN=) and TRANSFORMOUT= (or TOUT=) options in the CONVERT statement transform the input time series and output time series, respectively. Use the TIN= option to transform a time series prior to interpolating missing values. Use the TOUT= option to transform a time series for which missing values have been interpolated. These options are useful for constraining the interpolated time series values to be within a given range. The interpolation methods in PROC EXPAND do not always produce logical results. For example, an interpolated sales figure might be negative or an interpolated percentage might be outside the range of 0% to 100%. To avoid negative values, you can use a logarithmic transformation of the input series and then use an exponential transformation of the output series to rescale the values back to their original form. To constrain percentages within a range of 0% to 100%, you can divide the original values by 100 and apply the logit function to the input time series. After interpolating the missing values, you can apply the inverse logit function to the output time series and multiply the values by 100 to rescale them back to percentages between 0% and 100%. The following SAS code fragment shows how to perform these transformations to a variable, X:

```
convert x / tin=(/100 logit) tout=(ilogit *100);
```

You can also use the transformation options for purposes unrelated to interpolation of missing values. They provide a convenient way to perform many of the same tasks for which you might use a DATA step. For example, you can apply mathematical operations, such as addition, subtraction, multiplication, and division, to time series data. You can apply various functions to the data (log, exponential, logit, inverse logit, square, and square root). You can also apply lags, leads, differences, sums, and moving averages of any length to the data. When you use the transformation options for these purposes, you can suppress interpolation methods by specifying METHOD=NONE in the CONVERT statement. See the *SAS/ETS User's Guide, Version 6, Second Edition*, pp. 411-412, for the complete list of available transformation operations.

Further Reading

For more information on PROC EXPAND, see the *SAS/ETS User's Guide, Version 6, Second Edition.*

EXAMPLE 9

Using Macros for Forecasting Tasks

Featured Tools:

- BOXCOXAR macro
- DFPVALUE macro
- DFTEST macro
- LOGTEST macro

The examples in this chapter show how to use several SAS macros provided with SAS/ETS software. A *SAS macro* is a program that generates SAS statements. Macros make it easier to produce and execute complex SAS programs that would be time-consuming to write yourself.

This chapter shows how to use the following macros:

%BOXCOXAR investigates Box-Cox transformations useful for modeling and forecasting a time series.

%DFPVALUE computes probabilities for Dickey-Fuller test statistics.

%DFTEST performs Dickey-Fuller tests for unit roots in a time series process.

%LOGTEST tests to see if a log transformation is appropriate for modeling and forecasting a time series.

These macros are part of the SAS AUTOCALL facility and are automatically available for use in your SAS program. See the *SAS Guide to Macro Processing, Version 6, Second Edition* for more information about the SAS macro facility.

In addition to the four macros listed previously, three other macros are available in SAS/ETS software. The %AR, %MA, and %PDL macros are used only with the MODEL procedure. They define autoregressive, moving average, and polynomial distributed lag models, respectively, for PROC MODEL. For more information on these macros, see the *SAS/ETS User's Guide, Version 6, Second Edition.*

The %BOXCOXAR Macro

Transformations are a useful way to deal with nonlinear relationships or heteroscedasticity in time series data. The log transformation is commonly used to convert exponential growth relationships into straight-line relationships. It can also convert nonconstant variation into constant variation. The transformed series can be readily modeled and forecasted.

The Box-Cox transformation is a general class of power transformations that include the log transformation and no transformation as special cases. Many versions of the Box-Cox transformation have been investigated (Box and Cox 1964; Carroll and Ruppert 1988; Davidson and MacKinnon 1993). The %BOXCOXAR macro uses the following Box-Cox transformation:

$$X_t^{(\lambda)} = \frac{(X_t + c)^{\lambda} - 1}{\lambda} \qquad \text{for } \lambda \neq 0$$

$$X_t^{(\lambda)} = ln(X_t + c) \qquad \text{for } \lambda = 0$$

where

$X_t^{(\lambda)}$ is the transformed series.

X_t is the untransformed series.

c is a constant (0 by default).

λ is the parameter that determines the type of transformation.

The parameter λ controls the shape of the transformation. For example, $\lambda = 0$ produces a log transformation, $\lambda = .5$ produces a square-root transformation, and $\lambda = 1$ simply differs from the original series by $c - 1$.

The %BOXCOXAR macro transforms the specified series with each value of a range of λ values and fits an autoregressive model to the transformed series. The value of λ that produces the maximum log likelihood value is returned in the macro variable BOXCOXAR.

The %DFTEST and %DFPVALUE Macros

The %DFTEST macro performs the Dickey-Fuller unit root test. Use this macro to decide if a time series is stationary and to determine the order of differencing required for the time series analysis of a nonstationary series.

The %DFPVALUE macro computes the significance of the Dickey-Fuller test. The %DFTEST macro uses the %DFPVALUE macro to compute p-values for the unit root test. However, you can use the %DFPVALUE macro to compute p-values directly, if you wish.

You can also use the PROBDF function to compute significance probabilities for Dickey-Fuller test statistics. You can use the PROBDF function wherever SAS library functions can be used. The PROBDF function requires that you specify the Dickey-Fuller test statistic and the sample size.

The %DFTEST macro tests the null hypothesis that the time series has a unit root. The alternative hypothesis is that the time series is stationary, based on tables provided in Dickey (1976) and Dickey, Hasza, and Fuller (1984). You can also find tables in Appendix 2 of *SAS/ETS Software: Applications Guide 1, Version 6, First Edition.* Thus, a significant *p*-value indicates that the time series is stationary. The test applies to a simple unit root at lag 1 or to seasonal unit roots at lag 2, 4, or 12. See the *SAS/ETS User's Guide, Version 6, Second Edition* for more information on the %DFTEST macro as well as the theoretical background on the Dickey-Fuller test.

The %LOGTEST Macro

The %LOGTEST macro tests whether a logarithmic transformation is appropriate for modeling and forecasting a time series. It fits an autoregressive model to a series and fits the same model to the log of the series. The macro estimates both models by the maximum likelihood method and computes the maximum log likelihood values for both autoregressive models. The %LOGTEST macro expresses these log likelihood values in terms of the original data and compares them.

Program

Determining the Optimal Box-Cox Transformation

Create the Dow Jones Index data set. The complete Dow Jones Index data set is in "Introduction: The Example Data Sets."

```
data djm;
   input date:monyy5. djiam @@;
   format date monyy5.;
   title 'Dow Jones Index Data';
   title2 'Monthly Average';
   datalines;
jan84 1258.89 feb84 1164.46 mar84 1161.97 apr84 1152.71
more data lines
;
```

Find the optimal Box-Cox transformation for the Dow Jones Index time series. The first argument within the parentheses must be the name of the data set. The second argument must be the variable to be analyzed. These arguments can be followed by options in any order.

```
   /* nlambda=9 specifies 9        */
   /* equally spaced lambda values.*/
   /* The default is nlambda=2.    */
%boxcoxar(djm,djiam,dif=(1),nlambda=9)
```

Output 9.1
Standard Output from the %BOXCOXAR Macro.

Dow Jones Index Data
Monthly Average

LAMBDA	LOGLIK	RMSE	AIC	SBC
1.000	-695.398	5750.93	1402.80	1419.57
0.875	-694.226	5757.20	1400.45	1417.23
0.750	-693.293	5766.40	1398.59	1415.36
0.625	-692.613	5778.62	1397.23	1414.00
0.500	-692.205	5794.03	1396.41	1413.18
0.375	-692.083	5812.88	1396.17	1412.94
0.250	-692.264	5835.48	1396.53	1413.30
0.125	-692.764	5862.31	1397.53	1414.30
0.000	-693.598	5894.00	1399.20	1415.97

Explanation

Output 9.1 shows the standard output from the %BOXCOXAR macro, which prints five variables. The first variable, LAMBDA, is the list of λ values used in the Box-Cox transformation. The following four variables are statistics from the autoregressive model fit to the transformed series:

LOGLIK is the log likelihood value.

RMSE is the residual mean squared error, computed from predicted values that are transformed back to the original scale of the data.

AIC is the Akaike Information Criterion, a goodness-of-fit measure for which smaller values indicate better fit.

SBC is the Schwarz's Bayesian Criterion, a goodness-of-fit measure for which smaller values indicate better fit.

In this example, you specify first differences for the transformed series, and you request that nine different λ values (including the low value of 0 and the high value of 1) be used in the Box-Cox transformations. The λ values are equally spaced.

Of the nine λ values tried, the value of .375 produces the maximum log likelihood value of -692.083. It also produces the minimum AIC value of 1396.17 and the minimum SBC value of 1412.94. After you invoke the %BOXCOXAR macro for these data, the macro variable &BOXCOXAR contains the value .375.

Testing the Time Series for Stationarity

Perform the Dickey-Fuller unit root test for the Dow Jones Index time series. The first argument within the parentheses must be the name of the data set. The second argument must be the variable to be analyzed. ◙ These arguments can be followed by options in any order.

```
%dftest(djm,djiam,outstat=dfout)
```

Print the output data set.

```
proc print data=dfout;
run;
```

Apply a first difference to the data and rerun the unit root test.

```
%dftest(djm,djiam,dif=(1),outstat=dfout1)
```

Print the output data set.

```
proc print data=dfout1;
run;
```

Output 9.2
The Output Data Set from the First Invocation of the %DFTEST Macro

Dow Jones Index Data
Monthly Average

OBS	_TYPE_	_DEPVAR_	_NAME_	_MSE_	INTERCEP	AR_V	DLAG_V	AR_V1
1	OLS	AR_V		6115.56	25.284	-1	-0.00266	0.35033
2	COV	AR_V	INTERCEP	6115.56	584.579	.	-0.22346	0.02146
3	COV	AR_V	DLAG_V	6115.56	-0.223	.	0.00010	-0.00008
4	COV	AR_V	AR_V1	6115.56	0.021	.	-0.00008	0.00887
5	COV	AR_V	AR_V2	6115.56	0.042	.	-0.00005	-0.00309
6	COV	AR_V	AR_V3	6115.56	0.086	.	-0.00010	0.00131

OBS	AR_V2	AR_V3	_NOBS_	_TAU_	_TREND_	_DLAG_	❶ _PVALUE_
1	-0.13021	-0.037478	118	-0.27248	1	1	0.92446
2	0.04200	0.086184	118	-0.27248	1	1	0.92446
3	-0.00005	-0.000096	118	-0.27248	1	1	0.92446
4	-0.00309	0.001306	118	-0.27248	1	1	0.92446
5	0.00987	-0.003047	118	-0.27248	1	1	0.92446
6	-0.00305	0.008879	118	-0.27248	1	1	0.92446

Output 9.3
The Output Data Set from the Second Invocation of the %DFTEST Macro

Dow Jones Index Data
Monthly Average

OBS	_TYPE_	_DEPVAR_	_NAME_	_MSE_	INTERCEP	AR_V	DLAG_V	AR_V1
1	OLS	AR_V		6106.53	21.0395	-1	-0.90983	0.25239
2	COV	AR_V	INTERCEP	6106.53	63.3551	.	-0.51205	0.34324
3	COV	AR_V	DLAG_V	6106.53	-0.5120	.	0.02356	-0.01630
4	COV	AR_V	AR_V1	6106.53	0.3432	.	-0.01630	0.01788
5	COV	AR_V	AR_V2	6106.53	0.2474	.	-0.01180	0.01029
6	COV	AR_V	AR_V3	6106.53	0.1456	.	-0.00723	0.00688

OBS	AR_V2	AR_V3	_NOBS_	_TAU_	_TREND_	_DLAG_	❷ _PVALUE_
1	0.10913	0.09822	117	-5.92787	1	1	.000085160
2	0.24737	0.14560	117	-5.92787	1	1	.000085160
3	-0.01180	-0.00723	117	-5.92787	1	1	.000085160
4	0.01029	0.00688	117	-5.92787	1	1	.000085160
5	0.01268	0.00574	117	-5.92787	1	1	.000085160
6	0.00574	0.00879	117	-5.92787	1	1	.000085160

Explanation

Output 9.2 lists the output data set from the first invocation of the %DFTEST macro. The last variable in the data set, _PVALUE_ ❶, lists the probability value of the Dickey-Fuller unit root test. The value of .92446 exceeds .05, a result which supports the null hypothesis that the Dow Jones Index data has a unit root at lag 1. The results indicate that the time series is nonstationary.

Output 9.3 lists the output data set for the second invocation of the %DFTEST macro, which applies a first difference to the data before performing the unit root test. In this case, the value of the _PVALUE_ variable ❷ is less than .05 (in fact, it is less than .001), a result which supports the alternative hypothesis that the time series does not have a unit root. You conclude that the Dow Jones Index data can be made stationary when you apply a first difference to the data.

Testing the Need for a Log Transformation

Test whether a log transformation is appropriate for the Dow Jones Index data. The first argument within the parentheses must be the name of the data set. The second argument must be the variable to be analyzed. ◙ These arguments can be followed by options in any order.

```
%logtest(djm,djiam,dif=(1),print=yes)
```

Output 9.4
Standard Output from the %LOGTEST Macro

Dow Jones Index Data
Monthly Average

TRANS	LOGLIK	RMSE	AIC	SBC
NONE	-695.398	5750.93	1402.80	1419.57
LOG	-693.598	5894.00	1399.20	1415.97

Explanation

Output 9.4 lists the standard output from the %LOGTEST macro. The variable TRANS describes the type of transformation (NONE or LOG) applied to the time series before the autoregressive model is fit. The other four variables are statistics from the autoregressive model fit to the transformed series. See the "Explanation" that follows Output 9.1 for more details.

In this example, the log likelihood value for the log transformed time series is higher. Also, the values of AIC and SBC are smaller for the log transformed series. From these results, you conclude that a log transformation is appropriate for the Dow Jones Index time series.

A Closer Look

Options for the %BOXCOXAR and %LOGTEST Macros

You can specify any of the following options in both the %BOXCOXAR and %LOGTEST macros:

AR=
: specifies the order of the autoregressive model fit to the transformed series. The default is AR=5.

CONST=
: specifies a constant, *c*, to be added to the series before transformation. Use the CONST= option when some of the values of the series are 0 or negative. The default is CONST=0.

DIF=(*differencing-list*)
: specifies the degrees of differencing to apply to the transformed series before the autoregressive model is fit. The *differencing-list* is a list of positive integers separated by commas and enclosed in parentheses.

OUT=
: writes the results to an output data set. The output data set contains the same variables as the standard output.

PRINT= YES | NO
: specifies whether the results are printed. The default for the %BOXCOXAR macro is PRINT=YES; the default for the %LOGTEST macro is PRINT=NO.

You can specify any of the following options in the %BOXCOXAR macro:

LAMBDAHI=
: specifies the maximum value of lambda for the grid search. The default is LAMBDAHI=1.

LAMBDALO=
: specifies the minimum value of lambda for the grid search. The default is LAMBDALO=0.

NLAMBDA=
: specifies the number of lambda values considered, including the LAMBDALO= and LAMBDAHI= option values. The default is NLAMBDA=2.

Options for the %DFTEST and %DFPVALUE Macros

You can specify any of the following options in the %DFTEST macro:

AR=
: specifies the order of autoregressive model fit after any differencing specified by the DIF= and DLAG= options. The default is AR=3.

DIF= (*differencing-list*)
: specifies the degree of differencing to apply to the series. The *differencing-list* is a list of positive integers separated by commas and enclosed in parentheses.

OUT=
: writes residuals to an output data set.

OUTSTAT=
: writes the test statistic, parameter estimates, and other statistics to an output data set.

You can specify any of the following options in both the %DFTEST and %DFPVALUE macros:

DLAG= 1 | 2 | 4 | 12
: specifies the lag to be tested for a unit root. The default is DLAG=1.

TREND= 0 | 1 | 2
: specifies the degree of deterministic time trend included in the model. TREND=0 includes no deterministic term and assumes the series has a 0 mean. TREND=1 includes an intercept term. TREND=2 specifies an intercept term and a linear time trend term. The default is TREND=1.

Variations

Computing the *p*-Value for the Unit Root Test

If you know the value of τ (the Dickey-Fuller unit root test statistic) and the number of observations on which the test statistic is based, you can use the %DFPVALUE macro to compute the *p*-value for the Dickey-Fuller unit root test. The *p*-value is stored in the &DFPVALUE macro variable.

Compute the *p*-value for the Dickey-Fuller unit root test for the Dow Jones Index data. Use the values from Output 9.2. The first argument in the parentheses must be the τ value. The second argument must be the number of observations on which the statistic is based.

```
%dfpvalue(-.27248,118)
```

Displaying the Macro Variable Values

A simple way to display the values in the macro variables is to use %PUT statements that write the values to the SAS log. The following macro variables are displayed in Output 9.5:

&BOXCOXAR contains the value of λ for the optimal Box-Cox transformation.

&DFPVALUE contains the *p*-value of the test statistic for the Dickey-Fuller unit root test.

&LOGTEST contains the result (NONE or LOG) of the test for log transformation.

Display the values of the macro variables used in this example in the SAS log.

```
%put Optimal Value of Lambda for Box-Cox Transformation: &boxcoxar;
%put P-value from Dickey-Fuller Test: &dfpvalue;
%put Result of Test for Log Transformation: &logtest;
```

Output 9.5
Displaying Macro Variable Values in the SAS Log

```
   %put Optimal Value of Lambda for Box-Cox Transformation: &boxcoxar;
Optimal Value of Lambda for Box-Cox Transformation: 0.375
2   %put P-value from Dickey-Fuller Test: &dfpvalue;
P-value from Dickey-Fuller Test: 0.9244571438
3   %put Result of Test for Log Transformation: &logtest;
Result of Test for Log Transformation: LOG
```

Another way to display macro variable values is with PUT statements, which are part of the DATA step. You specify the output file for PUT statements with the FILE statement. These results are shown in Output 9.6. When you reference a macro variable within a text string, you must enclose the text string in double quotation marks.

Display the values of the macro variables in SAS output.

```
data _null_;
   file print;
   put // "Optimal Value of Lambda for Box-Cox Transformation: &boxcoxar" /
          "P-value from Dickey-Fuller Test: &dfpvalue" /
          "Result of Test for Log Transformation: &logtest";
run;
```

Output 9.6
Displaying Macro Variable Values in the SAS Output

```
                          Dow Jones Index Data
                            Monthly Average

   Optimal Value of Lambda for Box-Cox Transformation: 0.375
   P-value from Dickey-Fuller Test: 0.9244571058
   Result of Test for Log Transformation: LOG
```

Further Reading

- □ For more information on macros available in SAS/ETS software, see the *SAS/ETS User's Guide, Version 6, Second Edition.*
- □ For more information about the SAS macro facility, see the *SAS Guide to Macro Processing, Version 6, Second Edition.*

References

- □ Box, G.E.P. and Cox, D.R. (1964), "An Analysis of Transformations," *Journal of the Royal Statistics Society*, B-26, 211-252.
- □ Carroll, R.J. and Ruppert, D. (1988), *Transformation and Weighting in Regression*, Chapman and Hall.
- □ Davidson, R. and MacKinnon, J.G. (1993), *Estimation and Inference in Econometrics*, New York: Oxford University Press.

□ Dickey, D.A. (1976), "Estimation and Testing of Nonstationary Time Series," Unpublished Ph.D. Thesis, Ames: Iowa State University.

□ Dickey, D.A., Hasza, D.P., and Fuller, W.A. (1984), "Testing for Unit Roots in Seasonal Time Series," *Journal of the American Statistical Association,* 79, 355-367.

EXAMPLE 10

Fitting and Forecasting a Linear Model by OLS

Featured Tools:

- □ AUTOREG procedure
  - MODEL statement
    - ARCHTEST option
    - DW= option
    - DWPROB option
    - GODFREY= option
    - NORMAL option
  - OUTPUT statement
  - TEST statement
- □ GPLOT procedure

The Capital Asset Pricing Model (CAPM) relates the returns of an asset to the returns of the market portfolio (Black, Jensen, and Scholes 1972). The estimated equation can be used for forecasting the return on assets.

Using data of past returns, the CAPM in risk premium form can be estimated.

$$R_{i,t} - R_{f,t} = \alpha_i + \beta_i \times \left(R_{M,t} - R_{f,t}\right) + \epsilon_{i,t}$$

The parameters and variables of the CAPM equation for the *i*th asset are defined as follows:

α_i is the intercept parameter to be estimated.

β_i is the slope parameter to be estimated, a relative measure of systematic, nondiversifiable risk.

$\epsilon_{i,t}$ is the random error term for the *i*th asset in the *t*th period, interpreted as nonsystematic (diversifiable) risk; holding additional assets can eliminate this risk.

$R_{i,t}$ is the return on asset *i* in the *t*th period:

$$Returns_{i,t} = \frac{Price_{i,t} - Price_{i,t-1} + Dividends_{i,t}}{Price_{i,t-1}}$$

$R_{M,t}$ is the return on the market portfolio (all assets) for the *t*th period. The Center for Research on Securities Prices (CRSP) at the University of Chicago provides an R_M based on the value-weighted transactions of all stocks listed on the New York and American Stock exchanges.

$R_{f,t}$ is the return on a risk-free asset for the *t*th period. The return on U.S. Treasury bills is often used in empirical work.

Program

Estimating the Model

Create the RETURNS data set. The complete RETURNS data set is listed in "Introduction: The Example Data Sets." The monthly returns data are from the Center for Research in Security Prices (CRSP).

The RETURNS data set contains the market return (R_M), the risk-free return (R_F), and returns for individual stocks from JAN78 - DEC86.

The RETURNS data set contains twelve additional values for R_M and R_F, which are used as input values for generating the forecasts of the risk premiums for the individual stock returns.

```
data returns;
   input date r_m r_f r_ibm r_wyr;
   format date monyy.;
   informat date monyy.;
   mkt = r_m - r_f;
   ibm = r_ibm - r_f;
   wyr = r_wyr - r_f;
   label mkt='Risk Premium for Market'
         r_f='Risk-Free Rate of Return'
         ibm='Risk Premium for IBM'
         wyr='Risk Premium for Weyerhauser';
   title 'Returns Data';
datalines;
JAN78 -0.045 0.00487 -0.029 -0.116
FEB78  0.010 0.00494 -0.043 -0.135
MAR78  0.050 0.00526 -0.063  0.084
more data lines
;
```

Fit the CAPM regression using PROC AUTOREG.

```
proc autoreg data=returns;
```

Use a MODEL statement to fit the model.

```
   model ibm = mkt      /* Fit the CAPM Regression                */
```

Test the residuals for autocorrelation and for autoregressive conditional heteroscedasticity (ARCH effects) using the DW=, ARCHTEST, and GODFREY= options.

```
         / normal       /* Print the Jarque-Bera Statistic        */
           dw=12        /* Print the Durbin-Watson Statistics     */
           dwprob       /* Print Durbin-Watson p Values           */
           archtest     /* Test for the Absence of ARCH Effects */
           godfrey=12;  /* Godfrey Test for Autocorrelation       */
```

Test if the estimated slope parameter equals 1 using a TEST statement.

```
   test mkt=1;          /* Test if the Slope Parameter Equals 1 */
run;
```

Output 10.1
Model Estimated by Ordinary Least Squares (Partial Output)

```
                    Returns Data

                  Autoreg Procedure

Dependent Variable = IBM       Risk Premium for IBM


              Ordinary Least Squares Estimates

      ❶ SSE         0.265422   DFE             106
        MSE         0.002504   Root MSE    0.05004
        SBC          -333.07   AIC        -338.434
        Reg Rsq       0.2094   Total Rsq    0.2094
      ❷ Normal Test   2.1160   Prob>Chi-Sq  0.3471

              ❸ Durbin-Watson Statistics

                  Order     DW     PROB<DW
                    1    1.9149    0.3292
                    2    1.7707    0.1364
                    3    1.6628    0.0582
                    4    1.6559    0.0659
                    5    1.7102    0.1258
                    6    1.7016    0.1414
                    7    1.9086    0.5468
                    8    1.8096    0.3830
                    9    1.8621    0.5228
                   10    1.8715    0.5849
                   11    1.5506    0.0830
                   12    1.8509    0.6221
```

```
                    Returns Data

                  Autoreg Procedure

        ❹ Q and LM Tests for ARCH Disturbances

        Order      Q       Prob>Q        LM     Prob>LM

            1   0.1653    0.6843     0.1253    0.7234
            2   1.4913    0.4744     1.3162    0.5178
            3   2.3482    0.5034     2.3847    0.4965
            4   2.9172    0.5718     3.6615    0.4538
            5   3.3958    0.6392     3.7038    0.5928
            6   3.5282    0.7402     3.7097    0.7159
            7   3.5377    0.8312     3.8515    0.7967
            8   3.8273    0.8724     4.2802    0.8310
            9   4.6203    0.8661     4.8169    0.8500
           10   4.6255    0.9148     4.8939    0.8982
           11   5.0960    0.9264     5.2474    0.9186
           12   5.8397    0.9239     6.1794    0.9068
```

```
                         Returns Data

                      Autoreg Procedure

           ❺ Godfrey's Serial Correlation Test

               Alternative         LM    Prob>LM

                 AR(+  1)      0.1460     0.7024
                 AR(+  2)      1.2520     0.5347
                 AR(+  3)      2.8238     0.4196
                 AR(+  4)      3.8161     0.4315
                 AR(+  5)      4.0824     0.5376
                 AR(+  6)      4.2508     0.6428
                 AR(+  7)      4.9601     0.6648
                 AR(+  8)      5.0396     0.7533
                 AR(+  9)      5.2740     0.8098
                 AR(+ 10)      5.4195     0.8615
                 AR(+ 11)      7.8343     0.7281
                 AR(+ 12)      7.9496     0.7891
```

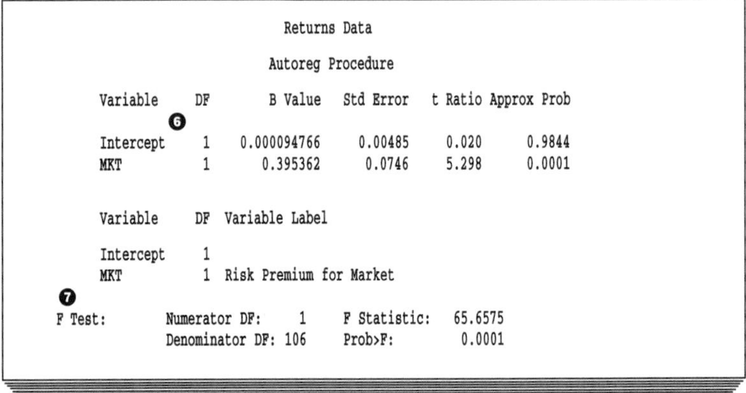

```
                         Returns Data

                      Autoreg Procedure

  Variable     DF        B Value   Std Error   t Ratio Approx Prob
              ❻
  Intercept     1    0.000094766     0.00485     0.020     0.9844
  MKT           1       0.395362      0.0746     5.298     0.0001

  Variable     DF  Variable Label

  Intercept     1
  MKT           1  Risk Premium for Market
❼
F Test:       Numerator DF:     1    F Statistic:   65.6575
              Denominator DF: 106    Prob>F:         0.0001
```

Explanation

❶ Goodness-of-fit statistics are listed, including

- □ error sum of squares (**SSE**).
- □ error degrees of freedom (**DFE**).
- □ mean square error (**MSE**) and **Root MSE**.
- □ Schwarz's Bayesian Criterion (**SBC**) and Akaike's Information Criterion (**AIC**). In general, the better the fit of the estimated model, the smaller these statistics will be.
- □ regression R-square (**Reg Rsq**) and total R-square (**Total Rsq**). The total R-square is 1 minus the ratio of SSE to SST, where SST is the total corrected sum of squares for the original (untransformed) response variable. The regression R-square is a measure of the fit of the structural part of the

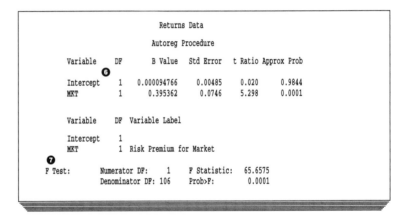

model after transforming for autocorrelation (as specified by the NLAG= option of the MODEL statement) and is the R-square for the transformed regression. The CAPM regression of this example has no autocorrelation correction specified and the `Reg Rsq` and `Total Rsq` measures are the same.

❷ The Jarque-Bera normality test statistic and *p*-value are listed. The high *p*-value indicates the null hypothesis of normality can be retained.

❸ Durbin-Watson *d*-statistics and *p*-values are listed. Durbin-Watson statistics are widely used as tests for autocorrelation, and when doing so, you should specify an order at least as large as the order of any potential seasonality because seasonality produces autocorrelation at the seasonal lag. The RETURNS data set contains monthly data, and so DW=12 was specified.

The generalized Durbin-Watson tests should not be used to decide on the autoregressive order, as the higher-order tests assume the absence of lower-order autocorrelation. If the first-order test indicates no first-order autocorrelation, the second-order test checks for second-order autocorrelation. Once autocorrelation is detected, further tests at higher orders are not appropriate.

Note that a significant Durbin-Watson statistic may indicate that the model is misspecified in terms of the included regressors or in functional form.

For the CAPM regression of this example, none of the Durbin-Watson *p*-values are less than .05. Example 13 provides examples of correcting the model for various orders of autocorrelation.

For additional discussion on generalized Durbin-Watson tests, see the *SAS/ETS User's Guide, Version 6, Second Edition*, pp. 222-224.

❹ Portmanteau *Q* and Lagrange Multiplier (LM) tests for ARCH disturbances are listed. The *Q*-statistics are calculated from the squared residuals and are used to test for nonlinear effects (for example, GARCH effects) present in the residuals. The null hypothesis for these tests is that the OLS residuals are a white noise process; that is, the residuals conform to the standard OLS regression assumptions. These statistics and the large *p*-values indicate that the null hypothesis can be retained.

❺ Statistics for Godfrey's general Lagrange multiplier tests for *p*-values and ARMA errors are listed. You can also use this test when there are lagged dependent regressors in the model. When GODFREY= r and NLAG= p are specified, the null hypothesis is that the errors are from an AR(p) process versus the alternative hypothesis that the errors are from an AR($p+r$) process. If the NLAG= option is not specified, the null hypothesis is that the errors are white noise versus the alternative that the errors are AR(r). Moreover, the ARMA(p,r) process is locally equivalent to the AR($p+r$) process for this test. For details, see Godfrey (1978a and 1978b).

For this model, none of the p-values are less than .05, indicating that the null hypotheses can be retained. You conclude that these Godfrey tests provide little evidence of autocorrelated errors.

6 Parameter estimates, standard errors, t-statistics, and the p-values for the null hypotheses that each parameter is equal to 0 are listed. The t-statistics and p-values indicate that the intercept (α) is not different from 0 and the slope parameter (β) is.

This model is fit by OLS. Because the NLAG= option was not specified, PROC AUTOREG did not make a correction for autocorrelation. For examples of estimation using the NLAG= option, see Example 13, "Fitting and Forecasting a Linear Model with an Error Correction."

7 Slope parameter hypothesis test, degrees of freedom, F-statistic, and p-value are listed. The low p-value indicates that the null hypothesis (that the parameter is 1.0) should be rejected.

Forecasting the Model

Forecast the estimated capital asset pricing model. Use an OUTPUT statement to create and name an output data set. The forecasts are generated from the estimated model using additional market returns and risk-free returns in the RETURNS data set.

```
proc autoreg data=returns noprint;
   model ibm = mkt;
   output out=rt_out   /* Names the Output Data Set      */
          predicted=p  /* Outputs Predicted Values       */
          residual=r   /* Outputs Residual Values        */
          lcl=l        /* Outputs Lower Confidence Limit */
          ucl=u;       /* Outputs Upper Confidence Limit */
run;
```

Print selected variables and observations with PROC PRINT. Use a WHERE statement to specify the observations to be printed.

```
proc print data=rt_out;
   where date > '01sep86'd;
   var date u p ibm l r;
run;
```

Output 10.2
Predicted and Residual Values, and the Lower and Upper 95% Confidence Limits

Returns Data

OBS	DATE	U	P	IBM	L	R
106	OCT86	0.10523	0.00556	-0.08518	-0.09411	-0.090739
107	NOV86	0.09812	-0.00157	0.03280	-0.10125	0.034366
108	DEC86	0.09631	-0.00339	-0.05982	-0.10309	-0.056428
109	JAN87	0.15848	0.05681	.	-0.04485	.
110	FEB87	0.12404	0.02407	.	-0.07591	.
111	MAR87	0.11279	0.01305	.	-0.08668	.
112	APR87	0.08919	-0.01061	.	-0.11041	.
113	MAY87	0.09962	-0.00006	.	-0.09973	.
114	JUN87	0.11327	0.01353	.	-0.08621	.
115	JUL87	0.11991	0.02004	.	-0.07983	.
116	AUG87	0.10387	0.00421	.	-0.09546	.
117	SEP87	0.09186	-0.00789	.	-0.10764	.
118	OCT87	0.00333	-0.10411	.	-0.21156	.
119	NOV87	0.07166	-0.02872	.	-0.12910	.
120	DEC87	0.12796	0.02786	.	-0.07223	.

Explanation

The following variables are listed in Output 10.2:

U are the upper confidence limits.

P are the predicted values.

IBM are the actual values.

L are the lower confidence limits.

R are the residual values.

Plotting Forecasts and Confidence Limits

Sort the variables prior to plotting.

```
proc sort data=rt_out out=rt_out1;
   by date;
run;
```

Plot the actual values, the predictions, and the confidence limits versus the market risk premium using PROC GPLOT.

```
proc gplot data=rt_out1;
```

The PLOT statement specifies plotting the vertical axis variable versus the horizontal axis variable.

```
   plot ibm*mkt=1
        p  *mkt=2
        l  *mkt=3
        u  *mkt=3 / overlay;
```

The OVERLAY option specifies plotting multiple variables on the same plot.

The SYMBOL statements define the plotted symbols.

```
   symbol1 v=star i=none h=1;       /* V= plotting symbol */
   symbol2 v=plus i=join h=1;       /* I=JOIN join points */
   symbol3 v=circle i=none h=1;     /* H= symbol height   */
```

```
   title2 ''Risk Premium versus Market'';
run;
```

Output 10.3
Two-Dimensional, High-Resolution Plot of Actual and Predicted Values with 95% Confidence Limits

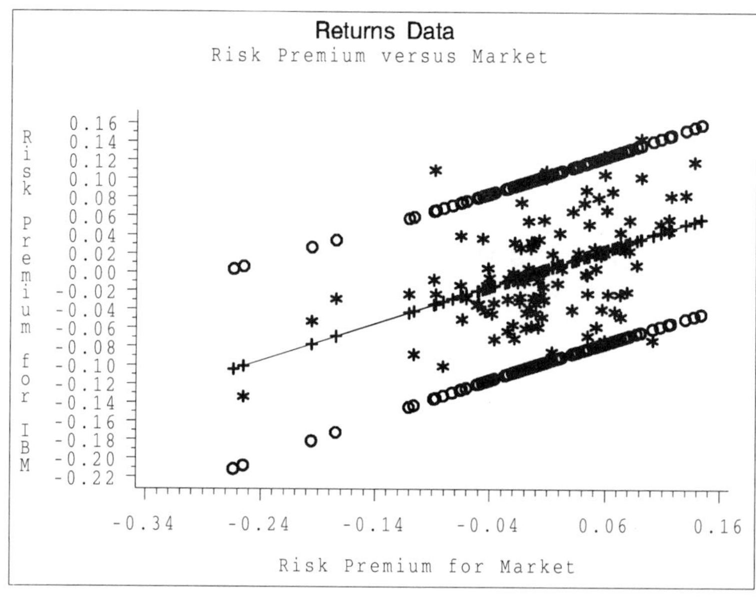

A Closer Look

Predicted Values and Confidence Limits

The AUTOREG procedure can produce two kinds of predicted values, residual values, and confidence limits for the dependent variable. In both cases, the residuals are the actual values minus the predicted values. If the NLAG= option is not specified, then there is no difference in the two kinds of predicted values. If the NLAG= option is specified, an autoregressive error correction is made, and the two kinds of predicted values differ.

- The first type of predicted value is obtained from only the structural part of the model, $\boldsymbol{x}_t'\boldsymbol{b}$. See the PREDICTEDM= option in the next section.
- The second type of predicted value uses both the structural part of the model and the predicted values of the error process. These conditional mean values are useful in predicting future values of the dependent variable. See the PREDICTED= option in the next section.

Options to Specify the Type of Predicted Values and Confidence Limits

The following options in the OUTPUT statement control the predicted and residuals values and the confidence limits that are generated by PROC AUTOREG:

OUT=*SAS-data-set*
: names the output SAS data set containing the predicted and residual values and the confidence limits.

ALPHACLI=*name*
: sets the confidence limit size for the estimates of future values of the response variable. The ALPHACLI= value must be between 0 and 1. The resulting confidence interval has 1 − *value* confidence. The default is ALPHACLI=.05, corresponding to a 95% confidence interval.

ALPHACLM=*name*
: sets the confidence limit size for the estimates of the structural or regression part of the model. The ALPHACLM= value must be between 0 and 1. The resulting confidence interval has 1 − *value* confidence. The default is ALPHACLM=.05, corresponding to a 95% confidence interval.

LCL=*name* and UCL=*name*
: writes the lower and upper confidence limits (respectively) for the predicted value as specified by the PREDICTED= option to the output data set. The size of the confidence interval is set by the ALPHACLI= option. When a GARCH model is estimated, the

confidence limits are calculated assuming that the disturbances have homoscedastic (constant) conditional variance.

LCLM=*name* and UCLM=*name*
: writes the lower and upper confidence limits (respectively) for the structural predicted value as specified by the PREDICTEDM= option to the output data set. The size of the confidence interval is set by the ALPHACLM= option.

PREDICTED=*name*
: writes the predicted values to the output data set. These values are formed from both the structural and autoregressive parts of the model. The PREDICTED= option can be abbreviated as P= .

PREDICTEDM=*name*
: writes the structural predicted values to the output data set. These values are formed from only the structural part of the model. The PREDICTEDM= option can be abbreviated as PM= .

RESIDUAL=*name*
: writes the residuals from the predicted values based on both the structural and autoregressive parts of the model to the output data set. The RESIDUAL= option can be abbreviated as R= .

RESIDUALM=*name*
: writes the residuals from the predicted values based on only the structural part of the model to the output data set. The RESIDUALM= option can be abbreviated as RM= .

Further Reading

- For more information on PROC AUTOREG, see *SAS/ETS User's Guide, Version 6, Second Edition*, and *SAS/ETS Software: Changes and Enhancements, Release 6.11.*
- For complete reference information on PROC GPLOT and other features available in SAS/GRAPH software, see *SAS/GRAPH Software: Reference, Version 6, First Edition, Volumes 1 and 2.*
- For more information on PROC PRINT and PROC SORT, see *SAS Procedures Guide, Version 6, Third Edition.*

References

- □ Black, F., Jensen, M., and Scholes, M. (1972), "The Capital Asset Pricing Model: Some Empirical Tests," *Studies in the Theory of Capital Markets*, ed. M. Jensen, New York: Praeger, 79-121.
- □ Godfrey, L. (1978a), "Testing against General Autoregressive and Moving Average Error Models When the Regressors Include Lagged Dependent Variables," *Econometrica*, 46, 1293-1301.
- □ Godfrey, L. (1978b), "Testing for Higher Order Serial Correlation in Regression Equations When the Regressors Include Lagged Dependent Variables," *Econometrica*, 46, 1303-1310.

EXAMPLE 11

Testing Forecasting Models for Break Points with Chow Tests

Featured Tools:

- AUTOREG procedure
  - MODEL statement
    - CHOW= option
    - PCHOW= option
  - TEST statement

The Capital Asset Pricing Model (CAPM) in risk premium form can be estimated for IBM Corporation stock returns contained in the RETURNS data set, and then used for forecasting.

$$R_{i,t} - R_{f,t} = \alpha_i + \beta_i \times \left(R_{M,t} - R_{f,t}\right) + \epsilon_{i,t}$$

For discussion of the CAPM, see Example 10, "Fitting and Forecasting a Linear Model by OLS," and Black, Jensen, and Scholes (1972).

Chow Tests

A linear regression model, $\mathbf{y} = \mathbf{X}\beta + \mathbf{u}$, can be hypothesized to have a break point, where there is a fundamental change in the relationship of the independent, right-side **X** variables to the dependent **y** variable.

The observations for the model are split into two subsets at the specified break point by the CHOW= option. There are n_1 and n_2 observations in the two subsets, and $\mathbf{y} = (\mathbf{y}_1,\mathbf{y}_2)$, $\mathbf{X} = (\mathbf{X}_1,\mathbf{X}_2)$, and $\mathbf{u} = (\mathbf{u}_1,\mathbf{u}_2)$.

The Chow test tests for equivalency of the k estimated parameters of separate linear regressions for each subset of observations.

$$\mathbf{y}_1 = \mathbf{X}_1\beta_1 + \mathbf{u}_1$$

$$\mathbf{y}_2 = \mathbf{X}_2\beta_2 + \mathbf{u}_2$$

The null hypothesis is that $\beta_1 = \beta_2$, conditional on the same error variance, $\mathbf{Var}(\mathbf{u}_1) = \mathbf{Var}(\mathbf{u}_2)$ (see Greene 1993, pp. 215-216). The test statistic has an F-distribution with k and $(n_1 + n_2 - 2k)$ degrees of freedom, and uses three sums of squared errors, calculated from OLS regressions (the model with all observations, the model with the n_1 observations, and the model with the n_2 observations).

$$F_{chow} = \frac{\left(u'u - u_1'u_1 - u_2'u_2\right) / k}{\left(u_1'u_1 + u_2'u_2\right) / \left(n_1 + n_2 - 2k\right)}$$

When break points are associated with known events, then input values can be created for right-side variables as expectations for the future are developed. Input values are often 0 for periods without the event and 1 for periods when the event occurs. Knowledge of break points may lead to more accurate forecast models.

Chow (1960) suggests another test statistic that tests the hypothesis that the mean of the prediction errors is 0. The predictive Chow test statistic has an F-distribution with n_2 and $(n_1 - k)$ degrees of freedom, and is calculated for the OLS regression residuals as follows:

$$F_{pchow} = \frac{\left(u'u - u_1'u_1\right) / n_2}{u_1'u_1 / \left(n_1 - k\right)}$$

The PCHOW= option in the SAS/ETS AUTOREG procedure compiles the predictive Chow test statistic.

For additional discussion on use of these tests, see Chow (1960) and Maddala (1992), pp. 170-177.

Program

Create the RETURNS data set. The complete RETURNS data set is listed in "Introduction: The Example Data Sets." The monthly returns data are from the Center for Research in Security Prices (CRSP).

```
data returns;
   input date r_m r_f r_ibm r_wyr;
   format date monyy.;
   informat date monyy.;
   mkt = r_m - r_f;
   ibm = r_ibm - r_f;
   wyr = r_wyr - r_f;
   label mkt='Risk Premium for Market'
         r_f='Risk-Free Rate of Return'
         ibm='Risk Premium for IBM'
         wyr='Risk Premium for Weyerhauser';
   title 'Returns Data';
datalines;
JAN78 -0.045 0.00487 -0.029 -0.116
FEB78  0.010 0.00494 -0.043 -0.135
MAR78  0.050 0.00526 -0.063  0.084
more data lines
;
```

Test the stability of parameter estimates with a Chow test. Use the CHOW= (obs_1, ... obs_n) option and the PCHOW= option. This example tests for a break point after the 48th observation, which is December 1981.

```
proc autoreg data=returns;
   model ibm = mkt / chow=(48)   /* Test for Regime Change
                                      after obs 48            */
                     pchow=(48); /* Test if Mean of Prediction
                                    Errors Is Zero            */
   title2;                       /* Resets the Program TITLE2  */
run;
```

Output 11.1
Chow Test of Parameter Stability Tests Created (Partial Output)

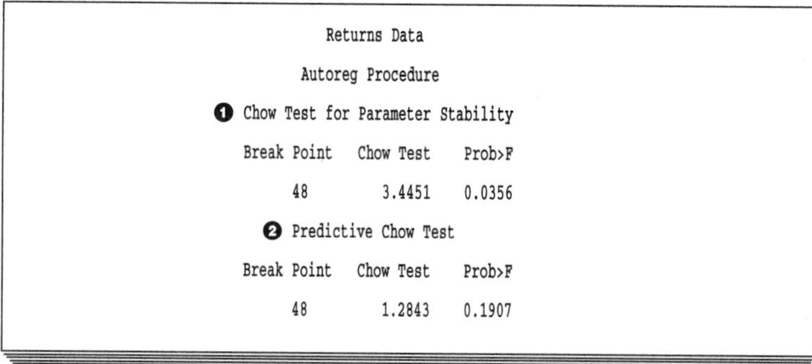

```
                    Returns Data

                 Autoreg Procedure

    ❶ Chow Test for Parameter Stability

    Break Point   Chow Test    Prob>F

        48          3.4451     0.0356

          ❷ Predictive Chow Test

    Break Point   Chow Test    Prob>F

        48          1.2843     0.1907
```

Explanation

❶ Use the **Chow Test** *F*-statistic to test the null hypothesis that there was no break point. The test is used to assess the stability of the estimated parameters. For this model, the *p*-value of .0356 indicates the rejection of the null hypothesis at the .05 level.

❷ Use the **Predictive Chow Test** *F*-statistic to test the null hypothesis that the mean of the prediction errors is 0. The high *p*-value indicates the retention of the null hypothesis at the .05 level.

Variation

Performing Chow Tests Using Dummy Variables

You can also perform Chow tests as tests of dummy variables. First, create dummy variables in a DATA step; then test if the dummy variable parameter estimates differ from 0.

Create the RETURNS0 data set in a DATA step.

The intercept dummy variable D is created with an IF-THEN/ELSE statement.

The slope dummy variable DUMMY is created with an assignment statement.

```
data returns0;
   set returns;

      /* Create Intercept Dummy */
   if date > '01DEC81'd then d=1;
   else d=0;

      /* Create Slope Dummy Variable */
   dummy=d*mkt;
run;
```

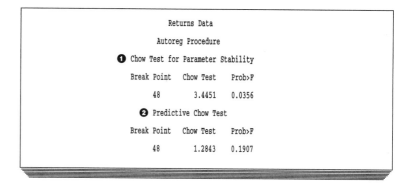

Fit the model using PROC AUTOREG.

```
proc autoreg data=returns0;
```

Use a MODEL statement to specify the model, including the dummy variables.

```
   model ibm = d mkt dummy;  /* Fit the CAPM Regression              */
```

Use a TEST statement to test for a regime change as a joint test of the estimated dummy variable parameters.

```
   test d,dummy;             /* Joint Test if Dummy Parms Are Zero */
run;
```

Output 11.2
Estimated Model with Dummy Variables and Parameter Tests

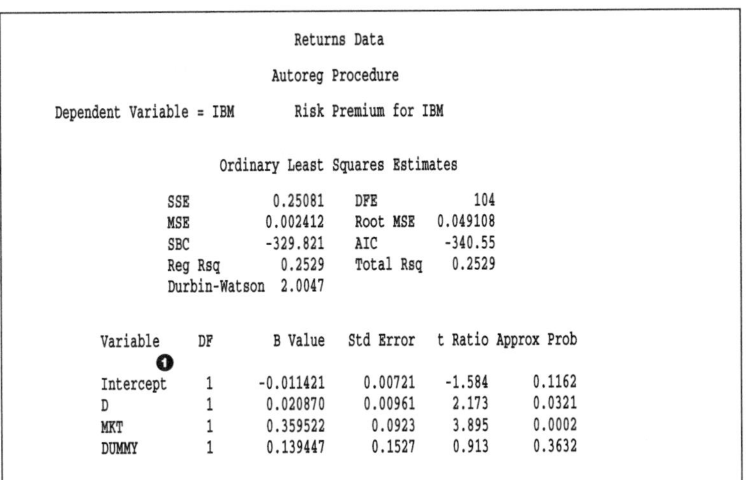

```
                          Returns Data

                        Autoreg Procedure

Dependent Variable = IBM        Risk Premium for IBM

                  Ordinary Least Squares Estimates

          SSE           0.25081    DFE            104
          MSE          0.002412    Root MSE  0.049108
          SBC          -329.821    AIC        -340.55
          Reg Rsq        0.2529    Total Rsq   0.2529
          Durbin-Watson  2.0047

      Variable     DF      B Value   Std Error   t Ratio Approx Prob
             ❶
      Intercept     1    -0.011421     0.00721    -1.584      0.1162
      D             1     0.020870     0.00961     2.173      0.0321
      MKT           1     0.359522      0.0923     3.895      0.0002
      DUMMY         1     0.139447      0.1527     0.913      0.3632
```

```
                          Returns Data

                        Autoreg Procedure
     ❷
F Test:       Numerator DF:     2    F Statistic:    3.0296
              Denominator DF: 104    Prob>F:         0.0526
```

Explanation

❶ The parameter estimates, standard errors, *t*-statistics, and *p*-values indicate that the slope parameter for the variable MKT and the intercept dummy D are different from 0 at the .10 level, while the intercept and dummy slope parameters are not.

From these test results, you conclude that the intercept coefficient is different in the two periods, while the slope coefficient is not.

❷ `F Test` lists the *F*-statistics and *p*-value for the null hypothesis that the intercept dummy coefficient and the coefficient of the dummy slope variable are jointly 0. The *p*-value is .0526. At the .10 level, the null hypothesis should be rejected. You conclude that at least one of the dummy coefficients is not equal to 0.

Further Reading

For more information on PROC AUTOREG, see the *SAS/ETS User's Guide, Version 6, Second Edition*, and *SAS/ETS Software: Changes and Enhancements, Release 6.11.*

References

- □ Black, F., Jensen, M., and Scholes, M. (1972), "The Capital Asset Pricing Model: Some Empirical Tests," *Studies in the Theory of Capital Markets*, ed. M. Jensen, New York: Praeger, 79-121.
- □ Chow, G. (1960), "Tests of Equality between Sets of Coefficients in Two Linear Regressions," *Econometrica*, 28, 531-534.
- □ Greene, W. (1993), *Econometric Analysis, Second Edition*, New York: Macmillian Publishing Co.
- □ Maddala, G.S. (1992), *Introduction to Econometrics, Second Edition*, New York: Macmillian Publishing Co.

EXAMPLE 12

Fitting and Forecasting Linear Models with Linear Restrictions

Featured Tools:

- AUTOREG procedure
  - MODEL statement
  - OUTPUT statement
  - RESTRICT statement

The Capital Asset Pricing Model (CAPM) in risk premium form can be estimated for IBM Corporation stock returns contained in the RETURNS data set, and then can be used for forecasting.

$$R_{i,t} - R_{f,t} = \alpha_i + \beta_i \times \left(R_{M,t} - R_{f,t}\right) + \epsilon_{i,t}$$

For discussion of the CAPM, see Example 10, "Fitting and Forecasting a Linear Model by OLS," and Black, Jensen, and Scholes (1972).

For some forecasting models, theory or physical reality indicate that model parameters should be linearly restricted. For example, in theory, the estimated intercept of the CAPM in risk premium form in an efficient market is expected to be 0. Use RESTRICT statements to impose linear parameter restrictions.

Program

Linearly Restricting Parameter Estimates

Restrict the model parameters. The appropriate RESTRICT statements with labels follow the MODEL statement specifying the equation containing the parameter (or parameters) to be restricted.

The RETURNS data set contains twelve additional market returns (R_M) and risk-free returns (R_F), which are used as input values for generating the forecasts of the risk premiums for the IBM Corporation stock returns.

```
proc autoreg data=returns;

      /* Restrict Intercept Parameter */
   model ibm = mkt;
   intercpt: restrict intercept=0;

      /* Forecast Restricted Model */
   output out=rstrict1  /* Names the Output Data Set       */
          alphacli=.1   /* Sets the Confidence Limit Size */
          p=p           /* Outputs Predicted Values       */
          r=r           /* Outputs Residual Values        */
          lcl=l         /* Outputs Lower Confidence Limit */
          ucl=u;        /* Outputs Upper Confidence Limit */

      /* Restrict Slope Parameter */
   model ibm = mkt;
   slope: restrict mkt=.75;

      /* Restrict Sum of Intercept and Slope Parms to 1 */
   model ibm = mkt;
   intcp_sl: restrict intercept + mkt=1;
run;
```

Print forecasts from the restricted model using PROC PRINT and a WHERE statement. The NOOBS option suppresses the printing of the observation number.

```
proc print data=rstrict1 noobs;
   where date > '01sep86'd;
   var date u p ibm l r;
   title2 'Restricted Model';
run;
```

Output 12.1
Restricting Model Parameters (Output from PROC AUTOREG)

```
                              Returns Data

                           Autoreg Procedure

Dependent Variable = IBM        Risk Premium for IBM

                     Ordinary Least Squares Estimates

          ❶ SSE            0.265423   DFE             107
            MSE            0.002481   Root MSE   0.049806
            SBC            -337.752   AIC        -340.434
            Reg Rsq          0.2094   Total Rsq    0.2094
            Durbin-Watson    1.9150

      Variable     DF       B Value   Std Error   t Ratio Approx Prob
                                ❷
      Intercept     1   -1.35525E-20        .          .          .
      MKT           1       0.395536     0.0737     5.364     0.0001

      Restriction  DF       L Value   Std Error   t Ratio Approx Prob

      INTERCPT     -1       0.010088     0.5139     0.020     0.9844
```

```
                              Returns Data

                           Autoreg Procedure

Dependent Variable = IBM        Risk Premium for IBM

                     Ordinary Least Squares Estimates

          ❸ SSE            0.321981   DFE             107
            MSE            0.003009   Root MSE   0.054856
            SBC             -316.89   AIC        -319.572
            Reg Rsq          0.0409   Total Rsq    0.0409
            Durbin-Watson    2.1026

      Variable     DF       B Value   Std Error   t Ratio Approx Prob

      Intercept     1     -0.002665     0.00528    -0.505     0.6146
      MKT           1      0.750000        .          .          .

      Restriction  DF       L Value   Std Error   t Ratio Approx Prob

      SLOPE        -1     -0.159481      0.0368    -4.335     0.0001
```

```
                         Returns Data

                      Autoreg Procedure

Dependent Variable = IBM      Risk Premium for IBM

               Ordinary Least Squares Estimates

        ❹ SSE          0.431662   DFE            107
          MSE          0.004034   Root MSE  0.063516
          SBC           -285.23   AIC       -287.912
          Reg Rsq             .   Total Rsq  -0.2858
          Durbin-Watson  2.1685

    Variable     DF      B Value   Std Error  t Ratio Approx Prob

    Intercept     1    -0.002081     0.00615   -0.339      0.7356
    MKT           1     1.002081     0.00615  163.026      0.0001

    Restriction  DF      L Value   Std Error  t Ratio Approx Prob

    INTCP_SL     -1    -0.274983      0.0428   -6.419      0.0001
```

Explanation

❶ The goodness-of-fit statistics for the intercept-restricted model are listed.

❷ The intercept parameter estimate is -1.35525E-20, which is 0 for practical purposes. The slope parameter estimate in the restricted model is .395536, which is slightly larger than the unrestricted model slope parameter estimate of .395362 in Output 10.1.

The `L Value`, which is shaded in Output 12.1, is the Lagrange multiplier used to impose the restriction. The restriction has a *t*-statistic of .020 and a *p*-value of .9844, which indicates that the data are consistent with this restriction. In general, the intercept term of the CAPM is expected to be 0.

This restriction (that the intercept is 0) can also be imposed with the NOINT option in the MODEL statement.

❸ The goodness-of-fit statistics for the slope-restricted model are listed.

The Lagrange multiplier used to impose the restriction has a *t*-statistic of -4.335 and a *p*-value of .0001, which indicates that the data are not consistent with this restriction.

❹ The goodness-of-fit statistics for the intercept and slope-restricted model are listed.

The Lagrange multiplier used to impose the restriction has a *t*-statistic of -6.419 and a *p*-value of .0001, which indicates that the data are not consistent with this restriction.

Output 12.2
Predicted and Residual Values, and the Lower and Upper 90% Confidence Limits

Returns Data
Restricted Model

DATE	U	P	IBM	L	R
OCT86	0.08812	0.00547	-0.08518	-0.07719	-0.090646
NOV86	0.08098	-0.00166	0.03280	-0.08430	0.034461
DEC86	0.07916	-0.00349	-0.05982	-0.08613	-0.056331
JAN87	0.14123	0.05674	.	-0.02774	.
FEB87	0.10695	0.02398	.	-0.05899	.
MAR87	0.09570	0.01296	.	-0.06977	.
APR87	0.07200	-0.01071	.	-0.09341	.
MAY87	0.08249	-0.00015	.	-0.08279	.
JUN87	0.09618	0.01344	.	-0.06930	.
JUL87	0.10282	0.01995	.	-0.06291	.
AUG87	0.08676	0.00411	.	-0.07853	.
SEP87	0.07469	-0.00799	.	-0.09067	.
OCT87	-0.01555	-0.10426	.	-0.19296	.
NOV87	0.05429	-0.02883	.	-0.11194	.
DEC87	0.11086	0.02778	.	-0.05531	.

Further Reading

For more information on PROC AUTOREG, see the *SAS/ETS User's Guide, Version 6, Second Edition*, and *SAS/ETS Software: Changes and Enhancements, Release 6.11.*

Reference

Black, F., Jensen, M., and Scholes, M. (1972), "The Capital Asset Pricing Model: Some Empirical Tests," *Studies in the Theory of Capital Markets*, ed. M. Jensen, New York: Praeger, 79-121.

EXAMPLE 13

Fitting and Forecasting a Linear Model with an AR Error Correction

Featured Tools:

- AUTOREG procedure
  - MODEL statement
    - BACKSTEP option
    - NLAG= option
  - OUTPUT statement
    - ALPHACLI= option

The Capital Asset Pricing Model (CAPM) in risk premium form can be estimated for IBM Corporation stock returns contained in the RETURNS data set, and then can be used for forecasting.

$$R_{i,t} - R_{f,t} = \alpha_i + \beta_i \times \left(R_{M,t} - R_{f,t}\right) + \epsilon_{i,t}$$

For discussion of the CAPM, see Example 10, "Fitting and Forecasting a Linear Model by OLS," and Black, Jensen, and Scholes (1972).

Correcting for Autocorrelation

The standard ordinary least squares (OLS) regression model assumes that the errors are independent of each other. Violation of this assumption has the following consequences:

- Statistical tests of the significance of estimated parameters, and the confidence limits for the predicted values are not correct.
- The estimates of the regression coefficients are not as efficient as they would be if the autocorrelation were taken into account.
- Because the OLS residuals are not independent, they contain information that can be used to improve the prediction of future values.

PROC AUTOREG can be used to fit regression models with autocorrelated error terms. The NLAG= option in the MODEL statement specifies the order (or subset orders) of autocorrelation. The autoregressive error correction model supported by PROC AUTOREG is as follows:

$$y_t = \mathbf{x}_t' \beta + \nu_t$$

$$\nu_t = -\phi_1 \nu_{t-1} - \phi_2 \nu_{t-2} - \ldots - \phi_p \nu_{t-p} + \epsilon_t$$

$$\epsilon_t \sim \mathrm{IN}\left(0, \sigma^2\right)$$

where

y_t	is the response or dependent variable, an ordered and equally spaced time series.
$\mathbf{x}_t$	are the regressor variables and may or may not be included in the model.
β	are the regression parameters.
$\phi_1, \phi_2, \ldots, \phi_p$	are the autoregressive parameters.
p	is the order of the AR process.
ϵ_t	are the identically and independently distributed random errors (the usual assumption being that they are normally distributed with mean 0 and variance σ^2).

In Example 10, the model is fit by OLS; then forecasts are generated, and the residuals are tested for autocorrelation with generalized Durbin-Watson tests and Godfrey's general Lagrange multiplier tests (Godfrey, 1978a and 1978b).

Program

Estimating the Model and Correcting for Autocorrelation

Correct for autocorrelation using the NLAG= option in the MODEL statement.

The RETURNS data set contains twelve additional market returns (R_M) and risk-free returns (R_F), which are used as input values for generating the forecasts of the risk premiums for the IBM Corporation stock returns.

The BACKSTEP option specifies the removal of insignificant autoregressive parameters from the model.

```
proc autoreg data=returns;

   /* Fit an AR(3) Model */
 model ibm = mkt       /* Fits the CAPM Regression            */
     / nlag=3          /* Specifies an AR(3) Error Term       */
       dw=1            /* Prints the Durbin Watson Statistic */
       dwprob;         /* Prints the Durbin Watson p Value    */

   /* Forecast the AR(3) Model */
 output out=rt_out2    /* Names the Output Data Set           */
       alphacli=.05    /* Sets the Confidence Limit Size      */
       p=p_ar3         /* Outputs Predicted Values            */
       r=r_ar3         /* Outputs Residual Values             */
       lcl=l_ar3       /* Outputs Lower Confidence Limit      */
       ucl=u_ar3;      /* Outputs Upper Confidence Limit      */

   /* Fit an AR(1,4) Subset Model */
 model ibm = mkt       /* Fits the CAPM Regression            */
     / nlag=(1 4);     /* Specifies an AR(1,4) Subset Model   */

   /* Forecast an AR(1,4) Subset Model */
 output out=rt_out3
       alphacli=.05
       p=p_ar14
       r=r_ar14
       lcl=l_ar14
       ucl=u_ar14;

   /* Fit an AR(13) Model */
 model ibm = mkt       /* Fits the CAPM Regression            */
     / nlag=13         /* Specifies an AR(13) Error Term      */
       backstep;       /* Removes Insignificant AR Terms      */
```

```
      /* Forecast an AR(13) Model */
   output out=rt_out4
          alphacli=.05
          p=p_ar13
          r=r_ar13
          lcl=l_ar13
          ucl=u_ar13;
run;
```

Match-merge output data sets in a DATA step. The BY statement specifies the merging by variable, which for this example is the DATE variable.

```
data rt_out5;
   merge rt_out2 rt_out3 rt_out4;
   by date;
run;
```

Print the AR model forecasts using PROC PRINT.

```
proc print data=rt_out5;
   where date > '01sep86'd;
   var date p_ar3 p_ar14 p_ar13;
   title2 'Forecasts from AR Models';
run;
```

Output 13.1
AR(3) Model Results (Partial Output)

```
                        Returns Data

                     Autoreg Procedure

               Preliminary MSE = 0.002395

     ❶ Estimates of the Autoregressive Parameters

      Lag   Coefficient     Std Error       t Ratio
        1   -0.02049213      0.097818        -0.209
        2   -0.09625275      0.097378        -0.988
        3   -0.12027855      0.097818        -1.230
```

```
                        Returns Data

                     Autoreg Procedure

                  ❷ Yule-Walker Estimates

      SSE            0.258048    DFE              103
      MSE            0.002505    Root MSE    0.050053
      SBC            -322.001    AIC         -335.412
      Reg Rsq          0.2351    Total Rsq     0.2313
      Durbin-Watson    2.0221    PROB<DW       0.5460

Variable     DF       B Value   Std Error   t Ratio Approx Prob

Intercept     1     -0.000530     0.00629    -0.084      0.9331
MKT           1      0.412324      0.0733     5.627      0.0001
```

Explanation

❶ The estimates of autoregressive parameters, standard errors, and *t*-statistics are listed. None of the autoregressive parameter estimates are different from 0 at the .05 level.

❷ The Yule-Walker estimates of the AR(3) model and goodness-of-fit statistics are listed. (The OLS estimates are shown in Output 10.1.) The intercept term is not different from 0, while the slope parameter is. The AR(3) model slope parameter is .412324, which is slightly larger than the OLS model slope parameter of .395362. If there are no additional violations of the standard assumptions, then the difference between these slope parameters is not meaningful because both are unbaised estimates.

Fitting the AR(1,4) Subset Model

Output 13.2
AR(1,4) Subset Model Results (Partial Output)

```
                         Returns Data

                       Autoreg Procedure

                   Preliminary MSE = 0.002427

            Estimates of the Autoregressive Parameters

        Lag    Coefficient        Std Error         t Ratio
          1    -0.02277592         0.098227          -0.232
          4    -0.10637936         0.098227          -1.083
```

```
                         Returns Data

                       Autoreg Procedure

                     Yule-Walker Estimates

        SSE             0.261735    DFE              104
        MSE             0.002517    Root MSE    0.050167
        SBC             -325.171    AIC         -335.899
        Reg Rsq           0.2172    Total Rsq     0.2204
        Durbin-Watson   2.0046

Variable      DF        B Value   Std Error   t Ratio Approx Prob

Intercept      1      -0.000143     0.00555    -0.026      0.9795
MKT            1       0.398396      0.0742     5.372      0.0001
```

Explanation

Only the first and fourth-order autoregressive parameters are estimated for this subset model. Be aware that even if the goodness-of-fit statistics were to indicate an acceptable fit by this specific subset model, the interpretation of the AR(1,4) subset model may be unacceptable in terms of observed and expected real world behavior.

Fitting the AR(13) Model

Output 13.3
AR(13) Model (Output from PROC AUTOREG)

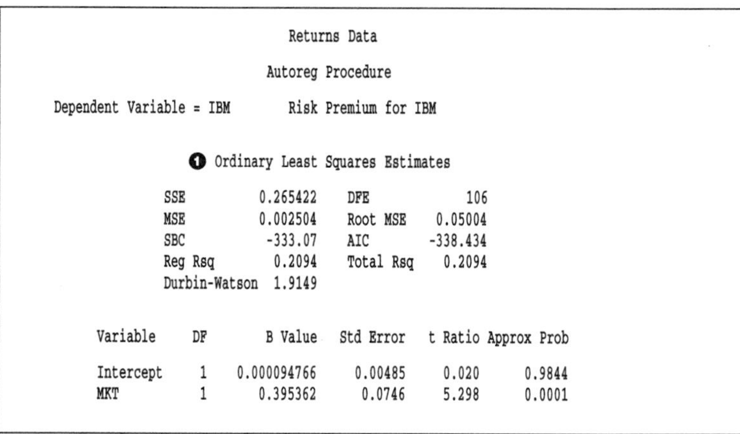

```
                                Returns Data

                              Autoreg Procedure

Dependent Variable = IBM        Risk Premium for IBM

                      ❶ Ordinary Least Squares Estimates

                SSE           0.265422    DFE             106
                MSE           0.002504    Root MSE    0.05004
                SBC            -333.07    AIC        -338.434
                Reg Rsq         0.2094    Total Rsq    0.2094
                Durbin-Watson   1.9149

        Variable     DF        B Value   Std Error   t Ratio Approx Prob

        Intercept     1    0.000094766     0.00485     0.020      0.9844
        MKT           1       0.395362      0.0746     5.298      0.0001
```

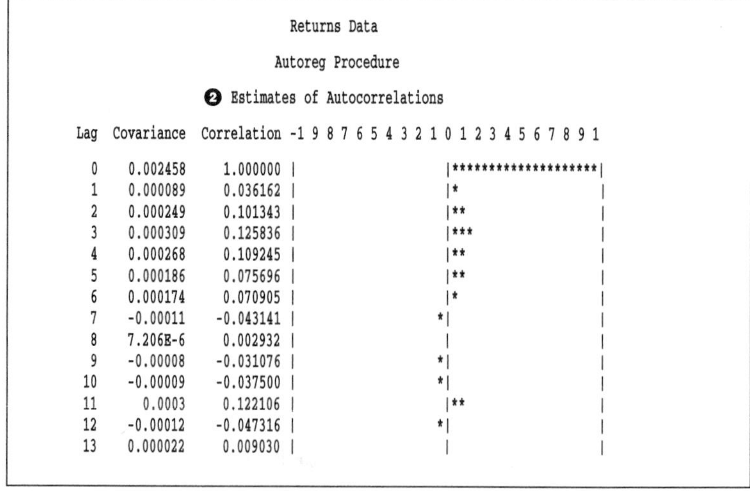

```
                               Returns Data

                             Autoreg Procedure

                      ❷ Estimates of Autocorrelations

 Lag  Covariance  Correlation -1 9 8 7 6 5 4 3 2 1 0 1 2 3 4 5 6 7 8 9 1

   0    0.002458     1.000000 |                    |********************|
   1    0.000089     0.036162 |                    |*                   |
   2    0.000249     0.101343 |                    |**                  |
   3    0.000309     0.125836 |                    |***                 |
   4    0.000268     0.109245 |                    |**                  |
   5    0.000186     0.075696 |                    |**                  |
   6    0.000174     0.070905 |                    |*                   |
   7    -0.00011    -0.043141 |                   *|                    |
   8    7.206E-6     0.002932 |                    |                    |
   9    -0.00008    -0.031076 |                   *|                    |
  10    -0.00009    -0.037500 |                   *|                    |
  11      0.0003     0.122106 |                    |**                  |
  12    -0.00012    -0.047316 |                   *|                    |
  13    0.000022     0.009030 |                    |                    |
```

```
                     Returns Data

                  Autoreg Procedure

    ❸ Backward Elimination of Autoregressive Terms

           Lag  Estimate    t-Ratio   Prob
             1 -0.009089    -0.0877 0.9303
            13 -0.016071    -0.1559 0.8765
            12  0.024307     0.2395 0.8112
            10  0.037135     0.3684 0.7134
             6 -0.036518    -0.3617 0.7184
             8  0.046884     0.4688 0.6403
             5 -0.053176    -0.5345 0.5942
             9  0.050683     0.5154 0.6074
             7  0.093916     0.9516 0.3436
             2 -0.090797    -0.9356 0.3517
             4 -0.110310    -1.1425 0.2559
            11 -0.121738    -1.2610 0.2101
             3 -0.125836    -1.2998 0.1965
```

Explanation

❶ The ordinary least squares (OLS) estimates and goodness-of-fit statistics are listed.

❷ The estimates of lag autocovariances and autocorrelations are listed.

❸ The history of the backward elimination of nonsignificant autoregressive terms is shown. The autoregressive term with the lowest *t*-statistic (and highest *p*-value) is eliminated, and the model is refit. Terms not significant at the .05 level continue to be so eliminated. The significance level criterion is specified with the SLSTAY= *value* option; the default value is .05. In this model, all autoregressive terms are eliminated.

Printing Forecasts from the AR Models

Output 13.4
Forecasts of AR Models

Returns Data
Forecasts from AR Models

OBS	DATE	P_AR3	P_AR14	P_AR13
106	OCT86	0.00006	0.00042	0.00556
107	NOV86	-0.00141	-0.01115	-0.00157
108	DEC86	-0.01377	0.00070	-0.00339
109	JAN87	0.04999	0.05417	0.05681
110	FEB87	0.02315	0.01432	0.02407
111	MAR87	0.00543	0.01637	0.01305
112	APR87	-0.01301	-0.01682	-0.01061
113	MAY87	-0.00160	-0.00073	-0.00006
114	JUN87	0.01243	0.01235	0.01353
115	JUL87	0.02000	0.02030	0.02004
116	AUG87	0.00354	0.00338	0.00421
117	SEP87	-0.00902	-0.00825	-0.00789
118	OCT87	-0.10927	-0.10526	-0.10411
119	NOV87	-0.03062	-0.02914	-0.02872
120	DEC87	0.02840	0.02777	0.02786

Explanation

The following variables are listed in Output 13.4:

DATE — are the monthly dates.

P_AR3 — are the forecasts for AR(3) model.

P_AR14 — are the forecasts for AR(1,4) model.

P_AR13 — are the forecasts for AR(13) model, which are the OLS forecasts as all AR terms were eliminated during estimation.

Further Reading

For more information on PROC AUTOREG, see the *SAS/ETS User's Guide, Version 6, Second Edition*, and *SAS/ETS Software: Changes and Enhancements, Release 6.11.*

References

- Black, F., Jensen, M., and Scholes, M. (1972), "The Capital Asset Pricing Model: Some Empirical Tests," *Studies in the Theory of Capital Markets*, ed. M. Jensen, New York: Praeger, 79-121.
- Godfrey, L. (1978a), "Testing against General Autoregressive and Moving Average Error Models When the Regressors Include Lagged Dependent Variables," *Econometrica*, 46, 1293-1301.
- Godfrey, L. (1978b), "Testing for Higher Order Serial Correlation in Regression Equations When the Regressors Include Lagged Dependent Variables," *Econometrica*, 46, 1303-1310.

EXAMPLE 14

Fitting Linear Models with Heteroscedastic Error Terms

Featured Tools:

- AUTOREG procedure
  - HETERO statement
    - LINK= option
    - STD= option
    - TEST= option
  - MODEL statement
- PLOT procedure

The Capital Asset Pricing Model (CAPM) in risk premium form can be estimated for the Weyerhauser Corporation stock returns contained in the RETURNS data set, and then can be used for forecasting.

$$R_{i,t} - R_{f,t} = \alpha_i + \beta_i \times \left(R_{M,t} - R_{f,t}\right) + \epsilon_{i,t}$$

For discussion of the CAPM, see Example 10, "Fitting and Forecasting a Linear Model by OLS," and Black, Jensen, and Scholes (1972).

The Heteroscedastic Regression Model

For OLS estimation to be appropriate, the assumptions of OLS must be satisfied. OLS parameter estimates are *efficient* (that is, they have minimum variance) if the error term is uncorrelated and has a constant variance (homoscedasticity). If the error term is autocorrelated or has nonconstant variance (heteroscedasticity), then you can make more efficient use of the data and more accurate forecast confidence limits by using models that account for autocorrelation or heteroscedasticity or both.

Regression models that have heteroscedastic error terms can be estimated by using the HETERO statement in the AUTOREG procedure. The heteroscedastic regression model supported by the HETERO statement is

$$y_t = \mathbf{x}_t\beta + \epsilon_t$$

$$\epsilon_t \sim \mathrm{IN}\left(0, \sigma_t^2\right)$$

$$\sigma_t^2 = \sigma^2 h_t$$

$$h_t = l\left(z_t'\eta\right)$$

The vector $\mathbf{z}_t$ is composed of the variables listed in the HETERO statement, η is a parameter vector, and l(.) is a link function that is specified with the LINK option.

Note: The errors are assumed to be uncorrelated, and the HETERO statement cannot be used if the NLAG= option is specified in the MODEL statement.

Program

Estimating the Model

Fit the CAPM regression by OLS using PROC AUTOREG. Test the residuals for autocorrelation using the DW=, DWPROB, and GF= options, and test the residuals for autoregressive conditional heteroscedasticity (ARCH effects) with the ARCHTEST option.

```
proc autoreg data=returns;
   model wyr = mkt     /* Fit the CAPM Regression             */
         / dw=12       /* Print the Durbin-Watson Statistics  */
           dwprob      /* Print Durbin-Watson p Values        */
           archtest    /* Test for the Absence of ARCH Effects */
           gf=12;      /* Godfrey Test for Autocorrelation    */
   output out=wyr_out1 /* Names the Output Data Set           */
           p=p_ols     /* Outputs the Predicted Values        */
           r=r_ols;    /* Outputs the Residual Values         */
run;
```

Plot the OLS CAPM residuals using PROC PLOT. The VPCT= option specifies the percentage of the SAS output page for the vertical height of the plot.

```
proc plot data=wyr_out1 vpct=150;
   plot r_ols * mkt;
   title2 'Weyerhauser CAPM Residuals versus Market';
run;
```

Fit the CAPM regression with a heteroscedastic error term using PROC AUTOREG.

The HETERO statement specifies the form of the heteroscedasticity.

The OUTPUT statement specifies an output data set. The P=, R=, LCL=, and UCL= options output the predicted and residual values, and the lower and upper 95% confidence limits.

```
proc autoreg data=returns;
   model wyr=mkt         /* OLS Estimation of the CAPM Regression */
         / itprint;      /* Prints Objective Function and Parameter
                              Estimates at Each Iteration         */
   hetero mkt            /* Specifies Variables Related to the
                              Heteroscedasticity                  */
         / link=exp      /* Specifies the Functional Form of
                              the Heteroscedasticity              */
           std=nonneg    /* Imposes Constraints on the Estimated
                              Residual Standard Deviation         */
           test=lm;      /* Test for Heteroscedasticity, Null
                              Hypothesis is Homoscedasticity,
                              Alternative Hypothesis is Specified
                              Form of Heteroscedasticity          */

   output out=wyr_out2 /* Names the Output Data Set             */
           p=p_het     /* Outputs Predicted Values              */
           r=r_het     /* Outputs Residual Values               */
           lcl=l       /* Outputs Lower Confidence Limit        */
           ucl=u;      /* Outputs Upper Confidence Limit        */
   title2;             /* Resets the Program Title2             */
run;
```

Print the forecasts using PROC PRINT. A WHERE statement is used to specify the observations to be printed.

```
proc print data=wyr_out2 noobs;
   where date > '01jul86'd;
   var date u p_het wyr l r_het;
   title2 'Heteroscedastic Model Forecasts';
run;
```

Output 14.1
OLS Estimated CAPM Regression and Tests of the Residuals from PROC AUTOREG

```
                         Returns Data

                      Autoreg Procedure

Dependent Variable = WYR       Risk Premium for Weyerhauser

                 Ordinary Least Squares Estimates

        SSE          0.434081    DFE               106
        MSE          0.004095    Root MSE     0.063993
        SBC          -279.944    AIC          -285.308
        Reg Rsq        0.3514    Total Rsq      0.3514

                ❶ Durbin-Watson Statistics

                   Order      DW     PROB<DW
                     1      2.3248    0.9558
                     2      2.0303    0.6024
                     3      1.8499    0.2799
                     4      2.0189    0.6541
                     5      1.9437    0.5307
                     6      2.0099    0.7055
                     7      1.5143    0.0243
                     8      2.0172    0.7843
                     9      1.4808    0.0240
                    10      2.0449    0.8686
                    11      1.6303    0.1695
                    12      1.5887    0.1396
```

```
                         Returns Data

                      Autoreg Procedure

          ❷ Q and LM Tests for ARCH Disturbances

        Order       Q      Prob>Q         LM     Prob>LM

          1      3.2765    0.0703     3.3082     0.0689
          2      3.5759    0.1673     4.5667     0.1019
          3      6.0263    0.1103     5.6424     0.1304
          4      8.3004    0.0812     7.9185     0.0946
          5     11.5964    0.0408    14.1483     0.0147
          6     13.2316    0.0395    14.1725     0.0278
          7     13.2398    0.0665    14.2426     0.0470
          8     13.7193    0.0894    14.9957     0.0592
          9     19.1650    0.0238    15.7276     0.0728
         10     19.7911    0.0313    16.1890     0.0943
         11     20.9128    0.0343    18.3050     0.0748
         12     20.9825    0.0506    18.4507     0.1027
```

```
                    Returns Data

                 Autoreg Procedure

         ❸ Godfrey's Serial Correlation Test

           Alternative          LM    Prob>LM

              AR(+  1)      3.2326     0.0722
              AR(+  2)      3.8964     0.1425
              AR(+  3)      3.8987     0.2726
              AR(+  4)      4.5507     0.3366
              AR(+  5)      5.3658     0.3729
              AR(+  6)      7.1439     0.3077
              AR(+  7)      8.2646     0.3098
              AR(+  8)      9.1857     0.3269
              AR(+  9)     11.2686     0.2577
              AR(+ 10)     13.1619     0.2148
              AR(+ 11)     13.3930     0.2684
              AR(+ 12)     13.7472     0.3171
```

```
                         Returns Data

                      Autoreg Procedure

Variable      DF        B Value   Std Error   t Ratio Approx Prob
        ❹
Intercept      1      -0.003558     0.00620    -0.574      0.5674
MKT            1       0.723119     0.0954      7.578      0.0001
```

Explanation

❶ Durbin-Watson *d*-statistics and *p*-values are listed. Durbin-Watson statistics are widely used as tests for autocorrelation, and are discussed in Example 10.

For this CAPM regression, only the *p*-values for the seventh and ninth order lags are less than .05. For purposes of this example, it is assumed that autocorrelation of the residuals is not a problem.

❷ Portmanteau *Q* and Lagrange Multiplier (LM) tests for ARCH disturbances are listed. The *Q*-statistics are calculated from the squared residuals and are used to test for nonlinear effects (for example, GARCH effects) present in the residuals. The null hypothesis for these tests is that the OLS residuals are a white noise process; that is, the residuals conform to the standard OLS regression assumptions. These statistics and the small *p*-values indicate that the null hypothesis should be rejected.

❸ Statistics for Godfrey's general Lagrange multiplier tests for ARMA errors and *p*-values are listed. These statistics are discussed in Example 10. For details, see Godfrey (1978a and 1978b).

For this model, none of the *p*-values is less than .05, indicating that the null hypotheses can be retained. You conclude that these Godfrey tests provide little evidence of autocorrelated errors.

4 OLS parameter estimates, standard errors, *t*-statistics for the null hypotheses that each parameter is equal to 0, and the *p*-values are listed. The *t*-statistics and *p*-values indicate that the intercept (α) is not different from 0 and the slope parameter (β) is different from 0.

For regression models with residuals that are not independent (that is, autocorrelated) or with residuals having nonconstant variances (that is, heteroscedasticity), the OLS parameter standard error estimates are biased, the hypothesis *t*-tests of the parameters are inaccurate, and forecast confidence limits are inaccurate.

Plotting the OLS Residuals

Output 14.2
Plot of Residual Values versus Market Risk Premiums Created with PROC PLOT

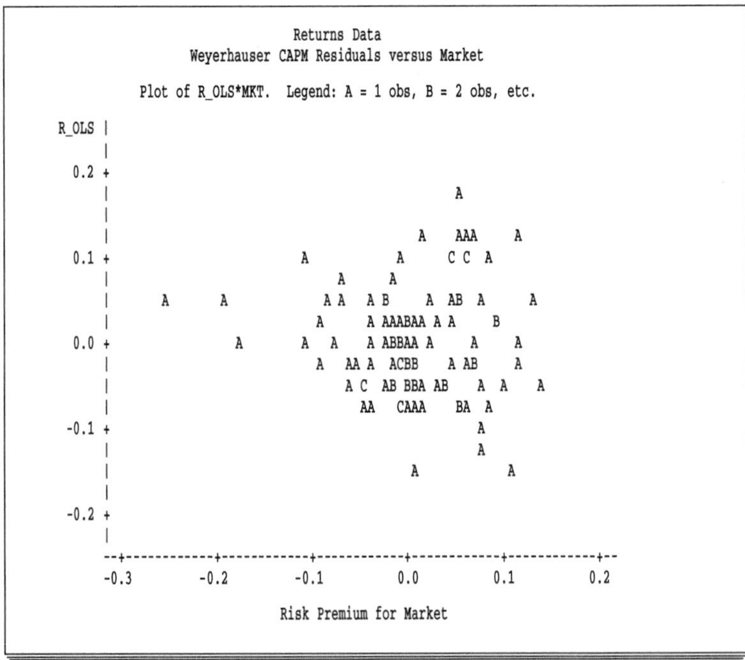

Explanation

In general, the scatter plot of the OLS residuals versus the market risk premium has greater variability as the market risk premium increases. Output 14.2 is a graphical representation of nonconstant residual variance, heteroscedasticity.

Fitting the Heteroscedastic Model

Output 14.3
The Heteroscedastic Model Results (Partial Output)

```
                              Returns Data

                           Autoreg Procedure
❶
Iter     Objective Halfstep   Intercept       MKT            HET0
                              HET1

   0 144.65407181       0    -0.00355801084 0.723119314665 0.063397675974
                                       1E-6

   1 148.44074838       0    -0.00355801084 0.723112350141 0.063189698453
                                   5.000001

   2 148.66224319       0    -0.00240740203 0.722564102648 0.056870728607
                             6.002104940192

   3 148.69101251       0    -0.00111845059 0.721614131177 0.056903746353
                             6.045681581388

   4 150.23360961       0    -0.00265891709 0.602405931748 0.054613270167
                             7.934428822567

   5 150.89236754       0    -0.00513879319 0.559812799123 0.058284256427
                              9.32596379043

   6 150.92946303       0    -0.00599147829 0.576977183758 0.058138961796
                             9.099606903672

   7 150.95357635       0    -0.00599714223 0.568751257466 0.057557236211
                             9.467519731351

   8 150.95407425       0    -0.00597021811 0.568018300015 0.057627219345
                             9.519306984865

   9 150.95408871       0    -0.00599521279 0.568007192696 0.057629153294
                             9.524685282099

  10 150.95408871       0     -0.0059955595 0.568001855128   0.0576291315
                             9.524752675695
```

```
                              Returns Data

                           Autoreg Procedure

               Multiplicative Heteroscedasticity Estimates

              SSE              0.446336    OBS                108
              MSE              0.004133    Root MSE    0.064286
              Log L            150.9541    Total Rsq     0.3331
              SBC               -283.18    AIC         -293.908
              Normality Test     3.2911    Prob>Chi-Sq   0.1929
            ❷ Hetero Test       14.2358    Prob>Chi-Sq   0.0002

    Variable      DF       B Value   Std Error    t Ratio Approx Prob
              ❸
    Intercept      1     -0.005996     0.00603     -0.994      0.3200
    MKT            1      0.568002      0.0698      8.137      0.0001
    HET0           1      0.057629     0.00481     11.987      0.0001
    HET1           1      9.524753      2.8970      3.288      0.0010
```

Explanation

❶ Objective function and parameter values at each iteration of the estimation process are listed. Parameter estimates converge when the maximum absolute value of change between iterations is less than the specified amount. You specify the convergence criterion with the CONVERGE=*value* option in the MODEL statement. The default is CONVERGE=.001.

❷ The Lagrange multiplier test for heteroscedasticity is listed. The null hypothesis is homoscedasticity (constant error variance), and the alternative hypothesis is heteroscedasticity of the form specified by the HETERO statement. For additional information on the HETERO statement, see "A Closer Look" later in this chapter.

For this example, the low p-value indicates rejection of the null hypothesis.

❸ Parameter estimates, standard errors, t-statistics for the null hypotheses that each parameter is equal to 0, and the p-values are listed.

The slope parameter of the OLS estimated model is .723119, and is .568002 for the heteroscedastic model. The lower β value may affect the weighting of this stock in linear programming portfolio optimization models. See Chapter 5, "Portfolio Creation with Linear Programming," in *Stock Market Analysis Using the SAS System: Portfolio Selection and Evaluation.*

The t-statistics and p-values indicate that the intercept (α) is not different from 0 while the slope parameter (β) and the two heteroscedasticity parameters are.

Printing the Forecasts

Output 14.4
Predicted and Residual Values, and the Lower and Upper 95% Confidence Limits

Returns Data
Heteroscedastic Model Forecasts

DATE	U	P_HET	WYR	L	R_HET
AUG86	0.14854	0.01989	0.11857	-0.10877	0.09868
SEP86	0.09360	-0.03505	-0.06216	-0.16371	-0.02711
OCT86	0.13051	0.00185	0.13082	-0.12680	0.12897
NOV86	0.12027	-0.00838	0.00180	-0.13703	0.01018
DEC86	0.11765	-0.01101	-0.04482	-0.13966	-0.03381
JAN87	0.20415	0.07549	.	-0.05317	.
FEB87	0.15710	0.02844	.	-0.10021	.
MAR87	0.14127	0.01262	.	-0.11604	.
APR87	0.10728	-0.02137	.	-0.15002	.
MAY87	0.12244	-0.00621	.	-0.13486	.
JUN87	0.14196	0.01331	.	-0.11535	.
JUL87	0.15132	0.02266	.	-0.10599	.
AUG87	0.12857	-0.00009	.	-0.12874	.
SEP87	0.11118	-0.01747	.	-0.14612	.
OCT87	-0.02704	-0.15571	.	-0.28438	.
NOV87	0.08126	-0.04739	.	-0.17604	.
DEC87	0.16255	0.03390	.	-0.09476	.

Explanation

The following variables are listed in Output 14.4:

U and L — are the upper and lower 95% confidence limits.

WYR and P — are the actual and predicted values.

R — are the residuals.

A Closer Look

Specifying the Form of the Heteroscedasticity

The HETERO statement specifies variables that are related to the heteroscedasticity of the residuals. The general syntax of the HETERO statement is

HETERO *variables* [/ *options*];

HETERO Statement Options

The following options enable you to specify the form of the heteroscedasticity and to constrain the estimated heteroscedasticity parameters and the residual standard deviation:

LINK=

specifies the form of the heteroscedasticity, $\sigma^2 h_t$.

EXP	specifies the exponential link function, $h_t = exp(z_t'\eta)$
SQUARE	specifies the square link function, $h_t = (1 + z_t'\eta)^2$
LINEAR	specifies the linear link function, $h_t = (1 + z_t'\eta)$

COEF=

imposes constraints on the estimated parameters η of the heteroscedasticity model.

NONNEG	specifies that the estimated heteroscedasticity parameters η must be nonnegative. When the HETERO statement is used in conjunction with the GARCH= option, the default is COEF=NONNEG.
UNIT	constrains the heteroscedasticity parameters η to equal 1.
ZERO	constrains the heteroscedasticity parameters η to equal 0 (zero).
UNREST	specifies unrestricted estimation of the heteroscedasticity parameters η. When the GARCH= option is not specified, the default is COEF=UNREST.

STD=

imposes constraints on the estimated standard deviation σ of the heteroscedasticity model.

NONNEG	specifies that the estimated standard deviation σ must be nonnegative.
UNIT	constrains the standard deviation parameter σ to equal 1.
UNREST	specifies unrestricted estimation of σ. This is the default.

TEST=

produces a Lagrange multiplier test for heteroscedasticity. The null hypothesis is homoscedasticity (constant variance); the alternative is heteroscedasticity of the form specified by the HETERO statement. Be aware that the test may give different results depending on the functional form specified by the LINK= option, and the power of the test depends on the variables specified in the HETERO statement.

NOCONST

specifies that the heteroscedasticity model not include the unit term for LINK=SQUARE and LINK=LINEAR options.

Examples

The following HETERO statement estimates the heteroscedasticity model $\sigma_t^2 = \sigma^2 x_t^2$:

```
hetero x / link=square coef=unit noconst;
```

The following HETERO statement estimates the heteroscedasticity model $\sigma_t^2 = x_t^2$:

```
hetero x / link=square coef=unit std=unit noconst;
```

To estimate the heteroscedasticity model $\sigma_t^2 = \sigma^2 x_t^\eta$, first log transform the variable X to LN_X in a DATA step, and then estimate the model using the following HETERO statement:

```
hetero ln_x / link=exp noconst;
```

For additional information on heteroscedastic models, see Greene (1993).

Further Reading

- For more information on PROC AUTOREG, see the *SAS/ETS User's Guide, Version 6, Second Edition*, and *SAS/ETS Software: Changes and Enhancements, Release 6.11*.
- For more information on PROC PLOT and PROC PRINT, see the *SAS Procedures Guide, Version 6, Third Edition*.

References

- Black, F., Jensen, M., and Scholes, M. (1972), "The Capital Asset Pricing Model: Some Empirical Tests," *Studies in the Theory of Capital Markets*, ed. M. Jensen, New York: Praeger, 79-121.
- Bollerslev, T. (1986), "Generalized Autoregressive Conditional Heteroskedasticity," *Journal of Econometrics*, 31, 307-327.
- Godfrey, L. (1978a), "Testing against General Autoregressive and Moving Average Error Models When the Regressors Include Lagged Dependent Variables," *Econometrica*, 46, 1293-1301.
- Godfrey, L. (1978b), "Testing for Higher Order Serial Correlation in Regression Equations When the Regressors Include Lagged Dependent Variables," *Econometrica*, 46, 1303-1310.
- Greene, W. (1993), *Econometric Analysis, Second Edition*, New York: Macmillan Publishing Co.

EXAMPLE 15

Fitting Linear Models with ARCH-GARCH Error Terms

Featured Tools:

- AUTOREG procedure
  - MODEL statement
    - GARCH= option
    - NLAG= option
- DATA step

The Capital Asset Pricing Model (CAPM) in risk premium form can be estimated for the Weyerhauser Corporation stock returns contained in the RETURNS data set, and then can be used for forecasting.

$$R_{i,t} - R_{f,t} = \alpha_i + \beta_i \times \left(R_{M,t} - R_{f,t}\right) + \epsilon_{i,t}$$

For discussion of the CAPM, see Example 10, "Fitting and Forecasting a Linear Model by OLS," and Black, Jensen, and Scholes (1972).

The Generalized Autoregressive Conditional Heteroscedastic (GARCH) Regression Model

Many economic and financial time series exhibit heteroscedasticity, a nonconstant series variance over time. The changes in variability are often based on recent past shocks, which cause large (small) fluctuations to cluster together. This information has been used to more accurately define the forecast error variance, first in Autoregressive Conditional Heteroscedasticity (ARCH) models introduced by Engle (1982), and then in Generalized ARCH (GARCH) models by Bollerslev (1986).

The following GARCH regression model combines an *m*th-order autoregressive errors model and a GARCH(*p*,*q*) variance model, and is supported by the GARCH= option of the MODEL statement:

$$y_t = \mathbf{x}_t'\beta + \nu_t$$

$$\nu_t = \epsilon_t - \phi_1\nu_{t-1} - \dots - \phi_m\nu_{t-m}$$

$$\epsilon_t = \sqrt{h_t}e_t$$

$$h_t = \omega + \sum_{i=1}^{q}\alpha_i\epsilon_{t-i}^2 + \sum_{j=1}^{p}\gamma_i h_{t-j}$$

$$e_t \sim \mathrm{IN}(0,1)$$

The most basic ARCH model is a short memory process with $q = 1$ and $p = 0$; that is, only 1 lagged squared residual is used to estimate the changing residual variance. Higher order ARCH models use many lagged squared residuals to estimate the residual variance. A basic GARCH model has $q = 1$ and $p = 1$; that is, 1 lagged squared residual and the most recent past estimate of the residual variance are used to estimate the current residual variance. Higher order GARCH models use many past estimates of the residual variance to estimate the current residual variance.

Program

Estimating and Forecasting GARCH Models

Fit the CAPM regression with an AR(1)-GARCH error term using PROC AUTOREG. The NLAG= option specifies the order of the autoregressive process. The GARCH= option specifies the GARCH form. The UCL= and LCL= options output the unconditional upper and lower 95% confidence limits.

```
proc autoreg data=returns;
   model wyr = mkt              /* OLS Estimation                       */
        / nlag=1                /* Specifies AR(1) Error Correction     */
          garch=(q=1,p=1);      /* Specifies the GARCH Model            */
   output out=wyr_out3          /* Names the Output Data Set            */
          p=p_garch             /* Outputs Predicted Values             */
          ucl=u                 /* Outputs Upper Confidence Limit       */
          lcl=l                 /* Outputs Lower Confidence Limit       */
          r=r_garch             /* Outputs Residual Values              */
          cpev=cpev;            /* Outputs the Conditional Prediction
                                       Error Variance                   */
run;
```

Estimate upper and lower forecast confidence limits using the conditional prediction error variance. In general, prediction errors of AR-GARCH models have complicated distributions.

```
data wyr_out4;
   set wyr_out3;
   u_garch=p_garch+2*sqrt(cpev);
   l_garch=p_garch-2*sqrt(cpev);
run;
```

Print the forecasts using PROC PRINT. A WHERE statement is used to specify the observations to be printed.

```
proc print data=wyr_out4 noobs;
   where date > '01jul86'd;
   var date u u_garch p_garch wyr l_garch l r_garch;
   title2 'AR(1)-GARCH Model Forecasts';
run;
```

Output 15.1
The AR(1)-GARCH Model Created with PROC AUTOREG (Partial Output)

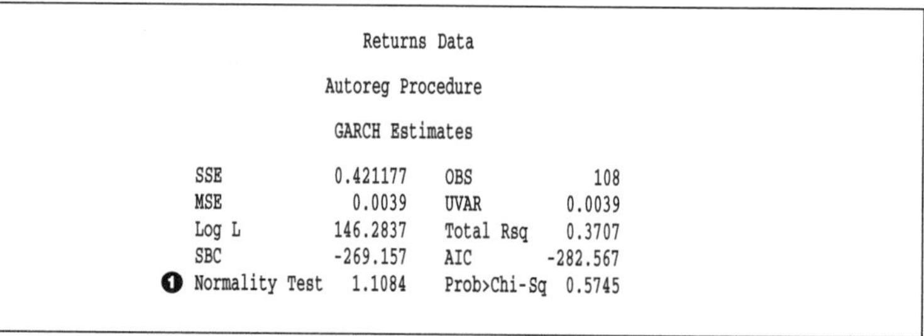

```
                    Returns Data

                 Autoreg Procedure

                  GARCH Estimates

   SSE             0.421177    OBS              108
   MSE               0.0039    UVAR          0.0039
   Log L           146.2837    Total Rsq     0.3707
   SBC             -269.157    AIC         -282.567
❶ Normality Test     1.1084    Prob>Chi-Sq   0.5745
```

```
                         Returns Data

                       Autoreg Procedure

Variable     DF        B Value   Std Error   t Ratio Approx Prob
       ❷
Intercept     1      -0.003540     0.00606    -0.584      0.5594
MKT           1       0.738970      0.1087     6.800      0.0001
A(1)          1       0.173396      0.1255     1.382      0.1671
ARCH0         1       0.003898    0.000572     6.810      0.0001
ARCH1         1              0    5.65E-15     0.000      1.0000
GARCH1        1       0.000548    2.232E-6   245.728      0.0001
```

Explanation

❶ The Jarque-Bera normality test statistic and p-value are listed. The high p-value indicates the retention of the null hypothesis of normally distributed residuals.

❷ Parameter estimates, standard errors, t-statistics for the null hypotheses that each parameter is equal to 0, and the p-values are listed.

The slope parameter of the OLS estimated model is .723119, and is .738970 for the AR(1)-GARCH model.

The t-statistics and p-values indicate that the intercept, AR(1) (ϕ_1), and ARCH1 (α_1) parameters are not different from 0 (at the .10 level) while the slope (β), ARCH0 (ω), and GARCH1 (γ_1) parameters are.

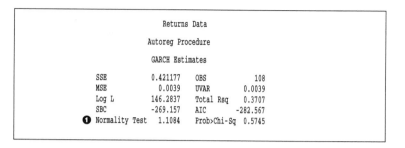

The fitted AR(1)-GARCH model is as follows:

$$WYR_t = -0.00354 + .73897MKT_t + \nu_t$$

$$\nu_t = \epsilon_t - .173396\nu_{t-1}$$

$$\epsilon_t = \sqrt{h_t}e_t$$

$$h_t = .003898 + \left(0 \times \epsilon^2_{t-1}\right) + .000548h_{t-1}$$

$$e_t \sim IN(0,1)$$

Printing the GARCH Forecasts

Output 15.2
Predicted and Residual Values, and the Lower and Upper 95% Confidence Limits

Returns Data
AR(1)-GARCH Model Forecasts

DATE	U	U_GARCH	P_GARCH	WYR	L_GARCH	L	R_GARCH
AUG86	0.15573	0.15321	0.02831	0.11857	-0.09658	-0.09910	0.09026
SEP86	0.07102	0.06822	-0.05668	-0.06216	-0.18158	-0.18438	-0.00548
OCT86	0.13751	0.13518	0.01028	0.13082	-0.11461	-0.11694	0.12054
NOV86	0.09907	0.09673	-0.02817	0.00180	-0.15307	-0.15541	0.02997
DEC86	0.11574	0.11337	-0.01152	-0.04482	-0.13642	-0.13878	-0.03330
JAN87	0.24010	0.23340	0.10850	.	-0.01640	-0.02310	.
FEB87	0.16976	0.16698	0.04022	.	-0.08654	-0.08932	.
MAR87	0.15011	0.14767	0.02086	.	-0.10596	-0.10839	.
APR87	0.10575	0.10324	-0.02358	.	-0.15039	-0.15291	.
MAY87	0.12536	0.12300	-0.00382	.	-0.13063	-0.13299	.
JUN87	0.15083	0.14839	0.02157	.	-0.10525	-0.10769	.
JUL87	0.16315	0.16056	0.03374	.	-0.09308	-0.09567	.
AUG87	0.13331	0.13096	0.00415	.	-0.12267	-0.12502	.
SEP87	0.11080	0.10835	-0.01847	.	-0.14528	-0.14774	.
OCT87	-0.05942	-0.07150	-0.19832	.	-0.32513	-0.33721	.
NOV87	0.07266	0.06942	-0.05740	.	-0.18421	-0.18745	.
DEC87	0.17805	0.17518	0.04836	.	-0.07846	-0.08134	.

Explanation

The following variables are listed in Output 15.2:

U_GARCH and L_GARCH
: are estimates of the upper and lower 95% confidence limits calculated using the conditional prediction error variance. Note that these estimates are not n-step ahead conditional confidence limits.

U and L
: are the upper and lower 95% confidence limits calculated using the unconditional prediction error variance.

WYR and P_GARCH	are the actual and predicted values.
R_GARCH	are the residuals.

A Closer Look

Specifying the GARCH Form

You can control the type of GARCH model fit with the GARCH= option. The general syntax of the GARCH= option is

GARCH=(P=*p*, Q=*q* [*options*]);

The P= option specifies the order of past residuals variances used to compute the conditional error variance. The Q= option specifies the order of lagged squared residuals.

Additional GARCH= Options

MEAN=

specifies the GARCH-M model, which includes an added regressor that is a function of the conditional variance h_t:

$$y_t = \mathbf{x}_t'\beta + \delta F(h_t) + \epsilon_t$$

$$\epsilon_t = \sqrt{h_t}e_t$$

where h_t follows the ARCH or GARCH process, and e_t has a normal or Student's *t*-distribution, depending on the DIST= option. The MEAN= option can be set to the following values:

LINEAR	specifies the linear function. $y_t = \mathbf{x}_t'\beta + \delta h_t + \epsilon_t$
LOG	specifies the log function. $y_t = \mathbf{x}_t'\beta + \delta ln(h_t) + \epsilon_t$
SQRT	specifies the square root function. MEAN=SQRT is the default value. $y_t = \mathbf{x}_t'\beta + \delta\sqrt{h_t} + \epsilon_t$

NOINT

suppresses the intercept parameter in the conditional variance model. This option is valid only with the TYPE=INTEGRATED option.

TR

uses the trust regional method for GARCH estimation. This algorithm is numerically stable, though computationally expensive. The dual quasi-Newton method is the default.

TYPE=

specifies the form of the GARCH model. The TYPE= option can be set to the following values:

EXP	specifies the exponential GARCH or EGARCH model.
INTEGRATED	specifies the integrated GARCH or IGARCH model.
NELSON	specifies the Nelson-Cao inequality constraints, which are less restrictive than the TYPE=NONNEG option (Bollerslev 1986).
NONNEG	constrains the GARCH parameters to nonnegative values. This is the default setting. (Note the ARCH1 parameter estimate in Output 15.1.)
STATIONARY	constrains the sum of the GARCH coefficients to be less than 1.

Additional MODEL Statement Option

The DIST= option in the MODEL statement specifies the distribution assumed for the error term. The general syntax of the DIST= option is

MODEL ... / GARCH=(...) DIST= *value*;

The DIST= option can be set to the following values:

T	specifies Student's *t*-distribution. The *t*-distribution is supported only for GARCH models, and is allowed when both the NLAG= option and the GARCH= option are specified. DIST=T is not allowed when GARCH=(TYPE=EXP) option is specified.
NORMAL	specifies the standard normal distribution. The default is DIST=NORMAL.

Variations

Examples of GARCH Models

An IGARCH(1,1) model is specified by the following MODEL statement:

```
model wyr = mkt / garch=(p=1,q=1,type=integrated);
```

The log form of the GARCH(1,1)-M model is specified with the following MODEL statement:

```
model wyr = mkt / garch=(p=1, q=1, mean=log);
```

Fitting ARCH-GARCH Subset Models with PROC AUTOREG

You can use PROC AUTOREG to fit AR-GARCH subset models. The following statements fit an AR(3,4)-GARCH(1,(3,6,8,10)) model:

```
proc autoreg data=returns;
   model wyr = mkt / nlag=(3 4) garch=(p=1,q=(3 6 8 10));
   title2 'An AR(3,4)-GARCH(1,(3,6,8,10)) Model';
run;
```

In fitting subset models, the results are often highly sensitive to the specification chosen. In general, it is a risky strategy to select a specific subset model based on a data sample rather than on underlying theory. This model may overfit the data, and there may be no particular reason to expect a very specific GARCH process to continue into the future.

Including Regressor Variables in GARCH Models

You can combine the HETERO statement with the GARCH= option in the MODEL statement to include regressor variables in the GARCH conditional variance model. For example, the GARCH(1,1) variance model with two input variables X1 and X2 is as follows:

$$\epsilon_t = \sqrt{h_t} e_t$$

$$h_t = \omega + \alpha_1 \epsilon^2_{t-1} + \gamma_1 h_{t-1} + \eta_1 \mathrm{X1}_t + \eta_2 \mathrm{X2}_t$$

The following statements estimate this GARCH model:

```
proc autoreg data=a;
   model y = x1 x2 x3 / garch=(p=1,q=1);
   hetero x1 x2;
run;
```

To impose the constraints $\eta_1 = \eta_2 = 1$, use the COEF=UNIT option of the HETERO statement.

Note: When you specify both the GARCH= option and the HETERO statement, the GARCH=(TYPE=EXP) option is not valid.

Further Reading

- For more information on PROC AUTOREG, see the *SAS/ETS User's Guide, Version 6, Second Edition*, and *SAS/ETS Software: Changes and Enhancements, Release 6.11.*
- For more information on DATA step features and functions, see *SAS Language: Reference, Version 6, First Edition.*

References

- Black, F., Jensen, M., and Scholes, M. (1972), "The Capital Asset Pricing Model: Some Empirical Tests," *Studies in the Theory of Capital Markets*, ed. M. Jensen, New York: Praeger, 79-121.
- Bollerslev, T. (1986), "Generalized Autoregressive Conditional Heteroskedasticity," *Journal of Econometrics*, 31, 307-327.
- Engle, R. (1982), "Autoregressive Conditional Heteroscedasticity Estimates of the Variance of United Kingdom Inflation," *Econometrica*, 50, 987-1007.

EXAMPLE 16

Assessing Forecast Accuracy

Featured Tools:

- □ AUTOREG procedure
- □ DATA step
- □ SUMMARY procedure

In Examples 14 and 15, the Capital Asset Pricing Model (CAPM) in risk premium form (Black, Jensen, and Scholes 1972) was estimated for the Weyerhauser Corporation using the stock returns contained in the RETURNS data set, and then was used for forecasting. The following models were fit and forecasted:

- □ ordinary least squares (OLS)
- □ heteroscedastic error term
- □ generalized autoregressive conditional heteroscedastic (GARCH) error term.

The forecast accuracy of these models can be assessed by using the actual values (Y) and forecast values (F) over N periods to calculate the following forecast goodness-of-fit statistics:

- □ Mean Average Deviation (MAD), also known as the Mean Forecast Error (ME)

$$MAD = \frac{1}{N} \sum_{t=0}^{N} (Y_t - F_t)$$

- □ Mean Absolute Error (MAE)

$$MAE = \frac{1}{N} \sum_{t=0}^{N} | Y_t - F_t |$$

- □ Mean Percent Error (MPE)

$$MPE = \frac{100}{N} \sum_{t=0}^{N} (Y_t - F_t) / Y_t$$

- □ Mean Absolute Percent Error (MAPE)

$$MAPE = \frac{100}{N} \sum_{t=0}^{N} | (Y_t - F_t) / Y_t |$$

- Mean Square Error (MSE)

$$\text{MSE} = \frac{1}{N}\sum_{t=0}^{N}(Y_t - F_t)^2$$

- Root Mean Square Error (RMSE) is the positive square root of MSE.

- Mean Square Percent Error (MSPE)

$$\text{MSPE} = \frac{100}{N}\sum_{t=0}^{N}((Y_t - F_t) / Y_t)^2$$

- Root Mean Square Percent Error (RMSPE) is the positive square root of MSPE.

The model generating values of these statistics closest to 0 is the most accurate forecasting model. For more information on these statistics, see Pindyck and Rubinfeld (1991) and Bails and Peppers (1982).

Program

Calculating Forecast Goodness-of-Fit Statistics

Create the RETURNS data set. The complete RETURNS data set is listed in "Introduction: The Example Data Sets." The monthly return data are from the Center for Research in Security Prices (CRSP). The last 12 observations contain missing values for the returns of the Weyerhauser Corporation; however, the RETURNS data set contains 12 additional market returns (R_M) and risk-free returns (R_F), which are used as input values for generating the forecasts.

```
data returns;
   input date r_m r_f r_ibm r_wyr;
   format date monyy.;
   informat date monyy.;
   mkt = r_m - r_f;
   ibm = r_ibm - r_f;
   wyr = r_wyr - r_f;
   label mkt='Risk Premium for Market'
         r_f='Risk-Free Rate of Return'
         ibm='Risk Premium for IBM'
         wyr='Risk Premium for Weyerhauser';
   title 'Returns Data';
datalines;
JAN78 -0.045 0.00487 -0.029 -0.116
FEB78  0.010 0.00494 -0.043 -0.135
MAR78  0.050 0.00526 -0.063  0.084
more data lines
;
```

Create the RETURNS1 data set. The RETURNS1 data set contains the actual monthly return values (for the 12 periods to be forecast) and are from the Center for Research in Security Prices (CRSP).

```
data returns1;
   input date r_m r_f r_ibm r_wyr;
   format date monyy.;
   informat date monyy.;
   mkt = r_m - r_f;
   ibm_a = r_ibm - r_f;
   wyr_a = r_wyr - r_f;
   label mkt='Risk Premium for Market'
         r_f='Risk-Free Rate of Return'
         ibm_a='Actual Risk Premium for IBM'
         wyr_a='Actual Risk Premium for Weyerhauser';
   title 'Returns1 Data';
datalines;
JAN87  0.148 0.00454  0.073  0.270
FEB87  0.065 0.00437  0.092  0.094
MAR87  0.037 0.00423  0.076  0.089
APR87 -0.025 0.00207  0.067 -0.027
MAY87  0.004 0.00438  0.006 -0.107
JUN87  0.038 0.00402  0.016  0.026
JUL87  0.055 0.00455 -0.009  0.021
AUG87  0.015 0.00460  0.053  0.081
SEP87 -0.015 0.00520 -0.105 -0.054
OCT87 -0.260 0.00358 -0.187 -0.271
NOV87 -0.070 0.00288 -0.087 -0.066
DEC87  0.073 0.00277  0.043  0.103
;
```

Fit the OLS, heteroscedastic, and GARCH models using PROC AUTOREG. Separate MODEL statements fit each model, and separate OUTPUT statements output the predicted values.

```
proc autoreg data=returns noprint;

      /* Fit the OLS CAPM Regression Model */
   model wyr = mkt;
   output out=wyr_out1 p=p_ols r=r_ols;

      /* Fit the Heteroscedastic Model      */
   model wyr=mkt;
   hetero mkt / link=exp std=nonneg;
   output out=wyr_out2 p=p_het r=r_het lcl=l ucl=u;

      /* Fit the AR(1)-GARCH(1,1) Model     */
   model wyr = mkt / nlag=1 garch=(q=1,p=1);
   output out=wyr_out3 p=p_gar r=r_gar;
run;
```

Create the RETURNS2 data set. The RETURNS2 data set consists of the actual values and the forecast values from the OLS, heteroscedastic, and GARCH models. The WYR_OUT1, WYR_OUT2, and WYR_OUT3 data sets contain the forecast values from the OLS, heteroscedastic, and GARCH models respectively.

```
data returns2;
   merge returns1 wyr_out1 wyr_out2 wyr_out3;
   where date > '31dec86'd;
   by date;
run;
```

Calculate the forecast errors. Use assignment statements in a DATA step.

```
data stats;
   set returns2;
   e_ols = wyr_a-p_ols;               /* Forecast Errors OLS Model    */
   e_het = wyr_a-p_het;               /* Forecast Errors HETERO Model */
   e_gar = wyr_a-p_gar;               /* Forecast Errors GARCH Model  */
   ae_ols = abs(e_ols);               /* Absolute Errors OLS Model    */
   ae_het = abs(e_het);               /* Absolute Errors HETERO Model */
   ae_gar = abs(e_gar);               /* Absolute Errors GARCH Model  */
   pe_ols = (e_ols*100)/wyr_a;        /* Percent Error OLS Model      */
   pe_het = (e_het*100)/wyr_a;        /* Percent Error HETERO Model   */
   pe_gar = (e_gar*100)/wyr_a;        /* Percent Error GARCH Model    */
   ape_ols = abs(e_ols/wyr_a)*100;    /* Absolute % Error OLS         */
   ape_het = abs(e_het/wyr_a)*100;    /* Absolute % Error HETERO      */
   ape_gar = abs(e_gar/wyr_a)*100;    /* Absolute % Error GARCH       */
   se_ols = e_ols**2;                 /* Square Error OLS Model       */
   se_het = e_het**2;                 /* Square Error HETERO Model    */
   se_gar = e_gar**2;                 /* Square Error GARCH Model     */
   spe_ols = ((e_ols/wyr_a)**2)*100; /* Square % Error OLS Model     */
   spe_het = ((e_het/wyr_a)**2)*100; /* Square % Error HETERO Model  */
   spe_gar = ((e_gar/wyr_a)**2)*100; /* Square % Error GARCH Model   */
run;
```

Calculate the mean values of the forecast error statistics using PROC SUMMARY.

```
proc summary data=stats mean;
   var e_ols e_het e_gar ae_ols ae_het ae_gar pe_ols pe_het
       pe_gar ape_ols ape_het ape_gar se_ols se_het se_gar
       spe_ols spe_het spe_gar;
   output out=stats1 mean=mad_ols mad_het mad_gar mae_ols
          mae_het mae_gar mpe_ols mpe_het mpe_gar
          mape_ols mape_het mape_gar mse_ols mse_het mse_gar
          mspe_ols mspe_het mspe_gar;
run;
```

Calculate the root mean square forecast error statistics using a DATA step.

```
data stats2;
   set stats1;
   rmse_ols = sqrt(mse_ols);    /* Root Mean Sq Error OLS Model       */
   rmse_het = sqrt(mse_het);    /* Root Mean Sq Error HETERO Model    */
   rmse_gar = sqrt(mse_gar);    /* Root Mean Sq Error GARCH Model     */
   rmspe_ol = sqrt(mspe_ols);   /* Root Mean % Sq Error OLS Model     */
   rmspe_ht = sqrt(mspe_het);   /* Root Mean % Sq Error HETERO Model */
   rmspe_gr = sqrt(mspe_gar);   /* Root Mean % Sq Error GARCH Model   */
   title2 'Forecast Goodness-of-Fit Statistics';
run;
```

Print the mean values of the forecast error statistics using PROC PRINT.

```
proc print data=stats2;
   var mad_ols mad_het mad_gar mae_ols mae_het mae_gar
       mpe_ols mpe_het mpe_gar mape_ols mape_het mape_gar
       mse_ols mse_het mse_gar mspe_ols mspe_het mspe_gar;
run;
```

Print the root mean square forecast error statistics using PROC PRINT.

```
proc print data=stats2;
   var rmse_ols rmse_het rmse_gar rmspe_ol rmspe_ht rmspe_gr;
run;
```

Output 16.1
Mean Forecast Error Statistics Created with PROC SUMMARY

```
                         Returns1 Data
              Forecast Goodness-of-Fit Statistics

OBS  MAD_OLS     MAD_HET     MAD_GAR     MAE_OLS     MAE_HET     MAE_GAR

 1  0.011802    0.014470    0.011333    0.055808    0.064665    0.054471

OBS  MPE_OLS  MPE_HET  MPE_GAR  MAPE_OLS  MAPE_HET  MAPE_GAR

 1  39.9517  54.9037  38.4551   56.6420   61.1956   55.9741

OBS  MSE_OLS    MSE_HET    MSE_GAR    MSPE_OLS    MSPE_HET    MSPE_GAR

 1 .0051809   .0069047   .0048817     41.9111     43.2048     41.9685
```

Explanation

The forecast error statistics for the GARCH model in Output 16.1 are slightly closer to 0 for the MAD, MAE, MPE, MAPE, and MSE than they are for the OLS model. The OLS model has the MSPE closest to 0. Based on these statistics, the GARCH model may be a slightly better forecasting model than the OLS model.

Note: A forecasting model that produces large positive errors and large negative errors may still have low values for the MAD and MPE forecast error statistics.

Output 16.2
Root Mean Square Forecast Error Statistics

```
                         Returns1 Data
                Forecast Goodness-of-Fit Statistics

OBS   RMSE_OLS   RMSE_HET   RMSE_GAR   RMSPE_OL   RMSPE_HT   RMSPE_GR

 1    0.071978   0.083094   0.069869    6.47388    6.57304    6.47831
```

Explanation

In Output 16.2, the GARCH model has root mean square error (RMSE) closest to 0, and the OLS model has root mean square percent error (RMSPE) closest to 0. The difference in magnitude is small. Based on these statistics, the OLS and GARCH models are nearly equivalent in forecast accuracy.

Further Reading

- For more information on PROC AUTOREG, see the *SAS/ETS User's Guide, Version 6, Second Edition,* and *SAS/ETS Software: Changes and Enhancements, Release 6.11.*
- For more information on DATA step features and functions, see *SAS Language: Reference, Version 6, First Edition.*
- For more information on PROC PRINT and PROC SUMMARY, see the *SAS Procedures Guide, Version 6, Third Edition.*

References

- Bails, D. and Peppers, L. (1982), *Business Fluctuations: Forecasting Techniques and Applications,* Englewood Cliffs, N.J.: Prentice Hall, Inc.
- Black, F., Jensen, M., and Scholes, M. (1972), "The Capital Asset Pricing Model: Some Empirical Tests," *Studies in the Theory of Capital Markets,* ed. M. Jensen, New York: Praeger, 79-121.
- Pindyck, R.S. and Rubinfeld, D.L. (1991), *Econometric Models and Economic Forecasts, Third Edition,* New York: McGraw-Hill Book Co.

EXAMPLE 17

Forecasting Using a Lagged Dependent Variable Model

Featured Tools:

- AUTOREG procedure
  - MODEL statement
  - LAGDEP= option
  - NLAG= option
- SIMLIN procedure

Consumption functions typically model consumption as a function of disposable income. One hypothesis is that consumption expenditures do not immediately adjust as disposable income changes. Past values of disposable income, DI, affect the current level of consumption, C. For example, the effect of a windfall gain (or loss) on consumption may be spread across several periods.

In infinite lag form, the habit persistence consumption model with $0 < w < 1$ has the form

$$C_t = d_0 + b_1\left(DI_t + wDI_{t-1} + w^2DI_{t-2} + \ldots\right)$$

Lag the model 1 period to yield

$$C_{t-1} = d_0 + b_1\left(DI_{t-1} + wDI_{t-2} + w^2DI_{t-3} + \ldots\right)$$

Use a Koyck transformation (Koyck 1954) to obtain the following equation. Multiply the lagged model by *w* and subtract it from the original expression:

$$C_t - wC_{t-1} = d_0(1 - w) + b_1DI_t$$

$$C_t = d_0(1 - w) + wC_{t-1} + b_1DI_t$$

The model is now

$$C_t = b_0 + wC_{t-1} + b_1DI_t$$

where $b_0 = d_0(1 - w)$.

The habit persistence model of consumption is equivalent to an adaptive expectations model and stock adjustment models. For details, see Pindyck and Rubinfeld (1991), pp. 204-210.

Program

Estimating a Consumption Function

Create the CONSUME data set. The complete CONSUME data set is in "Introduction: The Example Data Sets." The CONSUME data set contains values for all variables from SEP82 to DEC89, and values for all variables except C_N from DEC89 to JUN90.

```
data consume;
   format date monyy.;
   input date:monyy5. di_n c_n cpi @@;
      c = c_n/cpi;
     di = di_n/cpi;
    c_1 = lag(c);
   label di='Real Disposable Income in Billions 1982$'
         c='Real Consumption in Billions of 1982$'
         c_1='1 Month Lagged Real C in Billions 1982$';
   title 'Consume Data';
datalines;
SEP82 2283.2 2140.1  .979  OCT82 2299.8 2157.9  .982
NOV82 2321.7 2178.7  .980  DEC82 2332.7 2188.1  .976
JAN83 2344.3 2196.9  .978  FEB83 2339.2 2202.4  .979
more data lines
;
```

Estimate the model parameters using PROC AUTOREG. Use the LAGDEP= option in the MODEL statement to specify the lagged dependent variable, the calculation of the Durbin *h*-statistic, and the *p*-value of the Durbin *h*-statistic.

```
proc autoreg data=consume;
   model c = c_1 di / lagdep=c_1;
run;
```

Output 17.1
Consumption Function Estimated by Ordinary Least Squares with PROC AUTOREG

```
                          Consume Data

                       Autoreg Procedure

Dependent Variable = C           Real Consumption in Billions of 1982$


                   Ordinary Least Squares Estimates

            SSE          23449.84    DFE              84
            MSE          279.1648    Root MSE   16.70823
            SBC          747.2069    AIC        739.8092
            Reg Rsq        0.9936    Total Rsq    0.9936
        ❶   Durbin h     -3.47543    PROB<h       0.0003


    Variable    DF      B Value   Std Error  t Ratio Approx Prob
        ❷
    Intercept    1    -4.357187     27.2495   -0.160      0.8733
    C_1          1     0.826034      0.0527   15.661      0.0001
    DI           1     0.170119      0.0552    3.081      0.0028
```

Explanation

The estimated model in Output 17.1 is as follows:

$$C_t = -4.357187 + .826034C_{t-1} + .170119DI_t$$

❶ The Durbin *h*-statistic is -3.47543, and the *p*-value is .0003. This Durbin *h*-statistic indicates the presence of positive autocorrelation in a properly specified model. For additional information on the Durbin *h*-statistic, see pp.147-149 of Pindyck and Rubinfeld (1991).

❷ Parameter estimates, standard errors, *t*-statistics for the null hypotheses that each parameter is equal to 0, and the *p*-values are listed. At the .10 level all parameter estimates are different from 0 except the intercept.

Be aware that the residuals of infinite lag models (Geometric, Koyck, Exponential, and so on) often exhibit autocorrelation. This tendency is a major shortcoming of infinite lag models. For additional information, see Maddala (1977), pp. 359-373.

Fitting and Forecasting an Autoregressive Model

Fit an autoregressive model using PROC AUTOREG. Use the NLAG= option in the MODEL statement to specify the order of the autoregressive process or the subset of lags to be fit. Use the METHOD=option to specify the estimation method, ML (maximum-likelihood estimation), ULS (unconditional least-squares estimation), and YW (Yule-Walker estimation).

```
proc autoreg data=consume
    outest=con_est;  /* Outputs and Stores Parameter Estimates  */

   model c = c_1 di    /* Fits the Model */
       / lagdep=c_1  /* Specifies the Lagged Dependent Variable */
         nlag=13     /* Specifies the Order of AR Model         */
         method=ml   /* Specifies the Estimation Method         */
         backstep    /* Removes Insignificant AR Parameters     */
         dw=1;       /* Prints the Durbin-Watson d Statistic    */

   output out=con_out /* Names the Output Data Set              */
         p=p         /* Outputs Predicted Values                */
         lcl=l       /* Outputs Lower Confidence Limit          */
         ucl=u;      /* Outputs Upper Confidence Limit          */
run;
```

Print the forecasts using PROC PRINT. A WHERE statement is used to specify the observations to be printed.

```
proc print data=con_out noobs;
   where date > '01jun89'd;
   var date u p c l;
   title2 'Autoregressive Model Forecasts';
run;
```

Estimating the AR(1) Model

Output 17.2
First-Order Autoregressive Model Estimated by Maximum Likelihood with PROC AUTOREG (Partial Output)

```
                              Consume Data

                           Autoreg Procedure

                    ❶ Estimates of Autocorrelations

Lag  Covariance  Correlation -1 9 8 7 6 5 4 3 2 1 0 1 2 3 4 5 6 7 8 9 1

  0    269.5384     1.000000 |                    |********************|
  1    -83.6336    -0.310285 |              ******|                    |
  2    23.34116     0.086597 |                    |**                  |
  3    -9.06668    -0.033638 |                   *|                    |
  4    15.20586     0.056414 |                    |*                   |
  5    17.34147     0.064338 |                    |*                   |
  6    6.093793     0.022608 |                    |                    |
  7    15.02795     0.055754 |                    |*                   |
  8    40.09023     0.148737 |                    |***                 |
  9     -14.771    -0.054801 |                   *|                    |
 10    1.602652     0.005946 |                    |                    |
 11    -3.72742    -0.013829 |                    |                    |
 12    32.32951     0.119944 |                    |**                  |
 13    -3.24071    -0.012023 |                    |                    |
```

```
                    Consume Data

                  Autoreg Procedure

    ❷ Backward Elimination of Autoregressive Terms

            Lag   Estimate    t-Ratio    Prob
             13  -0.013118    -0.1105  0.9123
             11   0.015724     0.1258  0.9002
             10   0.025529     0.2184  0.8277
              3   0.034748     0.2921  0.7710
              2   0.050147     0.4424  0.6594
              9  -0.046495    -0.4122  0.6813
              4  -0.056353    -0.5057  0.6145
             12  -0.086624    -0.8279  0.4103
              6  -0.107870    -0.9411  0.3495
              5  -0.079426    -0.7641  0.4471
              7  -0.127098    -1.1705  0.2452
              8  -0.166554    -1.6089  0.1115
```

```
                    Consume Data

                  Autoreg Procedure

              Preliminary MSE = 243.5882

      Estimates of the Autoregressive Parameters

        Lag   Coefficient      Std Error        t Ratio
          1    0.31028467       0.104347          2.974


              Maximum Likelihood Estimates

        SSE            20236.41    DFE              83
        MSE            243.8122    Root MSE   15.61449
        SBC            739.0255    AIC        729.1618
        Reg Rsq          0.9971    Total Rsq    0.9945
        Durbin-Watson    2.1412
```

```
                    Consume Data

                  Autoreg Procedure

Variable      DF       B Value   Std Error   t Ratio Approx Prob
   ❸
Intercept      1     16.403308     19.1843     0.855      0.3950
C_1            1      0.910106      0.0408    22.323      0.0001
DI             1      0.082490      0.0427     1.930      0.0571
A(1)           1      0.400410      0.1050     3.814      0.0003
```

Explanation

The structural portion of the estimated model in Output 17.2 is as follows:

$$C_t = 16.403308 + .910106C_{t-1} + .082490DI_t$$

❶ Estimates of autocovariances and autocorrelations show that only the first-order autocorrelation parameter is of relatively large magnitude.

❷ Backward elimination of autoregressive terms eliminates all but the first-order term.

❸ Parameter estimates, standard errors, *t*-statistics for the null hypotheses that each parameter is equal to 0, and the *p*-values are listed. At the .10 level, all parameter estimates are different from 0 except the intercept.

Printing the Forecasts

Output 17.3
Predicted and Residual Values, and the Lower and Upper 95% Confidence Limits

Consume Data
Autoregressive Model Forecasts

DATE	U	P	C	L
JUL89	2893.29	2861.84	2868.97	2830.38
AUG89	2902.81	2871.46	2887.48	2840.12
SEP89	2918.12	2886.78	2879.68	2855.44
OCT89	2921.16	2889.83	2870.22	2858.50
NOV89	2915.09	2883.65	2873.79	2852.21
DEC89	2915.10	2883.58	2897.22	2852.05
JAN90	2930.86	2897.10	.	2863.34
FEB90	.	.	.	.
MAR90	.	.	.	.
APR90	.	.	.	.
MAY90	.	.	.	.
JUN90	.	.	.	.

Explanation

In Output 17.3, the following variables are listed:

U and L   are the upper and lower 95% confidence limits.

C and P   are the actual and predicted values.

Only 1 period ahead is forecast as PROC AUTOREG requires values for the right-side variables to forecast regression models. Values of the lagged endogenous variable C_1 are not available for forecasting after DEC89.

Variations

Using PROC SIMLIN

Forecast the model using PROC SIMLIN. The INTERIM and TOTAL options calculate the interim and total multipliers.

The LAGGED statement specifies the name of the lagged endogenous variable, the name of the endogenous variable that is lagged, and the degree of the lag. This statement specifies that the variable C_1 contain values of the endogenous variable C lagged 1 period.

```
proc simlin data=consume
            est=con_est    /* Specifies Input Data Set of
                                Estimated Model Parameters    */
            type=ols       /* Specifies Observation Type to
                                Read from the EST= Data Set   */
            interim=3      /* Computes Interim Multipliers    */
            total;         /* Computes Total Multipliers      */

   endogenous c;           /* Specifies Endogenous Variables  */
   exogenous di;           /* Specifies Exogenous Variables   */
   lagged c_1 c 1;         /* Specifies Lagged Variables      */
   output out=con_out1 predicted=c_pred;
   title2;                 /* Resets the Program Title2       */
run;
```

Print the EST= data set using PROC PRINT.

```
proc print data=con_est;
run;
```

Print the forecasts using PROC PRINT. A WHERE statement is used to specify the observations to be printed. The NOOBS option suppresses the printing of the observation number.

```
proc print data=con_out1 noobs;
   where date > '01jun89'd;
   var date di c c_pred c_1;
run;
```

Output 17.4
PROC SIMLIN Output: Reduced Form, Multipliers, and Statistics of Fit

```
                         Consume Data

                       SIMLIN Procedure

  ❶ Inverse Coefficient Matrix for Endogenous Variables

                                     C

                       C        1.0000

     ❷ Reduced Form for Lagged Endogenous Variables

                                   C_1

                       C        0.9101

            Reduced Form for Exogenous Variables

                              DI       INTERCEP

                 C        0.0825        16.4033
```

```
                 Consume Data

               SIMLIN Procedure

      ❸ Interim Multipliers for Interim 1

                       DI       INTERCEP

        C       0.0750747       14.92875

        Interim Multipliers for Interim 2

                       DI       INTERCEP

        C       0.0683260       13.58675

        Interim Multipliers for Interim 3

                       DI       INTERCEP

        C       0.0621839       12.36539
```

```
                 Consume Data

               SIMLIN Procedure

            ❹ Total Multipliers

                       DI       INTERCEP

        C       0.9176391       182.4743
```

```
                 Consume Data

               SIMLIN Procedure

            ❺ Statistics of Fit

                           Mean     Mean %   Mean Abs     Mean Abs
     Variable       N     Error      Error      Error      % Error

     C             87    1.8860     0.0503    19.1639      0.73024

                   Statistics of Fit

                 RMS       RMS %
Variable       Error       Error  Label

C            23.3793      0.8891  Real Consumption in Billions of 1982$
```

Explanation

❶ **`Inverse Coefficient Matrix for Endogenous Variables`** for this single equation model is 1 as no (contemporaneous) endogenous variables appear as regressor variables.

❷ **`Reduced Form for Lagged Endogenous Variables`** and **`Reduced Form for Exogenous Variables`** are the parameter estimates for this single equation model.

❸ **`Interim Multipliers`** for interim periods 1, 2, and 3 are the effect on the endogenous variables of a 1-unit change of the exogenous variables. The interim multiplier for the first interim period is the impact multiplier; that is, the contemporaneous change in C as DI changes by 1 unit. The interim multiplier for the second interim period is the impact on C of a 1-unit change in DI in the previous period. The interim multiplier for the third interim period is the impact on C of a 1-unit change in DI two periods back.

❹ **`Total Multipliers`** are the cumulative effect on the endogenous variables of a 1-unit change in the exogenous variables.

❺ **`Statistics of Fit`** for the historical data are listed: the mean error, mean percent error, mean absolute error, mean absolute percent error, the root mean square error, and the root mean percent error. The formulas for these statistics of fit are listed in Example 16, " Assessing Forecast Accuracy."

Printing an EST= Data Set

Output 17.5
The CON_EST Data Set Created by PROC AUTOREG

```
                          Consume Data

OBS  _MODEL_   _TYPE_   _DEPVAR_   _METHOD_   _NAME_    _MSE_      _SSE_

 1              OLS        C          ML              243.812   20236.41

OBS  INTERCEP    C    C_1        DI        _A_1    _A_2   _A_3   _A_4

 1   16.4033    -1   0.91011  0.082490  0.40041    .      .      .

OBS  _A_5  _A_6  _A_7  _A_8  _A_9  _A_10  _A_11  _A_12  _A_13

 1    .     .     .     .     .     .      .      .      .
```

Explanation

The CON_EST data set was created by PROC AUTOREG and was used as input for PROC SIMLIN to

- □ compute the reduced form of the model (see Output 17.4).
- □ calculate interim and total multipliers (see Output 17.4).
- □ calculate statistics of fit (see Output 17.4).
- □ forecast the model (see Output 17.6).

As shown in Output 17.5, the CON_EST data set contains 1 observation (which corresponds to the 1 equation of the model) and includes the following variables:

TYPE
: a character variable that identifies the type of observation.

DEPVAR
: a character variable containing the name of the dependent variable.

METHOD
: the estimation method. ML is maximum likelihood estimation.

MSE and _SSE_
: the mean square error and the sum of squared errors.

INTERCEP
: the estimated intercept.

C
: the coefficient of the endogenous variable C (when taken to the right side of the equation).

C_1 and DI
: the estimated slope parameters of the regressor variables C_1 and DI.

_A_1
: the first-order autoregressive parameter. The remaining autoregressive terms were eliminated when the model was estimated.

Printing the Forecasts

Output 17.6
Actual Input Values and Forecasts

Consume Data

DATE	DI	C	C_PRED	C_1
JUL89	3006.51	2868.97	2886.14	2880.68
AUG89	3002.41	2887.48	2890.76	2886.14
SEP89	2999.20	2879.68	2894.71	2890.76
OCT89	3003.90	2870.22	2898.69	2894.71
NOV89	3019.94	2873.79	2903.63	2898.69
DEC89	3032.43	2897.22	2909.16	2903.63
JAN90	3030.77	.	2914.06	2909.16
FEB90	3036.02	.	2918.95	2914.06
MAR90	3042.66	.	2923.94	2918.95
APR90	3037.63	.	2928.08	2923.94
MAY90	3040.02	.	2932.04	2928.08
JUN90	3037.49	.	2935.43	2932.04

Explanation

DATE	are the monthly dates.
DI	are the values for the variable DI.
C	are the values for the variable C.
C_PRED	are the predicted values.
C_1	are the lagged values for the variable C_PRED.

As shown in Output 17.6, PROC SIMLIN forecasts the model using the lagged predicted values of C as input values for the variable C_1.

Further Reading

- For more information on PROC AUTOREG, see the *SAS/ETS User's Guide, Version 6, Second Edition,* and *SAS/ETS Software: Changes and Enhancements, Release 6.11.*
- For more information on PROC SIMLIN, see the *SAS/ETS User's Guide, Version 6, Second Edition.*

References

- Koyck, L.M. (1954), *Distributed Lags and Investment Analysis*, Amsterdam: North-Holland.
- Pindyck, R.S. and Rubinfeld, D.L. (1991), *Econometric Models and Economic Forecasts, Third Edition*, New York: McGraw-Hill Inc.
- Maddala, G.S. (1977), *Econometrics*, New York: McGraw-Hill.

EXAMPLE 18

Static and Dynamic Forecasting Using a Lagged Dependent Variable Model

Featured Tools:

- MODEL procedure

  FIT statement

  SOLVE statement

The Koyck lag consumption function (developed and estimated in Example 17, "Forecasting Using a Lagged Dependent Variable Model") models current-period consumption as a linear function of previous-period consumption and current-period disposable income. The simplified model is as follows:

$$C_t = b_0 + wC_{t-1} + b_1 DI_t$$

For additional discussion, see Koyck (1954), and Pindyck and Rubinfeld (1991), pp.147-149.

You can estimate the Koyck lag consumption function and use it for static or dynamic forecasting and simulation with the SAS/ETS MODEL procedure. Static and dynamic solution modes refer to the value of the lagged endogenous variable that is to be used by the lagging functions in solving the model. A *static solution* refers to a solution obtained by using the actual values for the lagged endogenous variables when they are available. A *dynamic solution* refers to a solution obtained by using only solved values for the lagged variables. Static mode is used to simulate the behavior of the model without the complication of previous period solution errors. Dynamic mode is used both for forecasting and for simulating the dynamic properties of the model.

In PROC MODEL, *simulation* is the calculation of the endogenous (dependent) variables as a function of the input values of the other variables, even when actual data for some of the solution variables are available in the input data set. In forecast mode, PROC MODEL solves only for those variables that are missing in the input data set, if values are provided for all right-side variables.

Program

Static and Dynamic Forecasting

Create the CONSUME data set.

The CONSUME data set contains values for all variables from SEP82 to DEC89, and values for all variables except C_N from DEC89 to JUN90. Static solutions for consumption can be obtained only for JAN90 while dynamic solutions can be obtained for JAN90 through JUN90.

The complete CONSUME data set is in "Introduction: The Example Data Sets."

```
data consume;
   format date monyy.;
   input date:monyy5. di_n c_n cpi @@;
      c = c_n/cpi;
     di = di_n/cpi;
    c_1 = lag(c);
   label di='Real Disposable Income in Billions 1982$'
         c='Real Consumption in Billions of 1982$'
         c_1='1 Month Lagged Real C in Billions 1982$';
   title 'Consume Data';
datalines;
SEP82 2283.2 2140.1  .979  OCT82 2299.8 2157.9  .982
NOV82 2321.7 2178.7  .980  DEC82 2332.7 2188.1  .976
JAN83 2344.3 2196.9  .978  FEB83 2339.2 2202.4  .979
more data lines
;
```

Fit and forecast the model using PROC MODEL. Use FIT statements to estimate models and SOLVE statements to simulate or forecast models.

Use the SIMULATE option to specify that the solution values of variables be used, even when actual values are available in the input data set. SIMULATE is the default solution mode.

Use the FORECAST option to specify that the actual value of a solved variable is used as the solution value (rather than the predicted value from the model equations) whenever nonmissing values are available. In FORECAST mode, PROC MODEL solves only for those variables that are missing in the input data set if values are provided for all right-side variables.

```
proc model data=consume noprint;
   parms b0 w b1;                   /* Specifies the Model Parameters */
      c = b0 + w*lag(c) + b1*di;    /* Specifies the Model to Be Fit  */
   fit c                            /* Fit the Model                  */
         / outest=con_est1;         /* Stores the Estimated Model     */
   id date di;                      /* Specifies ID Variables and
                                         Stores in Output Data Set    */


      /* Static Simulation */
   solve c                         /* Solves the Specified Model     */
       / estdata=con_est1          /* Specifies the Input Data Set
                                        Containing the Fitted Model  */
         static                    /* Specifies Using Actual Values
                                      of Lagged Endogenous Variables */
         out=con_out2              /* Names the Output Data Set      */
         outpredict;               /* Includes Predicted Values in
                                        Output Data Set              */


      /* Static Forecasting */
   solve c                         /* Solves the Specified Model     */
       / estdata=con_est1          /* Specifies the Input Data Set
                                        Containing the Fitted Model  */
         static                    /* Specifies Using Actual Values
                                      of Lagged Endogenous Variables */
         forecast                  /* Specifies that the Solution
                                        Values Be Forecasts          */
         out=con_out3              /* Names the Output Data Set      */
         outpredict;               /* Includes Predicted Values in
                                        Output Data Set              */


      /* NAHEAD=3 Dynamic Simulation */
   solve c
       / estdata=con_est1

         dynamic                   /* Specifies Using Solved Values
                                      of Lagged Endogenous Variables */
         nahead=3                  /* Three Period Ahead Forecasting */
         out=con_out4
         outpredict;
```

```
      /* Dynamic Forecasting */
   solve c
      / estdata=con_est1
        dynamic                 /* Specifies Using Solved Values
                                   of Lagged Endogenous Variables */
        forecast                /* Specifies that the Solution
                                    Values Be Forecasts          */
        out=con_out5
        outpredict;
run;
```

Print the forecasts and simulations using PROC PRINT.

```
proc print data=con_out2;
   where date > '01sep89'd;
   title2 'Static Simulation';
run;

proc print data=con_out3;
   where date > '01sep89'd;
   title2 'Static Forecasting';
run;

proc print data=con_out4;
   where date > '01sep89'd;
   title2 'NAHEAD=3 Dynamic Simulation';
run;

proc print data=con_out5;
   where date > '01sep89'd;
   title2 'Dynamic Forecasting';
run;
```

Output 18.1
Static Simulation of the Koyck Lag Consumption Function

Consume Data
Static Simulation

OBS	DATE	DI	_TYPE_	_MODE_	_LAG_	_ERRORS_	C
85	OCT89	3003.90	PREDICT	SIMULATE	0	0	2885.38
86	NOV89	3019.94	PREDICT	SIMULATE	0	0	2880.29
87	DEC89	3032.43	PREDICT	SIMULATE	0	0	2885.36
88	JAN90	3030.77	PREDICT	SIMULATE	0	0	2904.44
89	FEB90	3036.02	PREDICT	SIMULATE	0	-1	.
90	MAR90	3042.66	PREDICT	SIMULATE	0	-1	.
91	APR90	3037.63	PREDICT	SIMULATE	0	-1	.
92	MAY90	3040.02	PREDICT	SIMULATE	0	-1	.
93	JUN90	3037.49	PREDICT	SIMULATE	0	-1	.

Explanation

The values of the variable C in Output 18.1 are static simulations. In the static mode, PROC MODEL uses the actual values of the lagged endogenous variables. In simulation mode, the model is solved if all right-side variables have values in the input data set. After JAN90, the values of the lagged endogenous variable are missing and static simulation solutions cannot be calculated.

The following variables are listed:

DATE	is the date variable.
DI	are the values for the variable DI.
TYPE	is a character variable identifying the type of observation (PREDICT, RESIDUAL, ACTUAL, or ERROR).
MODE	is a character variable identifying the solution _MODE_ (FORECAST or SIMULATE).
LAG	is a numeric variable containing the number of dynamic lags that contribute to the solution. The value of _LAG_ is always set to 0 for STATIC mode solutions.
ERRORS	is a numeric variable containing the number of errors that occurred during the execution of the program for the last iteration for the observation. Zero (0) indicates no error while -1 indicates an error occurred in the solution process.
C	are the solution values. For this example, the actual values for the variable C_1 (the lagged endogenous values) are missing after JAN90, and static simulation solutions cannot be calculated.

PROC MODEL Warning Message

When PROC MODEL encounters a missing lagged input value in the static simulation solution process, a warning is printed.

Output 18.2
PROC MODEL Warning Message Printed during Static Simulation if Lagged Input Value Is Missing

```
                              Consume Data

                            MODEL Procedure
                   Static Single-Equation Simulation

WARNING: Solution values are missing because of missing input values for
         observation 89 at NEWTON iteration 0.
```

Static Forecasting

Output 18.3
Static Forecasting of the Koyck Lag Consumption Function

Consume Data
Static Forecasting

OBS	DATE	DI	_TYPE_	_MODE_	_LAG_	_ERRORS_	C
85	OCT89	3003.90	PREDICT	FORECAST	0	0	2870.22
86	NOV89	3019.94	PREDICT	FORECAST	0	0	2873.79
87	DEC89	3032.43	PREDICT	FORECAST	0	0	2897.22
88	JAN90	3030.77	PREDICT	FORECAST	0	0	2904.44
89	FEB90	3036.02	PREDICT	FORECAST	0	-1	.
90	MAR90	3042.66	PREDICT	FORECAST	0	-1	.
91	APR90	3037.63	PREDICT	FORECAST	0	-1	.
92	MAY90	3040.02	PREDICT	FORECAST	0	-1	.
93	JUN90	3037.49	PREDICT	FORECAST	0	-1	.

Explanation

The values of the variable C in Output 18.3 are the static forecasts. In static mode, PROC MODEL uses the actual values of the lagged endogenous variable. In forecast mode, forecasts are generated for the endogenous variable C for observations containing missing values for C *and* if all right-side variables have values in the input data set. Errors in the solution process occur because values for the variable C_1 are missing after JAN90.

NAHEAD=3 Dynamic Simulation

Output 18.4
Three-Period Ahead Dynamic Forecasts of the Koyck Lag Consumption Function

Consume Data
NAHEAD=3 Dynamic Simulation

OBS	DATE	DI	_TYPE_	_MODE_	_LAG_	_ERRORS_	C
85	OCT89	3003.90	PREDICT	SIMULATE	2	0	2887.10
86	NOV89	3019.94	PREDICT	SIMULATE	2	0	2900.55
87	DEC89	3032.43	PREDICT	SIMULATE	2	0	2901.08
88	JAN90	3030.77	PREDICT	SIMULATE	2	0	2899.08
89	FEB90	3036.02	PREDICT	SIMULATE	2	0	2903.20
90	MAR90	3042.66	PREDICT	SIMULATE	2	0	2918.08

Explanation

The values of the variable C in Output 18.4 are the three-period ahead dynamic forecasts. In dynamic mode, PROC MODEL uses the solution values of lagged endogenous variables. The lagging function uses two lagged periods in calculating the values of the lagged endogenous variable, C_1. After MAR90, the values of C_1 are missing and the model cannot be solved. PROC MODEL prints the error message in Output 18.5.

PROC MODEL Error Message

Output 18.5
Error Message Printed if Required Data Is Missing for Solution

```
                              Consume Data

                             MODEL Procedure
         Dynamic Single-Equation 3-Periods-Ahead Forecasting Simulation

ERROR: Solution values are missing because of missing input values for
       observation 89 at NEWTON iteration 0.

NOTE: Additional information on the values of the variables at this
      observation, which may be helpful in determining the cause of the
      failure of the solution process, is printed below.
```

```
                              Consume Data

                             MODEL Procedure
         Dynamic Single-Equation 3-Periods-Ahead Forecasting Simulation

Observation 89. Iteration 0. _LAG_=0  DATE=FEB1990 DI=3036 Missing=1 NEWTON
               CC=-1
Iteration Errors: Missing.

                  --- Listing of Program Data Vector ---
_N_:                     1   ACTUAL.C:               .   B0:            -4.35719
B1:                0.17012   C:              0.0001000   DATE:           FEB1990
DI:                   3036   ERROR.C:                .   PRED.C:               .
RESID.C:                 .   W:                0.82603

NOTE: Simulation aborted.
```

Dynamic Forecasting

Output 18.6
Dynamic Forecasting of the Koyck Lag Consumption Function

Consume Data
Dynamic Forecasting

OBS	DATE	DI	_TYPE_	_MODE_	_LAG_	_ERRORS_	C
85	OCT89	3003.90	PREDICT	FORECAST	84	0	2870.22
86	NOV89	3019.94	PREDICT	FORECAST	85	0	2873.79
87	DEC89	3032.43	PREDICT	FORECAST	86	0	2897.22
88	JAN90	3030.77	PREDICT	FORECAST	87	0	2904.44
89	FEB90	3036.02	PREDICT	FORECAST	88	0	2911.29
90	MAR90	3042.66	PREDICT	FORECAST	89	0	2918.08
91	APR90	3037.63	PREDICT	FORECAST	90	0	2922.83
92	MAY90	3040.02	PREDICT	FORECAST	91	0	2927.17
93	JUN90	3037.49	PREDICT	FORECAST	92	0	2930.32

Explanation

The values of the variable C in Output 18.6 are dynamic forecasts. In dynamic mode, PROC MODEL uses the solution values of lagged endogenous variables. In forecast mode, forecasts are generated for the endogenous variable C for observations containing missing values for C *if* all right-side variables have values. Current-period values for the right-side variable C-1 are the previous-period forecasts of the variable C.

A Closer Look

Using PROC MODEL for Fitting and Forecasting

The MODEL procedure analyzes models in which the relationships among the variables comprise a system of one or more equations. Primary uses of the MODEL procedure are estimation, simulation, and forecasting of linear and nonlinear simultaneous equation models.

SAS programming statements are used to define the model. All parameters and arithmetic operators should be included in the model. The FIT statement estimates models, and the SOLVE statement simulates and forecasts models. Other statements include the PARAMETERS statement, which specifies the model parameters; the ENDOGENOUS and EXOGENOUS statements, which specify the endogenous and exogenous variables of the model; and the INSTRUMENTS statement, which specifies the instruments for instrumental variables estimation methods. PROC MODEL supports BY-group processing, ARRAY processing in DO-END groups, IF-THEN/ELSE statements, and WHERE and WHEN statements.

Solution Modes

In simulating the model, either solved values or actual values from the data set can be used to supply lagged values of an endogenous variable. A dynamic solution refers to a solution obtained by using only solved values for the lagged endogenous variable values. A static solution refers to a solution obtained by using the actual values when available for the lagged endogenous variable values.

The following are commonly used solution modes:

- Static simultaneous simulation mode can be used to examine the within-period performance of the model without the complications of previous period errors. Use the STATIC option of the SOLVE statement.
- Dynamic simultaneous simulation mode is often called ex-post simulation, historical simulation, or ex-post forecasting. Use the DYNAMIC option of the SOLVE statement. This is the default mode.
- NAHEAD=*n* dynamic simultaneous simulation mode can be used to assess how well *n*-period-ahead forecasting would have performed over the historical period. Use the NAHEAD=*n* option of the SOLVE statement.
- Dynamic simultaneous forecast mode is used for forecasting the model. To forecast the model, an input data set containing future expected values of the exogenous variables is needed. When the solution mode is specified as forecast (with the FORECAST option), PROC MODEL only solves for those variables whose values are missing in the input data set.

Further Reading

For more information on PROC MODEL, see the *SAS/ETS User's Guide, Version 6, Second Edition*, and *SAS/ETS Software: Changes and Enhancements, Release 6.11.*

References

- Koyck, L.M. (1954), *Distributed Lags and Investment Analysis*, Amsterdam: North-Holland.
- Pindyck, R.S. and Rubinfeld, D.L. (1991), *Econometric Models and Economic Forecasts, Third Edition*, New York: McGraw-Hill Inc.
- Maddala, G.S. (1977), *Econometrics*, New York: McGraw-Hill.

EXAMPLE 19

Fitting and Forecasting Polynomial Distributed Lag Models

Featured Tools:

- PDLREG procedure
  - MODEL statement
  - OUTPUT statement
- MODEL procedure
  - FIT statement
  - PDL macro
  - SOLVE statement

Polynomial distributed lag (PDL) regression models arise in time series data because the effects of some regressor variables are distributed over time. If the regressor variable X changes at time t, the dependent variable Y typically experiences some immediate effect at time t, and possibly a delayed effect at times t+1, t+2, and so on up to time $t+p$ for some limit p.

For example, Almon's model of capital expenditures (1965) formalized the generally accepted notion that investment takes time and planning: many current capital expenditures are planned months or even years in advance, funds are allocated, and then the investment in new capital assets occurs.

The regression model supported by the SAS/ETS PDLREG procedure can include any number of regressors with distributed lags and any number of simple regressors without distributed lags (covariates). A simple model is as follows:

$$y_t = \alpha + \sum_{i=0}^{p} \beta_i x_{t-i} + \gamma z_t + u_t$$

The distribution of the lagged effects is modeled by Almon lag polynomials (1965). The coefficients b_i of the lagged values of the regressor are assumed to lie on a polynomial curve of degree $d(\leq p)$.

$$b_i = \alpha_0^* + \sum_{j=0}^{d} \alpha_j^* i^j$$

For numerically efficient estimation, Emerson (1968) suggests a method of constructing orthogonal polynomials. The preceding equation is transformed as follows with $f_j(i)$ as a polynomial of degree j in the lag length i, and α_j as a coefficient estimated from the data:

$$b_i = \alpha_0 + \sum_{j=0}^{d} \alpha_j f_j(i)$$

For computational details of constructing orthogonal polynomials, see the *SAS/ETS User's Guide, Version 6, Second Edition*, pp. 710-711.

To fit a PDL model, you need to specify the length of the lag and the degree of polynomial for the lag. The theory underlying the model and the data may suggest the appropriate length of lag and the appropriate degree for the polynomial.

A general approach to fitting polynomial lag models is to initially estimate a polynomial lag of a high degree and then to examine the *t*-statistic of the highest degree. If the highest degree is not significantly different from 0 (at the specified level of significance), refit the model with a polynomial of 1 less degree. Continue fitting with lower degree polynomials until the highest degree is significantly different from 0.

If theory offers no range of lag lengths, Maddala (1977) suggests fitting different lag lengths and choosing the optimal length based on either the adjusted R^2 or a minimum standard error criterion.

Be aware that by specifying a PDL model, the effect of the regressor variable is distributed over the given range. Even if the correct model is no lag, there will be the impression of a lag.

Program

Estimating the PDL Model

Create the ALMON data set. The complete ALMON data set is found in "Introduction: The Example Data Sets."

The Almon data contain quarterly values of capital expenditures (Y) and appropriations (X) for the U.S. for the period First Quarter 1953 to Fourth Quarter 1966. Values for expenditures in 1967 are missing, but can be forecasted using the estimated model and the input values for appropriations.

```
data almon;
   input y x @@;
   retain date '1oct52'd;
   date=intnx('qtr',date,1);
   format date yyq.;
   qtr = mod( _n_-1, 4 ) + 1;
   q1  = qtr=1;
   q2  = qtr=2;
   q3  = qtr=3;
   label y='Capital Expenditures'
         x='Appropriations';
   title 'National Industrial Conference Board Data';
datalines;
2071 1660   2077 1926   2078 2181   2043 1897   2062 1695
2067 1705   1964 1731   1981 2151   1914 2556   1991 3152
2129 3763   2309 3903   2614 3912   2896 3571   3058 3199
more data lines
;
```

Fit the PDL model using PROC PDLREG.

Use a MODEL statement to specify the model. The PDL lag for the variable X is defined by the three arguments P, D, and Q, which are the number of lags (the lag length) and the maximum and minimum degrees of the lag polynomial, respectively.

```
proc pdlreg data=almon;

   model y=q1 q2 q3 x(9,3,2) /* Specifies the PDL Model: 9 Lags,
                                Maximum Degree 3, Minimum Degree 2 */
         / dw=4             /* Prints Durbin Watson d Statistics  */
           dwprob           /* Prints Durbin Watson p Values      */
           nlag=2;          /* Specifies AR(2) Error Correction   */
run;
```

Output 19.1
OLS Estimates of PDL Models (Partial Output)

```
                    National Industrial Conference Board Data

                                PDLREG Procedure

Dependent Variable = Y          Capital Expenditures

                          Ordinary Least Squares Estimates

          ❶ SSE          612503.6    DFE              39
            MSE          15705.22    Root MSE   125.3205
            SBC           609.514    AIC        594.7129
            Reg Rsq        0.9860    Total Rsq    0.9860

                      ❷ Durbin-Watson Statistics

                          Order       DW      PROB<DW
                            1       0.4023     0.0001
                            2       0.9840     0.0001
                            3       1.4174     0.0509
                            4       1.7283     0.1608
```

```
                    National Industrial Conference Board Data

                                PDLREG Procedure

        Variable     DF       B Value   Std Error   t Ratio Approx Prob
           ❸
        Intercept     1    -39.071606     82.2778    -0.475      0.6375
        Q1            1      8.364166     52.4057     0.160      0.8740
        Q2            1    -16.913521     51.4664    -0.329      0.7442
        Q3            1     -7.532690     51.2336    -0.147      0.8839
        X**0          1      0.319291     0.00792    40.306      0.0001
        X**1          1     -0.092306      0.0161    -5.717      0.0001
        X**2          1     -0.094944      0.0259    -3.667      0.0007
        X**3          1      0.050785      0.0456     1.115      0.2718
```

```
                    National Industrial Conference Board Data

                                PDLREG Procedure

                   Parameter       Std       t    Approx
        Variable       Value     Error   Ratio      Prob
           ❹
        X(0)         0.07409     0.027    2.74    0.0093
        X(1)         0.12769     0.008   15.78    0.0001
        X(2)         0.15383     0.016    9.72    0.0001
        X(3)         0.15800     0.015   10.31    0.0001
        X(4)         0.14568     0.010   14.63    0.0001
        X(5)         0.12236     0.010   11.67    0.0001
        X(6)         0.09352     0.016    5.86    0.0001
        X(7)         0.06464     0.016    4.00    0.0003
        X(8)         0.04120     0.010    4.18    0.0002
        X(9)         0.02868     0.031    0.92    0.3609
```

```
                National Industrial Conference Board Data

                            PDLREG Procedure

                      Estimate of Lag Distribution
Variable       0                                   0.158
   ❺
X(0)           |*******************                      |
X(1)           |*********************************        |
X(2)           |****************************************  |
X(3)           |*****************************************|
X(4)           |**************************************   |
X(5)           |********************************         |
X(6)           |************************                 |
X(7)           |*****************                        |
X(8)           |***********                              |
X(9)           |*******                                  |
```

```
                National Industrial Conference Board Data

                            PDLREG Procedure

                  ❻ Ordinary Least Squares Estimates

          SSE          632021.1    DFE              40
          MSE          15800.53    Root MSE   125.7001
          SBC          610.9883    AIC        596.1872
          Reg Rsq        0.9856    Total Rsq    0.9856

Variable       DF        B Value    Std Error   t Ratio Approx Prob

Intercept       1     -33.332595      82.3654    -0.405      0.6879
Q1              1       8.136737      52.5641     0.155      0.8778
Q2              1     -21.582827      51.4511    -0.419      0.6771
Q3              1      -9.664213      51.3530    -0.188      0.8517
X**0            1       0.318467      0.00791    40.257      0.0001
X**1            1      -0.100345       0.0145    -6.926      0.0001
X**2            1      -0.097392       0.0259    -3.764      0.0005
X**3            0              0            .         .           .
```

```
                National Industrial Conference Board Data

                            PDLREG Procedure

             Parameter       Std        t    Approx
Variable         Value     Error    Ratio      Prob

X(0)           0.09956     0.015     6.82    0.0001
X(1)           0.12242     0.007    18.58    0.0001
X(2)           0.13680     0.004    32.78    0.0001
X(3)           0.14271     0.007    20.80    0.0001
X(4)           0.14014     0.009    16.19    0.0001
X(5)           0.12909     0.009    15.00    0.0001
X(6)           0.10957     0.007    15.83    0.0001
X(7)           0.08157     0.006    14.82    0.0001
X(8)           0.04509     0.009     4.87    0.0001
X(9)           0.00013     0.018     0.01    0.9940
```

```
                     National Industrial Conference Board Data

                                 PDLREG Procedure

                             Estimate of Lag Distribution
        Variable       0                                        0.1427

        X(0)           |******************************             |
        X(1)           |*************************************      |
        X(2)           |*****************************************  |
        X(3)           |*******************************************|
        X(4)           |****************************************** |
        X(5)           |***************************************    |
        X(6)           |*********************************          |
        X(7)           |************************                   |
        X(8)           |**************                             |
        X(9)           |                                           |
```

Explanation

❶ Ordinary least squares (OLS) goodness-of-fit statistics for the cubic PDL lag model are listed.

❷ The generalized Durbin-Watson statistics and *p*-values for this model indicate positive autocorrelation of the OLS residuals.

❸ The parameter estimates for the structural model, standard error estimates, *t*-statistics, and approximate *p*-values for the null hypothesis that the parameter is equal to 0 are listed. For this model, the parameter estimates for the intercept, the dummy variables Q1, Q2, Q3, and the cubic term are not significantly different from 0 at the .05 level. A quadratic polynomial lag may be appropriate for these data.

❹ The parameter estimates for the lag coefficients, standard error estimates, *t*-statistics, and approximate *p*-values for the null hypothesis that the estimated parameter is equal to 0 are listed. For this model, all of the lag coefficients except the ninth are significantly different from 0 at the .05 level. An eight-period lag may be appropriate for these data.

❺ The plot of the lag distribution indicates that the lags appear to follow a quadratic polynomial function.

❻ Ordinary least squares estimates for the quadratic PDL lag model are listed.

Estimation with Correction for Autocorrelation

Output 19.2
Yule-Walker Estimates of PDL Models with AR(2) Correction (Partial Output from PROC PDLREG)

```
                    National Industrial Conference Board Data

                               PDLREG Procedure

                      ❶ Estimates of Autocorrelations

Lag  Covariance  Correlation -1 9 8 7 6 5 4 3 2 1 0 1 2 3 4 5 6 7 8 9 1

  0    13031.99     1.000000 |                    |********************|
  1    10406.41     0.798528 |                    |****************    |
  2    6447.545     0.494747 |                    |**********          |

                        Preliminary MSE = 3987.759

                Estimates of the Autoregressive Parameters

                Lag    Coefficient       Std Error          t Ratio
                  1    -1.11344145        0.151075           -7.370
                  2     0.39436701        0.151075            2.610
```

```
                    National Industrial Conference Board Data

                               PDLREG Procedure

                             Yule-Walker Estimates

                SSE            182785.1    DFE               37
                MSE            4940.137    Root MSE    70.28611
                SBC            561.7331    AIC         543.2316
                Reg Rsq          0.9595    Total Rsq     0.9958

    Variable      DF        B Value    Std Error   t Ratio Approx Prob
       ❷
    Intercept      1     -42.303940        131.1    -0.323      0.7487
    Q1             1       8.487712      18.6175     0.456      0.6511
    Q2             1     -16.803911      23.4092    -0.718      0.4774
    Q3             1      -7.388083      18.2045    -0.406      0.6872
    X**0           1       0.320937       0.0135    23.727      0.0001
    X**1           1      -0.078128       0.0259    -3.014      0.0046
    X**2           1      -0.092115       0.0364    -2.533      0.0157
    X**3           1       0.074824       0.0376     1.992      0.0538
```

```
                National Industrial Conference Board Data

                            PDLREG Procedure

                 Parameter      Std       t    Approx
Variable             Value    Error   Ratio      Prob
   ❸
X(0)               0.05816    0.026    2.21    0.0333
X(1)               0.12687    0.012   10.35    0.0001
X(2)               0.15928    0.015   10.48    0.0001
X(3)               0.16349    0.015   10.95    0.0001
X(4)               0.14755    0.013   11.67    0.0001
X(5)               0.11957    0.014    8.55    0.0001
X(6)               0.08760    0.017    5.02    0.0001
X(7)               0.05973    0.018    3.39    0.0017
X(8)               0.04404    0.016    2.76    0.0088
X(9)               0.04860    0.033    1.49    0.1457
```

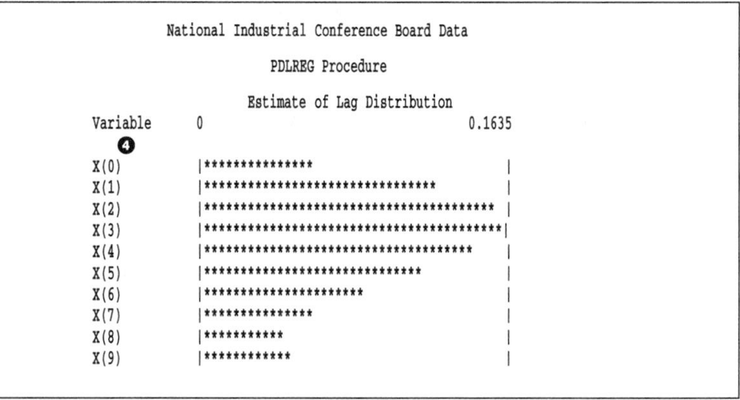

```
               National Industrial Conference Board Data

                           PDLREG Procedure

                      Estimate of Lag Distribution
Variable      0                                          0.1635
   ❹
X(0)          |****************                          |
X(1)          |*********************************         |
X(2)          |*****************************************  |
X(3)          |******************************************|
X(4)          |**************************************    |
X(5)          |*******************************           |
X(6)          |***********************                   |
X(7)          |****************                          |
X(8)          |************                              |
X(9)          |*************                             |
```

```
               National Industrial Conference Board Data

                           PDLREG Procedure

                       ❺ Yule-Walker Estimates

          SSE             202381    DFE              38
          MSE           5325.815    Root MSE   72.97818
          SBC           566.5196    AIC        548.0181
          Reg Rsq         0.9552    Total Rsq    0.9954

Variable     DF        B Value   Std Error   t Ratio Approx Prob

Intercept     1     -62.802148       135.7    -0.463      0.6461
Q1            1       9.925574     19.3160     0.514      0.6103
Q2            1     -19.141870     24.2752    -0.789      0.4353
Q3            1      -8.184849     18.8972    -0.433      0.6674
X**0          1       0.323265      0.0140    23.103      0.0001
X**1          1      -0.078895      0.0269    -2.931      0.0057
X**2          1      -0.100803      0.0375    -2.689      0.0106
X**3          0              0           .         .           .
```

```
                    National Industrial Conference Board Data

                                PDLREG Procedure

                   Parameter       Std        t    Approx
Variable               Value     Error    Ratio      Prob

X(0)                 0.08867     0.022     3.99    0.0003
X(1)                 0.11508     0.011    10.32    0.0001
X(2)                 0.13271     0.008    17.52    0.0001
X(3)                 0.14158     0.010    13.51    0.0001
X(4)                 0.14166     0.013    11.10    0.0001
X(5)                 0.13298     0.013    10.46    0.0001
X(6)                 0.11552     0.011    10.74    0.0001
X(7)                 0.08928     0.010     9.02    0.0001
X(8)                 0.05428     0.016     3.47    0.0013
X(9)                 0.01049     0.028     0.38    0.7052
```

```
                   National Industrial Conference Board Data

                               PDLREG Procedure

                         Estimate of Lag Distribution
Variable       0                                              0.1417

X(0)           |**************************                         |
X(1)           |*********************************                  |
X(2)           |**************************************             |
X(3)           |******************************************|
X(4)           |******************************************|
X(5)           |**************************************             |
X(6)           |*********************************                  |
X(7)           |**************************                         |
X(8)           |****************                                   |
X(9)           |***                                                |
```

Explanation

❶ Estimates of autocorrelations and autocovariance, the preliminary mean square (which results from solving the Yule-Walker equations), the estimates of the autoregressive parameters, their standard errors, and the *t*-ratios are listed.

❷ The parameter estimates for the structural model, standard error estimates, *t*-statistics, and approximate *p*-values for the null hypothesis that the parameter is equal to 0 are listed. For this model, the parameter estimates for the intercept, the dummy variables Q1, Q2, Q3, are not significantly different from 0 at the .05 level.

❸ The parameter estimates for the lag coefficients, standard error estimates, *t*-statistics, and approximate *p*-values for the null hypothesis that the estimated parameter is equal to 0 are listed. For this model, all of the lag coefficients except the ninth are significantly different from 0 at the .05 level.

❹ The plot of the lag distribution indicates that the lags appear to follow a quadratic polynomial function.

❺ Yule-Walker estimates for the quadratic PDL lag model are listed.

Forecasting the Model

Forecast the PDL model using PROC PDLREG. The NOPRINT option suppresses the printed output.

Use an OUTPUT statement to output the predicted values, residual values, and upper and lower confidence limits.

```
proc pdlreg data=almon noprint;
   model y=x(8,2)          /* Specifies the PDL Model               */
         / nlag=2;         /* Specifies AR(2) Error Correction      */
   output out=pdl_out1     /* Names the Output Data Set             */
          predicted=p      /* Outputs Predicted Values              */
          residual=r       /* Outputs Residual Values               */
          lcl=l            /* Outputs Lower 95% Confidence Limit */
          ucl=u;           /* Outputs Upper 95% Confidence Limit */
run;
```

Print the forecasts using PROC PRINT and a WHERE statement. The NOOBS option suppresses the printing of the observation number.

```
proc print data=pdl_out1 noobs;
   where date > '01dec65'd;
   var date u p y l r;
   title2 'PDL Model Forecasts';
run;
```

Output 19.3
Printing PDL Model Forecasts and Confidence Limits

National Industrial Conference Board Data
PDL Model Forecasts

DATE	U	P	Y	L	R
66Q1	5300.26	5085.85	5160	4871.43	74.154
66Q2	5661.63	5431.73	5319	5201.83	-112.732
66Q3	5725.18	5496.80	5574	5268.43	77.196
66Q4	5989.48	5754.21	5749	5518.94	-5.210
67Q1	6127.17	5833.48	.	5539.78	.
67Q2	6162.83	5837.25	.	5511.67	.
67Q3	6139.41	5798.49	.	5457.58	.
67Q4	6078.27	5722.08	.	5365.89	.

Explanation

The following variables are listed in Output 19.3:

DATE	is the date variable.
U and L	are the upper and lower 95% confidence limits.
P and Y	are the predicted and actual values.
R	are the residual values.

Variation

Estimating and Forecasting a PDL Model Using PROC MODEL

Fit and forecast the PDL model using the %PDL macro in PROC MODEL.

```
proc model data=almon;
   parms intercpt a1 a2 a3;  /* Specify the Model Parameters    */
   %pdl (xpdl,9,2)           /* Specify a Quadratic, 9 Lag PDL */

     /* Specify the Model to Estimate  */
   y = intercpt + a1*q1 + a2*q2 + a3*q3 + %pdl (xpdl,x);
```

Use a FIT statement to estimate the PDL model.

Use a SOLVE statement to simulate or forecast the estimated model.

```
   fit y;                    /* Fit (Estimate) the Model        */
   id date;                  /* Specify an ID Variable          */
   solve y                   /* Solve the Estimated Model       */
       / forecast            /* Specifies Forecast Solutions    */
         out=pdl_out2        /* Names the Output Data Set       */
         outpredict;         /* Outputs the Predicted Values    */
   title2;                   /* Resets the Program Title2       */
run;
quit;
```

Print the forecasts using PROC PRINT.

```
proc print data=pdl_out2 noobs;
   where date > '01dec65'd;
run;
```

Output 19.4
Model Summary and Parameter Estimates

```
            National Industrial Conference Board Data

                        MODEL Procedure

                      ❶ Model Summary

                    Model Variables        1
                    Parameters             7
                    ID Variables           1
                    Equations              1

                    Number of Statements  22

                    Program Lag Length     9

     Model Variables: Y

     Parameters: INTERCPT A1 A2 A3 XPDL_0 XPDL_1 XPDL_2

     Equations: Y
```

```
           National Industrial Conference Board Data

                        MODEL Procedure

               ❷ The Equation to Estimate is:

     Y = F( INTERCPT(1), A1(Q1), A2(Q2), A3(Q3), XPDL_0, XPDL_1,
            XPDL_2 )

               The estimation lag length is 9.
```

```
           National Industrial Conference Board Data

                        MODEL Procedure
                         OLS Estimation

                  ❸ OLS Estimation Summary

                   Dataset Option      Dataset
                   DATA=                 ALMON

                   Parameters Estimated      7

                      Minimization Summary
                   Method                GAUSS
                   Iterations                1

                   Final  Convergence  Criteria
                   R                         0
                   PPC                2.47E-12
                   RPC(INTERCPT)      330026.7
                   Object           0.99863252
                   Trace(S)         15800.5264
```

```
               National Industrial Conference Board Data

                          MODEL Procedure
                           OLS Estimation

                ❹ Objective Value   13447.2565

                       Observations Processed
                    Read                      60
                    Solved                    51
                     First                    10
                     Last                     60
                    Used                      47
                    Missing                    4
                    Lagged                     9
```

```
               National Industrial Conference Board Data

                          MODEL Procedure
                           OLS Estimation

          ❺ Nonlinear OLS Summary of Residual Errors

              DF    DF
Equation Model Error       SSE        MSE  Root MSE R-Square Adj R-Sq

Y            7    40    632021  15800.53    125.70   0.9856   0.9834
```

```
               National Industrial Conference Board Data

                          MODEL Procedure
                           OLS Estimation

             ❻ Nonlinear OLS Parameter Estimates

                                  Approx.       'T'   Approx.
        Parameter    Estimate     Std Err     Ratio  Prob>|T|

        INTERCPT   -33.332595    82.36539     -0.40    0.6879
        A1           8.136737    52.56411      0.15    0.8778
        A2         -21.582827    51.45110     -0.42    0.6771
        A3          -9.664213    51.35301     -0.19    0.8517
        XPDL_0       0.099561     0.01459      6.82    0.0001
        XPDL_1       0.027098     0.01000      2.71    0.0099
        XPDL_2    -0.00423842   0.0011260     -3.76    0.0005
```

```
                National Industrial Conference Board Data

                            MODEL Procedure
                            OLS Estimation

                                   Approx.       'T'    Approx.
Term          Estimate             Std Err      Ratio   Prob>|T|
 ❼
XPDL_L0       0.099561             0.01459       6.82     0.0001
XPDL_L1       0.122421           0.0065876      18.58     0.0001
XPDL_L2       0.136804           0.0041728      32.78     0.0001
XPDL_L3       0.142710           0.0068599      20.80     0.0001
XPDL_L4       0.140139           0.0086562      16.19     0.0001
XPDL_L5       0.129092           0.0086054      15.00     0.0001
XPDL_L6       0.109567           0.0069193      15.83     0.0001
XPDL_L7       0.081566           0.0055030      14.82     0.0001
XPDL_L8       0.045088           0.0092508       4.87     0.0001
XPDL_L9     0.00013263             0.01756       0.01     0.9940
```

```
                National Industrial Conference Board Data

                            MODEL Procedure
                    Dynamic Single-Equation Forecast

                       ❽ Solution Summary

                    Dataset Option        Dataset
                    DATA=                   ALMON
                    OUT=                 PDL_OUT2

                    Variables Solved            1

                    Forecast Lag Length         9

                    Solution Method        NEWTON
                    CONVERGE=                1E-8
                    Maximum CC                  0
                    Maximum Iterations          1
                    Total Iterations           51
                    Average Iterations          1

                       Observations Processed
                    Read                       60
                    Lagged                      9
                    Solved                     51
                     First                     10
                     Last                      60

                    Variables Solved For: Y
```

Explanation

❶ **`Model Summary`** lists the model variables, parameters estimated, ID variables, equations, and the program lag length.

❷ **`The Equation to Estimate is:`** shows the dependent variable Y as a linear function of the parameters and variables.

❸ **`OLS Estimation Summary`** lists the data set options specified, the number of parameters estimated, and the convergence criteria. The convergence criteria of PROC MODEL are described in Example 25, "Linear System Diagnostics and Autoregressive Error Correction."

❹ `Objective Value` lists the objective function value and summarizes the processing of observations: observations read, the first observation solved, the last observation solved, and the number of observations used, missing and lagged.

❺ `Nonlinear OLS Summary of Residual Errors` lists the model and error degrees of freedom, `SSE` (sum of squared errors), `MSE` (mean square error), `Root MSE` (root mean square error), `R-Square`, and `Adj R-SQ` (adjusted R-Square).

❻ `Nonlinear OLS Parameter Estimates` lists the parameter estimates for the structural model, approximate standard error estimates, *t*-statistics, and approximate *p*-values for the null hypothesis that the parameter is equal to 0. For this quadratic PDL model, the parameter estimates for the intercept, the dummy variables Q1, Q2, Q3, are not significantly different from 0 at the .05 level.

The estimated parameter values of the intercept, A1, A2, and A3, match the parameter estimates of Output 19.1, while those of the polynomial distributed lag do not. This is because PROC PDLREG uses an orthogonal reparameterization of the polynomial distributed lag parameters, and PROC MODEL does not.

❼ The parameter estimates for the lag coefficients, standard error estimates, *t*-statistics, and approximate *p*-values for the null hypothesis that the estimated parameter is equal to 0 are listed. These parameter estimates match those of Output 19.1.

❽ `Solution Summary` lists the data set options, the variables solved for, the forecast lag length, the solution method, and a summary of the observations processed.

Printing the Forecasts

Output 19.5
Contents of PDL_OUT2 Data Set: Forecasts and Actual Values

National Industrial Conference Board Data

DATE	_TYPE_	_MODE_	_LAG_	_ERRORS_	Y	Q1	Q2	Q3	X
66Q1	PREDICT	FORECAST	43	0	5160.00	1	0	0	6109
66Q2	PREDICT	FORECAST	44	0	5319.00	0	1	0	6542
66Q3	PREDICT	FORECAST	45	0	5574.00	0	0	1	5785
66Q4	PREDICT	FORECAST	46	0	5749.00	0	0	0	5707
67Q1	PREDICT	FORECAST	47	0	5807.76	1	0	0	5412
67Q2	PREDICT	FORECAST	48	0	5795.85	0	1	0	5465
67Q3	PREDICT	FORECAST	49	0	5785.80	0	0	1	5550
67Q4	PREDICT	FORECAST	50	0	5739.06	0	0	0	5465

Explanation

The following variables are listed in Output 19.5:

DATE	is the date variable.
TYPE	is a character variable identifying the type of observation (PREDICT, RESIDUAL, ACTUAL, or ERROR).
MODE	is a character variable identifying the solution _MODE_ (FORECAST or SIMULATE).
LAG	is a numeric variable containing the number of dynamic lags that contribute to the solution. The value of _LAG_ is always set to 0 for STATIC mode solutions.
ERRORS	is a numeric variable containing the number of errors that occurred during the execution of the program for the last iteration for the observation. Zero (0) indicates no error, while -1 indicates an error occurred in the solution process.
Y	is the forecast value. The values for 66Q1 through 66Q4 are the actual values while the values for 67Q1 through 67Q4 are forecasts. When you specify the FORECAST option, the actual value of the variable is used as the solution value whenever nonmissing data are available in the input data set. Thus, in FORECAST mode, PROC MODEL solves only for those variables that are missing in the input data set.
Q1, Q2, Q3	are the values of the quarterly dummy variables.
X	is the value of the variable X, which is the quarterly capital appropriation.

Further Reading

- □ For more information on PROC PDLREG, see the *SAS/ETS User's Guide, Version 6, Second Edition.*
- □ For more information on PROC MODEL, see the *SAS/ETS User's Guide, Version 6, Second Edition*, and *SAS/ETS Software: Changes and Enhancements, Release 6.11.*

References

- Almon, S. (1965), "The Distributed Lag between Capital Appropriations and Expenditures," *Econometrica*, 33, 178-196.
- Emerson, P.L. (1968), "Numerical Construction of Orthogonal Polynomials from a General Recurrence Formula," *Biometrics*, 24, 695-701.
- Maddala, G.S. (1977), *Econometrics*, New York: McGraw-Hill.

EXAMPLE 20

Fitting and Forecasting Restricted Polynomial Distributed Lag Models

Featured Tools:

- □ PDLREG procedure
  - MODEL statement
  - RESTRICT statement
- □ MODEL procedure
  - FIT statement
  - PDL macro
  - RESTRICT statement
  - SOLVE statement

The regression model supported by the SAS/ETS PDLREG procedure can include any number of regressors with distributed lags and any number of simple regressors without distributed lags (covariates). A simple model is as follows:

$$y_t = \alpha + \sum_{i=0}^{p} \beta_i x_{t-i} + \gamma z_t + u_t$$

The distribution of the lagged effects is modeled by Almon lag polynomials (1965). The coefficients b_i of the lagged values of the regressor are assumed to lie on a polynomial curve of degree $d(\leq p)$.

$$b_i = \alpha_0^* + \sum_{j=0}^{d} \alpha_j^* i^j$$

For numerically efficient estimation, Emerson (1968) suggests a method of constructing orthogonal polynomials. The preceding equation is transformed as follows with $f_j(i)$ as a polynomial of degree j in the lag length i, and α_j as a coefficient estimated from the data:

$$b_i = \alpha_0 + \sum_{j=0}^{d} \alpha_j f_j(i)$$

In PROC PDLREG, polynomial distributed lag (PDL) regression models can be restricted as follows:

- □ restricting the intercept parameter or slope parameters of covariate regressors with a RESTRICT statement.
- □ restricting the PDL endpoints in the MODEL statement.

Program

Estimating Restricted PDL Models

Create the ALMON data set. The complete ALMON data set is found in "Introduction: The Example Data Sets."

```
data almon;
   input y x @@;
   retain date '1oct52'd;
   date=intnx('qtr',date,1);
   format date yyq.;
   qtr = mod( _n_-1, 4 ) + 1;
   q1  = qtr=1;
   q2  = qtr=2;
   q3  = qtr=3;
   label y='Capital Expenditures'
         x='Appropriations';
   title 'National Industrial Conference Board Data';
datalines;
2071 1660   2077 1926   2078 2181   2043 1897   2062 1695
2067 1705   1964 1731   1981 2151   1914 2556   1991 3152
2129 3763   2309 3903   2614 3912   2896 3571   3058 3199
more data lines
;
```

Fit restricted PDL models using PROC PDLREG.

```
proc pdlreg data=almon;
```

Use a RESTRICT statement to restrict the estimated intercept parameter or the slope parameters of covariate regressors or both. The appropriate RESTRICT statement follows the MODEL statement that specifies the model to be restricted.

Use a MODEL statement to specify the model. The unrestricted PDL lag for the variable X is defined by the three arguments P, D, and Q, which are the number of lags (the lag length) and the maximum and minimum degrees of the lag polynomial, respectively. The optional endpoint restriction can have values FIRST ($b_{-1} = 0$), LAST ($b_{p+1} = 0$), or BOTH.

```
     /* Restrict Covariate Regressor Parameters */
  model y=q1 q2 q3 x(8,2) /* Specifies the PDL Model: 8 Lags,
                             Maximum Degree 2, Minimum Degree 2 */
        / nlag=2;         /* Specifies AR(2) Error Correction   */
  restrict q1=q2=q3=0;    /* Restrict Slope Parameters to Zero  */
  output out=pdl_out3     /* Names the Output Data Set          */
        p=p               /* Outputs Predicted Values           */
        r=r               /* Outputs Residual Values            */
        lcl=l             /* Outputs Lower 95% Confidence Limit */
        ucl=u;            /* Outputs Upper 95% Confidence Limit */

     /* Restrict PDL Endpoints */
  model y=x(8,2,2,both)   /* Specifies the PDL Model: 8 Lags,
                             Maximum Degree 2, Minimum Degree 2
                             Both PDL Endpoints Restricted to 0 */
        / nlag=2;         /* Specifies AR(2) Error Correction   */
  output out=pdl_out4     /* Names the Output Data Set          */
        p=p               /* Outputs Predicted Values           */
        r=r               /* Outputs Residual Values            */
        lcl=l             /* Outputs Lower 95% Confidence Limit */
        ucl=u;            /* Outputs Upper 95% Confidence Limit */
run;
```

Print the forecasts using PROC PRINT and a WHERE statement. The NOOBS option suppresses the printing of the observation number.

```
proc print data=pdl_out3 noobs;
  where date > '01dec65'd;
  var date u p y l r;
  title2 'Forecasts of PDL Model';
  title3 'Slope Parameter Restrictions';
run;

proc print data=pdl_out4 noobs;
  where date > '01dec65'd;
  var date u p y l r;
  title3 'PDL Endpoint Restrictions';
run;
```

Output 20.1
Autocorrelation Estimates and Yule-Walker Parameter Estimates for the Restricted PDL Models. (Partial Output)

```
                National Industrial Conference Board Data

                            PDLREG Procedure

                   ❶ Estimates of Autocorrelations

Lag  Covariance  Correlation -1 9 8 7 6 5 4 3 2 1 0 1 2 3 4 5 6 7 8 9 1

  0    13265.21     1.000000 |                    |********************|
  1    10357.45     0.780798 |                    |****************    |
  2     6353.82     0.478984 |                    |**********          |

                       Preliminary MSE =  4597.96

                Estimates of the Autoregressive Parameters

                 Lag    Coefficient       Std Error        t Ratio
                   1    -1.04215227        0.145402         -7.167
                   2     0.33472674        0.145402          2.302
```

```
                National Industrial Conference Board Data

                            PDLREG Procedure

                          Yule-Walker Estimates

            ❷ SSE            214835.3    DFE                42
              MSE            5115.126    Root MSE     71.52011
              SBC            564.1321    AIC          552.9049
              Reg Rsq          0.9584    Total Rsq      0.9952
              Durbin-Watson    1.9528
```

```
                National Industrial Conference Board Data

                            PDLREG Procedure

         Variable      DF         B Value   Std Error   t Ratio Approx Prob
           ❸
         Intercept      1       -8.841145       117.8    -0.075      0.9405
         Q1             1   1.776357E-15           .         .           .
         Q2             1   2.664535E-15           .         .           .
         Q3             1               0           .         .           .
         X**0           1        0.332996      0.0128    25.959      0.0001
         X**1           1       -0.048148      0.0263    -1.828      0.0746
         X**2           1       -0.107615      0.0342    -3.144      0.0031

         Restriction   DF         L Value   Std Error   t Ratio Approx Prob

         RESTRICT      -1      480.739770       354.8     1.355      0.1784
         RESTRICT      -1      -32.415799       299.6    -0.108      0.9154
         RESTRICT      -1      147.390119       355.1     0.415      0.6833
```

```
                 National Industrial Conference Board Data

                            PDLREG Procedure

                   Parameter      Std        t    Approx
        Variable       Value    Error    Ratio      Prob
           ❹
        X(0)         0.07863    0.021     3.66    0.0007
        X(1)         0.11534    0.010    11.23    0.0001
        X(2)         0.13978    0.008    17.27    0.0001
        X(3)         0.15196    0.011    13.64    0.0001
        X(4)         0.15188    0.012    12.18    0.0001
        X(5)         0.13953    0.011    12.44    0.0001
        X(6)         0.11492    0.010    11.97    0.0001
        X(7)         0.07804    0.014     5.48    0.0001
        X(8)         0.02890    0.026     1.09    0.2802
```

```
                 National Industrial Conference Board Data

                            PDLREG Procedure

                        Estimate of Lag Distribution
        Variable      0                                        0.152
           ❺
        X(0)          |*********************                   |
        X(1)          |******************************          |
        X(2)          |*************************************   |
        X(3)          |****************************************|
        X(4)          |****************************************|
        X(5)          |*************************************   |
        X(6)          |******************************          |
        X(7)          |*********************                   |
        X(8)          |********                                |
```

```
                 National Industrial Conference Board Data

                            PDLREG Procedure

                      ❻ Estimates of Autocorrelations

     Lag  Covariance  Correlation -1 9 8 7 6 5 4 3 2 1 0 1 2 3 4 5 6 7 8 9 1

      0    17989.24     1.000000 |                    |********************|
      1    14774.04     0.821271 |                    |****************    |
      2     9592.99     0.533263 |                    |***********         |

                       Preliminary MSE = 4753.568

               Estimates of the Autoregressive Parameters

                 Lag    Coefficient       Std Error        t Ratio
                   1    -1.17757638        0.135829         -8.670
                   2     0.43384659        0.135829          3.194
```

```
                National Industrial Conference Board Data

                            PDLREG Procedure

                      ❼ Yule-Walker Estimates

            SSE             226819.7     DFE                44
            MSE             5154.993     Root MSE     71.79828
            SBC             559.3564     AIC          551.8716
            Reg Rsq           0.9420     Total Rsq      0.9950
            Durbin-Watson     2.0655
```

```
                National Industrial Conference Board Data

                            PDLREG Procedure

 Variable     DF        B Value    Std Error    t Ratio Approx Prob
     ❽
 Intercept     1     -52.107058        124.4     -0.419      0.6774
 X**0          1       0.341002       0.0128     26.739      0.0001
 X**1          1   -4.16334E-17            .          .           .
 X**2          1      -0.108810      0.00407    -26.739      0.0001

 Restriction  DF        L Value    Std Error    t Ratio Approx Prob

 X(-1)        -1         187785       159588      1.177      0.2437
 X(9)         -1        -184549       136433     -1.353      0.1791
```

```
                National Industrial Conference Board Data

                            PDLREG Procedure

               Parameter       Std        t     Approx
 Variable          Value     Error    Ratio       Prob

 X(0)            0.05580    0.0021    26.74     0.0001
 X(1)            0.09920    0.0037    26.74     0.0001
 X(2)            0.13020    0.0049    26.74     0.0001
 X(3)            0.14880    0.0056    26.74     0.0001
 X(4)            0.15500    0.0058    26.74     0.0001
 X(5)            0.14880    0.0056    26.74     0.0001
 X(6)            0.13020    0.0049    26.74     0.0001
 X(7)            0.09920    0.0037    26.74     0.0001
 X(8)            0.05580    0.0021    26.74     0.0001
```

```
                 National Industrial Conference Board Data

                            PDLREG Procedure

                      Estimate of Lag Distribution
Variable       0                                           0.155

X(0)           |****************                              |
X(1)           |***************************                   |
X(2)           |***********************************           |
X(3)           |*****************************************     |
X(4)           |*******************************************   |
X(5)           |*****************************************     |
X(6)           |***********************************           |
X(7)           |***************************                   |
X(8)           |****************                              |
```

Explanation

In Output 20.1, the estimation results of the PDL model with restricted covariate regressor parameter estimates are presented first, and the estimation results of the PDL model with restricted PDL endpoints are presented second.

❶ Estimates of autocorrelations and autocovariance, the preliminary mean square (which results from solving the Yule-Walker equations), the estimates of the autoregressive parameters, their standard errors, and the *t*-ratios are listed.

❷ The statistics of fit of the PDL model with restricted covariate regressor parameter estimates are listed.

❸ The parameter estimates for the structural model, standard error estimates, *t*-statistics, and approximate *p*-values are listed.

Restricted parameter estimates are computed by introducing a Lagrange parameter λ for each restriction (Pringle and Raynor 1971). The estimates of the Lagrange parameters are printed in the parameter estimates table.

The Lagrange parameter λ measures the sensitivity of the SSE to the restriction. If the restriction is changed by a small amount ϵ, the SSE is changed by $2\lambda\epsilon$.

The *t*-ratio tests the significance of the restrictions. For this model, the high *p*-values of the *t*-ratio tests indicate that the restrictions are not statistically significant at the .05 level.

Note that estimated slope parameters can also be restricted to 0 by excluding the associated variable from the model specification.

❹ The parameter estimates for the lag coefficients, standard error estimates, *t*-statistics, and approximate *p*-values are listed.

❺ The plot of the lag distribution indicates that the lags appear to follow a quadratic function.

❻ Estimates of autocorrelations and autocovariance for the endpoint restricted PDL model are listed.

❼ Yule-Walker estimates for the endpoint restricted PDL model are listed.

❽ The parameter estimates for the structural model, standard error estimates, *t*-statistics, and approximate *p*-values are listed.

For this model, the high *p*-values of the *t*-ratio tests indicate that the restrictions are not statistically significant at the .05 level. You conclude that the data are consistent with these endpoint restrictions.

Printing the Forecasts

Output 20.2
Printing the Restricted PDL Model Forecasts and Confidence Limits

National Industrial Conference Board Data
Forecasts of PDL Model
Slope Parameter Restrictions

DATE	U	P	Y	L	R
66Q1	5300.26	5085.85	5160	4871.43	74.154
66Q2	5661.63	5431.73	5319	5201.83	-112.732
66Q3	5725.18	5496.80	5574	5268.43	77.196
66Q4	5989.48	5754.21	5749	5518.94	-5.210
67Q1	6127.17	5833.48	.	5539.78	.
67Q2	6162.83	5837.25	.	5511.67	.
67Q3	6139.41	5798.49	.	5457.58	.
67Q4	6078.27	5722.08	.	5365.89	.

National Industrial Conference Board Data
Forecasts of PDL Model
PDL Endpoint Restrictions

DATE	U	P	Y	L	R
66Q1	5306.17	5086.66	5160	4867.15	73.341
66Q2	5670.59	5436.61	5319	5202.63	-117.608
66Q3	5745.89	5498.93	5574	5251.97	75.071
66Q4	6024.73	5766.73	5749	5508.72	-17.725
67Q1	6198.47	5882.14	.	5565.81	.
67Q2	6267.99	5920.85	.	5573.71	.
67Q3	6261.59	5904.02	.	5546.45	.
67Q4	6206.83	5848.96	.	5491.08	.

Explanation

The following variables are listed in Output 20.2:

DATE	is the date variable.
U and L	are the upper and lower 95% confidence limits.
P and Y	are the predicted values and the actual values, respectively, for each model.
R	is the residual value.

Variation

Fitting and Forecasting Using the %PDL Macro

Use the %PDL macro to fit PDL models with PROC MODEL.

Use a FIT statement to estimate the PDL model.

Use a SOLVE statement to simulate or forecast the estimated model.

```
   /* Restrict Covariate Regressor Parameters */
proc model data=almon noprint;
   parms intercpt a1 a2 a3;  /* Specify the Model Parameters   */
   %pdl (xpdl,8,2)           /* Specify a Quadratic, 8 Lag PDL */

      /* Specify the Model to Estimate  */
   y = intercpt + a1*q1 + a2*q2 + a3*q3 + %pdl (xpdl,x);
   restrict a1,a2,a3=0;      /* Restrict Slope Parameters      */
   fit y;                    /* Fit (Estimate) the Model       */
   id date;                  /* Specify an ID Variable         */

   solve y                   /* Solve the Estimated Model      */
        / forecast           /* Specifies Forecast Solutions   */
          out=pdl_out5       /* Names the Output Data Set      */
          outpredict;        /* Outputs the Predicted Values   */
   title2;                   /* Resets the Program Title2      */
   title3;                   /* Resets the Program Title3      */
run;
quit;
```

```
   /* Restrict PDL Endpoints */
proc model data=almon noprint;
   parms int;                  /* Specify the Model Parameters   */
   %pdl (xpdl,8,2,r=both)      /* Specify a Quadratic, 8 Lag PDL */
                               /* Restrict the PDL Endpoints     */
   y = int + %pdl (xpdl,x);    /* Specify the Model to Estimate  */
   fit y;                      /* Fit (Estimate) the Model       */
   id date;                    /* Specify an ID Variable         */
   solve y                     /* Solve the Estimated Model      */
        / forecast             /* Specifies Forecast Solutions   */
          out=pdl_out6         /* Names the Output Data Set      */
          outpredict;          /* Outputs the Predicted Values   */
run;
quit;
```

Print the forecasts using PROC PRINT.

```
proc print data=pdl_out5 noobs;
   where date > '01dec65'd;
   title2 'Forecasts of PDL Model';
   title3 'Slope Parameter Restrictions';
run;

proc print data=pdl_out6 noobs;
   where date > '01dec65'd;
   title3 'PDL Endpoint Restrictions';
run;
```

Printing the Forecasts

Output 20.3
Input Values and Forecasts from Restricted PDL Models

National Industrial Conference Board Data
Forecasts of PDL Model
Slope Parameter Restrictions

DATE	_TYPE_	_MODE_	_LAG_	_ERRORS_	Y	Q1	Q2	Q3	X
66Q1	PREDICT	FORECAST	44	0	5160.00	1	0	0	6109
66Q2	PREDICT	FORECAST	45	0	5319.00	0	1	0	6542
66Q3	PREDICT	FORECAST	46	0	5574.00	0	0	1	5785
66Q4	PREDICT	FORECAST	47	0	5749.00	0	0	0	5707
67Q1	PREDICT	FORECAST	48	0	5794.40	1	0	0	5412
67Q2	PREDICT	FORECAST	49	0	5809.38	0	1	0	5465
67Q3	PREDICT	FORECAST	50	0	5784.16	0	0	1	5550
67Q4	PREDICT	FORECAST	51	0	5723.21	0	0	0	5465

National Industrial Conference Board Data
Forecasts of PDL Model
PDL Endpoint Restrictions

DATE	_TYPE_	_MODE_	_LAG_	_ERRORS_	Y	X
66Q1	PREDICT	FORECAST	44	0	5160.00	6109
66Q2	PREDICT	FORECAST	45	0	5319.00	6542
66Q3	PREDICT	FORECAST	46	0	5574.00	5785
66Q4	PREDICT	FORECAST	47	0	5749.00	5707
67Q1	PREDICT	FORECAST	48	0	5892.80	5412
67Q2	PREDICT	FORECAST	49	0	5938.03	5465
67Q3	PREDICT	FORECAST	50	0	5923.20	5550
67Q4	PREDICT	FORECAST	51	0	5867.54	5465

Explanation

The following variables are listed in Output 20.3:

DATE — is the date variable.

TYPE — is a character variable identifying the type of observation (PREDICT, RESIDUAL, ACTUAL, or ERROR).

MODE — is a character variable identifying the solution _MODE_ (FORECAST or SIMULATE).

LAG — is numeric variable containing the number of dynamic lags that contribute to the solution. The value of _LAG_ is always set to 0 for STATIC mode solutions.

ERRORS — is a numeric variable containing the number of errors that occurred during the execution of the program for the last iteration for the observation. Zero (0) indicates no error while -1 indicates an error occurred in the solution process.

Y — is the forecast value. The values for 66Q1 through 66Q4 are the actual values while the values for 67Q1 through 67Q4 are forecasts. When the FORECAST option is specified, the actual value of the variable is used as the solution value whenever nonmissing data are available in the input data set. Thus, in FORECAST mode, PROC MODEL solves only for those variables that are missing in the input data set.

Q1, Q2, Q3 — are the values of the quarterly dummy variables.

X — is the value of the variable X, which is the quarterly capital appropriation.

Further Reading

- For more information on PROC MODEL, see the *SAS/ETS User's Guide, Version 6, Second Edition*, and *SAS/ETS Software: Changes and Enhancements, Release 6.11.*
- For more information on PROC PDLREG, see the *SAS/ETS User's Guide, Version 6, Second Edition.*

References

- Almon, S. (1965), "The Distributed Lag between Capital Appropriations and Expenditures," *Econometrica*, 33, 178-196.
- Emerson, P.L. (1968), "Numerical Construction of Orthogonal Polynomials from a General Recurrence Formula," *Biometrics*, 24, 695-701.
- Maddala, G.S. (1977), *Econometrics*, New York: McGraw-Hill.
- Pringle, R.M. and Raynor, A.A. (1971), *Generalized Inverse Matrices with Applications to Statistics*, New York: Hafner Publishing Company.

EXAMPLE 21

Fitting and Forecasting a Linear System by SUR and ITSUR

Featured Tools:

- SYSLIN procedure
  - SUR option
  - ITSUR option
  - MODEL statement
  - OUTPUT statement
  - PREDICTED= option
  - RESIDUAL= option

Foreign exchange rates (units of foreign currency per U.S. dollar) depend, in part, on the amount of trade between countries, the difference in their inflation rates, and the difference in their real short-term interest rates. Thus, a model of exchange rates between the U.S. and France (FR), Germany (WG), and Italy (IT) is

$$\text{RATE\_FR}_t = a_1 + b_1\,\text{IM\_FR}_t + c_1\,\text{DI\_FR}_t + d_1\,\text{DR\_FR}_t + \epsilon_{1,t}$$

$$\text{RATE\_WG}_t = a_2 + b_2\,\text{IM\_WG}_t + c_2\,\text{DI\_WG}_t + d_2\,\text{DR\_WG}_t + \epsilon_{2,t}$$

$$\text{RATE\_IT}_t = a_3 + b_3\,\text{IM\_IT}_t + c_3\,\text{DI\_IT}_t + d_3\,\text{DR\_IT}_t + \epsilon_{3,t}$$

The variables are defined as follows:

RATE_*xx* are the exchange rates of foreign currencies per U.S. dollar.

IM_*xx* are the imports to the U.S. from the foreign country in 1984 U.S. dollars.

Real Imports = *Nominal Imports* / *CPI_US*

DI_*xx* are the difference in the U.S. and the foreign country inflation rate as measured by the difference of the percentage increase in the U.S. consumer price index (CPI) and the CPI of the foreign country.

$$\textit{US Inflation Rate} = \text{IR\_US} = \frac{\text{CPI\_US}_t - \text{CPI\_US}_{t-1}}{\text{CPI\_US}_{t-1}}$$

$$\text{DI\_}xx = \text{IR\_}xx - \text{IR\_US}$$

DR_*xx* are the difference in the U.S. and the foreign country real money market rates. The real money market rate in each country is the observed money market rate minus the inflation rate.

$$\text{DR\_}xx = (\text{MM\_}xx - \text{IR\_}xx) - (\text{MM\_US} - \text{IR\_US})$$

The variables can be classified as follows:

- *Dependent* or *endogenous variables* are determined within the system. In this example, the endogenous variables appear on the left side of the equations: RATE_FR, RATE_WG, RATE_IT.
- *Independent* or *exogenous variables* are determined outside of the system. A variable is strictly exogenous if it is independent of the contemporaneous, future, and past errors. In this example, all of the right-side variables are exogenous.
- *Predetermined variables* are the exogenous variables and the variables representing past values of the endogenous variables. In this example, there are no lagged endogenous variables.

For this exchange rate model, there are three equations with twelve parameters to estimate. The equations seem to be unrelated because no dependent variable also serves as a right-side variable. The seemingly unrelated equations could be fit separately by ordinary least squares (OLS). However, there are unmodeled events (very good and very bad weather for the northern hemisphere, similar macroeconomic conditions, energy and political crises, and so on) that occurred which affect these countries. These unmodeled events imply that the error terms across equations are correlated. The model can be fitted more efficiently if the cross-equation error correlations are explicitly accounted for. Zellner (1962) extended OLS estimation by viewing the system as one large equation and applying generalized least squares. The resulting estimation technique is seeming unrelated regressions, SUR.

SUR estimation, also called *joint generalized least squares* (JGLS) or Zellner estimation, is a generalization of OLS for multi-equation systems. Like OLS, the SUR method assumes that all the regressors are independent variables, but SUR uses the contemporaneous correlations among the errors of different equations to improve the regression estimates. The regression parameters are estimated through generalized least squares, using the estimated covariances. For additional information on SUR estimation, see Pindyck and Rubinfeld (1991), pp. 308-311 and pp. 326-327, and Greene (1993), pp. 487-489.

Note: SUR produces the same results as OLS in either of two situations: if the cross-equation errors are not contemporaneously correlated (that is, the error-covariance matrix is diagonal), or if the identical set of regressors appears in each equation. The efficiency gain from using a systems estimation method is greater as the contemporaneous correlations among the errors of different equations are greater (in absolute value) and as the correlation between the matrices of the independent variables of the different equations are smaller (in absolute value).

Program

Estimating the Model

Create the EXCH1 data set. The complete EXCH1 data set is in "Introduction: The Example Data Sets."

The EXCH1 data set contains

- □ values for 1977 to initialize the lagging functions
- □ values for all variables from 1978 to 1991 to estimate the model
- □ values for the right-side variables from 1992 and 1993 to forecast the exchange rates (RATE_FR, RATE_WG, and RATE_IT).

```
data exch1;
input year rate_fr rate_wg rate_it cpi_us cpi_fr cpi_wg cpi_it
      imn_fr / imn_wg imn_it mm_us mm_fr mm_wg mm_it prod_us
      prod_fr prod_wg prod_it;
     ius = 100*dif(cpi_us)/lag(cpi_us);
     ifr = 100*dif(cpi_fr)/lag(cpi_fr);
     iwg = 100*dif(cpi_wg)/lag(cpi_wg);
     iit = 100*dif(cpi_it)/lag(cpi_it);
   im_fr = imn_fr/cpi_us;
   im_wg = imn_wg/cpi_us;
   im_it = imn_it/cpi_us;
   di_fr = ius - ifr;
   di_wg = ius - iwg;
   di_it = ius - iit;
   dr_fr = (mm_fr-ifr)-(mm_us-ius);
   dr_wg = (mm_wg-iwg)-(mm_us-ius);
   dr_it = (mm_it-iit)-(mm_us-ius);
label im_fr = 'Imports to US from France in 1984 $'
      im_wg = 'Imports to US from WG in 1984 $'
      im_it = 'Imports to US from Italy in 1984 $'
      di_fr = 'Difference in Inflation Rates US-France'
      di_wg = 'Difference in Inflation Rates US-WG'
      di_it = 'Difference in Inflation Rates US-Italy'
      dr_fr = 'Difference in Money Mkt Rates US-France'
      dr_wg = 'Difference in Money Mkt Rates US-WG'
      dr_it = 'Difference in Money Mkt Rates US-Italy';
title 'Exchange Rate Model';
datalines;
1977 4.9161 2.3236  882.78 0.606 0.527 0.769 0.401  3032
   7238  3037   .     .     .     .    78.2  92    88.0  83.8
1978 4.5091 2.0096  849.13 0.652 0.575 0.790 0.451  4051
   9962  4102  7.93  8.16  3.70 11.49  82.6  94    90.4  85.4
more data lines
;
```

Fit the model using the estimation technique of seeming unrelated regressions. Use the SUR option to specify the estimation technique of seeming unrelated regressions.

Use a MODEL statement to define each exchange rate equation.

Use an OUTPUT statement after each MODEL statement to output the predicted and residual values from that equation. Note that the PREDICTED= and RESIDUAL= options can be abbreviated as P= and R=, respectively.

```
proc syslin data=exch1 sur out=sur_pred;

   France:  model rate_fr = im_fr di_fr dr_fr;
            output predicted=pred_fr residual=r_fr;

   Germany: model rate_wg = im_wg di_wg dr_wg;
            output p=pred_wg r=r_wg;

   Italy:   model rate_it = im_it di_it dr_it;
            output p=pred_it r=r_it;
run;
```

Printing the predicted and residual values using PROC PRINT. A WHERE statement is used to specify the observations to be printed.

```
proc print data=sur_pred;
   where year > 1989;
   var year rate_fr pred_fr r_fr rate_wg pred_wg r_wg
            rate_it pred_it r_it;
run;
```

Output 21.1
Model Estimated by Ordinary Least Squares (Partial Output)

```
                         Exchange Rate Model

                          SYSLIN Procedure
                   Ordinary Least Squares Estimation

Model: FRANCE
Dependent variable: RATE_FR

                      ❶ Analysis of Variance

                            Sum of        Mean
  Source          DF       Squares      Square      F Value      Prob>F

  Model            3      22.71710     7.57237       12.133      0.0011
  Error           10       6.24111     0.62411
  C Total         13      28.95821
                      ❷
          Root MSE         0.79001     R-Square      0.7845
          Dep Mean         6.19408     Adj R-SQ      0.7198
          C.V.            12.75423
```

```
                         Exchange Rate Model

                           SYSLIN Procedure
                   Ordinary Least Squares Estimation

                       ❸ Parameter Estimates

                    Parameter      Standard    T for H0:
Variable  DF         Estimate         Error  Parameter=0   Prob > |T|

INTERCEP   1        -2.231866      1.884598       -1.184       0.2637
IM_FR      1         0.000945      0.000225        4.202       0.0018
DI_FR      1        -0.665379      0.135506       -4.910       0.0006
DR_FR      1        -0.083746      0.178782       -0.468       0.6495
```

```
                         Exchange Rate Model

                           SYSLIN Procedure
                   Ordinary Least Squares Estimation

Model: GERMANY
Dependent variable: RATE_WG

                        ❶ Analysis of Variance

                          Sum of         Mean
Source          DF       Squares       Square      F Value        Prob>F

Model            3       1.60830      0.53610        6.375        0.0109
Error           10       0.84097      0.08410
C Total         13       2.44927

        Root MSE ❷  0.29000      R-Square       0.6566
        Dep Mean    2.11267      Adj R-SQ       0.5536
        C.V.       13.72647
```

```
                         Exchange Rate Model

                           SYSLIN Procedure
                   Ordinary Least Squares Estimation

                       ❸ Parameter Estimates

                    Parameter      Standard    T for H0:
Variable  DF         Estimate         Error  Parameter=0   Prob > |T|

INTERCEP   1         2.664662      0.457061        5.830       0.0002
IM_WG      1  -0.000028805    0.000021650       -1.331       0.2129
DI_WG      1        -0.007720      0.046356       -0.167       0.8710
DR_WG      1        -0.127693      0.046662       -2.737       0.0210
```

```
                         Exchange Rate Model

                           SYSLIN Procedure
                    Ordinary Least Squares Estimation

Model: ITALY
Dependent variable: RATE_IT

                   ❶ Analysis of Variance

                            Sum of          Mean
   Source          DF      Squares        Square      F Value       Prob>F

   Model            3 1090157.3148 363385.77158       15.088       0.0005
   Error           10 240849.80748  24084.98075
   C Total         13 1331007.1222
                     ❷
         Root MSE     155.19337      R-Square       0.8190
         Dep Mean    1293.98214      Adj R-SQ       0.7648
         C.V.          11.99347
```

```
                         Exchange Rate Model

                           SYSLIN Procedure
                    Ordinary Least Squares Estimation

                     ❸ Parameter Estimates

                     Parameter        Standard    T for H0:
    Variable  DF      Estimate           Error   Parameter=0     Prob > |T|

    INTERCEP   1  -1369.459943      661.998444        -2.069         0.0654
    IM_IT      1      0.248858        0.074240         3.352         0.0073
    DI_IT      1   -144.956410       24.815955        -5.841         0.0002
    DR_IT      1     37.003941       32.488967         1.139         0.2813
```

Explanation

The SYSLIN procedure prints preliminary OLS parameter values and statistics to help you analyze and evaluate the estimated model as shown in Output 21.1. For each estimated equation, the following are printed. The OLS models provide residuals from which the cross-equation variance-covariance matrix is estimated.

❶ **`Analysis of Variance`** (ANOVA) includes

- □ sums of squares for the model, error, and corrected total
- □ degrees of freedom for each component of variation
- □ mean squares for the model and error components
- □ the *F*-statistic and *p*-value for the null hypothesis that all parameters are jointly equal to 0.

❷ The goodness-of-fit statistics include the root mean square, R-square, and adjusted R-square.

❸ The parameter estimates, standard errors, *t*-statistics for the null hypotheses that each parameter estimate is equal to 0, and the *p*-values are listed.

Cross Model Covariance and Correlations

Output 21.2
The Cross Model Covariance and Correlation Matrices and the Cross Model Inverse Covariance and Correlation Matrices (Partial Output)

```
                         Exchange Rate Model

                           SYSLIN Procedure
                 Seemingly Unrelated Regression Estimation

                     ❶ Cross Model Covariance

Sigma               FRANCE            GERMANY              ITALY

FRANCE        0.6241113746       0.1876022093       76.874606825
GERMANY       0.1876022093       0.0840972716       21.525711319
ITALY         76.874606825       21.525711319       24084.980748

                     ❷ Cross Model Correlation

Corr                FRANCE            GERMANY              ITALY

FRANCE                   1       0.8188718589        0.627016121
GERMANY       0.8188718589                  1       0.4782923193
ITALY          0.627016121       0.4782923193                  1
```

```
                         Exchange Rate Model

                           SYSLIN Procedure
                 Seemingly Unrelated Regression Estimation

                   ❸ Cross Model Inverse Correlation

Inv Corr             FRANCE            GERMANY              ITALY

FRANCE         3.8815962783       -2.611975721       -1.184535516
GERMANY        -2.611975721       3.0542510311       0.1769260749
ITALY          -1.184535516       0.1769260749       1.6581004817

                   ❹ Cross Model Inverse Covariance

Inv Sigma            FRANCE            GERMANY              ITALY

FRANCE          6.219396788       -11.40110994       -0.009661485
GERMANY        -11.40110994        36.31807515       0.0039312235
ITALY          -0.009661485       0.0039312235       0.0000688438
```

Explanation

In Output 21.2, the following items are printed:

❶ the cross model covariance matrix.

❷ the cross model correlation matrix.

Note that the off-diagonal elements are nonzero, suggesting that the SUR estimates are more efficient than the OLS estimates.

❸ the cross model inverse correlation matrix.

❹ the cross model inverse covariance matrix.

SUR Estimation

Output 21.3
Model Estimated by Seemingly Unrelated Regressions Method (Partial Output)

```
                          Exchange Rate Model

                            SYSLIN Procedure
                 Seemingly Unrelated Regression Estimation

        System Weighted MSE:  0.83429 with 30 degrees of freedom.
        System Weighted R-Square:  0.7403
```

```
                          Exchange Rate Model

                            SYSLIN Procedure
                 Seemingly Unrelated Regression Estimation

    Model: FRANCE
    Dependent variable: RATE_FR
                             Parameter Estimates

                         Parameter      Standard    T for H0:
       Variable  DF       Estimate         Error  Parameter=0     Prob > |T|

       INTERCEP   1      -0.157400      1.471375       -0.107         0.9169
       IM_FR      1       0.000706      0.000171        4.119         0.0021
       DI_FR      1      -0.563960      0.120423       -4.683         0.0009
       DR_FR      1       0.057474      0.128591        0.447         0.6644
```

```
                          Exchange Rate Model

                            SYSLIN Procedure
                 Seemingly Unrelated Regression Estimation

    Model: GERMANY
    Dependent variable: RATE_WG
                             Parameter Estimates

                         Parameter      Standard    T for H0:
       Variable  DF       Estimate         Error  Parameter=0     Prob > |T|

       INTERCEP   1       2.850373      0.345446        8.251         0.0001
       IM_WG      1   -0.000034846   0.000017055       -2.043         0.0683
       DI_WG      1      -0.037225      0.038085       -0.977         0.3514
       DR_WG      1      -0.063523      0.035583       -1.785         0.1045
```

```
                      Exchange Rate Model

                        SYSLIN Procedure
               Seemingly Unrelated Regression Estimation

Model: ITALY
Dependent variable: RATE_IT
                       Parameter Estimates

                    Parameter      Standard    T for H0:
    Variable  DF     Estimate         Error  Parameter=0    Prob > |T|

    INTERCEP   1  -774.062495    578.538069       -1.338        0.2105
    IM_IT      1     0.188700      0.064609        2.921        0.0153
    DI_IT      1  -119.038682     22.812110       -5.218        0.0004
    DR_IT      1    46.286407     29.343623        1.577        0.1458
```

Explanation

Note that, in Output 21.3, the SUR estimated parameter standard errors are smaller than the OLS estimated parameter standard errors, which suggests that SUR estimators are more efficient.

Actual and Predicted Values

Output 21.4
Printing Predicted, Actual, and Residual Values

```
                         Exchange Rate Model

 OBS   YEAR   RATE_FR    PRED_FR      R_FR      RATE_WG    PRED_WG

  14   1990    5.4467    6.04366   -0.59696     1.6166    1.83416
  15   1991    5.6468    6.43914   -0.79234     1.6610    1.90875
  16   1992     .        7.41094     .           .        1.85580
  17   1993     .        7.14768     .           .        1.99271

 OBS     R_WG      RATE_IT    PRED_IT      R_IT

  14   -0.21756    1198.27    1312.08   -113.814
  15   -0.24775    1241.28    1319.40    -78.116
  16     .           .        1532.44      .
  17     .           .        1372.42      .
```

Explanation

The variables listed in Output 21.4 are as follows:

YEAR
: contains the date in years.

RATE_FR, RATE_WG, and RATE_IT
: are the actual exchange rate values.

PRED_FR, PRED_WG, PRED_IT
are the predicted exchange rates from the SUR estimated model.

R_FR, R_WG, and R_IT
are the residual values (actual value−predicted value).

Variation

Iterated SUR (ITSUR) Estimation

The SUR estimation method is a two-step process. The model equations are fit separately by OLS, and the residuals are used to estimate the cross-equation covariance matrix Σ, which in turn is used to re-estimate the model parameters by generalized least squares. The residuals of the fitted model can be used to form another estimate of Σ, which can be used to estimate the model parameters. The covariance matrix and parameters can be estimated in alternating fashion until convergence is achieved. This estimation method is known as *iterated SUR*, or ITSUR.

Estimate the model by the ITSUR method.

Use the MAXITER=*n* and CONVERGE=*n* options to specify the maximum number of iterations and the convergence criterion for iterated methods. The default values are MAXITER=30 and CONVERGE=.0001.

```
proc syslin data=exch1
            itsur           /* Specifies ITSUR Estimation      */
            maxiter=150     /* Specifies Number of Iterations  */
            converge=.00025 /* Specifies Convergence Criterion */
            out=itsur_p     /* Creates & Names Output Data Set */
            noprint;        /* Suppresses Printed Output       */

   France:  model rate_fr = im_fr di_fr dr_fr;
            output p=pred_fr r=r_fr;
   Germany: model rate_wg = im_wg di_wg dr_wg;
            output p=pred_wg r=r_wg;
   Italy:   model rate_it = im_it di_it dr_it;
            output p=pred_it r=r_it;
run;
```

Print the forecasts using PROC PRINT.

```
proc print data=itsur_p;
   where year > 1989;
   var year rate_fr pred_fr r_fr rate_wg pred_wg r_wg
            rate_it pred_it r_it;
   title2 'Estimated by the ITSUR Method';
run;
```

Actual and Predicted Values

Output 21.5
Printing Actual, Predicted, and Residual Values.

```
                    Exchange Rate Model
               Estimated by the ITSUR Method

OBS   YEAR   RATE_FR   PRED_FR      R_FR     RATE_WG   PRED_WG

 14   1990    5.4467   5.90328   -0.45658    1.6166    1.77667
 15   1991    5.6468   5.84671   -0.19991    1.6610    1.69707
 16   1992     .       5.62155     .           .       1.44874
 17   1993     .       5.66953     .           .       1.54493

OBS     R_WG      RATE_IT    PRED_IT     R_IT

 14   -0.16007    1198.27    1285.59   -87.3194
 15   -0.03607    1241.28    1257.33   -16.0546
 16     .            .       1231.76      .
 17     .            .       1249.35      .
```

Explanation

The variables listed in Output 21.5 follow the same pattern as those listed in Output 21.4.

Further Reading

For more information on PROC SYSLIN, see the *SAS/ETS User's Guide, Version 6, Second Edition.*

References

- □ *Economic Report of the President*, Washington, D.C.: U.S. Government Printing Office, 1995.
- □ Greene, W. (1993), *Econometric Analysis, Second Edition*, New York: Macmillan Publishing Co.
- □ Pindyck, R.S. and Rubinfeld, D.L. (1991), *Econometric Models and Economic Forecasts, Third Edition*, New York: McGraw-Hill Inc.
- □ *Statistical Abstracts of the U.S.*, Department of Commerce, Washington, D.C.: U.S. Government Printing Office, various years.
- □ Zellner, A. (1962), "An Efficient Method of Estimating Seeming Unrelated Regressions and Tests for Aggregation Bias," *Journal of the American Statistical Association*, 57, 348-368.

EXAMPLE 22

Testing and Restricting Parameter Estimates in a Linear System Forecasting Model

Featured Tools:

- SYSLIN procedure
  - TEST statement
  - STEST statement
  - RESTRICT statement
  - SRESTRICT statement

The foreign exchange rate model developed in Example 21 ("Fitting and Forecasting a Linear System by SUR and ITSUR") and estimated using the EXCH1 data set is

$$\text{RATE\_FR}_t = a_1 + b_1\,\text{IM\_FR}_t + c_1\,\text{DI\_FR}_t + d_1\,\text{DR\_FR}_t + \epsilon_{1,t}$$

$$\text{RATE\_WG}_t = a_2 + b_2\,\text{IM\_WG}_t + c_2\,\text{DI\_WG}_t + d_2\,\text{DR\_WG}_t + \epsilon_{2,t}$$

$$\text{RATE\_IT}_t = a_3 + b_3\,\text{IM\_IT}_t + c_3\,\text{DI\_IT}_t + d_3\,\text{DR\_IT}_t + \epsilon_{3,t}$$

When fitting a system of linear equations, you may be interested in testing hypotheses about the estimated parameters in one or more of the equations. You may also be interested in restricting the parameter estimates in one or more equations.

- To perform a hypothesis test of the estimated parameters in a single equation, use a TEST statement. The appropriate TEST statement follows the MODEL statement specifying the equation containing the parameter (or parameters) to be tested.
- To perform hypothesis tests using the estimated parameters of multiple equations, use the STEST statement. The appropriate STEST statement follows the MODEL statements specifying the equations containing the parameters used in the test.
- To restrict the parameter estimates in a single equation, use a RESTRICT statement. The appropriate RESTRICT statement follows the MODEL statement specifying the equation containing the parameter (or parameters) to be restricted.
- To restrict the parameter estimates in multiple equations, use an SRESTRICT statement. The appropriate SRESTRICT statement follows the MODEL statements specifying the equations containing the parameters to be restricted.

Program

Test and Restrict Model Parameters

Perform tests if the slope parameters of variables in a single equation are equal in magnitude. The first TEST statement tests if the slope parameters of DI_FR and DR_FR are equal. The second TEST statement tests if the slope parameters of DI_WG and DR_WG are equal. Each TEST statement follows the appropriate MODEL statement. Use labels to distinguish test results for different tests in printed output.

```
proc syslin data=exch1 sur;

   France:  model rate_fr = im_fr di_fr dr_fr;
   France:  test di_fr = dr_fr;

   Germany: model rate_wg = im_wg di_wg dr_wg;
   Germany: test di_wg = dr_wg;

   Italy:   model rate_it = im_it di_it dr_it;
run;
```

Test if the slope parameters for the variables DI_FR and DI_WG are equal in magnitude. The STEST statement follows the MODEL statements specifying equations for the French and German exchange rates.

```
proc syslin data=exch1 sur;
   France:  model rate_fr = im_fr di_fr dr_fr;
   Germany: model rate_wg = im_wg di_wg dr_wg;
   stest France.di_fr = Germany.di_wg;

   Italy:   model rate_it = im_it di_it dr_it;
run;
```

Restrict the slope parameters for the variables in a single equation to be equal in magnitude. The first RESTRICT statement restricts the slope parameters of DI_FR and DR_FR to be equal. The second RESTRICT statement restricts the slope parameters of DI_WG and DR_WG to be equal. Each RESTRICT statement follows the appropriate MODEL statement.

```
proc syslin data=exch1 sur;

   France:  model rate_fr = im_fr di_fr dr_fr;
            restrict di_fr = dr_fr;

   Germany: model rate_wg = im_wg di_wg dr_wg;
            restrict di_wg = dr_wg;

   Italy:   model rate_it = im_it di_it dr_it;
run;
```

Restrict the slope parameters for the variables DI_FR and DI_WG to be equal in magnitude. The SRESTRICT statement follows the MODEL statements specifying equations for the French and German exchange rates.

```
proc syslin data=exch1 sur;

   France:  model rate_fr = im_fr di_fr dr_fr;
   Germany: model rate_wg = im_wg di_wg dr_wg;
   srestrict France.di_fr = Germany.di_wg;

   Italy:   model rate_it = im_it di_it dr_it;
   srestrict France.dr_fr = Germany.dr_wg = Italy.dr_it;
run;
```

TEST Statement Results

Output 22.1
Performing Tests of Estimated Parameters in a Single Equation (Partial Output)

```
                          Exchange Rate Model

                            SYSLIN Procedure
                  Seemingly Unrelated Regression Estimation

Model: FRANCE
Dependent variable: RATE_FR
                          Parameter Estimates

                      Parameter      Standard    T for H0:
    Variable  DF       Estimate         Error   Parameter=0     Prob > |T|

    INTERCEP   1      -0.157400      1.471375        -0.107         0.9169
    IM_FR      1       0.000706      0.000171         4.119         0.0021
    DI_FR      1      -0.563960      0.120423        -4.683         0.0009
    DR_FR      1       0.057474      0.128591         0.447         0.6644

Test: FRANCE
      Numerator:    8.492595   DF:     1  F Value:  10.1794
      Denominator: 0.834291    DF:    30   Prob>F:   0.0033
```

```
                          Exchange Rate Model

                            SYSLIN Procedure
                  Seemingly Unrelated Regression Estimation

Model: GERMANY
Dependent variable: RATE_WG
                          Parameter Estimates

                      Parameter      Standard    T for H0:
    Variable  DF       Estimate         Error   Parameter=0     Prob > |T|

    INTERCEP   1       2.850373      0.345446         8.251         0.0001
    IM_WG      1  -0.000034846    0.000017055        -2.043         0.0683
    DI_WG      1      -0.037225      0.038085        -0.977         0.3514
    DR_WG      1      -0.063523      0.035583        -1.785         0.1045

Test: GERMANY
      Numerator:    0.164444   DF:     1  F Value:   0.1971
      Denominator: 0.834291    DF:    30   Prob>F:   0.6603
```

Explanation

As shown in Output 22.1, the first test tests the estimated parameters of the French exchange rate equation, and has the null hypothesis that the slope coefficient of DI_FR equals the slope coefficient of DR_FR. The F-statistic is 10.1794 with 1 and 30 degrees of freedom, and has a p-value of .0033, which indicates that the null hypothesis can be rejected at the .05 level.

The second test tests the estimated parameters of the German exchange rate equation, and has the null hypothesis that the slope coefficient of DI_WG equals the slope coefficient of DR_WG. The F-statistic is .1971 with 1 and 30 degrees of freedom, and has a p-value of .6603, which indicates that the null hypothesis can be retained at the .05 level.

STEST Statement Results

Output 22.2
Cross Model Hypothesis Test of Estimated Parameters (Partial Output)

```
                         Exchange Rate Model

                          SYSLIN Procedure
                Seemingly Unrelated Regression Estimation

Test:
     Numerator:   27.02962  DF:     1  F Value:  32.3983
     Denominator: 0.834291  DF:    30   Prob>F:   0.0001
```

Explanation

As shown in Output 22.2, the F-statistic is 32.3983, (27.02962/0.834291), with 1 and 30 degrees of freedom, and has a p-value of .0001, which indicates that the null hypothesis of equal parameter values can be rejected at the .05 level.

RESTRICT Statement Results

Output 22.3
Restricting the Estimated Parameters in a Single Equation (Partial Output)

```
                         Exchange Rate Model

                           SYSLIN Procedure
                Seemingly Unrelated Regression Estimation

                         Parameter Estimates

                   Parameter     Standard    T for H0:
Variable  DF        Estimate        Error  Parameter=0   Prob > |T|

INTERCEP   1       -1.343708     1.943116       -0.692       0.5050
IM_FR      1        0.000880     0.000227        3.876       0.0031
DI_FR      1       -0.308662     0.081807       -3.773       0.0036
DR_FR      1       -0.308662     0.081807       -3.773       0.0036
RESTRICT  -1       -9.675411     3.832895       -2.524       0.0032
```

```
                         Exchange Rate Model

                           SYSLIN Procedure
                Seemingly Unrelated Regression Estimation

Model: GERMANY
Dependent variable: RATE_WG
                         Parameter Estimates

                   Parameter     Standard    T for H0:
Variable  DF        Estimate        Error  Parameter=0   Prob > |T|

INTERCEP   1        2.848989     0.358008        7.958       0.0001
IM_WG      1  -0.000034400    0.000019563       -1.758       0.1092
DI_WG      1       -0.040558     0.017961       -2.258       0.0475
DR_WG      1       -0.040558     0.017961       -2.258       0.0475
RESTRICT  -1       24.711850    14.291069        1.729       0.0817
```

Explanation

The first restriction, shown in Output 22.3, restricts the estimated parameters of the French exchange rate equation: the restriction is that the slope coefficient of DI_FR equals the slope coefficent of DR_FR. The parameter estimate for the restriction is the Lagrange multiplier used to impose the restriction. The restriction has a *t*-statistic of -2.524 and a *p*-value of .0032, which indicates that this restriction is statistically significant at the .05 level.

The second restriction restricts the estimated parameters of the German exchange rate equation: the restriction is that the slope coefficient of DI_WG equals the slope coefficent of DR_WG. The parameter estimate for the restriction is the Lagrange multiplier used to impose the restriction. The restriction has a t-statistic of 1.729 and a p-value of .0817, which indicates that the data are marginally consistent with this restriction.

SRESTRICT Statement Results

Output 22.4
Cross Model Parameter Restrictions (Partial Output)

```
                     Exchange Rate Model
           Seemingly Unrelated Regression Estimation

                      Parameter Estimates

                  Parameter      Standard    T for H0:
Variable  DF       Estimate         Error  Parameter=0     Prob > |T|

INTERCEP   1       4.829752      0.950291        5.082         0.0005
IM_FR      1       0.000171      0.000113        1.517         0.1603
DI_FR      1   ❶   0.015993      0.033028        0.484         0.6387
DR_FR      1   ❷   0.007851      0.029535        0.266         0.7958
```

```
                     Exchange Rate Model
           Seemingly Unrelated Regression Estimation

                      Parameter Estimates

                  Parameter      Standard    T for H0:
Variable  DF       Estimate         Error  Parameter=0     Prob > |T|

INTERCEP   1       2.588481      0.335785        7.709         0.0001
IM_WG      1   -0.000029715   0.000016995       -1.748         0.1110
DI_WG      1   ❶   0.015993      0.033028        0.484         0.6387
DR_WG      1   ❷   0.007851      0.029535        0.266         0.7958
```

```
                     Exchange Rate Model
           Seemingly Unrelated Regression Estimation

                      Parameter Estimates

                  Parameter      Standard    T for H0:
Variable  DF       Estimate         Error  Parameter=0     Prob > |T|

INTERCEP   1    -227.030678    390.097120       -0.582         0.5735
IM_IT      1       0.158817      0.039136        4.058         0.0023
DI_IT      1     -57.421634     19.270544       -2.980         0.0138
DR_IT      1   ❷   0.007851      0.029535        0.266         0.7958
```

```
                    Exchange Rate Model
         Seemingly Unrelated Regression Estimation

Cross Model Restrictions:

                    Parameter Estimates

                 Parameter     Standard    T for H0:
Variable  DF      Estimate        Error  Parameter=0    Prob > |T|
          ❸
RESTRICT  -1    -58.696909    11.269833       -5.208        0.0001
RESTRICT  -1    -17.987853    10.950174       -1.643        0.1015
RESTRICT  -1     -0.021596     0.039344       -0.549        0.6098
```

Explanation

❶ Slope parameters for DI_FR and DI_WG are equal in magnitude and sign, as specified in the first SRESTRICT statement.

❷ Slope parameters for DR_FR, DR_WG, and DR_IT are equal in magnitude and sign, as specified in the second SRESTRICT statement.

❸ The Lagrange multiplier values, standard errors, *t*-statistics, and *p*-values for these restrictions are printed.

A Closer Look

Specifying RESTRICT, SRESTRICT, STEST, and TEST Statements

- □ Each RESTRICT, SRESTRICT, STEST, and TEST statement is written as a linear equation.
- □ When no equal sign appears in the specified statement, the linear combination is set equal to 0.
- □ The keyword INTERCEPT is used to refer to the intercept parameter.
- □ In RESTRICT and TEST statements, parameters are referred to by the name of the corresponding regressor variable in the preceding MODEL statement.
- □ In SRESTRICT and STEST statements, parameters are referred to as *label.variable*, where *label* is the model label, or if no model label is specified the dependent variable can be used as the model label.
- □ Variable names can be multiplied by constants.
- □ Note that the parameters associated with the variables are restricted or tested, not the variables themselves.

- Each statement can be given a label to distinguish results for each statement in the printed output.
- If RESTRICT or SRESTRICT statements are used, the tests computed by STEST and TEST statements are conditional on the restrictions imposed. The validity of the tests may be compromised if incorrect restrictions are imposed on the estimates.
- If multiple restrictions appear in a single RESTRICT or SRESTRICT statement, they should be separated by commas. Restrictions should be consistent and not redundant.
- If multiple tests appear in a single STEST or TEST statement, they should be separated by commas, and a joint F-test is performed for the specified tests.
- The PRINT option can be specified in STEST and TEST statements after a slash (/) to print the intermediate calculations for the hypothesis tests.

Valid RESTRICT Statements

The RESTRICT statement imposes linear restrictions on the parameter estimates for the preceding MODEL statement. More than one RESTRICT statement can follow a MODEL statement. The following are examples of valid RESTRICT statements:

```
sum_pos: restrict x1 + x2 = 1;
         restrict x1 + x2 = -1;
x1_int:  restrict 2*x1 = intercept;
x1x2x3:  restrict x1 = x2 = x3 = 1;
```

Valid SRESTRICT Statements

The SRESTRICT statement imposes linear restrictions on the parameter estimates in two or more MODEL statements. More than one SRESTRICT statement can follow the appropriate MODEL statements. The restrictions should be consistent and not redundant. The results of SRESTRICT statements are printed after the parameter estimates for all the models in the system.

The following example code contains examples of valid SRESTRICT statements for the exchange rate model:

```
proc syslin data=exch1 sur;
   France:    model rate_fr = im_fr di_fr dr_fr;
   Germany:   model rate_wg = im_wg di_wg dr_wg;
   fr_wg:     srestrict France.di_fr = 2*Germany.di_wg;
   Italy:     model rate_it = im_it di_it dr_it;
   fr_it:     srestrict France.intercept=Italy.intercept;
   fr_wg_it:  srestrict France.dr_fr = Germany.dr_wg = Italy.dr_it;
run;
```

Valid STEST Statements

The STEST statement performs an *F*-test for the joint hypotheses specified in the statement. The following example code contains examples of valid STEST statements for the exchange rate model:

```
proc syslin data=exch1 sur;
   France:    model rate_fr = im_fr di_fr dr_fr;
   Germany:   model rate_wg = im_wg di_wg dr_wg;
   fr_wg:     stest 2*France.di_fr = Germany.di_wg;
   Italy:     model rate_it = im_it di_it dr_it;
   fr_it:     stest France.intercept=Italy.intercept;
   fr_wg_it:  stest 10*France.dr_fr = 25*Germany.dr_wg = Italy.dr_it;
run;
```

Valid TEST Statements

The TEST statement performs an *F*-test for the joint hypotheses of the parameters in the preceding MODEL. The following are examples of valid TEST statements:

```
sum_neg: test x1 + x2 = -1;
x1_int:  test 2*x1 = intercept;
x1x2x3:  test x1 = x2 = x3 = 1;
joint:   test x1 + x2 = -1, 2*x1 = intercept;
```

Further Reading

For more information on PROC SYSLIN, see the *SAS/ETS User's Guide, Version 6, Second Edition.*

References

- *Economic Report of the President*, Washington, D.C.: U.S. Government Printing Office, 1995.
- *Statistical Abstracts of the U.S.*, Department of Commerce, Washington, D.C.: U.S. Government Printing Office, various years.

EXAMPLE 23

Producing Goodness-of-Fit Statistics for Forecasts of a Linear System of Equations

Featured Tools:

- □ SYSLIN procedure
- □ SIMLIN procedure

The foreign exchange rate model developed in Example 21 ("Fitting and Forecasting a Linear System by SUR and ITSUR") and estimated using the EXCH1 data set is

$$\text{RATE\_FR}_t = a_1 + b_1\,\text{IM\_FR}_t + c_1\,\text{DI\_FR}_t + d_1\,\text{DR\_FR}_t + \epsilon_{1,t}$$

$$\text{RATE\_WG}_t = a_2 + b_2\,\text{IM\_WG}_t + c_2\,\text{DI\_WG}_t + d_2\,\text{DR\_WG}_t + \epsilon_{2,t}$$

$$\text{RATE\_IT}_t = a_3 + b_3\,\text{IM\_IT}_t + c_3\,\text{DI\_IT}_t + d_3\,\text{DR\_IT}_t + \epsilon_{3,t}$$

You can use goodness-of-fit statistics to assess how well the fitted model reflects the actual data. In this example, you first estimate the linear system by SUR using the SAS/ETS SYSLIN procedure. The parameter estimates are written to an output data set and then used by the SAS/ETS SIMLIN procedure to produce forecasts and goodness-of-fit statistics.

Program

Fit the model using the estimation technique of seeming unrelated regressions. Use the SUR option in the PROC SYSLIN statement to specify the estimation technique of seeming unrelated regressions. Use the OUTEST= option to write the parameter estimates to an output data set.

```
proc syslin data=exch1
            sur              /* Specifies SUR Estimation      */
            outest=est_xch1  /* Writes Estimates to Data Set */
            noprint;         /* Suppresses Printed Output     */

   France:  model rate_fr = im_fr di_fr dr_fr;
   Germany: model rate_wg = im_wg di_wg dr_wg;
   Italy:   model rate_it = im_it di_it dr_it;
run;
```

Print the OUTEST= data set using PROC PRINT.

```
proc print data=est_xch1;
run;
```

Forecast the linear model and assess the forecasts using PROC SIMLIN. The EST= option specifies the input data set containing the structural coefficients of the system. The TYPE= option specifies the type of estimates to be read from the EST= data set.

```
proc simlin data=exch1 est=est_xch1 type=sur;
   endogenous rate_fr rate_wg rate_it;
   exogenous im_fr di_fr dr_fr im_wg di_wg dr_wg
             im_it di_it dr_it;
   output out=exchout1 predicted = fore_fr1 fore_wg1 fore_it1
                       residual = r_fr1 r_wg1 r_it1;
run;
```

Print the forecasts using PROC PRINT.

```
proc print data=exchout1;
   where year > 1989;
   var year fore_fr1 r_fr1 fore_wg1 r_wg1 fore_it1 r_it1;
   title2 'Estimated by the SUR Method';
run;
```

Output 23.1
An OUTEST= Data Set Created with PROC SYSLIN

Exchange Rate Model

OBS	_TYPE_	_MODEL_	_DEPVAR_	_SIGMA_	INTERCEP	RATE_FR	RATE_WG
1	OLS	FRANCE	RATE_FR	0.790	-2.23	-1	.
2	OLS	GERMANY	RATE_WG	0.290	2.66	.	-1
3	OLS	ITALY	RATE_IT	155.193	-1369.46	.	.
4	SUR	FRANCE	RATE_FR	0.880	-0.16	-1	.
5	SUR	GERMANY	RATE_WG	0.319	2.85	.	-1
6	SUR	ITALY	RATE_IT	163.657	-774.06	.	.

OBS	RATE_IT	IM_FR	DI_FR	DR_FR	IM_WG	DI_WG
1	.	.00094455	-0.66538	-0.083746	.	.
2	.	.	.	.	-.000028805	-0.007720
3	-1	.	.	.	.	.
4	.	.00070594	-0.56396	0.057474	.	.
5	.	.	.	.	-.000034846	-0.037225
6	-1	.	.	.	.	.

Exchange Rate Model

OBS	DR_WG	IM_IT	DI_IT	DR_IT
1	.	.	.	.
2	-0.12769	.	.	.
3	.	0.24886	-144.956	37.0039
4	.	.	.	.
5	-0.06352	.	.	.
6	.	0.18870	-119.039	46.2864

Explanation

The EST_XCH1 data set variables, shown in Output 23.1, are as follows:

TYPE identifies the estimation type for the observations. In this example there are two types of observations, OLS and SUR.

MODEL is the model label, or the dependent variable if no label is specified in the MODEL statement.

DEPVAR is the name for the dependent variable in the model.

SIGMA contains the root mean square error for the model, which is an estimate of the standard deviation of the error term.

INTERCEP is the intercept parameter estimate.

regressors are the slope parameters associated with the regressor variables.

Reduced Form Coefficients and Statistics of Fit

Output 23.2
PROC SIMLIN Output: Reduced Form and Statistics of Fit

```
                     Exchange Rate Model

                      SIMLIN Procedure

   ❶ Inverse Coefficient Matrix for Endogenous Variables

                      RATE_FR        RATE_WG        RATE_IT

         RATE_FR       1.0000              0              0
         RATE_WG            0         1.0000              0
         RATE_IT            0              0         1.0000
```

```
                        Exchange Rate Model

                         SIMLIN Procedure

              ❷ Reduced Form for Exogenous Variables

                IM_FR        DI_FR        DR_FR        IM_WG        DI_WG

RATE_FR      0.000706      -0.5640       0.0575            0            0
RATE_WG             0            0            0    -0.000035      -0.0372
RATE_IT             0            0            0            0            0

                DR_WG        IM_IT        DI_IT        DR_IT     INTERCEP

RATE_FR             0            0            0            0      -0.1574
RATE_WG       -0.0635            0            0            0       2.8504
RATE_IT             0       0.1887    -119.0387      46.2864    -774.0625
```

```
                         Exchange Rate Model

                          SIMLIN Procedure

                      ❸  Statistics of Fit

                     Mean    Mean %  Mean Abs   Mean Abs       RMS     RMS %
Variable   N        Error     Error     Error    % Error     Error     Error

RATE_FR   14  5.837E-15   -1.6193    0.5387    8.19790    0.7435   10.0503
RATE_WG   14  1.935E-15   -1.8062    0.1932    8.75310    0.2693   11.1938
RATE_IT   14  1.218E-12   -1.4923  102.7017    7.62063  138.3156    9.5544
```

Explanation

Given a linear system with g endogenous variables (y_t), g equations, l lagged endogenous variables (y_t^L), and k exogenous variables (x_t), including the intercept, the structural equations can be written as

$$\mathbf{G}\mathbf{y}_t = \mathbf{C}\mathbf{y}_t^L + \mathbf{B}\mathbf{x}_t$$

The **G** matrix is assumed to be nonsingular.

The SIMLIN procedure computes the reduced form coefficients of the endogenous variables by premultiplying by the inverse of the **G** matrix.

$$\mathbf{y}_t = \mathbf{G}^{-1}\mathbf{C}\mathbf{y}_t^L + \mathbf{G}^{-1}\mathbf{B}\mathbf{x}_t$$

$$\mathbf{y}_t = \Pi_1\mathbf{y}_t^L + \Pi_2\mathbf{x}_t$$

The circled numbers in Output 23.2 correspond to the following:

❶ `Inverse Coefficient Matrix for Endogenous Variables` is the inverse of the **G** matrix. For this model the **G** matrix is an identity matrix, as no contemporaneous endogenous variables appear as regressor variables. The seemingly unrelated equations are estimated jointly because of the contemporaneously correlated error terms.

❷ `Reduced Form for Exogenous Variables` is the matrix $\Pi_2 = \mathbf{G}^{-1}\mathbf{B}$. Because $\mathbf{G} = \mathbf{I}$, this matrix contains the OLS parameter estimates. Because this model has no lagged endogenous variables, the Π_1 matrix has no nonzero elements.

For models with lagged endogenous variables, multipliers are also calculated that show the effect of changes in exogenous variables on the endogenous variables. Use the INTERIM=*n* and TOTAL options in the PROC SIMLIN statement to calculate and print the interim multipliers for interims 1 to *n*, and the total multipliers, respectively.

❸ The `Statistics of Fit` table includes the `Mean Error`, `Mean % Error` (mean percent error), `Mean Abs Error` (mean absolute error), `Mean Abs % Error` (mean absolute percent error), `RMS Error` (root mean square error), and `RMS % Error` (root mean percent error). The closer these statistics are to 0, the closer the forecasts match the actual values. Note that the RATE_IT equation has the largest errors in levels, but the closest to 0 in percentages.

Also the statistics of fit can assist in selecting among forecasting models. Statistics closer to 0 indicate the model that best predicts the historical data. As additional data becomes available the forecasts can be compared with the actual values, and additional insights may be obtained.

The mathematical formulas for these statistics are listed in Example 16, "Assessing Forecast Accuracy." For additional information on statistics of fit, see p. 735 of the *SAS/ETS User's Guide, Version 6, Second Edition.*

Printing the Forecasts of the SUR Estimated Model

Output 23.3
Printing the Predicted and Residual Values

```
                          Exchange Rate Model
                        Estimated by the SUR Method

OBS  YEAR  FORE_FR1    R_FR1    FORE_WG1    R_WG1    FORE_IT1    R_IT1

 14  1990   6.04366  -0.59696   1.83416  -0.21756    1312.08  -113.814
 15  1991   6.43914  -0.79234   1.90875  -0.24775    1319.40   -78.116
 16  1992   7.41094    .        1.85580    .         1532.44     .
 17  1993   7.14768    .        1.99271    .         1372.42     .
```

Further Reading

For more information on PROC SIMLIN and PROC SYSLIN, see the *SAS/ETS User's Guide, Version 6, Second Edition.*

References

- *Economic Report of the President*, Washington, D.C.: U.S. Government Printing Office, 1995.
- *Statistical Abstracts of the U.S.*, Department of Commerce, Washington, D.C.: U.S. Government Printing Office, various years.

EXAMPLE 24

Fitting a Linear System by Instrumental Methods

Featured Tools:

- SYSLIN procedure
  - 3SLS option
  - IT3SLS option
  - FIML option

The foreign exchange rate model developed in Example 21 ("Fitting and Forecasting a Linear System by SUR and ITSUR") was estimated by OLS and SUR methods. Estimating the model by the methods of OLS and SUR implies that the regressor variables are assumed to conform to the standard assumption of being uncorrelated with the error term. However, if you believe that the level of real imports is contemporaneously influenced by the exchange rate, then the variables IM_FR, IM_WG, and IM_IT are correlated with the error term, and OLS and SUR estimation yields biased parameter estimates. (In a larger exchange rate model with more equations, the level of each country's imports could appear as dependent variables.) In this case, appropriate methods for estimating each equation separately are two-stage least squares (2SLS) and limited information maximum likelihood (LIML).

In addition to single equation methods, system estimation can be performed. For simultaneous equation models with regressor variables correlated with the error terms of one or more equations, appropriate estimation methods are three-stage least squares (3SLS) and full information maximum likelihood (FIML).

3SLS estimation combines the instrumental regression method of 2SLS to account for regressors correlated with the error term, and the estimation of the covariance matrix of SUR to account for the cross-equation correlation of the error terms. In the first stage of 3SLS estimation, instrumental regressions are used to create regressors uncorrelated with the error terms. An instrument is a variable correlated with a regressor but not with error terms; nor is an instrument dependent on the endogenous variables. Predicted values from an instrumental regression are linear combinations of instruments and of the regressors that are not correlated with the error term. In the second stage, substituting these predictions for the regressors, each equation is estimated by OLS, and the residuals are used to estimate the covariance matrix of equation errors. In the third stage, the model parameters are estimated by generalized least squares.

Note: 3SLS estimation produces the same results as 2SLS if the cross-equation errors are not contemporaneously correlated.

Program

3SLS Estimation

To fit the exchange rate model using the systems estimation method of 3SLS, specify the 3SLS option in the PROC SYSLIN statement. The ENDOGENOUS statement specifies the variables that are dependent (endogenous) variables in the first-stage regressions. You only need to declare an endogenous variable in the ENDOGENOUS statement if it is used as a right-side variable; although RATE_FR, RATE_WG and RATE_IT are endogenous in this model, it is not necessary to list them in the ENDOGENOUS statement. The INSTRUMENTS statement specifies the instrumental variables.

By default, the SAS/ETS SYSLIN procedure prints results of second and third stages of 3SLS estimation.

Fit the model using the estimation technique of 3SLS. The FIRST option specifies the printing of the first-stage regression statistics for endogenous regressors.

```
proc syslin data=exch1 3sls first out=p_3sls;
   endogenous im_fr im_wg im_it;
   instruments year di_fr dr_fr di_wg dr_wg di_it dr_it
               prod_us prod_fr prod_wg prod_it;
   France:  model rate_fr = im_fr di_fr dr_fr;
            output p=p_fr r=r_fr;
   Germany: model rate_wg = im_wg di_wg dr_wg;
            output p=p_wg r=r_wg;
   Italy:   model rate_it = im_it di_it dr_it;
            output p=p_it r=r_it;
run;
```

Print the predicted and residual values using PROC PRINT. A WHERE statement is used to specify the observations to be printed.

```
proc print data=p_3sls;
   where year > 1989;
   var year rate_fr p_fr r_fr rate_wg p_wg r_wg
            rate_it p_it r_it;
   title2 'Predicted Values from 3SLS Model';
run;
```

First-Stage Regression Statistics

Output 24.1
Instrumental Variables Regression for Endogenous Regressor, IM_FR (Partial Output)

```
                          Exchange Rate Model

                            SYSLIN Procedure
                     First Stage Regression Statistics

Model:
Dependent variable: IM_FR Imports to US from France in 1984 $

                        ❶ Analysis of Variance

                              Sum of         Mean
   Source          DF        Squares        Square      F Value       Prob>F

   Model           11 42447336.734 3858848.7940      144.302       0.0069
   Error            2  53483.04226  26741.52113
   C Total         13 42500819.776
                                              ❷
           Root MSE    163.52835      R-Square        0.9987
           Dep Mean   8099.61627      Adj R-SQ        0.9918
           C.V.          2.01896
```

```
                          Exchange Rate Model

                            SYSLIN Procedure
                     First Stage Regression Statistics

                        ❸ Parameter Estimates

                       Parameter       Standard    T for H0:
    Variable  DF        Estimate          Error  Parameter=0    Prob > |T|

    INTERCEP   1         -483176         542732       -0.890        0.4673
    YEAR       1      251.376910     280.530110        0.896        0.4648
    DI_FR      1      225.571390     325.638507        0.693        0.5601
    DR_FR      1      284.874881     542.639573        0.525        0.6520
    DI_WG      1      325.032351     433.403226        0.750        0.5315
    DR_WG      1     -806.013352     642.697469       -1.254        0.3365
    DI_IT      1      140.383318     274.964360        0.511        0.6604
    DR_IT      1     -266.815375     442.991387       -0.602        0.6082
    PROD_US    1      -95.378691     193.436544       -0.493        0.6708
    PROD_FR    1     -461.448589     293.372859       -1.573        0.2564
    PROD_WG    1      384.726960     273.721305        1.406        0.2951
    PROD_IT    1      101.303845      83.890517        1.208        0.3506
```

Explanation

The SYSLIN procedure prints the parameter values and statistics to help you analyze and evaluate the estimated model. As shown in Output 24.1, for each estimated equation, the following are printed:

❶ **`Analysis of Variance`** (ANOVA) includes

- □ sums of squares for the model, error, and corrected total
- □ degrees of freedom for each component of variation
- □ mean squares for the model and error components
- □ the *F*-statistic and *p*-value for the null hypothesis that all parameters are jointly equal to 0.

❷ The goodness-of-fit statistics include the **`Root MSE`** (root mean square error), **`R-square`**, and **`Adj R-Sq`** (adjusted R-square). A first-stage regression R-square of 1.0 indicates that none of the information in the endogenous regressor is lost when it is replaced by the predicted values in the second-stage regressions. An R-square of less than 1.0 indicates that some of the information has been lost, and an R-square of 0 indicates that all of the information has been lost.

❸ The parameter estimates, standard errors, *t*-statistics for the null hypotheses that each parameter is equal to 0, and the *p*-values are listed.

2SLS Estimation

Output 24.2
Model Estimated by Two-Stage Least Squares (Partial Output)

```
                         Exchange Rate Model

                          SYSLIN Procedure
                 Two-Stage Least Squares Estimation

Model: FRANCE
Dependent variable: RATE_FR

                      ❶ Analysis of Variance

                           Sum of         Mean
   Source          DF     Squares       Square      F Value       Prob>F

   Model            3    22.32894      7.44298       11.921       0.0012
   Error           10     6.24381      0.62438
   C Total         13    28.95821
                    ❷
         Root MSE         0.79018     R-Square       0.7815
         Dep Mean         6.19408     Adj R-SQ       0.7159
         C.V.            12.75699
```

```
                    Exchange Rate Model

                     SYSLIN Procedure
              Two-Stage Least Squares Estimation

                  ❸ Parameter Estimates

                  Parameter      Standard    T for H0:
Variable  DF       Estimate         Error  Parameter=0    Prob > |T|

INTERCEP   1      -2.109124      1.889028       -1.117        0.2903
IM_FR      1       0.000930      0.000225        4.126        0.0021
DI_FR      1      -0.663871      0.135544       -4.898        0.0006
DR_FR      1      -0.076260      0.178978       -0.426        0.6791
```

```
                    Exchange Rate Model

                     SYSLIN Procedure
              Two-Stage Least Squares Estimation

Model: GERMANY
Dependent variable: RATE_WG

                  ❶ Analysis of Variance

                        Sum of         Mean
Source          DF     Squares       Square      F Value       Prob>F

Model            3     1.57455      0.52485        6.227       0.0117
Error           10     0.84291      0.08429
C Total         13     2.44927
                 ❷
       Root MSE        0.29033     R-Square       0.6513
       Dep Mean        2.11267     Adj R-SQ       0.5467
       C.V.           13.74230
```

```
                    Exchange Rate Model

                     SYSLIN Procedure
              Two-Stage Least Squares Estimation

                  ❸ Parameter Estimates

                  Parameter      Standard    T for H0:
Variable  DF       Estimate         Error  Parameter=0    Prob > |T|

INTERCEP   1       2.598933      0.460585        5.643        0.0002
IM_WG      1   -0.000025516   0.000021833       -1.169        0.2696
DI_WG      1      -0.005056      0.046458       -0.109        0.9155
DR_WG      1      -0.130412      0.046766       -2.789        0.0192
```

```
                         Exchange Rate Model

                           SYSLIN Procedure
                  Two-Stage Least Squares Estimation

Model: ITALY
Dependent variable: RATE_IT

                       ❶ Analysis of Variance

                            Sum of          Mean
   Source          DF      Squares        Square       F Value       Prob>F

   Model            3 1081581.2076 360527.06921         14.968       0.0005
   Error           10 240858.89311  24085.88931
   C Total         13 1331007.1222
                      ❷
             Root MSE    155.19629      R-Square       0.8179
             Dep Mean   1293.98214      Adj R-SQ       0.7632
             C.V.         11.99370
```

```
                        Exchange Rate Model

                          SYSLIN Procedure
                  Two-Stage Least Squares Estimation

                       ❸ Parameter Estimates

                     Parameter       Standard    T for H0:
    Variable  DF      Estimate          Error   Parameter=0    Prob > |T|

    INTERCEP   1  -1356.765470     668.686582       -2.029        0.0699
    IM_IT      1      0.247416       0.075009        3.298        0.0080
    DI_IT      1   -144.642893      24.925352       -5.803        0.0002
    DR_IT      1     37.489067      32.688625        1.147        0.2781
```

Explanation

For each estimated equation, PROC SYSLIN printed the following statistics, as shown in Output 24.2:

❶ **`Analysis of Variance`** (ANOVA) includes the partitioned sums of squares, degrees of freedom, and mean squares.

❷ Goodness-of-fit statistics include the **`Root MSE`** (root mean square), **`R-square`**, and **`Adj R-Sq`** (adjusted R-square).

❸ The parameter estimates, standard errors, *t*-statistics for the null hypotheses that each parameter is equal to 0, and the *p*-values are listed.

3SLS Estimation

Output 24.3
The Cross Model Covariance and Correlation Matrices, the Cross Model Inverse Covariance and Correlation Matrices, and the Parameter Estimates for each equation of the Model (Partial Output)

```
                    Exchange Rate Model

                     SYSLIN Procedure
              Three-Stage Least Squares Estimation

          ❶ Cross Model Covariance

Sigma            FRANCE          GERMANY            ITALY

FRANCE       0.6243808487      0.186253624     77.565243762
GERMANY       0.186253624     0.0842913492     21.729439952
ITALY        77.565243762     21.729439952     24085.889311


          ❷ Cross Model Correlation

Corr             FRANCE          GERMANY            ITALY

FRANCE                  1     0.8118736424     0.6325007309
GERMANY      0.8118736424                1     0.4822538321
ITALY        0.6325007309     0.4822538321                1
```

```
                    Exchange Rate Model

                     SYSLIN Procedure
              Three-Stage Least Squares Estimation

          ❸ Cross Model Inverse Correlation

Inv Corr          FRANCE          GERMANY            ITALY

FRANCE        3.7707859521     -2.490404663     -1.184017679
GERMANY       -2.490404663     2.9478288814     0.1535809952
ITALY         -1.184017679     0.1535809952     1.6748270238

          ❹ Cross Model Inverse Covariance

Inv Sigma         FRANCE          GERMANY            ITALY

FRANCE        6.0392402491     -10.85559498     -0.009654995
GERMANY       -10.85559498     34.971902927     0.0034085105
ITALY         -0.009654995     0.0034085105     0.0000695356
```

```
                    Exchange Rate Model

                     SYSLIN Procedure
              Three-Stage Least Squares Estimation

   System Weighted MSE:  0.84577 with 30 degrees of freedom.
   System Weighted R-Square:  0.7328
```

```
                    Exchange Rate Model

                      SYSLIN Procedure
             Three-Stage Least Squares Estimation

Model: FRANCE
Dependent variable: RATE_FR
                   ❺ Parameter Estimates

                   Parameter       Standard    T for H0:
   Variable  DF     Estimate          Error   Parameter=0   Prob > |T|

   INTERCEP   1    -0.164234       1.492112        -0.110       0.9145
   IM_FR      1     0.000707       0.000174         4.060       0.0023
   DI_FR      1    -0.563193       0.120859        -4.660       0.0009
   DR_FR      1     0.056075       0.130033         0.431       0.6754
```

```
                    Exchange Rate Model

                      SYSLIN Procedure
             Three-Stage Least Squares Estimation

Model: GERMANY
Dependent variable: RATE_WG
                   ❺ Parameter Estimates

                   Parameter       Standard    T for H0:
   Variable  DF     Estimate          Error   Parameter=0   Prob > |T|

   INTERCEP   1     2.839620       0.354141         8.018       0.0001
   IM_WG      1 -0.000034365    0.000017511        -1.962       0.0781
   DI_WG      1    -0.036435       0.038378        -0.949       0.3648
   DR_WG      1    -0.064392       0.035964        -1.790       0.1036
```

```
                    Exchange Rate Model

                      SYSLIN Procedure
             Three-Stage Least Squares Estimation

Model: ITALY
Dependent variable: RATE_IT
                   ❺ Parameter Estimates

                   Parameter       Standard    T for H0:
   Variable  DF     Estimate          Error   Parameter=0   Prob > |T|

   INTERCEP   1  -765.624719     583.645597        -1.312       0.2189
   IM_IT      1     0.187881       0.065217         2.881       0.0164
   DI_IT      1  -118.621885      22.865330        -5.188       0.0004
   DR_IT      1    46.332675      29.492823         1.571       0.1473
```

Explanation

In Output 24.3, the following items are listed:

❶ The cross model covariance matrix is printed.

❷ The cross model correlation matrix is printed. Note that the off-diagonal elements are nonzero, suggesting that the 3SLS estimate are more efficient than the 2SLS estimates.

❸ The cross model inverse correlation matrix is printed.

❹ The cross model inverse covariance matrix is printed.

❺ For each equation, the parameter estimates standard errors, *t*-statistics for the null hypotheses that each parameter is equal to 0, and the *p*-values are listed.

CAUTION!

The system estimation method of 3SLS is more sensitive to specification error bias than nonsystem estimation methods. One poorly specified equation can affect the parameter estimates in all equations because individual parameter estimates (by construction) are sensitive to the specification of the entire model system.

In theory, with a large number of observations, 3SLS estimates are unbiased and more efficient than OLS estimates. Yet, the small-sample properties of system method estimates may not be good. With small sample sizes, 2SLS may be preferred to 3SLS. This is because cross-equation covariances are estimated, not known. For the same reason, OLS may be preferred to SUR in small samples.

For additional information on 3SLS estimation, see Pindyck and Rubinfeld (1991), pp. 314-327. ■

Forecasts from the 3SLS Estimated Model

Output 24.4
Printing Actual, Predicted, and Residual Values

```
                       Exchange Rate Model
                  Predicted Values from 3SLS Model

OBS   YEAR   RATE_FR     P_FR       R_FR     RATE_WG     P_WG

 14   1990    5.4467   6.04239   -0.59569    1.6166   1.83372
 15   1991    5.6468   6.43535   -0.78855    1.6610   1.90445
 16   1992     .       7.40392     .          .       1.84988
 17   1993     .       7.14194     .          .       1.98769

OBS     R_WG      RATE_IT     P_IT       R_IT

 14   -0.21712    1198.27   1312.43   -114.160
 15   -0.24345    1241.28   1320.02    -78.738
 16     .           .       1533.12      .
 17     .           .       1373.14      .
```

Explanation

The variables listed in Output 24.4 are as follows:

YEAR
: contains the date in years.

RATE_FR, RATE_WG, and RATE_IT
: are the actual exchange rate values.

P_FR, P_WG, and P_IT
: are the predicted exchange rate values from the 3SLS estimated model.

R_FR, R_WG, and R_IT
: are the residual values (actual values−predicted value).

Iterated 3SLS (IT3SLS) Estimation

As in ITSUR, the residuals of the fitted equations can be used to form another estimate of the covariance matrix of equation errors, which can then be used to re-estimate the model parameters. The covariance matrix and parameters can be estimated in alternating fashion until convergence is achieved. This estimation method is known as *iterated 3SLS*, or *IT3SLS*.

Forecasting the IT3SLS Estimated Model

To fit the exchange rate model using the systems estimation method of IT3SLS, specify the IT3SLS option in the PROC SYSLIN statement.

Fit the model using the estimation technique of IT3SLS. Use the MAXITER= option to specify the maximum number of iterations. The default number of iterations is 30. The NOPRINT option suppresses the printed output.

```
proc syslin data=exch1 it3sls maxiter=300 out=p_it3sls noprint;
   endogenous im_fr im_wg im_it;
   instruments year di_fr dr_fr di_wg dr_wg di_it dr_it
               prod_us prod_fr prod_wg prod_it;
   France:  model rate_fr = im_fr di_fr dr_fr;
            output p=p_fr r=r_fr;
   Germany: model rate_wg = im_wg di_wg dr_wg;
            output p=p_wg r=r_wg;
   Italy:   model rate_it = im_it di_it dr_it;
            output p=p_it r=r_it;
run;
```

Print the predicted and residual values with PROC PRINT. A WHERE statement is used to specify the observations to be printed.

```
proc print data=p_it3sls;
   where year > 1989;
   var year rate_fr p_fr r_fr rate_wg p_wg r_wg
            rate_it p_it r_it;
   title2 'Predicted Values from IT3SLS Model';
run;
```

Output 24.5
Printing Actual, Predicted, Residual Values of the IT3SLS Estimated Model

Exchange Rate Model
Predicted Values from IT3SLS Model

OBS	YEAR	RATE_FR	P_FR	R_FR	RATE_WG	P_WG
14	1990	5.4467	6.60680	-1.16010	1.6166	2.01845
15	1991	5.6468	6.82455	-1.17775	1.6610	2.10055
16	1992	.	7.31620	.	.	2.04984
17	1993	.	7.17806	.	.	2.04159

OBS	R_WG	RATE_IT	P_IT	R_IT
14	-0.40185	1198.27	1386.25	-187.983
15	-0.43955	1241.28	1387.63	-146.352
16	.	.	1516.11	.
17	.	.	1439.55	.

Explanation

The variables listed in Output 24.5 follow the same pattern as those listed in Output 24.4.

A Closer Look

3SLS Estimation: Selection of Instrumental Variables

Instruments are used to purge the regressors of their correlation with the residuals. Possible instruments include variables in the model that are independent of the error terms, lags of variables in the model that are independent of the error terms, and low degree polynomials of the exogenous variables. Instruments must not depend on any endogenous variable, nor depend on any of the estimated parameters, nor be lags of endogenous variables if there is any serial correlation of the error terms.

In the exchange rate model, the level of real imports is suspected of being correlated with the error term and, hence, suggests an instrumental variables method or a maximum likelihood method. Possible instrumental variables include industrial production indexes; employment levels and rates in the U.S., France, Germany, and Italy; and real gross national or real gross domestic products (GNP or GDP). These variables may be correlated with the level of real imports while not being correlated with the model error terms nor being dependent on any of the endogenous variables.

Appropriate Number of Instrumental Variables

You need at least as many linearly-independent instruments as the maximum number of parameters in any equation, or else some of the parameters cannot be estimated. You can, however, use too many instruments. To get the benefit of instrumental variables, you must have more observations than instruments. Instrumental variables techniques are most successful in eliminating simultaneous equation bias in large samples. The larger the excess of observations over instruments, the more bias is reduced. Adding more instruments can initially improve the efficiency, but after some point efficiency declines as the excess of observations over instruments becomes smaller and the bias grows.

For each equation in the exchange rate model, there are 3 slope parameters and an intercept parameter to estimate, but only 14 observations with no missing values with which to fit the model. You need enough instruments to estimate the parameters, but fewer than the number of observations.

Variations

Using the DW Option

Print the Durbin-Watson *d*-statistics and the first-order autocorrelation coefficient using the DW option in the MODEL statement.

```
proc syslin data=exch1 3sls;
   endogenous im_fr im_wg im_it;
   instruments year di_fr dr_fr di_wg dr_wg di_it dr_it
               prod_us prod_fr prod_wg prod_it;
   France:  model rate_fr = im_fr di_fr dr_fr / dw;
   Germany: model rate_wg = im_wg di_wg dr_wg / dw;
   Italy:   model rate_it = im_it di_it dr_it / dw;
run;
```

Output 24.6
Durbin-Watson Statistics (Partial Output)

```
                        Exchange Rate Model

                          SYSLIN Procedure
                Three-Stage Least Squares Estimation

Model: FRANCE
Dependent variable: RATE_FR

                     Durbin-Watson               0.872
                     (For Number of Obs.)           14
                     1st Order Autocorrelation   0.508


Model: GERMANY
Dependent variable: RATE_WG

                     Durbin-Watson               0.754
                     (For Number of Obs.)           14
                     1st Order Autocorrelation   0.590


Model: ITALY
Dependent variable: RATE_IT

                     Durbin-Watson               1.710
                     (For Number of Obs.)           14
                     1st Order Autocorrelation   0.120
```

Explanation

The Durbin-Watson *d*-statistic is often used as a test for first-order autocorrelation, AR(1). The *d*-statistic has a range from 0 to 4. The null hypothesis is that the residuals are not a first-order autoregressive process. A value close to 2.0 indicates you should retain the null hypothesis. In general, values close to 0 indicate positive AR(1), and values close to 4.0 indicate negative AR(1).

The Durbin-Watson *d*-statistics for the French, German, and Italian exchange rate equations are .872, .754, and 1.710, respectively. The

Savin-White tables (Savin and White 1977) show that at the .05 level of significance, with 14 observations and 3 regressor variables, the lower d_L and upper d_U bounds on the critical value are .767 and 1.779. The d-statistics for the French and Italian equations are in this inconclusive range while the German equation is in the critical region.

Assuming the model is properly specified, these d-statistics indicate the usefulness of specifying the error terms as autoregressive processes. In Example 25, "Linear System Diagnostics and Autoregressive Error Correction," the exchange rate model is estimated with autoregressive error terms.

Note: As an alternative to estimation with autoregressive error terms, you might want to explore the results of including additional regressor variables and employing different functional forms for the model because model misspecification can produce a Durbin-Watson d-statistic that is in the critical region.

Full Information Maximum Likelihood (FIML) Estimation

FIML estimation is a system generalization of limited information maximum likelihood (LIML) estimation. FIML estimation involves minimizing the determinant of the covariance matrix associated with the residuals of the reduced form of the equation system. *LIML estimation* involves assuming that the errors are normally distributed and then maximizing the likelihood function subject to the restrictions on a particular equation. FIML estimation involves assuming that the errors are normally distributed and then maximizing the likelihood function subject to the restrictions on all of the parameters in the model, not just those in the equation being estimated. FIML estimation is implemented as an instrumental variables method. For additional information on FIML estimation, see Hausman (1975).

FIML Estimation of the Exchange Rate Model

To fit the exchange rate model using the systems estimation method of FIML, specify the FIML option in the PROC SYSLIN statement and then use an INSTRUMENTS statement to specify the instrumental variables.

Fit the model using the estimation technique of FIML. Use the MAXITER= option to specify the maximum number of iterations. The default is MAXITER=30. You can use the CONVERGE= option to specify a convergence criterion for iterative estimation methods (ITSUR, IT3SLS, and FIML). The default is CONVERGE=.0001.

```
proc syslin data=exch1 fiml maxiter=100 out=p_fiml;
   instruments year di_fr dr_fr di_wg dr_wg di_it dr_it
               prod_us prod_fr prod_wg prod_it
               cpi_us cpi_fr cpi_wg cpi_it;
   France:  model rate_fr = im_fr di_fr dr_fr;
            output p=p_fr r=r_fr;
   Germany: model rate_wg = im_wg di_wg dr_wg;
            output p=p_wg r=r_wg;
   Italy:   model rate_it = im_it di_it dr_it;
            output p=p_it r=r_it;
run;
```

Print the predicted and residual values using PROC PRINT.

```
proc print data=p_fiml;
   where year > 1989;
   var year rate_fr p_fr r_fr rate_wg p_wg r_wg
            rate_it p_it r_it;
   title2 'Predicted Values from FIML Model';
run;
```

Output 24.7
FIML Estimation Results: Parameter Estimates, Standard Errors, *t*-statistics, and *p*-values

```
                         Exchange Rate Model

                           SYSLIN Procedure
             Full-Information Maximum Likelihood Estimation

Model: FRANCE
Dependent variable: RATE_FR
                           SYSLIN Procedure
             Full-Information Maximum Likelihood Estimation

                         Parameter Estimates

                   Parameter      Standard    T for H0:
   Variable  DF     Estimate         Error  Parameter=0     Prob > |T|

   INTERCEP   1     7.150101      0.790731        9.042         0.0001
   IM_FR      1    -0.000114   0.000080737       -1.409         0.1891
   DI_FR      1     0.037787      0.067538        0.559         0.5881
   DR_FR      1    -0.047465      0.064106       -0.740         0.4761
```

```
                         Exchange Rate Model

                           SYSLIN Procedure
             Full-Information Maximum Likelihood Estimation

Model: GERMANY
Dependent variable: RATE_WG
                         Parameter Estimates

                   Parameter      Standard    T for H0:
   Variable  DF     Estimate         Error  Parameter=0     Prob > |T|

   INTERCEP   1     2.860614      0.233889       12.231         0.0001
   IM_WG      1 -0.000054857   0.000010388       -5.281         0.0004
   DI_WG      1     0.075803      0.020655        3.670         0.0043
   DR_WG      1    -0.042983      0.017480       -2.459         0.0337
```

Exchange Rate Model

SYSLIN Procedure
Full-Information Maximum Likelihood Estimation

Model: ITALY
Dependent variable: RATE_IT

Parameter Estimates

Variable	DF	Parameter Estimate	Standard Error	T for H0: Parameter=0	Prob > |T|
INTERCEP	1	900.881279	189.777968	4.747	0.0008
IM_IT	1	0.041506	0.020396	2.035	0.0692
DI_IT	1	-14.388588	8.548138	-1.683	0.1232
DR_IT	1	-8.151837	12.803537	-0.637	0.5386

Forecasts from the FIML Estimated Model

Output 24.8
Printing Actual, Predicted, and Residual Values

Exchange Rate Model
Predicted Values from FIML Model

OBS	YEAR	RATE_FR	P_FR	R_FR	RATE_WG	P_WG
14	1990	5.4467	5.90283	-0.45613	1.6166	1.77652
15	1991	5.6468	5.84621	-0.19941	1.6610	1.69686
16	1992	.	5.62076	.	.	1.44845
17	1993	.	5.66879	.	.	1.54472

OBS	R_WG	RATE_IT	P_IT	R_IT
14	-0.15992	1198.27	1285.52	-87.2456
15	-0.03586	1241.28	1257.27	-15.9869
16	.	.	1231.61	.
17	.	.	1249.24	.

Explanation

The variables listed in Output 24.8 follow the same pattern as those listed in Output 24.4.

Further Reading

For more information on PROC SYSLIN, see the *SAS/ETS User's Guide, Version 6, Second Edition.*

References

□ *Economic Report of the President*, Washington, D.C.: U.S. Government Printing Office, 1995.

□ Hausman, J.A. (1975), "An Instrumental Variable Approach to Full Information Estimators for Linear and Certain Nonlinear Econometric Models," *Econometrica*, 43, 727-738.

□ Pindyck, R.S. and Rubinfeld, D.L. (1991), *Econometric Models and Economic Forecasts, Third Edition*, New York: McGraw-Hill Inc.

□ Savin, N.E. and White, K.J. (1977), "The Durbin-Watson Test for Serial Correlation with Extreme Sample Sizes or Many Regressors," *Econometrica*, 45, 1989-1996.

□ *Statistical Abstracts of the U.S.*, Department of Commerce, Washington, D.C.: U.S. Government Printing Office, various years.

EXAMPLE 25

Linear System Diagnostics and Autoregressive Error Correction

Featured Tools:

- □ MODEL procedure
  - FIT statement
  - %AR macro
  - SOLVE statement

The foreign exchange rate model developed in Examples 21 through 24 was estimated by OLS, SUR, and instrumental variables methods. In Example 24, the Durbin-Watson statistics are printed and, if used as a test for first-order autocorrelation of the residuals, they indicate the usefulness of modeling the equation error terms as autoregressive processes.

This example uses the SAS/ETS MODEL procedure to:

- □ analyze the structure of the model with the GRAPH option
- □ fit the model with a FIT statement
- □ perform tests of the residuals with various options
- □ model the error terms as autoregressive processes with the %AR macro
- □ forecast the model with a SOLVE statement.

Program

Analyzing the Model and the Residuals

Analyze the model with the GRAPH option in the PROC MODEL statement.

```
proc model data=exch1 graph;
```

Specify the model parameters with a PARAMETERS statement.

```
   parameters a1-a3 b1-b3 c1-c3 d1-d3;
```

Specify the model with assignment statements, including parameters and arithmetic operators.

```
   France:  rate_fr = a1+b1*im_fr+c1*di_fr+d1*dr_fr;
   Germany: rate_wg = a2+b2*im_wg+c2*di_wg+d2*dr_wg;
   Italy:   rate_it = a3+b3*im_it+c3*di_it+d3*dr_it;
```

Fit the model with a FIT statement. Specify the SUR estimation method with the SUR option in the FIT statement.

```
   fit rate_fr rate_wg rate_it
       / sur     /* specifies SUR estimation                 */
```

Test the residuals using the DW, GF=, WHITE, BREUSCH=, and NORMAL options.

```
         dw      /* prints DW statistics                     */
         gf=2    /* Godfrey test for serial correlation      */
         white   /* White's test for heteroscedasticity      */
         breusch=(im_fr di_fr dr_fr)  /* Breusch-Pagan test */
         normal; /* normality tests of residuals             */

run;
```

Output 25.1
Analysis of the Model Structure (Partial Output)

```
                    Exchange Rate Model

                      MODEL Procedure

                   ❶ Model Summary

                 Model Variables        3
                 Parameters            12
                 Equations              3

                 Number of Statements   3

        Model Variables: RATE_FR RATE_WG RATE_IT

        Parameters: A1 A2 A3 B1 B2 B3 C1 C2 C3 D1 D2 D3

        Equations: RATE_FR RATE_WG RATE_IT
```

```
                    Exchange Rate Model

                      MODEL Procedure

              ❷ Model Structure Analysis
      (Based on Assignments to Endogenous Model Variables)

        Endogenous Variables: RATE_FR RATE_WG RATE_IT

                    Exchange Rate Model

                      MODEL Procedure

             Adjacency Matrix for Graph of System

                    Variable     1 2 3

                    RATE_FR  1:  X . .
                    RATE_WG  2:  . X .
                    RATE_IT  3:  . . X

               NOTE: The System is Independent.
```

```
                    Exchange Rate Model

                      MODEL Procedure

          ❸ The 3 Equations to Estimate are:

   RATE_FR = F( A1(1), B1(IM_FR), C1(DI_FR), D1(DR_FR) )
   RATE_WG = F( A2(1), B2(IM_WG), C2(DI_WG), D2(DR_WG) )
   RATE_IT = F( A3(1), B3(IM_IT), C3(DI_IT), D3(DR_IT) )
```

Explanation

In Output 25.1 the following items are listed:

❶ `Model Summary` lists the model variables, parameters, equations, and number of statements in the PROC MODEL program. If starting values were specified, then the values used to begin the optimizing process are also printed.

❷ `Model Structure Analysis` lists the endogenous variables, prints the adjacency matrix for the graph of the system, and notes the structure of the model. The graph of the model structure can be quite useful in analyzing the lag and dependency structures of models. Model variables are classified into endogenous (dependent) and exogenous (independent) groups based on the presence of the variable on the left-side of an assignment statement defining the model. The endogenous variables are grouped into simultaneously determined blocks. In terms of the endogenous variables, the exchange rate model is independent, and each equation could be estimated separately.

❸ `The 3 Equations to Estimate are:` lists the dependencies of the equations to be estimated. For linear models, each parameter depends on a variable. For nonlinear models, parameters may depend on variables, functions of variables, and other parameters.

Analyzing the Fit of the Model and the Residuals

Output 25.2
Estimation Results and Analysis of the Residuals (Partial Output)

```
                Exchange Rate Model

                  MODEL Procedure
                   SUR Estimation

             ❶ SUR Estimation Summary

              Dataset Option       Dataset
              DATA=                  EXCH1

              Parameters Estimated      12

               ❷ Minimization Summary
              Method                 GAUSS
              Iterations                 1

              Final  Convergence  Criteria
              R                1.05367E-8
              PPC                5.11E-14
              RPC(C2)              3.8211
              Object            0.1657094
              Trace(S)         26784.5737
```

```
                    Exchange Rate Model

                      MODEL Procedure
                       SUR Estimation

                 Objective Value    1.7877654

                    Observations Processed
                 Read                      17
                 Solved                    17
                 Used                      14
                 Missing                    3
```

```
                    Exchange Rate Model

                      MODEL Procedure
                       SUR Estimation

        ❸ Nonlinear SUR Summary of Residual Errors
                                                                  ❹
            DF   DF                                              Durbin
Equation Model Error      SSE       MSE  Root MSE R-Square Adj R-Sq Watson

RATE_FR      4    10   7.7384   0.77384   0.87968   0.7328   0.6526  0.873
RATE_WG      4    10   1.0152   0.10152   0.31863   0.5855   0.4611  0.752
RATE_IT      4    10   267837  26783.70    163.66   0.7988   0.7384  1.718
```

```
                    Exchange Rate Model

                      MODEL Procedure
                       SUR Estimation

             ❺ Nonlinear SUR Parameter Estimates

                                Approx.      'T'   Approx.
        Parameter    Estimate   Std Err    Ratio  Prob>|T|

        A1          -0.157400    1.47138    -0.11    0.9169
        A2           2.850373    0.34545     8.25    0.0001
        A3        -774.062495  578.53807    -1.34    0.2105
        B1         0.00070594  0.0001714     4.12    0.0021
        B2        -0.00003485 0.00001705    -2.04    0.0683
        B3           0.188700    0.06461     2.92    0.0153
        C1          -0.563960    0.12042    -4.68    0.0009
        C2          -0.037225    0.03809    -0.98    0.3514
        C3        -119.038682   22.81211    -5.22    0.0004
        D1           0.057474    0.12859     0.45    0.6644
        D2          -0.063523    0.03558    -1.79    0.1045
        D3          46.286407   29.34362     1.58    0.1458
```

```
                    Exchange Rate Model

                      MODEL Procedure
                       SUR Estimation

              ❻ Heteroscedasticity Test

Equation     Test            Statistic   DF     Prob  Variables

RATE_FR      White's Test         9.89    9   0.3597  Cross of all vars
             Breusch-Pagan        2.00    3   0.5721  IM_FR, DI_FR,
DR_F, 1
RATE_WG      White's Test         8.27    9   0.5068  Cross of all vars
             Breusch-Pagan        2.81    3   0.4213  IM_FR, DI_FR,
DR_F, 1
RATE_IT      White's Test        13.27    9   0.1509  Cross of all vars
             Breusch-Pagan        1.80    3   0.6154  IM_FR, DI_FR,
DR_F, 1
```

```
                    Exchange Rate Model

                      MODEL Procedure
                       SUR Estimation

                ❼ Autocorrelation Test

Equation     Lag  Statistic          Value    Prob

RATE_FR        1  Godfrey's AR       1.845  0.1744
               2  Godfrey's AR       4.503  0.1052
RATE_WG        1  Godfrey's AR        3.52  0.0606
               2  Godfrey's AR       8.657  0.0132
RATE_IT        1  Godfrey's AR       0.175  0.6753
               2  Godfrey's AR       3.958  0.1382
```

```
                    Exchange Rate Model

                      MODEL Procedure
                       SUR Estimation

                   ❽ Normality Test

Equation     Test Statistic    Value     Prob

RATE_FR      Shapiro-Wilk W    0.767   0.0016
RATE_WG      Shapiro-Wilk W    0.797   0.0040
RATE_IT      Shapiro-Wilk W    0.861   0.0310
System       Mardia Skewness   19.37   0.0358
             Mardia Kurtosis   0.352   0.7251
             Henze-Zirkler T   2.258   0.0239
```

Explanation

In Output 25.2 the following items are listed:

❶ `SUR Estimation Summary` lists the specified data set options and the number of parameters estimated.

❷ `Minimization Summary` lists the minimization method, number of iterations, the final convergence criteria, and the number of observations read, solved, used, and missing.

- □ The primary convergence criterion is `R`, which measures the degree to which the residuals are orthogonal to the Jacobian columns, and which approaches 0 as the gradient of the objective function becomes small. The criterion R can be viewed as a nonlinear models generalization of minimizing the error sum of squares (SSE) for linear models. Note that in linear regression, least squares residuals, $\mathbf{Y} - \mathbf{X}\beta$, are orthogonal to the regressors $\mathbf{X}$; that is, $\mathbf{X}'(\mathbf{Y} - \mathbf{X}\beta) = \mathbf{X}'\mathbf{Y} - \mathbf{X}'\mathbf{X}\beta = \mathbf{0}$. For details, see pp. 563-566, in the *SAS/ETS User's Guide, Version 6, Second Edition.*
- □ `PPC` and `RPC` are the prospective and retrospective parameter change measures. `PPC` measures the maximum relative change in the parameters implied by the parameter-change vector computed for the next iteration, and `RPC` measures the relative change in the parameters computed from the previous iteration. The parameter with the maximum relative change is printed with the `PPC` and `RPC` values (unless the values are very near to 0).
- □ `Object` measures the relative change in the objective function value between iterations. The `Trace(S)` is the trace (the sum of the diagonal elements) of the S matrix computed from the current residuals. The S matrix is the estimate of the covariance matrix of equation errors.

❸ `Nonlinear SUR Summary of Residual Errors` lists the degrees of freedom, `SSE` (sum of squared errors), `MSE` (mean square error), `Root MSE` (root mean square error), `R-square`, and `Adj R-Sq` (adjusted R-square).

❹ `Durbin Watson` lists the *d*-statistics. The Savin-White tables (Savin and White 1977) show that at the .05 level of significance, with 14 observations and 3 regressor variables, the lower d_L and upper d_U bounds on the critical value are .767 and 1.779. When used as a test for first-order autocorrelation, the calculated

d-statistics for these equations indicate that the null hypothesis of no first-order autocorrelation should be rejected for at least the RATE_WG equation.

5 `Nonlinear SUR Parameter Estimates` lists the parameter estimates, the approximate standard errors, t-statistics, and approximate p-values for the null hypotheses that each parameter is equal to 0.

You may want to examine the parameter estimates in Example 21, "Fitting and Forecasting a Linear System by SUR and ITSUR," to confirm that the SUR estimates of PROC MODEL and PROC SYSLIN match. In general if the model is linear, the nonlinear estimation methods of PROC MODEL reduce to the corresponding linear systems regression methods, the estimates converge on the first iteration, and the PROC MODEL estimates match those of PROC SYSLIN.

6 `Heteroscedasticity Test` lists the test statistics and p-values for White's test for heteroscedasticity of the residuals of each equation (White 1980) and for the modified Breusch-Pagan test, which assumes that the error variance varies with the listed set of regressors. For more information on heteroscedasticity tests, see Greene (1993), pp. 392-396.

The null hypothesis is that the error variances are constant (homoscedastic). White's test makes no assumption about the form of the heteroscedasticity and, hence, may be significant when the errors are homoscedastic while the model is misspecified in other ways (see Thursby 1982).

None of these tests indicate rejection at the .05 level of the null hypothesis of constant error variance.

7 `Autocorrelation Test` lists Godfrey's test for serial correlation for lags 1 through n (Godfrey 1978a and 1978b). The tests are performed separately for each estimated equation, and the null hypothesis is that the residuals are uncorrelated. If the residuals in fact have only first-order autocorrelation, the lag 1 test will have the most power for rejecting the null hypothesis. If the residuals have second-order but not higher-order autocorrelation, the lag 2 test may be more likely to reject; the same is true for third-order autocorrelation and the lag 3 test, and so on.

These statistics and p-values indicate that at least the RATE_WG equation error term should be modeled as an autoregressive process.

8 `Normality Test` lists the multivariate and univariate test statistics for normality tests of the equation residuals. Three multivariate tests are Mardia's skewness test and kurtosis test (Mardia 1980) and Henze-Zirkler $T_{n,\beta}$ test (Henze and Zirkler 1990). Two

univariate tests are the Shapiro-Wilk W-test, performed when the number of observations is less than or equal to 2000 (Shapiro and Wilk 1965), and the Kolmogorov-Smirnov test, performed when the number of observations is greater than 2000. The null hypothesis for all of these tests is that the residuals are normally distributed.

The low p-values of the Shapiro-Wilk W-statistics indicate the rejection of the null hypothesis that the error terms are random samples from a normal distribution. The low p-values for the multivariate Mardia skewness and Henze-Zirkler T-statistics indicate further evidence that the errors are not from a normal distribution.

Program

SUR Estimation with Autoregressive Error Terms

Fit the model with AR error terms using PROC MODEL. The second-order autoregressive error terms are specified using the %AR macro. This example uses three arguments in each use of the %AR macro. The first argument names the process. The second argument specifies the order of the autoregressive process. The third argument specifies the list of equations to which the process is to be applied. Three separate uses of the %AR macro create three univariate second-order error processes, one for each equation.

Specify the SUR estimation method with the SUR option in the FIT statement.

```
proc model data=exch1 graph outmodel=xchmodel;

   parameters a1-a3 b1-b3 c1-c3 d1-d3;

   France:  rate_fr = a1+b1*im_fr+c1*di_fr+d1*dr_fr;
   Germany: rate_wg = a2+b2*im_wg+c2*di_wg+d2*dr_wg;
   Italy:   rate_it = a3+b3*im_it+c3*di_it+d3*dr_it;

   %ar(ar_fr,2,rate_fr)
   %ar(ar_wg,2,rate_wg)
   %ar(ar_it,2,rate_it)

   fit rate_fr rate_wg rate_it

      start=(ar_fr_l1 -.5 .5 ar_fr_l2 -.5 .5
             ar_wg_l1 -.5 .5 ar_wg_l2 -.5 .5
             ar_it_l1 -.5 .5 ar_it_l2 -.5 .5)

      / sur maxiter=150 converge=1E-7
        outest=est_xch outcov outs=s1 dw;

run;
```

Output 25.3
SUR Estimation with Autoregressive Error Terms (Partial Output)

```
                    Exchange Rate Model

                      MODEL Procedure
                       SUR Estimation

                   SUR Estimation Summary

                Dataset Option      Dataset
                DATA=                 EXCH1
                OUTEST=             EST_XCH
                OUTS=                    S1

                Parameters Estimated      18
```

```
                    Exchange Rate Model

                      MODEL Procedure
                       SUR Estimation
                    Minimization Summary
                Method                 GAUSS
                Iterations               118

                Final  Convergence  Criteria
                R                  7.3757E-8
                PPC(C2)             1.636E-7
                RPC(C2)              2.26E-7

                Object           1.9396E-14
                Trace(S)         21242.1976
                Objective Value  1.33942851

                   Observations  Processed
                Read                      17
                Solved                    17
                Used                      14
                Missing                    3
```

```
                    Exchange Rate Model

                      MODEL Procedure
                       SUR Estimation

           Nonlinear SUR Summary of Residual Errors
                                                                    ❶
              DF    DF                                                Durbin
Equation Model Error      SSE       MSE  Root MSE R-Square Adj R-Sq Watson

RATE_FR      6     8   4.3266   0.54083   0.73541   0.8506   0.7572  1.864
RATE_WG      6     8   0.3805   0.04756   0.21809   0.8446   0.7475  1.832
RATE_IT      6     8   169933  21241.61    145.75   0.8723   0.7925  2.065
```

```
                    Exchange Rate Model

                     MODEL Procedure
                      SUR Estimation

          ❷ Nonlinear SUR Parameter Estimates

                                 Approx.       'T'   Approx.
Parameter      Estimate          Std Err     Ratio   Prob>|T|

A1            -1.718479          1.99011     -0.86    0.4130
A2             2.699315          0.43965      6.14    0.0003
A3             -1628.73        560.68185     -2.90    0.0197
B1           0.00088565        0.0002345      3.78    0.0054
B2          -0.00003153       0.00002181     -1.45    0.1863
B3             0.275967          0.06276      4.40    0.0023
C1            -0.610669          0.15801     -3.86    0.0048
C2          -0.00471637          0.04055     -0.12    0.9103
C3          -154.544221         17.62168     -8.77    0.0001
D1            -0.077662          0.17373     -0.45    0.6667
D2            -0.119454          0.04852     -2.46    0.0392
D3            28.973698         25.81041      1.12    0.2942
AR_FR_L1       0.486216          0.31545      1.54    0.1618
AR_FR_L2      -0.360763          0.31475     -1.15    0.2848
AR_WG_L1       0.744279          0.25092      2.97    0.0180
AR_WG_L2      -0.523291          0.27142     -1.93    0.0900
AR_IT_L1      -0.220473          0.27943     -0.79    0.4529
AR_IT_L2      -0.520012          0.25688     -2.02    0.0775
```

Explanation

❶ `Durbin-Watson` lists the *d*-statistics, which appear to be close to the value of 2.0.

❷ **`Nonlinear SUR Parameter Estimates`** lists the parameter estimates (including the parameters of the autoregressive error terms), the approximate standard errors, the *t*-ratios, and the approximate *p*-values.

The first and second-order autoregression parameters (AR_WG_L1 and AR_WG_L2) for the RATE_WG equation and the second-order autoregression parameter (AR_IT_L2) for the RATE_IT equation are significant at the .10 level. The remaining autoregressive parameters are not.

For more information about the %AR macro, see pp. 599-605 of the *SAS/ETS User's Guide, Version 6, Second Edition.*

Forecasting the SUR Estimated Model

You can use the exchange rate model stored in the model file XCHMODEL in PROC MODEL to forecast exchange rates for 1992 and 1993.

Forecast exchange rates. Use a SOLVE statement in PROC MODEL to forecast the exchange rate system of equations. The ID statement specifies variables to identify observations. The RANGE statement specifies the range of observations to be read from the DATA= data set.

```
proc model model=xchmodel noprint;
   solve rate_fr rate_wg rate_it / data=exch1
         estdata=est_xch forecast out=out1exch;
   id year;
   range year=1992 to 1993;
run;
```

Print the exchange rate forecasts.

```
proc print data=out1exch;
   where year > 1991;
   var year _mode_ rate_fr rate_wg rate_it;
run;
```

Output 25.4
Exchange Rate Forecasts

Exchange Rate Model

OBS	YEAR	_MODE_	RATE_FR	RATE_WG	RATE_IT
1	1992	FORECAST	6.72548	1.46518	1383.74
2	1993	FORECAST	6.53884	1.68420	1255.45

A Closer Look

Overview of PROC MODEL

The MODEL procedure analyzes models in which the relationships among the variables comprise a system of one or more equations. Primary uses of the MODEL procedure are estimation, simulation, and forecasting of linear and nonlinear simultaneous equation models.

SAS programming statements are used to define the model. All parameters and arithmetic operators should be included in the model. The FIT statement is used to estimate models, and the SOLVE statement is used to simulate and forecast models. Other statements include the PARAMETERS statement (which specifies the model parameters), the ENDOGENOUS and EXOGENOUS statements (which specify the endogenous and exogenous variables of the model), and the INSTRUMENTS statement (which specifies the instruments for instrumental variables estimation methods). PROC MODEL supports BY-group processing, ARRAY processing in DO-END groups, IF-THEN/ELSE statements, and WHERE and WHEN statements.

Fitting the Model

The PROC MODEL statements and options are used as follows:

PROC MODEL
: invokes the MODEL procedure. The following options in the PROC MODEL statement are specified:

  - The GRAPH option prints an analysis of the structure of the model given by assignments to model variables appearing in the model program. It also prints the graph of the dependency structure of the model.
  - The OUTMODEL= *model-name* option specifies the name of an output model file to which the model is to be written.

PARAMETERS
: specifies the model parameters. The PARAMETERS statement can be abbreviated as PARMS and PARM.

model assignment statements
: specify the model to be fit or solved. You must write out the model, including all arithmetic operators and parameters.

FIT
: estimates the model parameters. The following options in the FIT statement are specified:

  - The START= (*parameter values* ...) option specifies starting values for the parameters to be estimated. For this example, starting values are specified for the autoregression parameters. By default, parameters have starting values of .0001, which for some nonlinear models can result in failure to achieve convergence. If more than 1 starting value is specified for 1 or more parameters, a grid search is performed over all combinations of the values, and the best combination is used to start the iterations.

- The SUR option specifies the estimation method of seemingly unrelated regressions (SUR).

  Other estimation methods supported by PROC MODEL are OLS, ITOLS, 2SLS, IT2SLS, ITSUR, 3SLS, IT3SLS, FIML, GMM, and ITGMM. (Unless there are cross-equation parameter restrictions, ITOLS reduces to OLS and IT2SLS reduces to 2SLS.)

- The MAXITER= *n* option specifies the maximum number of iterations allowed. The default is 40.

- The CONVERGE= *value* option specifies the convergence criterion. The convergence measure must be less than the specified value before convergence is assumed. The default value is CONVERGE=.001.

  You may also specify CONVERGE= (*value1, value2*), where *value1* is the convergence measure for parameter estimation, and *value2* is the convergence measure for the S covariance matrix of equation errors (when the specified estimation method iterates the S matrix). For additional information on convergence criteria, see pp. 563-566 of the *SAS/ETS User's Guide, Version 6, Second Edition.*

- The OUTEST= *SAS-data-set* option names the SAS data set to contain the parameter estimates and, optionally, the covariances of the estimates.

- The OUTCOV option writes the covariance matrix of the estimates to the OUTEST= data set in addition to the parameter estimates. The OUTCOV option is applicable only if the OUTEST= option is also specified.

- The OUTS= *SAS-data-set* option names the SAS data set to contain the estimated covariance matrix of the equation errors, the S matrix. This is the covariance of the residuals computed from the parameter estimates.

- The DW option prints Durbin-Watson *d*-statistics.

Options Specified in Forecasting the Model

The following options are used in this example:

MODEL= *model-name*
: (in the PROC MODEL statement) reads the model from one or more input model files created by previous PROC MODEL executions.

DATA= *SAS-data-set*
: (in the SOLVE statement) specifies the input data set. The model is solved for each observation read from the DATA= data set.

ESTDATA= *SAS-data-set*
: (in the SOLVE statement) names a data set whose first observation provides values for some or all of the parameters.

FORECAST
: (in the SOLVE statement) specifies that the actual value of the solved variable is used as the solution value (instead of the predicted value from the model equations) whenever nonmissing data are available in the input data set. In FORECAST mode, PROC MODEL solves only for those variables that are missing in the input data set.

OUT= *SAS-data-set*
: in the SOLVE statement specifies the data set name to which the predicted (solution) values (and other values as specified by the OUTACTUAL, OUTALL, OUTERRORS, OUTLAGS, OUTPREDICT, and OUTRESID options) are stored.

Variations

Fit and Forecast in One Run

In one run of PROC MODEL, you can estimate the model parameters and forecast the model.

Estimate model parameters and create forecasts.

```
proc model data=exch1;
   parameters a1-a3 b1-b3 c1-c3 d1-d3;
   France:  rate_fr = a1+b1*im_fr+c1*di_fr+d1*dr_fr;
   Germany: rate_wg = a2+b2*im_wg+c2*di_wg+d2*dr_wg;
   Italy:   rate_it = a3+b3*im_it+c3*di_it+d3*dr_it;
   %ar(ar_fr,2,rate_fr)
   %ar(ar_wg,2,rate_wg)
   %ar(ar_it,2,rate_it)
   fit rate_fr rate_wg rate_it
       start=(ar_fr_l1 -.5 .5 ar_fr_l2 -.5 .5
              ar_wg_l1 -.5 .5 ar_wg_l2 -.5 .5
              ar_it_l1 -.5 .5 ar_it_l2 -.5 .5)
       / sur maxiter=150 converge=1E-7
         outest=est_xch outcov outs=s1 dw;
   solve rate_fr rate_wg rate_it / data=exch1
         estdata=est_xch forecast out=out2exch;
   id year;
   range year=1992 to 1993;
run;
```

Print forecasts using PROC PRINT.

```
proc print data=out2exch;
   where year > 1989;
   var year rate_fr rate_wg rate_it;
run;
```

Iterated SUR (ITSUR) Estimation

You specify iterated SUR (ITSUR) estimation with the ITSUR option in the FIT statement or in the PROC MODEL statement. The estimation method of ITSUR estimates the covariance matrix and parameters in alternating fashion until convergence is achieved.

3SLS and IT3SLS Estimation

As described in Example 24, you can estimate the exchange rate model using the methods of 3SLS and IT3SLS estimation. Specify 3SLS and IT3SLS with the 3SLS and IT3SLS options in either the FIT statement or the PROC MODEL statement. You also use the following statements:

ENDOGENOUS
: specifies the endogenous variables. The ENDOGENOUS statement can be abbreviated as ENDOG and ENDO.

EXOGENOUS
: specifies the exogenous variables. The EXOGENOUS statement can be abbreviated as EXOG and EXO.

INSTRUMENTS
: specifies the instrumental variables to be used in the first stage, instrumental regressions.

Estimate the model by 3SLS.

```
proc model data=exch1 outmodel=xchmodel;
   endogenous im_fr im_wg im_it;
   exogenous di_fr di_wg di_it dr_fr dr_wg dr_it;
   instruments di_fr di_wg di_it dr_fr dr_wg dr_it
               prod_us prod_fr prod_wg prod_it;
   parms a1-a3 b1-b3 c1-c3 d1-d3;
   France:  rate_fr = a1+b1*im_fr+c1*di_fr+d1*dr_fr;
   Germany: rate_wg = a2+b2*im_wg+c2*di_wg+d2*dr_wg;
   Italy:   rate_it = a3+b3*im_it+c3*di_it+d3*dr_it;
   %ar(ar_fr,2,rate_fr)
   %ar(ar_it,2,rate_it)
   fit rate_fr rate_wg rate_it
       start=(ar_fr_l1 -.5 .5 ar_fr_l2 -.5 .5
              ar_wg_l1 -.5 .5 ar_wg_l2 -.5 .5
              ar_it_l1 -.5 .5 ar_it_l2 -.5 .5)
       / 3sls maxiter=150 converge=1E-7;
run;
```

Further Reading

For more information on PROC MODEL, see the *SAS/ETS User's Guide, Version 6, Second Edition*, and *SAS/ETS Software: Changes and Enhancements, Release 6.11.*

References

- *Economic Report of the President*, Washington, D.C.: U.S. Government Printing Office, 1995.
- Godfrey, L. (1978a), "Testing against General Autoregressive and Moving Average Error Models When the Regressors Include Lagged Dependent Variables," *Econometrica*, 46, 1293-1301.
- Godfrey, L. (1978b), "Testing for Higher Order Serial Correlation in Regression Equations When the Regressors Include Lagged Dependent Variables," *Econometrica*, 46, 1303-1310.
- Greene, W. (1993), *Econometric Analysis, Second Edition*, New York: Macmillan Publishing Co.
- Henze, N. and Zirkler, B. (1990), "A Class of Invariant Consistent Tests for Multivariate Normality," *Communications in Statistics Theory and Methods*, 19 (10), 3595-3617.
- Mardia, K. (1980), "Measures of Multivariate Skewness and Kurtosis with Applications," *Biometrika*, 57 (3), 519-529.
- Savin, N.E. and White, K.J. (1977), "The Durbin-Watson Test for Serial Correlation with Extreme Sample Sizes or Many Regressors," *Econometrica*, 45, 1989-1996.
- Shapiro, S. and Wilk, M. (1965), "An Analysis of Variance Test for Normality (complete samples)," *Biometrika*, 52, 591-611.
- *Statistical Abstracts of the U.S.*, Department of Commerce, Washington, D.C.: U.S. Government Printing Office, various years.
- Thursby, J. (1982), "Misspecification, Heteroscedasticity, and the Chow and Goldfeld-Quandt Test," *Review of Economics and Statistics*, 64, 314-321.
- White, H. (1980), "A Heteroskedasticity-Consistant Covariance Matrix Estimator and a Direct Test for Heteroskedasticity," *Econometrica*, 48 (4), 817-838.

EXAMPLE 26

Creating Forecast Confidence Limits with Monte Carlo Simulation

Featured Tools:

- MODEL procedure
  - FIT statement
  - %AR macro
  - SOLVE statement
- UNIVARIATE procedure

This example shows you how to perform Monte Carlo simulations using the SAS/ETS MODEL procedure and the foreign exchange rate model developed in Examples 21 through 25. You can use the Monte Carlo simulations to generate confidence limits for the model's forecasts. The confidence limits are implied by the model's relationship to the implicit random error term and the parameters.

Program

Fit the Model and Perform Monte Carlo Simulations

Estimate the model using the method of SUR as specified by the SUR option in the FIT statement. The OUTMODEL=*model-name* option specifies the name of an output model file to which the model is to be written.

Correct the model for autocorrelation using the %AR macro.

```
proc model data=exch1 outmodel=xchmodel noprint;

      /* Specifies the Model Parameters */
   parameters a1-a3 b1-b3 c1-c3 d1-d3;

      /* Specifies the Model Equations */
   France:  rate_fr = a1+b1*im_fr+c1*di_fr+d1*dr_fr;
   Germany: rate_wg = a2+b2*im_wg+c2*di_wg+d2*dr_wg;
   Italy:   rate_it = a3+b3*im_it+c3*di_it+d3*dr_it;

      /* Specifies AR(2) Error Terms */
   %ar(ar_fr,2,rate_fr)
   %ar(ar_wg,2,rate_wg)
   %ar(ar_it,2,rate_it)

      /* Fits the Model Equations */
   fit rate_fr rate_wg rate_it

      /* Specifies Grid of Starting Values for AR Parameters */
       start=(ar_fr_l1 -.5 .5 ar_fr_l2 -.5 .5
              ar_wg_l1 -.5 .5 ar_wg_l2 -.5 .5
              ar_it_l1 -.5 .5 ar_it_l2 -.5 .5)

       / sur            /* Specifies SUR Estimation                 */
         maxiter=150    /* Specifies Maximum Number of Iterations */
         converge=1E-7  /* Specifies Convergence Criterion          */
         outest=est_xch /* Stores the Parameter Estimates           */
         outcov         /* Stores Parameter Covariance Matrix       */
         outs=s1;       /* Stores the Errors Covariance Matrix      */
run;
```

Create the forecasts and perform Monte Carlo simulation using the SOLVE statement in PROC MODEL.

```
proc model model=xchmodel; /* Specifies Model File    */

   solve rate_fr rate_wg rate_it

      / data=exch1

        estdata=est_xch   /* Specifies Data Set with Parameter
                               Values */

        sdata=s1          /* Specifies Data Set of Covariance
                               Matrix of the Equation Errors */

        random=100        /* Specifies Number of Simulations with
                              Different Random Perturbations */

        seed=123          /* Provides Seed for Generating
                               Pseudo-Random Numbers */
        forecast

        out=out3exch;     /* Creates Output Data Set */

   id year;

   range year=1992 to 1993;

run;
```

Sort the Monte Carlo simulations. Use PROC SORT to sort the observations by the variable YEAR.

```
proc sort data=out3exch;
   by year;
run;
```

Calculate the mean, 5th, and 95th percentiles. The mean value of the Monte Carlo simulations can be used as the point estimate of the forecasts. The 5th and 95th percentiles can be used as lower and upper confidence limits of the forecasts.

```
proc univariate data=out3exch noprint;
   by year;
   var rate_fr rate_wg rate_it;
   output out=out4exch mean=mean_fr mean_wg mean_it
                       p5=p5fr p5wg p5it
                       p95=p95fr p95wg p95it;
run;
```

Print the forecasts and Monte-Carlo-generated confidence limits.

```
proc print data=out4exch;
   var year p5fr mean_fr p95fr
            p5wg mean_wg p95wg
            p5it mean_it p95it;
run;
```

Output 26.1
Monte Carlo Generated Confidence Limits

Exchange Rate Model

OBS	YEAR	P5FR	MEAN_FR	P95FR	P5WG	MEAN_WG
1	1992	4.73344	6.77959	8.69012	0.78298	1.41770
2	1993	4.38803	6.55391	8.24272	1.00404	1.61906

OBS	P95WG	P5IT	MEAN_IT	P95IT
1	1.99581	1012.79	1401.56	1827.52
2	2.20296	963.29	1251.57	1517.85

A Closer Look

Generating Forecast Confidence Limits with Monte Carlo Simulation

You can generate confidence limits for the forecasts using the RANDOM= option in the SOLVE statement to specify Monte Carlo (or stochastic) simulation.

The Monte Carlo simulation of this example follows these steps:

1. A random set of additive error values are generated, one for each observation and each equation.
2. One set of perturbations of the parameters are computed.
3. The new parameter values and the additive error terms are used to compute a new forecast.
4. New forecasts are generated the specified number of times.
5. PROC SORT is used to sort the forecasts by the variable YEAR.
6. PROC UNIVARIATE is used to calculate the mean, the 5th percentile, and the 95th percentile of each distribution of forecasts.

Options Specified in Performing Monte Carlo Simulation

The following PROC MODEL options are used in this example:

MODEL= *model-name*
(in the PROC MODEL statement) reads the model from one or more input model files created by previous PROC MODEL executions.

DATA= *SAS-data-set*
(in the SOLVE statement) specifies the input data set. The model is solved for each observation read from the DATA= data set.

ESTDATA= *SAS-data-set*
(in the SOLVE statement) names a data set whose first observation provides values for some or all of the parameters or the parameter covariance matrix.

SDATA= *SAS-data-set*

(in the SOLVE statement) specifies a data set that provides the covariance matrix of the equation errors. The covariance matrix read from the SDATA= data set is used to generate multivariate normal pseudo-random shocks to the equations when the RANDOM= option requests Monte Carlo simulation.

RANDOM= *n*

(in the SOLVE statement) repeats the solution *n* times with different random perturbations of the equation errors if the SDATA= option is used, and with different random perturbations of the parameters if the ESTDATA= option is used and the ESTDATA= data set contains a parameter covariance matrix. If RANDOM=0, the random-number generator functions always return 0. The default is RANDOM=0.

SEED= *n*

(in the SOLVE statement) specifies an integer to use as the seed in generating pseudo-random numbers to shock the parameters and equations when the ESTDATA= or the SDATA= options are specified. If *n* is negative or 0, the time of day from the computer's clock is used as the seed. The SEED= option is only relevant if the RANDOM= option is used. The default is SEED=0.

FORECAST

(in the SOLVE statement) specifies that the actual value of the solved variable is used as the solution value whenever nonmissing data are available in the input data set. In FORECAST mode, PROC MODEL solves only for those variables that are missing in the input data set.

OUT= *SAS-data-set*

(in the SOLVE statement) specifies the data set name to which the predicted (solution) values are stored.

Variation

All in One Run: Estimation, Forecasting, and Monte Carlo Simulation

In one run of PROC MODEL, you can estimate the model parameters, forecast the model, and perform Monte Carlo simulation.

With some multiple equation models and some nonlinear models, it may be more efficient to use separate runs of PROC MODEL to

- □ fit and evaluate alternative models.
- □ analyze the residuals of the model.

□ analyze the properties of the model.

□ use the model for forecasting and simulation.

Estimate model parameters, forecast, and perform Monte Carlo simulation.

```
proc model data=exch1;
   parameters a1-a3 b1-b3 c1-c3 d1-d3;
   France:  rate_fr = a1+b1*im_fr+c1*di_fr+d1*dr_fr;
   Germany: rate_wg = a2+b2*im_wg+c2*di_wg+d2*dr_wg;
   Italy:   rate_it = a3+b3*im_it+c3*di_it+d3*dr_it;
   %ar(ar_fr,2,rate_fr)
   %ar(ar_wg,2,rate_wg)
   %ar(ar_it,2,rate_it)
   fit rate_fr rate_wg rate_it
       start=(ar_fr_l1 -.5 .5 ar_fr_l2 -.5 .5
              ar_wg_l1 -.5 .5 ar_wg_l2 -.5 .5
              ar_it_l1 -.5 .5 ar_it_l2 -.5 .5)
       / sur maxiter=150 converge=1E-7
         outest=est_xch outcov outs=s1 dw;
   solve rate_fr rate_wg rate_it / data=exch1
         estdata=est_xch sdata=s1 random=100 seed=123
         forecast out=out5exch;
   id year;
   range year=1992 to 1993;
   title 'Exchange Rate Model';
run;
```

Sort the Monte Carlo forecasts using PROC SORT.

```
proc sort data=out5exch;
   by year;
run;
```

Print forecasts using PROC PRINT.

```
proc print data=out5exch;
   where _REP_ = 0;
   var year rate_fr rate_wg rate_it;
run;
```

Calculate the mean forecasts and the 5th and 95th percentiles.

```
proc univariate data=out5exch noprint;
   by year;
   var rate_fr rate_wg rate_it;
   output out=out6exch mean=mean_fr mean_wg mean_it
                       p5=p5fr p5wg p5it
                       p95=p95fr p95wg p95it;
run;
```

Print the forecasts and confidence limits.

```
proc print data=out6exch;
   var year p5fr mean_fr p95fr
            p5wg mean_wg p95wg
            p5it mean_it p95it;
run;
```

Further Reading

- For more information on PROC MODEL, see the *SAS/ETS User's Guide, Version 6, Second Edition*, and *SAS/ETS Software: Changes and Enhancements, Release 6.11.*
- For more information on PROC PRINT, PROC SORT, and PROC UNIVARIATE, see the *SAS Procedures Guide, Version 6, Third Edition.*

References

- *Economic Report of the President*, Washington, D.C.: U.S. Government Printing Office, 1995.
- *Statistical Abstracts of the U.S.*, Department of Commerce, Washington, D.C.: U.S. Government Printing Office, various years.

EXAMPLE 27

Fitting and Forecasting a Nonlinear Model

Featured Tools:

- MODEL procedure
  - FIT statement
  - SOLVE statement
- UNIVARIATE procedure
- G3GRID procedure
- G3D procedure
- GCONTOUR procedure

The Constant Elasticity of Substitution (CES) production function was developed by Arrow, Chenery, Minhas, and Solow (1961) and is a generalization of the Cobb-Douglas (CD) production function. The CD production function implies that the elasticity of input substitution is 1. The CES production function allows the elasticity of input substitution to be a constant, but not necessarily 1.

For output Q, capital K, and labor L, the CES production function has the form

$$Q_i = \gamma\left[\delta K_i^{-\rho} + (1 - \delta)L_i^{-\rho}\right]^{-\nu/\rho}$$

The parameters are

γ is an efficiency parameter (an indicator of the state of technology).

δ is a distribution parameter (defining the relative factor shares).

ν is the returns to scale parameter.

ρ is the parameter associated with the elasticity of substitution.

If $\rho = 0$, then the CES production function reduces to the CD production function. As ρ approaches infinity, the CES production function approaches the Leontief (fixed proportions) production function. See pp. 428-430 of Chiang (1984).

Program

Creating a 3-D Plot of the Data

Create the CES data set in a DATA step. The complete CES production function data set is in "Introduction: The Example Data Sets."

```
data ces;
   input id k l q @@;
   label k ='Capital Input'
         l ='Labor Input'
         q ='Output';
   title 'CES Production Function';
datalines;
01 8 23 106.00  02 9 14  81.08  03 4 38  72.80  04 2 97  57.34
05 6 11  66.79  06 6 43  98.23  07 3 93  82.68  08 6 49  99.77
09 8 36 110.00  10 8 43 118.93  11 4 61  95.05  12 8 31 112.83
13 3 57  64.54  14 6 97 137.22  15 4 93  86.17  16 2 72  56.25
17 3 61  81.10  18 3 97  65.23  19 9 89 149.56  20 3 25  65.43
21 1 81  36.06  22 4 11  56.92  23 2 64  49.59  24 3 10  43.21
25 6 71 121.24
;
```

Interpolate a grid of points for plotting. The GRID statement specifies the x, y, and z-axis variables. Use the SPLINE option for spline interpolation, and the SMOOTH= option to specify a smoothing constant.

```
proc g3grid data=ces out=ces_grid;
   grid k*l=q / spline smooth=.025
                axis1=1 to 9 by .5
                axis2=10 to 100 by 10;
run;
```

Create a three dimensional, high-resolution plot using the G3D procedure. The PLOT statement plots the x-axis and y-axis variables versus the z-axis variables.

```
goptions cback=white colors=(black) border;

proc g3d data=ces_grid;
   plot k*l=q
      / rotate=75   /* rotates the plot about the z-axis      */
        tilt=80     /* tilts the plot about the x-axis        */
        zmin=10     /* specifies min values for the z-axis    */
        zmax=160    /* specifies max values for the z-axis    */
        yticknum=3  /* specifies number of y-axis tick marks */
        xticknum=5; /* specifies number of x-axis tick marks */
   title 'Production Function Surface plot';
run;
quit;
```

Output 27.1
Three-Dimensional, High-Resolution Plot

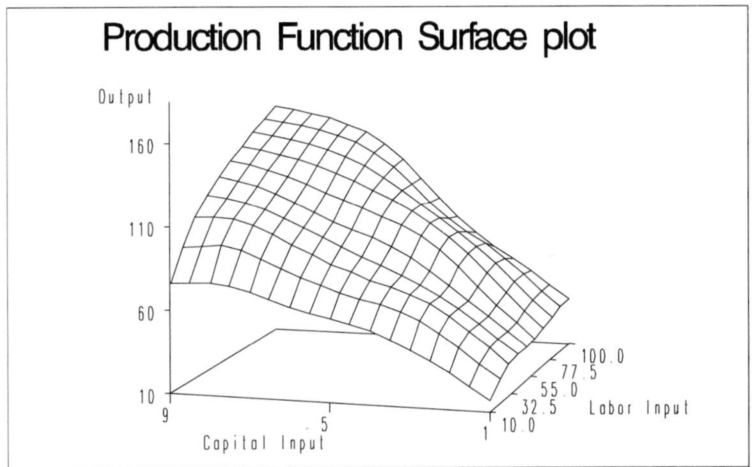

Explanation

Output 27.1 displays the nonlinear output surface produced by combinations of capital and labor. Cross-sections from front to back (holding capital constant) show the marginal physical product of labor. For a given level of capital, more labor increases output but at a rate that eventually decreases. Cross-sections from right to left (holding labor constant) show the marginal physical product of capital. Capital also exhibits diminishing marginal returns. Cross-sections at different output levels (cross-sections parallel to the capital and labor plane) are *isoquants*, different combinations of inputs that produce the same level of output.

Estimating the Model Parameters

The following PROC MODEL statements estimate the parameters of the CES production function and create an output data set containing the predicted (PREDQ) and residual values (RESIDQ).

Estimate the model parameters.

```
proc model data=ces outmodel=cesmodel;
   parms g r v d;
      q = g*(((d*k)**r) + ((1-d)*l)**r)**(v/r);
```

Use a FIT statement to fit the specified model. The START= option specifies parameter starting values, and the CONVERGE= option specifies the convergence criterion.

```
   fit q start = (g=15 d=.6 r=-.3 v=.5) / converge =.00005
         outest=est_ces outcov outs=s2 outactual out=ces_out;

   predq=pred.q;
   residq=actual.q-pred.q;
```

Use an OUTVARS statement to specify the variables created in PROC MODEL to be included in the output data set.

```
   outvars residq predq id;
   title 'CES Production Function';
run;
```

Print the actual, predicted, and residual values using PROC PRINT.

```
proc print data=ces_out;
   var q predq k l residq;
run;
```

Output 27.2
Model Summary and Estimated Model Parameters

```
                 CES Production Function

                     MODEL Procedure

                   ❶ Model Summary

                Model Variables        1
                Parameters             4
                OUTVARS Variables      3
                Equations              1

                Number of Statements   3

      Model Variables: Q

      Parameters: G: 15  R: -0.3  V: 0.5  D: 0.6

      Equations: Q

                 The Equation to Estimate is:

                     Q = F( G, R, V, D )
```

```
                    CES Production Function

                        MODEL Procedure
                         OLS Estimation

                ❷ OLS Estimation Summary

                 Dataset Option       Dataset
                 DATA=                    CES
                 OUT=                 CES_OUT
                 OUTEST=              EST_CES
                 OUTS=                     S2

                 Parameters Estimated       4

                  ❸ Minimization Summary
                 Method                 GAUSS
                 Iterations                 9
                 Subiterations              6
                 Average Subiterations   0.67

                 Final  Convergence  Criteria
```

```
                    CES Production Function

                        MODEL Procedure
                      ❹ OLS Estimation

                 R                 7.73905E-6
                 PPC(R)              0.000018
                 RPC(R)              0.000183
                 Object            8.94945E-9
                 Trace(S)          46.6646711
                 Objective Value   39.1983237

                    Observations Processed
                 Read                      25
                 Solved                    25
```

```
                    CES Production Function

                        MODEL Procedure
                         OLS Estimation

          ❺ Nonlinear OLS Summary of Residual Errors

             DF    DF
Equation Model Error      SSE       MSE  Root MSE R-Square Adj R-Sq Label

Q            4    21 979.9581  46.66467   6.83115   0.9537   0.9471 Output
```

```
                    CES Production Function

                        MODEL Procedure
                         OLS Estimation

              ❻ Nonlinear OLS Parameter Estimates

                                  Approx.        'T'   Approx.
   Parameter     Estimate        Std Err      Ratio  Prob>|T|

   G            55.669378       22.93564       2.43    0.0243
   R            -0.596285        0.30170      -1.98    0.0614
   V             0.827183        0.05595      14.78    0.0001
   D             0.655464        0.15403       4.26    0.0004


     Number of Observations         Statistics for System
     Used                  25       Objective      39.1983
     Missing                0       Objective*N   979.9581
```

Explanation

❶ `Model Summary` lists the model variables, parameters, equations, and number of statements in the PROC MODEL program. The specified starting values that were used to begin the optimizing process are also printed.

❷ `OLS Estimation Summary` lists the data set options and the number of parameters estimated.

❸ `Minimization Summary` lists the method used and the number of iterations and subiterations.

❹ `OLS Estimation` lists the final convergence criteria and the number of observations processed. Observations with missing values are not used in the estimation process.

For explanation of convergence criteria, see Example 25.

❺ `Nonlinear OLS Summary of Residual Errors` lists the degrees of freedom, `SSE` (error sum of squares), `MSE` (mean square error), `Root MSE` (root mean square error), `R-Square`, and `Adj R-Sq` (adjusted R-Square).

❻ `Nonlinear OLS Parameter Estimates` lists the parameter estimates, the approximate standard errors, individual *t*-statistics for the null hypotheses that each parameter separately is equal to 0, and the approximate *p*-value.

Printing Actual, Predicted, and Residual Values

Output 27.3
Actual, Predicted, and Residual Values

CES Production Function

OBS	Q	PREDQ	K	L	RESIDQ
1	106.00	98.380	8	23	7.6204
2	81.08	84.793	9	14	-3.7131
3	72.80	78.776	4	38	-5.9763
4	57.34	57.716	2	97	-0.3763
5	66.79	65.052	6	11	1.7380
6	98.23	102.861	6	43	-4.6314
7	82.68	76.571	3	93	6.1095
8	99.77	106.293	6	49	-6.5228
9	110.00	114.367	8	36	-4.3670
10	118.93	120.619	8	43	-1.6887
11	95.05	86.878	4	61	8.1721
12	112.83	109.049	8	31	3.7806
13	64.54	71.186	3	57	-6.6460
14	137.22	122.803	6	97	14.4172
15	86.17	93.266	4	93	-7.0957
16	56.25	55.801	2	72	0.4493
17	81.10	71.985	3	61	9.1148
18	65.23	76.992	3	97	-11.7618
19	149.56	155.480	9	89	-5.9198
20	65.43	60.205	3	25	5.2250
21	36.06	34.099	1	81	1.9613
22	56.92	54.556	4	11	2.3644
23	49.59	54.980	2	64	-5.3898
24	43.21	46.057	3	10	-2.8465
25	121.24	115.585	6	71	5.6545

Forecasting

Creating an Input Data Set

Create the CES_NEW data set. The CES_NEW data set provides values for the variables K and L, which can be used to solve the estimated production function for values of Q.

```
data ces_new;
input id k l q @@;
label k ='Capital Input'
      l ='Labor Input'
      q ='Output';
datalines;
26 5 30    .    27 6 35    .    28 7 40    .    29 6 45    .
;
```

Forecasting and Plotting

Forecast output for the observations in the CES_NEW data set. Use the SOLVE statement in PROC MODEL, the MODEL= option, and the FORECAST option to forecast the output levels.

```
proc model data=ces_new model=cesmodel noprint;

   solve q / out=fore forecast;
run;
```

Print the forecasts and the input data using PROC PRINT.

```
proc print data=fore;
   var _mode_ q k l;
run;
```

Use PROC G3GRID to create a grid of points for plotting the CES production function isoquants.

```
proc g3grid data=fore out=fore1;
   grid k*l=predq / spline smooth=.025
                    axis1=1 to 9 by .5
                    axis2=10 to 100 by 10;
run;
```

```
goptions cback=white colors=(black) border;
```

Use PROC GCONTOUR to plot the CES production function isoquants.

```
proc gcontour data=fore1;
   plot k*l=predq / legend=legend1;
   title 'CES Production Function Isoquants';
   legend1 label=(j=l 'Predicted' j=l 'Quantity');
run;
```

Output 27.4
Input Values and Forecasts for CES_NEW Data

CES Production Function

OBS	_MODE_	Q	K	L
1	FORECAST	84.354	5	30
2	FORECAST	97.318	6	35
3	FORECAST	109.913	7	40
4	FORECAST	104.064	6	45

Isoquant Plot

Output 27.5
PROC GCONTOUR Plot of CES Production Isoquants

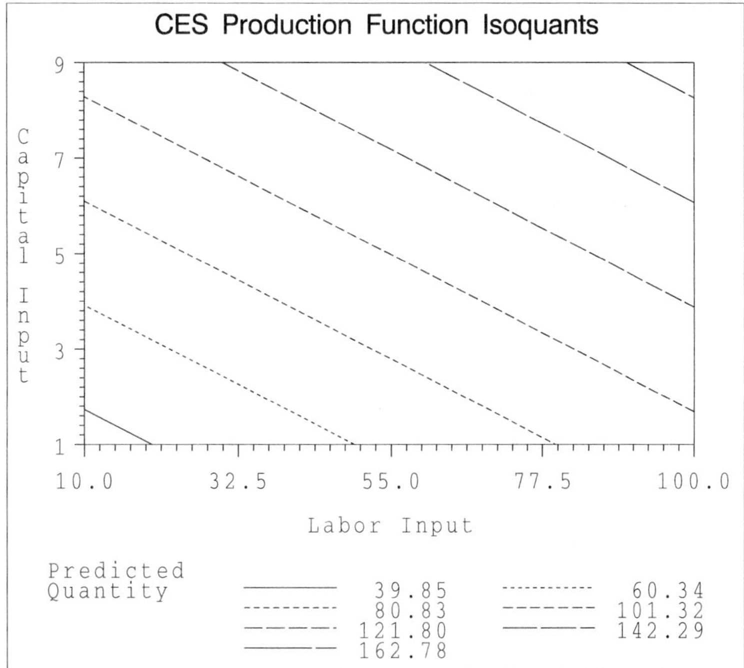

Explanation

The plot shows the CES production functions isoquants; that is, the combinations of capital and labor that produce the same level of output. The legend lists the output levels produced.

Generating Confidence Limits with Monte Carlo Techniques

Monte Carlo techniques are used to generate confidence limits using the steps described in Example 26, "Creating Forecast Confidence Limits with Monte Carlo Simulation."

Generate Monte Carlo forecasts. The RANDOM=*n* option specifies the number of forecasts to generate. The SEED=*n* option specifies the seed number in generating pseudo-random numbers to perturb the parameters and the equation errors.

```
proc model data=ces_new model=cesmodel noprint;
   solve q / estdata=est_ces sdata=s2 random=100
             seed=246 jacobi out=montcrlo forecast;
run;
```

Sort the Monte-Carlo-generated forecasts using PROC SORT. Use a BY statement to specify sorting by the variable ID.

```
proc sort data=montcrlo;
   by id;
run;
```

Calculate the Monte-Carlo-generated forecast mean, 5th percentile, and 95th percentile using PROC UNIVARIATE. Use an OUTPUT statement to create an output data set containing the calculated values.

```
proc univariate data=montcrlo noprint;
   by id;
   var q;
   output out=bounds mean=mean p5=p5 p95=p95;
run;
```

Print the Monte-Carlo-generated forecast mean, 5th percentile, and 95th percentile using PROC PRINT.

```
proc print data=bounds;
   var id p95 mean p5;
run;
```

Plot the Monte-Carlo-generated forecast mean, 5th percentile, and 95th percentile. Use the OVERLAY option in PROC PLOT to plot multiple variables in one plot.

```
proc plot data=bounds vpct=150;
   plot mean * id = 'M'
        p5 * id = 'L'
        p95 * id = 'U' / overlay;
   title ''Monte Carlo Generated Confidence Intervals on a Forecast'';
run;
```

Forecast Mean and Percentiles

Output 27.6
Monte-Carlo-Generated Forecast Mean, 5th, and 95th Percentiles

CES Production Function

OBS	ID	P95	MEAN	P5
1	26	88.600	65.4493	13.9578
2	27	103.995	75.1928	21.6621
3	28	113.999	83.5461	24.7278
4	29	108.378	78.8318	17.0859

Scatter Plot

Output 27.7
PROC PLOT Scatter Plot of Forecast Mean, 5th and 95th Percentiles

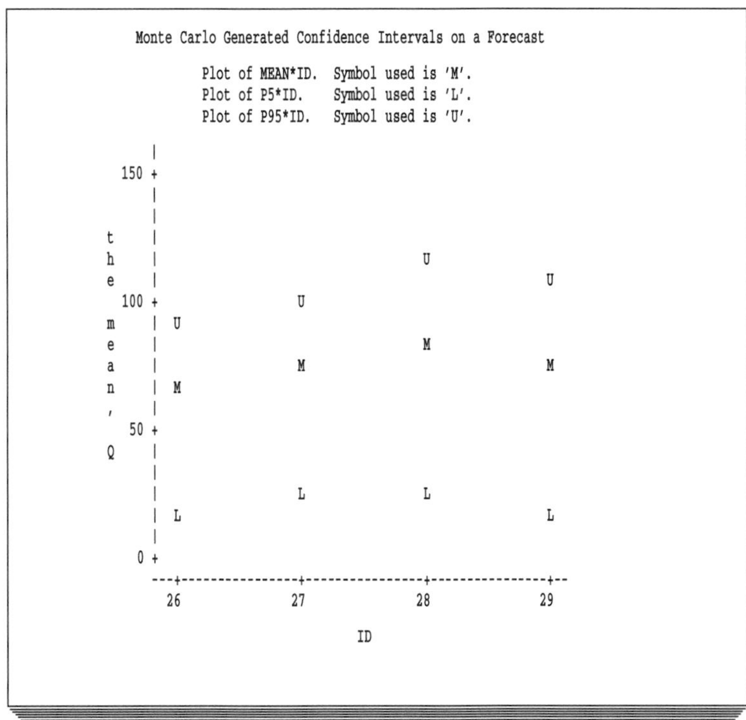

Variation

Fit and Forecast in One Run

In one run of PROC MODEL, you can fit the CES production function, generate forecasts, and perform Monte Carlo analysis.

With some multiple equation models and some nonlinear models, it may be more efficient to use separate runs of PROC MODEL to

- □ fit and evaluate alternative models.
- □ analyze the residuals of the model.
- □ analyze the properties of the model.
- □ use the model for forecasting and simulation.

Estimate, forecast, and perform Monte Carlo analysis in one run.

```
proc model data=ces;
   parms g r v d;
       q = g*(((d*k)**r) + ((1-d)*l)**r)**(v/r);
   fit q start = (g=15 d=.6 r=-.3 v=.5) / converge =.00005
         outest=est outcov outs=s3 outactual;
   solve q / data=ces_new estdata=est_ces sdata=s2 random=100
             seed=246 jacobi out=montcrlo forecast;
   id id;
   range id=25;
   title 'CES Production Function';
run;
```

Further Reading

- For more information on PROC MODEL, see the *SAS/ETS User's Guide, Version 6, Second Edition*, and *SAS/ETS Software: Changes and Enhancements, Release 6.11.*
- For complete reference information on PROC G3D, PROC G3GRID, and other features available in SAS/GRAPH software, see *SAS/GRAPH Software: Reference, Version 6, First Edition, Volumes 1 and 2.*
- For more information on PROC PLOT, PROC PRINT, PROC SORT, and PROC UNIVARIATE, see the *SAS Procedures Guide, Version 6, Third Edition.*

References

- Arrow, K.J., Chenery, H.B., Minhas, B.S., and Solow, R.M. (1961), "Capital-Labor Substitution and Economic Efficiency," *Review of Economics and Statistics*, (43), 225-250.
- Chiang, A. (1984), *Fundamental Methods of Mathematical Economics, Third Edition*, New York: McGraw-Hill Book Company.
- Kmenta, Jan (1986), *Elements of Econometrics, Second Edition*, New York: Macmillan Publishing Co., Inc.

EXAMPLE 28

Restricting and Testing Parameters of a Nonlinear Forecasting Model

Featured Tools:

- MODEL procedure
  - BOUNDS statement
  - ESTIMATE statement
  - FIT statement
  - RESTRICT statement
  - TEST statement

The Constant Elasticity of Substitution (CES) production function is estimated and used for forecasting in Example 27 ("Fitting and Forecasting a Nonlinear Model") with the CES data set and the SAS/ETS MODEL procedure.

The CES production function was developed by Arrow, Chenery, Minhas, and Solow (1961) and is a generalization of the Cobb-Douglas (CD) production function. The CD production function implies that the elasticity of input substitution is 1. The CES production function allows the elasticity of input substitution to be a constant, but not necessarily 1.

For output Q, capital K, and labor L, the CES production function has the form

$$Q_i = \gamma\left[\delta K_i^{-\rho} + (1 - \delta)L_i^{-\rho}\right]^{-\nu / \rho}$$

The parameters are

γ is an efficiency parameter (an indicator of the state of technology).

δ is a distribution parameter (defining the relative factor shares).

ν is the returns to scale parameter.

ρ is the parameter associated with the elasticity of substitution.

The following parameter restrictions are meaningful:

$\gamma > 0$

$0 < \delta < 1$

$\nu = 1$

$-1 < \rho$, but not equal to 0.

Under these restrictions, the elasticity of substitution $\sigma = 1 / (1 + \rho)$. See pp. 426-428 of Chiang (1984).

Program

Create the CES data set. The complete CES production function data set is in "Introduction: The Example Data Sets."

```
data ces;
   input id k l q @@;
   label k ='Capital Input'
         l ='Labor Input'
         q ='Output';
   title 'CES Production Function';
datalines;
01 8 23 106.00  02 9 14  81.08  03 4 38  72.80  04 2 97  57.34
05 6 11  66.79  06 6 43  98.23  07 3 93  82.68  08 6 49  99.77
09 8 36 110.00  10 8 43 118.93  11 4 61  95.05  12 8 31 112.83
13 3 57  64.54  14 6 97 137.22  15 4 93  86.17  16 2 72  56.25
17 3 61  81.10  18 3 97  65.23  19 9 89 149.56  20 3 25  65.43
21 1 81  36.06  22 4 11  56.92  23 2 64  49.59  24 3 10  43.21
25 6 71 121.24
;
```

Estimate and test the model parameters. The ESTIMATE statement prints estimates and standard errors of linear and nonlinear functions of the model parameters.

The TEST statement performs hypothesis tests of linear and nonlinear functions of the parameter estimates.

Use a FIT statement to fit the specified model.

```
proc model data=ces;

   parms g r v d;

   estimate 'Elas_Sub' 1/(1+r);

   test     'Unity'    1/(1+r)=1;
   test     'Dis_parm' v=1, / all;

      q = g*(((d*k)**r) + ((1-d)*l)**r)**(v/r);

   fit q start = (g=15 d=.6 r=-.3 v=.5) / converge =.00005
         outactual out=ces_out1;
   predq=pred.q;
   residq=actual.q-pred.q;
   outvars residq predq id;
   title2 'Unrestricted Model';
run;
```

Print the actual, predicted, and residual values using PROC PRINT.

```
proc print data=ces_out1;
   var q predq k l residq;
run;
```

Estimate, restrict, and test the model parameters.

```
proc model data=ces;
   parms g r v d;
```

Use a BOUNDS statement to impose boundary constraints on the model parameters.

```
   bounds g > 0,
          0 < d < 1;
```

Use a RESTRICT statement to impose linear and nonlinear restrictions on model parameters.

```
   restrict 'Dis_parm' v=1;

   test     'Unity'    1/(1+r)=1;

       q = g*(((d*k)**r) + ((1-d)*l)**r)**(v/r);

   fit q start = (g=.5 d=.6 r=-.5) / converge =.000001
         outactual out=ces_out2;

   predq=pred.q;
   residq=actual.q-pred.q;
   outvars residq predq id;
   title2 'Restricted Model';
run;
```

Print the actual, predicted, and residual values using PROC PRINT.

```
proc print data=ces_out2;
   var q predq k l residq;
run;
```

Output 28.1
Summary of Residual Errors, Parameter Estimates, and Test Results (Partial Output)

CES Production Function
Unrestricted Model

❶ Nonlinear OLS Summary of Residual Errors

Equation	DF Model	DF Error	SSE	MSE	Root MSE	R-Square	Adj R-Sq	Label
Q	4	21	979.9581	46.66467	6.83115	0.9537	0.9471	Output

CES Production Function
Unrestricted Model

❷ Nonlinear OLS Parameter Estimates

Parameter	Estimate	Approx. Std Err	'T' Ratio	Approx. Prob>|T|	Label
G	55.669378	22.93564	2.43	0.0243	
R	-0.596285	0.30170	-1.98	0.0614	
V	0.827183	0.05595	14.78	0.0001	
D	0.655464	0.15403	4.26	0.0004	

```
                  CES Production Function
                     Unrestricted Model

                              Approx.        'T'   Approx.
Term           Estimate       Std Err      Ratio  Prob>|T|  Label
   ❸
Elas_Sub       2.476993       1.85107       1.34    0.1952  1/(1+R)

                        ❹ Test Results

   Test         Type        Statistic      Prob.       Label

   Unity        Wald             0.76     0.3840       1/(1+R)=1
   Dis_parm     Wald            11.36     0.0008       V=1
                L.R.            10.93     0.0009       V=1
                L.M.             8.90     0.0029       V=1
```

Explanation

❶ **`Nonlinear OLS Summary of Residual Errors`** lists the degrees of freedom, **`SSE`** (error sum of squares), **`MSE`** (mean square errors), **`Root MSE`** (root mean square error), **`R-Square`**, and **`Adj R-Sq`** (adjusted R-Square).

❷ **`Nonlinear OLS Parameter Estimates`** lists the parameter estimates, the approximate standard errors, individual *t*-statistics for the null hypotheses that each parameter separately is equal to 0, and the approximate *p*-value.

❸ The term **`Elas_Sub`** is the estimate of the specified function of the parameter ρ. The specified function is an the estimate of the elasticity of substitution. Also listed are the approximate standard error, the *t*-statistic, and the approximate *p*-value.

❹ **`Test Results`** lists the test label, type of test (Wald, Likelihood Ratio and Lagrange Multiplier), test statistics, and approximate *p*-values. In this example, two tests are specified.

The null hypothesis of the first test is that the elasticity of substitution is equal to 1. The resulting *p*-value is .3840, and at the .10 level the null hypothesis can be retained.

The null hypothesis of the second test is that the distribution parameter, which defines the relative factor shares, is equal to 1. Three types of tests are performed. The largest *p*-value is .0029, and at the .10 level the null hypothesis should be rejected. You conclude that if this restriction is imposed, it would be statistically significant.

Printing the Predicted and Residual Values for the Unrestricted Model

Output 28.2
Actual, Predicted, and Residual Values

CES Production Function
Unrestricted Model

OBS	Q	PREDQ	K	L	RESIDQ
1	106.00	98.380	8	23	7.6204
2	81.08	84.793	9	14	-3.7131
3	72.80	78.776	4	38	-5.9763
4	57.34	57.716	2	97	-0.3763
5	66.79	65.052	6	11	1.7380
6	98.23	102.861	6	43	-4.6314
7	82.68	76.571	3	93	6.1095
8	99.77	106.293	6	49	-6.5228
9	110.00	114.367	8	36	-4.3670
10	118.93	120.619	8	43	-1.6887
11	95.05	86.878	4	61	8.1721
12	112.83	109.049	8	31	3.7806
13	64.54	71.186	3	57	-6.6460
14	137.22	122.803	6	97	14.4172
15	86.17	93.266	4	93	-7.0957
16	56.25	55.801	2	72	0.4493
17	81.10	71.985	3	61	9.1148
18	65.23	76.992	3	97	-11.7618
19	149.56	155.480	9	89	-5.9198
20	65.43	60.205	3	25	5.2250
21	36.06	34.099	1	81	1.9613
22	56.92	54.556	4	11	2.3644
23	49.59	54.980	2	64	-5.3898
24	43.21	46.057	3	10	-2.8465
25	121.24	115.585	6	71	5.6545

Estimating and Testing the Restricted Model

Output 28.3
Summary of Residual Errors, Parameter Estimates, and Test Results (Partial Output)

CES Production Function
Restricted Model

❶ Nonlinear OLS Summary of Residual Errors

Equation	DF Model	DF Error	SSE	MSE	Root MSE	R-Square	Adj R-Sq	Label
Q	3	22	1405	63.87732	7.99233	0.9336	0.9276	Output

```
                    CES Production Function
                        Restricted Model

               ❷ Nonlinear OLS Parameter Estimates

                              Approx.       'T'   Approx.
Parameter    Estimate         Std Err     Ratio  Prob>|T|  Label

G            12724.42        157122.7      0.08    0.9362
R           -0.133984         0.19352     -0.69    0.4960
V            1.000000               0        .        .
D            0.022383         0.18684      0.12    0.9057
Dis_parm    37.156152        14.28372      2.60    0.0060  V=1
```

```
                    CES Production Function
                        Restricted Model

                        ❸ Test Results

  Test       Type       Statistic      Prob.      Label

  Unity      Wald            0.25     0.6137      1/(1+R)=1
```

Explanation

❶ **`Nonlinear OLS Summary of Residual Errors`** lists the degrees of freedom, **`SSE`** (error sum of squares), **`MSE`** (mean square error), **`Root MSE`** (root mean square error), **`R-Square`**, and **`Adj R-Sq`** (adjusted R-Square).

❷ **`Nonlinear OLS Parameter Estimates`** lists the parameter estimates, the approximate standard errors, individual *t*-statistics for the null hypotheses that each parameter separately is equal to 0, and the approximate *p*-value.

Because the parameter ν is restricted to the value of 1, it is not estimated, and there is 1 less degree of freedom assigned to the model. You may want to compare the parameter estimates of the restricted and unrestricted models.

The parameter **`Dis_parm`** is the value of the Lagrange multiplier used to impose the restriction that the distribution parameter ν is 1. The resulting *t*-statistic is 2.60 and the *p*-value is 0.0060, indicating that the restriction is statistically significant.

❸ **`Test Results`** lists the test label, type of test, test statistic, and approximate *p*-value. In this example, one test is specified.

The null hypothesis is that the elasticity of substitution is equal to 1. The resulting *p*-value is .6137, and at the .10 level the null hypothesis can be retained.

Printing the Predicted and Residual Values for the Restricted Model

Output 28.4
Actual, Predicted, and Residual Values

CES Production Function
Restricted Model

OBS	Q	PREDQ	K	L	RESIDQ
1	106.00	98.476	8	23	7.5238
2	81.08	89.196	9	14	-8.1160
3	72.80	72.681	4	38	0.1189
4	57.34	57.905	2	97	-0.5655
5	66.79	63.085	6	11	3.7047
6	98.23	99.832	6	43	-1.6017
7	82.68	76.981	3	93	5.6992
8	99.77	104.020	6	49	-4.2497
9	110.00	114.517	8	36	-4.5165
10	118.93	121.378	8	43	-2.4483
11	95.05	83.836	4	61	11.2140
12	112.83	108.964	8	31	3.8657
13	64.54	67.046	3	57	-2.5057
14	137.22	127.932	6	97	9.2876
15	86.17	94.711	4	93	-8.5405
16	56.25	53.464	2	72	2.7858
17	81.10	68.368	3	61	12.7318
18	65.23	77.878	3	97	-12.6478
19	149.56	165.564	9	89	-16.0045
20	65.43	52.339	3	25	13.0908
21	36.06	33.036	1	81	3.0240
22	56.92	48.490	4	11	8.4296
23	49.59	51.771	2	64	-2.1810
24	43.21	38.841	3	10	4.3691
25	121.24	116.581	6	71	4.6586

A Closer Look

Specifying the TEST Statement

The TEST statement performs linear and nonlinear hypothesis tests about the model parameters. The syntax for the TEST statement is

TEST ['*name*'] *test1* [, *test2* ...] [,/ *options*];

The arguments of the statement are defined as follows:

- *name* is an optional string used to identify the results in the printed output and in the OUT= data set.
- Each *test* is composed of expressions involving the estimated parameters.
- *options* are the statement options.

If options are specified, a comma is required before the slash (/), because the slash (/) can also be used within a test expression to indicate division.

The following options are available in the TEST statement:

WALD
: specifies that a Wald test be computed.

LM, RAO, or LAGRANGE
: specifies that a Lagrange multiplier test be computed.

LR or LIKE
: specifies that a likelihood ratio test be computed.

ALL
: specifies all three types of tests.

OUT=*SAS-data-set*
: specifies the name of an output SAS data set that contains the test results.

Each test is written as an expression optionally followed by an equal sign (=) and a second expression. Test expressions can be composed of parameter names, arithmetic operators, functions, and constants. Parameters named in test expressions must be among the parameters estimated by the associated FIT statement. Logical operators (such as "&") *cannot* be used in TEST statement expressions.

If you specify only one expression in a test, that expression is tested against the value 0. When you specify multiple tests on the same TEST statement, a joint test is performed. For example, the following TEST statement tests the joint hypothesis that parameters A and B are equal to 0:

```
test a, b;
```

To perform separate tests, use separate TEST statements. For example, the following TEST statements test the two separate hypotheses that the parameter A is equal to 0, and that the parameter B is equal to 0:

```
test a;
test b;
```

Further Reading

For more information on PROC MODEL, see the *SAS/ETS User's Guide, Version 6, Second Edition*, and *SAS/ETS Software: Changes and Enhancements, Release 6.11.*

References

- Arrow, K.J., Chenery, H.B., Minhas, B.S., and Solow, R.M. (1961), "Capital-Labor Substitution and Economic Efficiency," *Review of Economics and Statistics*, (43), 225-250.
- Chiang, A. (1984), *Fundamental Methods of Mathematical Economics, Third Edition*, New York: McGraw-Hill Book Company.
- Kmenta, Jan (1986), *Elements of Econometrics, Second Edition*, New York: Macmillan Publishing Co., Inc.

EXAMPLE 29

Producing Forecasts Automatically Using the Time Series Forecasting System

Featured Tool:

- Time Series Forecasting System

The Time Series Forecasting System provides convenient point-and-click windows to drive the time series analysis and forecasting tools of SAS/ETS software. You can use the system in a fully automated mode to produce automatic forecasts of time series. Alternatively, you can use the system's diagnostic features and time series modeling tools interactively to develop customized models that produce the best forecasts for your time series. The system provides both graphical and statistical features to help you choose the best forecasting method for each series.

The Time Series Forecasting System is part of SAS/ETS software. To use it, you must have a license for SAS/ETS. To use the graphical display features of the system, you must also license SAS/GRAPH software. To use the features for browsing SAS data sets, you need to license SAS/FSP software.

This example uses the CITIDAY data set from the SASHELP library. This data set contains daily financial data from a variety of sources.

Invoking the Time Series Forecasting System

You can invoke the Time Series Forecasting System in the following ways:

- If you use the SAS Display Manager System with pull-down menus, pull down the `Globals` menu from the menu bar, select the `Analyze` item, and then select `Forecasting`.
- If you use display manager with a command line, enter the command `forecast` on the command line.
- If you use SAS/ASSIST software, select FORECASTING from the SAS/ASSIST `Planning Tools` menu.

Any of these methods brings up the Time Series Forecasting main window, as shown in Display 29.1.

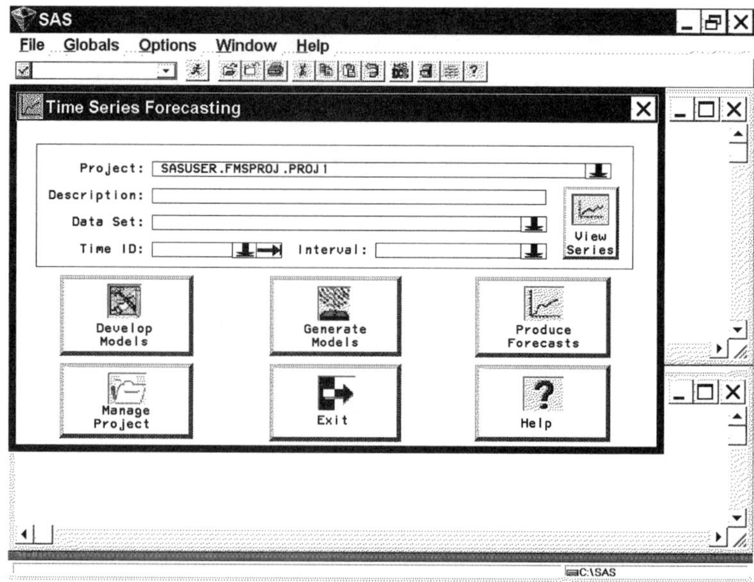

Display 29.1
Time Series Forecasting System Main Window

The top of the main window contains a data selection area in which you specify a project file and the input data set that contains the time series variables you want to forecast. This area also contains View Series, which enables you to browse or graph variables in the input data set.

The lower part of the main window contains six buttons:

Develop Models
: brings up the Develop Models window, which you use to develop forecasting models interactively for individual time series.

Generate Models
: brings up the Generate Models window, which you use to search automatically for the best forecasting model for one or more time series.

Produce Forecasts
: brings up the Produce Forecasts window, which you use to compute forecasts for all the variables in the input data set for which forecasting models have been fit.

Manage Project
: brings up the Manage Forecasting Project window, which lists the time series for which you have fit forecasting models. You can drill down on a series to see the forecasting models for the series. You can also delete unwanted models or series.

Exit
: exits the Time Series Forecasting System.

displays help information about the Time Series Forecasting System.

Specifying the Input Data Set

As the first step in the forecasting process, you must specify the input data set.

The `Data Set` field in the Time Series Forecasting main window gives the name of the input data set that contains the time series to forecast. Initially, this field is blank. You can type in the name of the data set in this field, or you can select the control item (a box with an arrow that points downward) at the right of the `Data Set` field to select the data set from a list. When you select the control arrow, it brings up the Data Set Selection window, as shown in Display 29.2.

Display 29.2
Data Set Selection Window

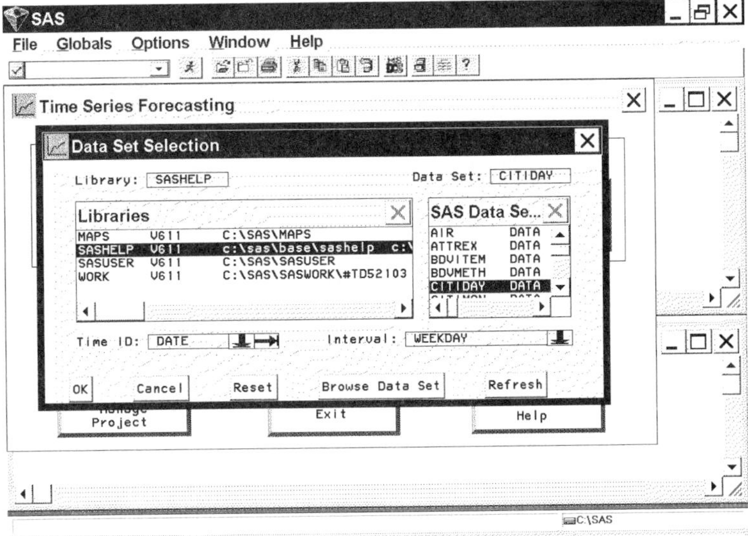

In the Data Set Selection window, you first select `SASHELP` from the `Libraries` selection list. Then you select `CITIDAY` from the `SAS Data Sets` selection list. Select OK to complete your selection of the data set and return to the Time Series Forecasting main window.

Generating Models Automatically

To generate models automatically, select Generate Models from the Time Series Forecasting main window. This brings up the Generate Forecasting Models window, shown in Display 29.3.

Display 29.3
Generate Forecasting Models Window

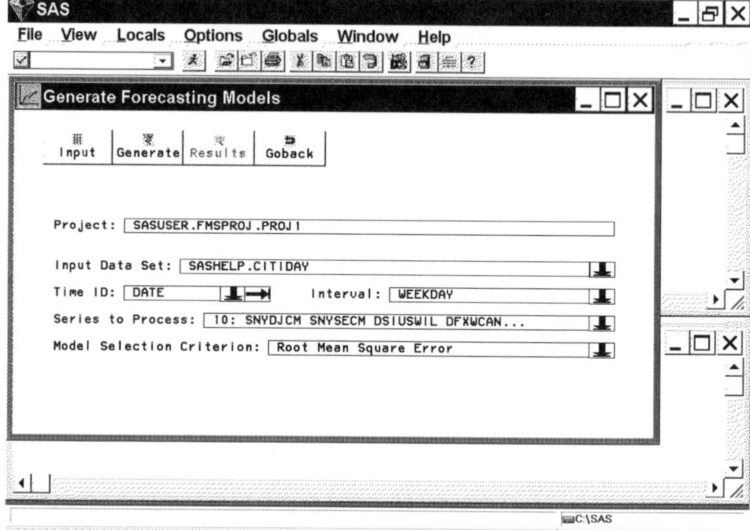

The `Series to Process` field shows the number and lists the names of the variables in the input data set for which models will be fit. By default, all numeric variables (except the time ID variable) are processed. You can specify that models be generated for only a subset of these variables.

Select the control arrow at the right of the `Series to Process` field. This brings up the Series to Process window, shown in Display 29.4.

Display 29.4
Series to Process Window

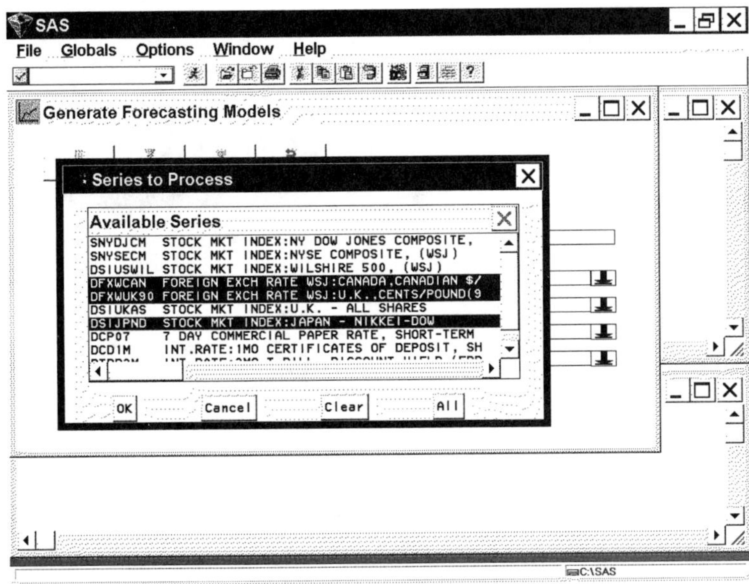

Display 29.4 shows the Series to Process window with three series selected. In this example, you select DFXWCAN and DFXWUK90, two exchange rate series, and DSIJPND, the Nikkei-Dow stock market index series. Select OK to complete your selection and return to the Generate Forecasting Models window.

The **`Model Selection Criterion`** field shows the goodness-of-fit measure that the system will use to select the best fitting model for each series. By default, the selection criterion is the root mean square error. However, you can control the selection criterion.

Select the control arrow to the right of the **`Model Selection Criterion`** field in the Generate Forecasting Models window (see Display 29.3). This brings up the Model Selection Criterion window, shown in Display 29.5, which contains a list of statistics of fit.

Display 29.5
Model Selection Criterion Window

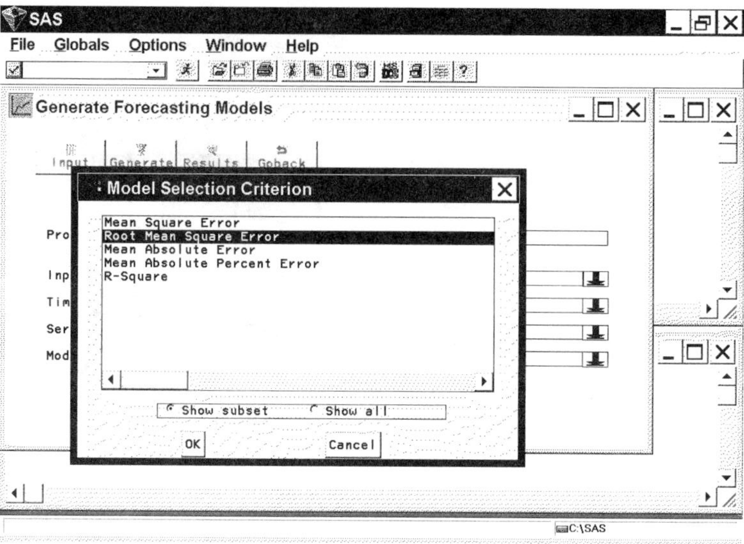

You can click on a different selection criterion from the Model Selection Criterion window. After you make a selection, select OK to complete your selection and return to the Generate Forecasting Models window.

When you have all the options set appropriately, you can start the estimation process for the automatic models. Select Generate at the top of the Generate Forecasting Models window (see Display 29.3) to generate the models.

The Time Series Forecasting System displays a notice to confirm that you want to fit models for the number of series you specified in the Generate Forecasting Models window. Select OK if you want to continue with the model generation process, or select Cancel to return to the Generate Forecasting Models window.

The system now fits several forecasting models to each of the series you selected. While the models are being fit, the system displays notices to indicate what it is doing so that you can observe its progress.

For each series, the system saves the model that produces the best value of the model selection criterion that you selected. You can have the system save all the models that it fits by selecting `Automatic Fit` from the `Options` pull-down menu.

After the model-fitting process is complete, the results are displayed in the Generate Models Results window, shown in Display 29.6.

Display 29.6
Generate Models Results Window

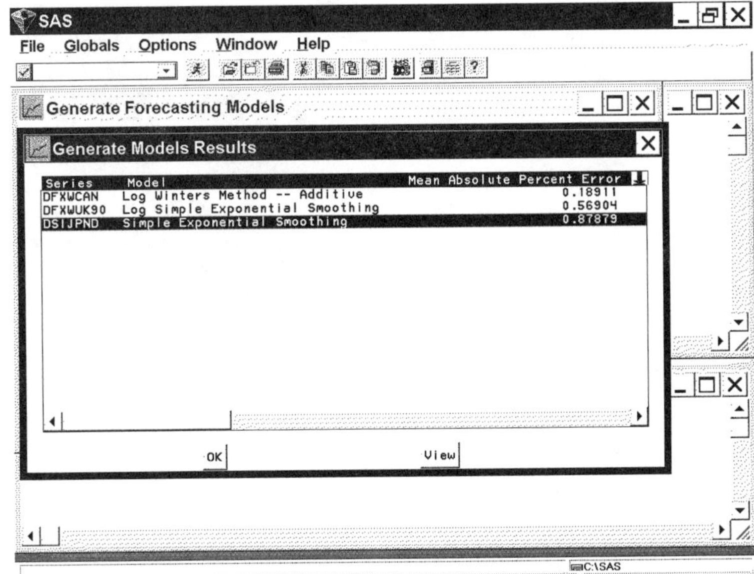

Display 29.6 shows the list of series names and descriptive labels for the forecasting models chosen for them. Select OK to return to the Generate Forecasting Models window. You can now generate models for other series in this data set or change to a different data set and generate models for series in the new data set.

Select Goback from the Generate Forecasting Models window (see Display 29.3) to return to the Time Series Forecasting System main window.

Producing Forecasts

After you generate models, you can use the Time Series Forecasting System to produce forecasts for the models.

Select Produce Forecasts from the Time Series Forecasting System main window. This brings up the Produce Forecasts window, shown in Display 29.7.

Display 29.7
Produce Forecasts Window

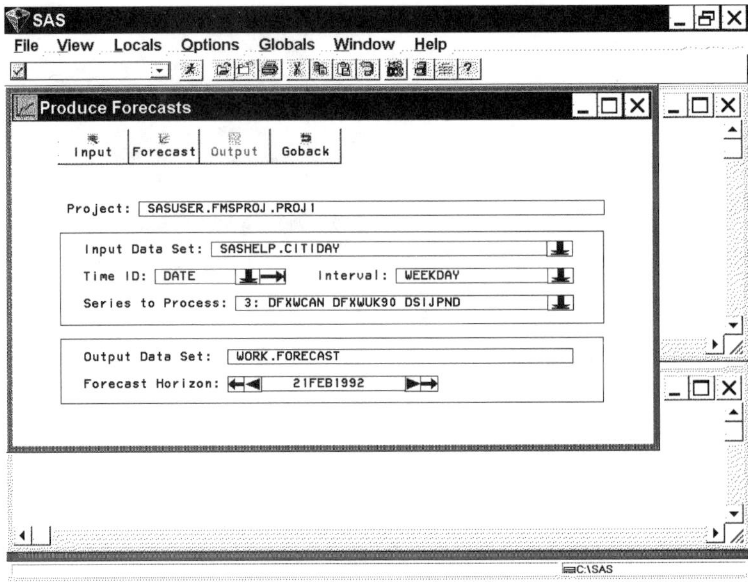

The Produce Forecasts window shows the input data set information and indicates the variables in the input data set for which forecasting models exist. Forecasts will be produced for these series. If you want to produce forecasts for only some of these series, use the control arrow at the right of the `Series to Process` field to select the series to forecast.

The `Output Data Set` field contains the name of the SAS data set in which the system will store the forecasts. The default output data set is WORK.FORECAST.

The `Forecast Horizon` field shows the date of the last forecast period. By default, this is set to a fixed number of periods from the date of the last observation in the input data set. To change the forecast horizon, position the cursor in the field and type in a new date, or click on the arrows at either end of the field.

Select [Forecast] to produce the forecasts. The system displays a notice to indicate that the forecasts have been stored in the output data set. Select [OK] to dismiss this notice.

The Time Series Forecasting System can save the forecasts to a SAS data set in three different formats. The output data set format is controlled by the `Forecast Data Set` option in the `Options` pull-down menu or the menu bar. You can select the following output formats. The simple format is the default.

`Simple`

The data set contains time ID variables and the forecast variables, and it contains one observation per time period. Observations for earlier time periods contain actual values copied from the input data set; later observations contain the forecasts.

`Interleaved`

The data set contains time ID variables, the variable TYPE, and the forecast variables. There are several observations per time period, with the meaning of each observation identified by the TYPE variable.

`Concatenated`

The data set contains the variable SERIES, time ID variables, and the variables ACTUAL, PREDICT, ERROR, UPPER, LOWER and STD. There is one observation per time period per forecast series. The variable SERIES contains the name of the forecast series. The data set is sorted by SERIES and DATE.

Producing Forecasts in Simple Format

To see the simple format forecast data set, select Output from the top of the Produce Forecasts window. This brings up an FSVIEW window to display the data set, shown in Display 29.8.

By default, the Time Series Forecasting System displays the simple format forecast data set in an FSVIEW window.

Display 29.8
Forecast Data Set - Simple Format

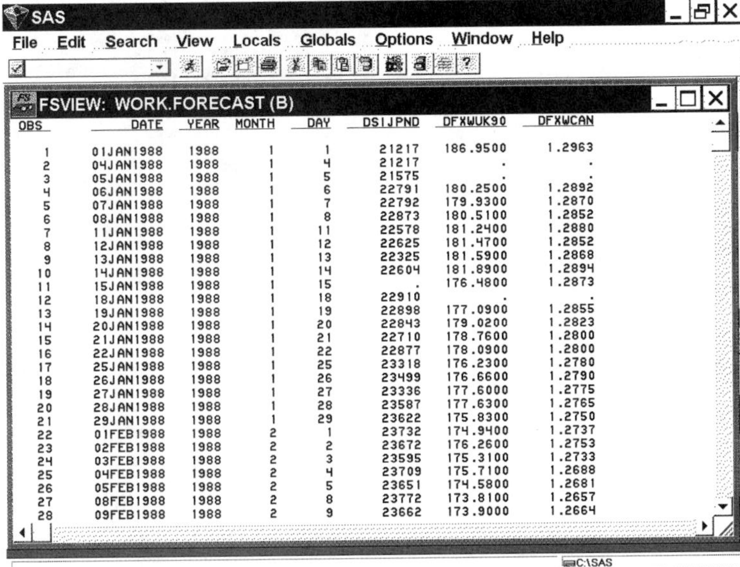

OBS	DATE	YEAR	MONTH	DAY	DSIJPND	DFXWUK90	DFXWCAN
1	01JAN1988	1988	1	1	21217	186.9500	1.2963
2	04JAN1988	1988	1	4	21217	.	.
3	05JAN1988	1988	1	5	21575	.	.
4	06JAN1988	1988	1	6	22791	180.2500	1.2892
5	07JAN1988	1988	1	7	22792	179.9300	1.2870
6	08JAN1988	1988	1	8	22873	180.5100	1.2852
7	11JAN1988	1988	1	11	22578	181.2400	1.2880
8	12JAN1988	1988	1	12	22625	181.4700	1.2852
9	13JAN1988	1988	1	13	22325	181.5900	1.2868
10	14JAN1988	1988	1	14	22604	181.8900	1.2894
11	15JAN1988	1988	1	15	.	176.4800	1.2873
12	18JAN1988	1988	1	18	22910	.	.
13	19JAN1988	1988	1	19	22898	177.0900	1.2855
14	20JAN1988	1988	1	20	22843	179.0200	1.2823
15	21JAN1988	1988	1	21	22710	178.7600	1.2800
16	22JAN1988	1988	1	22	22877	178.0900	1.2800
17	25JAN1988	1988	1	25	23318	176.2300	1.2780
18	26JAN1988	1988	1	26	23499	176.6600	1.2790
19	27JAN1988	1988	1	27	23336	177.6000	1.2775
20	28JAN1988	1988	1	28	23587	177.6300	1.2765
21	29JAN1988	1988	1	29	23622	175.8300	1.2750
22	01FEB1988	1988	2	1	23732	174.9400	1.2737
23	02FEB1988	1988	2	2	23672	176.2600	1.2753
24	03FEB1988	1988	2	3	23595	175.3100	1.2733
25	04FEB1988	1988	2	4	23709	175.7100	1.2688
26	05FEB1988	1988	2	5	23651	174.5800	1.2681
27	08FEB1988	1988	2	8	23772	173.8100	1.2657
28	09FEB1988	1988	2	9	23662	173.9000	1.2664

Select **End** from the **File** pull-down menu to close the FSVIEW window.

Producing Forecasts in Interleaved Format

From the Produce Forecasts window, select **Options** from the menu bar; then select **Forecast Data Set** and then **Interleaved** as the option value. Now select [Forecast] again. The system displays a warning notice that the data set WORK.FORECAST already exists. Select [Replace] from this notice to replace the data set.

The forecasts are stored in the data set WORK.FORECAST again, this time in the interleaved format. Dismiss the notice that the forecast was stored.

Select [Output] to bring up an FSVIEW window to display the data set, shown in Display 29.9.

Display 29.9
Forecast Data Set - Interleaved Format

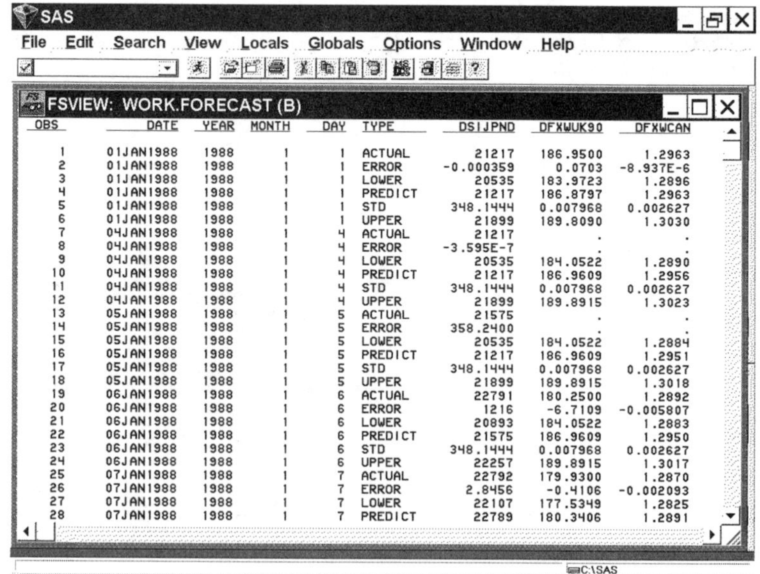

OBS	DATE	YEAR	MONTH	DAY	TYPE	DSIJPND	DFXWUK90	DFXWCAN
1	01JAN1988	1988	1	1	ACTUAL	21217	186.9500	1.2963
2	01JAN1988	1988	1	1	ERROR	-0.000359	0.0703	-8.937E-6
3	01JAN1988	1988	1	1	LOWER	20535	183.9723	1.2896
4	01JAN1988	1988	1	1	PREDICT	21217	186.8797	1.2963
5	01JAN1988	1988	1	1	STD	348.1444	0.007968	0.002627
6	01JAN1988	1988	1	1	UPPER	21899	189.8090	1.3030
7	04JAN1988	1988	1	4	ACTUAL	21217	.	.
8	04JAN1988	1988	1	4	ERROR	-3.595E-7	.	.
9	04JAN1988	1988	1	4	LOWER	20535	184.0522	1.2890
10	04JAN1988	1988	1	4	PREDICT	21217	186.9609	1.2956
11	04JAN1988	1988	1	4	STD	348.1444	0.007968	0.002627
12	04JAN1988	1988	1	4	UPPER	21899	189.8915	1.3023
13	05JAN1988	1988	1	5	ACTUAL	21575	.	.
14	05JAN1988	1988	1	5	ERROR	358.2400	.	.
15	05JAN1988	1988	1	5	LOWER	20535	184.0522	1.2884
16	05JAN1988	1988	1	5	PREDICT	21217	186.9609	1.2951
17	05JAN1988	1988	1	5	STD	348.1444	0.007968	0.002627
18	05JAN1988	1988	1	5	UPPER	21899	189.8915	1.3018
19	06JAN1988	1988	1	6	ACTUAL	22791	180.2500	1.2892
20	06JAN1988	1988	1	6	ERROR	1216	-6.7109	-0.005807
21	06JAN1988	1988	1	6	LOWER	20893	184.0522	1.2883
22	06JAN1988	1988	1	6	PREDICT	21575	186.9609	1.2950
23	06JAN1988	1988	1	6	STD	348.1444	0.007968	0.002627
24	06JAN1988	1988	1	6	UPPER	22257	189.8915	1.3017
25	07JAN1988	1988	1	7	ACTUAL	22792	179.9300	1.2870
26	07JAN1988	1988	1	7	ERROR	2.8456	-0.4106	-0.002093
27	07JAN1988	1988	1	7	LOWER	22107	177.5349	1.2825
28	07JAN1988	1988	1	7	PREDICT	22789	180.3406	1.2891

In Display 29.9, observations with the value of **PREDICT** for the TYPE variable contain the predicted values from the forecasting model. These predicted values are listed under the forecast variables. These are within-sample one-step-ahead predictions for observations within the historical period or multistep predictions for observations within the forecast period.

Select **End** from the **File** pull-down menu to close the FSVIEW window.

Producing Forecasts in Concatenated Format

Select **Options** and **Forecast Data Set**, and set the Forecast Data Set option to **Concatenated**. Re-create the forecast data set, and then select [Output]. This brings up an FSVIEW window that shows the forecast output data set in concatenated format, as shown in Display 29.10. Use the scroll bar at the bottom of the FSVIEW window to scroll the display to see the variables not currently visible.

Display 29.10
Forecast Data Set - Concatenated Format

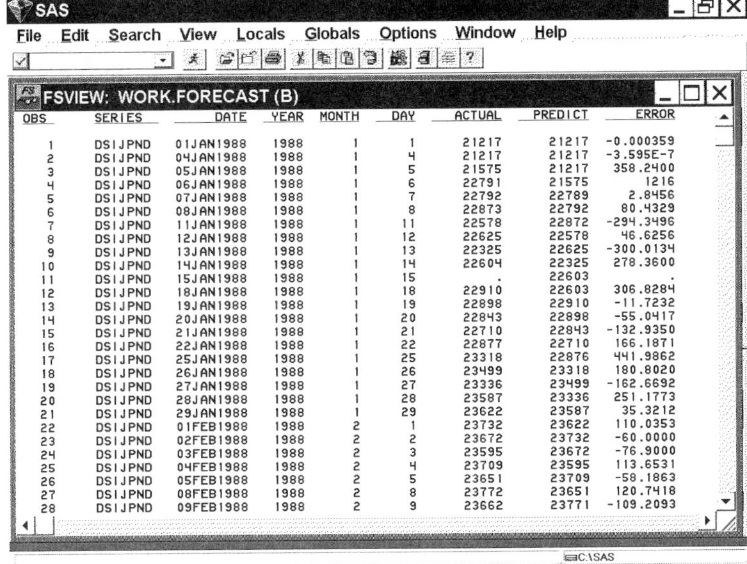

OBS	SERIES	DATE	YEAR	MONTH	DAY	ACTUAL	PREDICT	ERROR
1	DSIJPND	01JAN1988	1988	1	1	21217	21217	-0.000359
2	DSIJPND	04JAN1988	1988	1	4	21217	21217	-3.595E-7
3	DSIJPND	05JAN1988	1988	1	5	21575	21217	358.2400
4	DSIJPND	06JAN1988	1988	1	6	22791	21575	1216
5	DSIJPND	07JAN1988	1988	1	7	22792	22789	2.8456
6	DSIJPND	08JAN1988	1988	1	8	22873	22792	80.4329
7	DSIJPND	11JAN1988	1988	1	11	22578	22872	-294.3496
8	DSIJPND	12JAN1988	1988	1	12	22625	22578	46.6256
9	DSIJPND	13JAN1988	1988	1	13	22325	22625	-300.0134
10	DSIJPND	14JAN1988	1988	1	14	22604	22325	278.3600
11	DSIJPND	15JAN1988	1988	1	15	.	22603	.
12	DSIJPND	18JAN1988	1988	1	18	22910	22603	306.8284
13	DSIJPND	19JAN1988	1988	1	19	22898	22910	-11.7232
14	DSIJPND	20JAN1988	1988	1	20	22843	22898	-55.0417
15	DSIJPND	21JAN1988	1988	1	21	22710	22843	-132.9350
16	DSIJPND	22JAN1988	1988	1	22	22877	22710	166.1871
17	DSIJPND	25JAN1988	1988	1	25	23318	22876	441.9862
18	DSIJPND	26JAN1988	1988	1	26	23499	23318	180.8020
19	DSIJPND	27JAN1988	1988	1	27	23336	23499	-162.6692
20	DSIJPND	28JAN1988	1988	1	28	23587	23336	251.1773
21	DSIJPND	29JAN1988	1988	1	29	23622	23587	35.3212
22	DSIJPND	01FEB1988	1988	2	1	23732	23622	110.0353
23	DSIJPND	02FEB1988	1988	2	2	23672	23732	-60.0000
24	DSIJPND	03FEB1988	1988	2	3	23595	23672	-76.9000
25	DSIJPND	04FEB1988	1988	2	4	23709	23595	113.6531
26	DSIJPND	05FEB1988	1988	2	5	23651	23709	-58.1863
27	DSIJPND	08FEB1988	1988	2	8	23772	23651	120.7418
28	DSIJPND	09FEB1988	1988	2	9	23662	23771	-109.2093

The variable PREDICT contains within-sample one-step-ahead predictions for observations within the historical period or multistep predictions for observations within the forecast period.

Select **End** from the **File** pull-down menu to close the FSVIEW window.

Further Reading

For more information on the Time Series Forecasting System, see *SAS/ETS Software: Time Series Forecasting System, Version 6, First Edition.*

EXAMPLE 30

Developing Forecasting Models Using the Time Series Forecasting System

Featured Tool:

- Time Series Forecasting System

The previous example showed how to use the Time Series Forecasting System in a fully automated mode to produce automatic forecasts of multiple time series. This example shows how you can use the Time Series Forecasting System to work with one time series at a time to fit forecasting models and choose the best forecasting model for a given series.

This example uses the USECON and CITIMON data sets from the SASHELP library.

Invoking the Time Series Forecasting System

You can invoke the Time Series Forecasting System in the following ways:

- If you use the SAS Display Manager System with pull-down menus, pull down the `Globals` menu from the menu bar, select the `Analyze` item, and then select `Forecasting`.
- If you use the display manager with a command line, enter the command `forecast` on the command line.
- If you use SAS/ASSIST software, select FORECASTING in the SAS/ASSIST `Planning Tools` menu.

Any of these methods brings up the Time Series Forecasting System main window, as shown in Display 30.1.

Display 30.1
Time Series Forecasting System Main Window

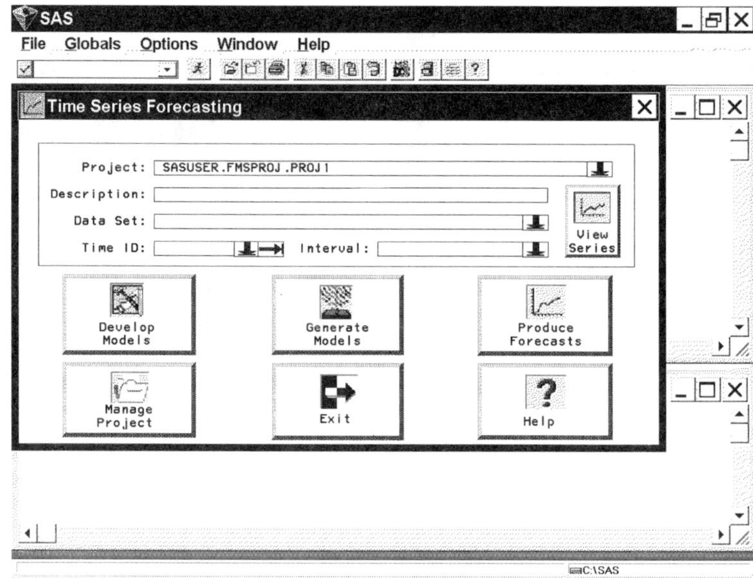

Developing Time Series Models Interactively

Specifying the Time Series to Process

Select the control arrow at the right of the `Data Set` field to bring up the Data Set Selection window. Select **`SASHELP`** from the **`Libraries`** selection list. Then select **`USECON`** from the **`SAS Data Sets`** list. After you choose the data set, select [OK] to complete your selection and return to the Time Series Forecasting main window.

In the Data Set Selection window, you select the USECON data set from the SASHELP library. This data set contains monthly data on the U.S. economy.

From the Time Series Forecasting System main window, select [Develop Models]. This brings up the Series Selection window, as shown in Display 30.2.

Display 30.2
Series Selection Window

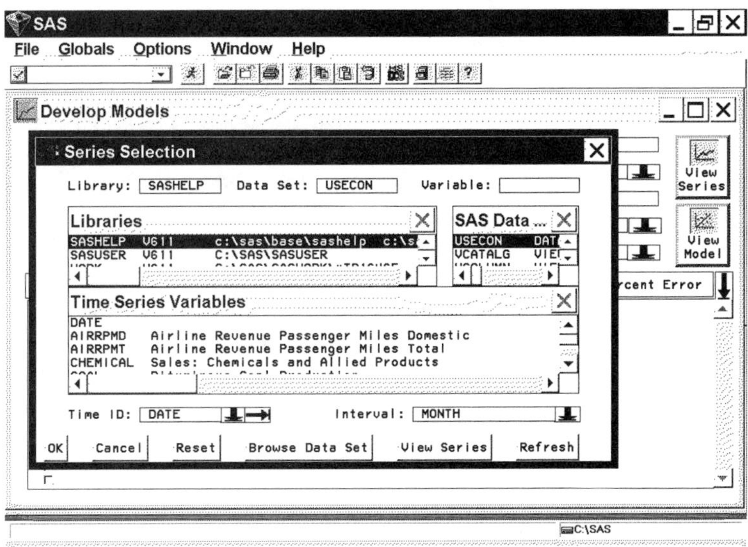

Select the series **CHEMICAL Sales: Chemicals and Allied Products**. When you select OK, you complete your selection of the time series and bring up the Develop Models window, as shown in Display 30.3.

Description of the Develop Models Window

Display 30.3
Develop Models Window

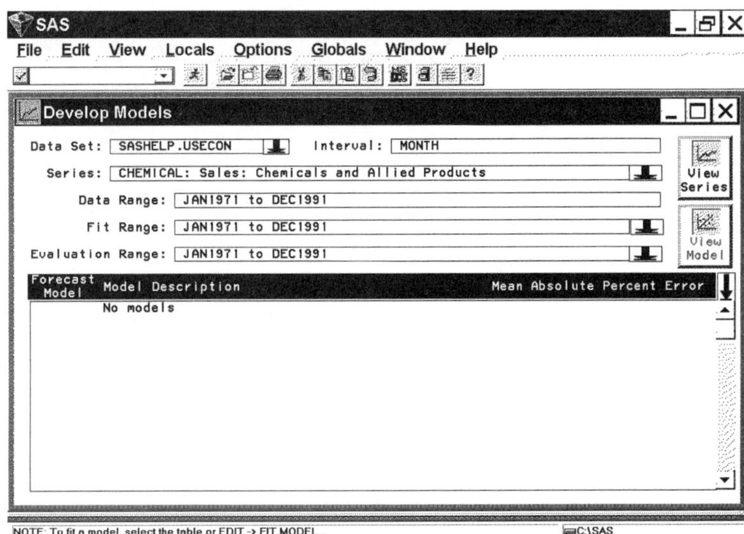

The **Data Set**, **Interval**, and **Series** fields in the upper part of the Develop Models window indicate the series with which you are currently working. The **Data Range**, **Fit Range**, and **Evaluation Range** fields show the time period over which data are available for the current series and what parts of that time period will be used to fit forecasting models to the series and to evaluate how well the models fit the data. You can change the settings of the fields by selecting the control arrows to the right of the fields.

The bottom part of the Develop Models window consists of a list of forecasting models to fit to the series. Initially, the list is empty, as indicated by the message **No models**. You can fit any number of forecasting models to each series and designate which of them you want to use to produce forecasts.

Choosing a Method to Fit Models

Select **Fit Model** from the **Edit** pull-down menu to display a menu of model-fitting choices. You can also click on a blank line in the list of models to access the same menu, shown in Display 30.4.

Display 30.4
Menu of Model-Fitting Choices

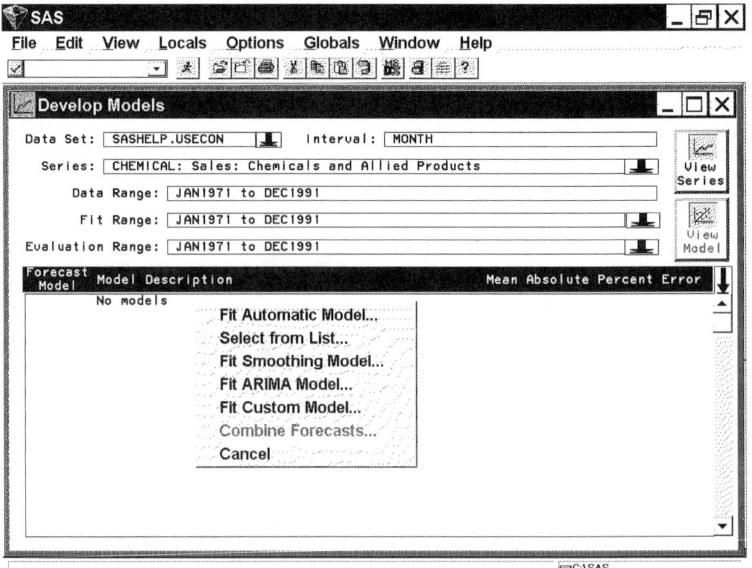

You have several different ways to develop your own forecasting models in the Time Series Forecasting System. The following model-fitting choices are available on the menu:

`Fit Automatic Model`
: performs the same automatic model selection process that the Generate Forecasting Models window performs. See Example 29, "Producing Forecasts Automatically Using the Time Series Forecasting System," for details on this process.

`Select from List`
: displays the Models to Fit window, which presents a list of commonly used forecasting models for convenient point-and-click selection.

`Fit Smoothing Model`
: displays the Smoothing Model Specification window, which enables you to specify many different kinds of exponential smoothing models as well as Winters method forecasting models.

`Fit ARIMA Model`
: displays the ARIMA Model Specification window, which enables you to specify many different kinds of autoregressive integrated moving average (ARIMA) models, including seasonal ARIMA models and ARIMA models with regressors, transfer functions, and other predictors.

`Fit Custom Model`
: displays the Custom Model Specification window, which enables you to construct a forecasting model by specifying separate options for transforming the data, modeling the trend, modeling seasonality, modeling autocorrelation of the errors, and modeling the effect of regressors and other independent predictors.

`Combine Forecasts`
: displays the Forecast Combination Model Specification window, which enables you to specify models that produce forecasts by combining, or averaging, the forecasts from other models. (This option is not available unless you have fit at least two models.)

Fitting a Predefined Model

Select `Select from List` from the menu of model-fitting choices (see Display 30.4) to bring up the Models to Fit window, shown in Display 30.5.

Display 30.5
Models to Fit Window

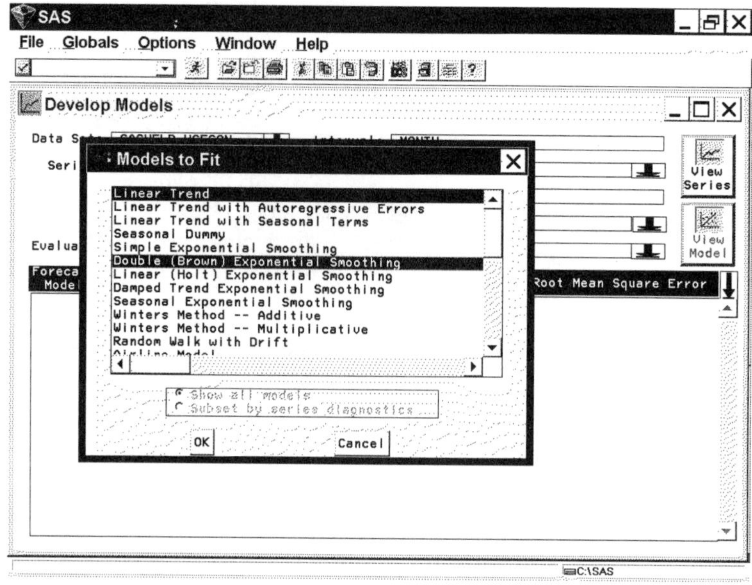

The Models to Fit window lists models that can be fit through either the ARIMA Model Specification or the Smoothing Model Specification windows. The advantage of using the Models to Fit window is that you can click on the model you want without defining it explicitly, as you would need to do in the ARIMA Model Specification window or the Smoothing Model Specification window.

Select **`Linear Trend`** and **`Double (Brown) Exponential Smoothing`** from the list of models. To begin the estimation process for the models, select OK after you choose the models.

Display 30.5 shows the Models to Fit window with two models selected. After the models are fit, the labels of the two models and their goodness-of-fit statistic are added to the model list in the Develop Models window, as shown in Display 30.6.

Display 30.6
Fitted Models List in Develop Models Window

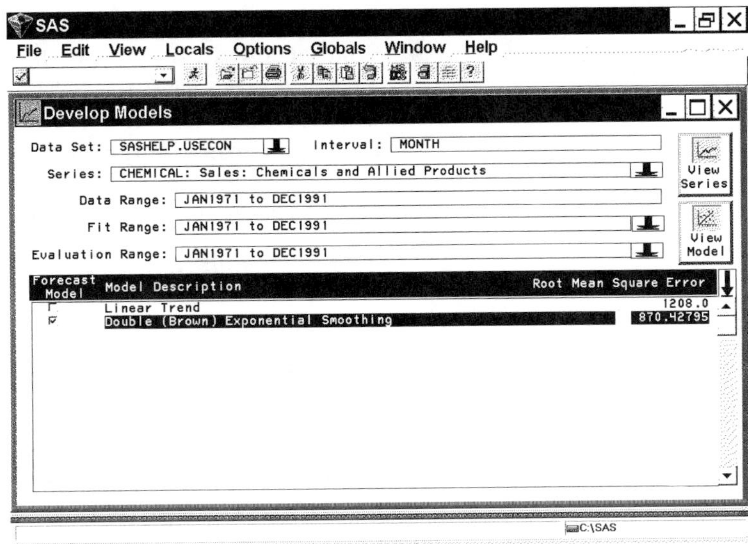

The model list in the Develop Models window contains three columns:

- The left column, labeled **`Forecast Model`**, consists of check boxes that indicate which one of the models in the list is selected as the model to use to produce the forecasts for the series. The system selects the one model with the best fit, as measured by the selected goodness-of-fit statistic, as the forecast model. To choose a different model as the forecast model, select its Forecast Model button.
- The column labeled **`Model Description`** shows the descriptive labels for the fitted models.
- The column labeled **`Root Mean Square Error`** shows the goodness-of-fit statistic used to decide which model fits best. You can use a different goodness-of-fit statistic. Select the control arrow to the right of the column heading for the statistics to bring up the Model Selection Criterion window, which was described in Example 29 and shown in Display 29.5.

Fitting a Smoothing Model

The sections that describe the Smoothing Model Specification window and the ARIMA Model Specification window use the RCARD series from the CITIMON data set in the SASHELP library. This series represents domestic retail sales of passenger cars. Return to the Time Series Forecasting System main window to start this part of the example.

Select [Develop Models] from the Time Series Forecasting System main window (see Display 30.1). This brings up the Series Selection window (see Display 30.2). Select **SASHELP** from the **Libraries** list. Select **CITIMON** from the **SAS Data Sets** list. Then select **RCARD** from the **Time Series Variables** list.

Select **Fit Smoothing Model** from the menu of model-fitting choices (see Display 30.4) to bring up the Smoothing Model Specification window, shown in Display 30.7.

Display 30.7
Smoothing Model Specification Window

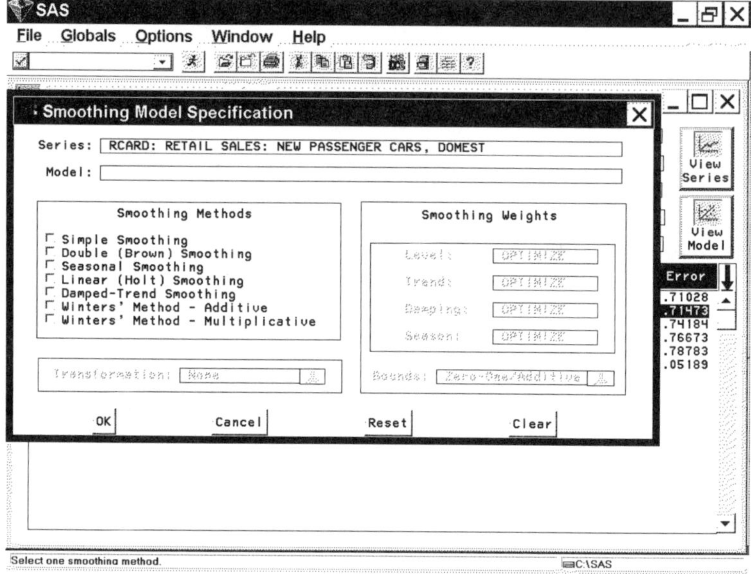

The Smoothing Model Specification window enables you to specify a smoothing method, a transformation, smoothing weights, and bounds for the smoothing weights for the time series named at the top of the window.

Select [OK] to fit the smoothing model you specify in this window and to return to the Develop Models window. The model is added to the list of fitted models in the Develop Models window.

Fitting an ARIMA Model

Select **Fit ARIMA Model** from the menu of model-fitting choices (see Display 30.4) to bring up the ARIMA Model Specification window, shown in Display 30.8.

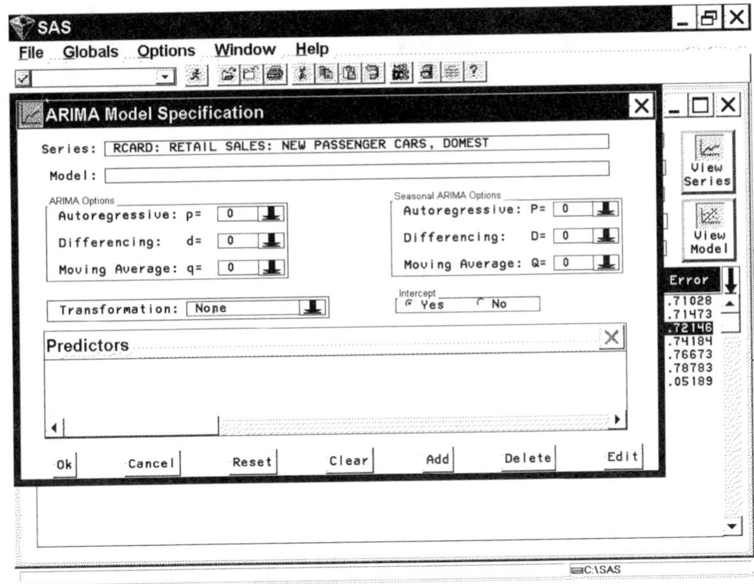

Display 30.8
ARIMA Model Specification Window

The ARIMA Model Specification window enables you to specify nonseasonal and seasonal ARIMA factors, a transformation, an intercept, and predictors for the time series named at the top of the window.

Select OK to fit the ARIMA model you specify in this window and to return to the Develop Models window. The model is added to the list of fitted models in the Develop Models window.

Using Graphical Features of the System

At the upper right of the Develop Models window are two buttons, View Series and View Model. These buttons bring up interactive graphical tools to view the data and display information about the fit of forecasting models.

Select View Series from the Develop Models window to bring up the Time Series Viewer window, shown in Display 30.9.

Display 30.9
Time Series Viewer Window

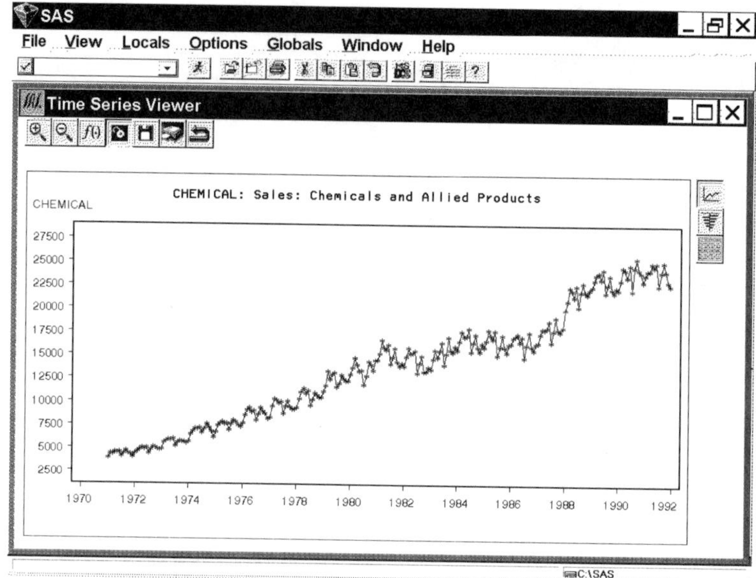

Icons in the vertical toolbar on the right side of the Time Series Viewer window also enable you to view

- plots of the sample autocorrelations
- a listing of the complete input data set.

The Time Series Viewer appears in a separate resizable window. You can leave the Time Series Viewer window up while you work in other parts of the Time Series Forecasting System.

To close the Time Series Viewer window, select **`End`** from the **`File`** pull-down menu, or select the last button in the horizontal toolbar.

Select [View Model] from the Develop Models window to bring up the Model Viewer window, shown in Display 30.10. You must first have selected a model from the list of fitted models in the Develop Models window.

Display 30.10
Model Viewer Window

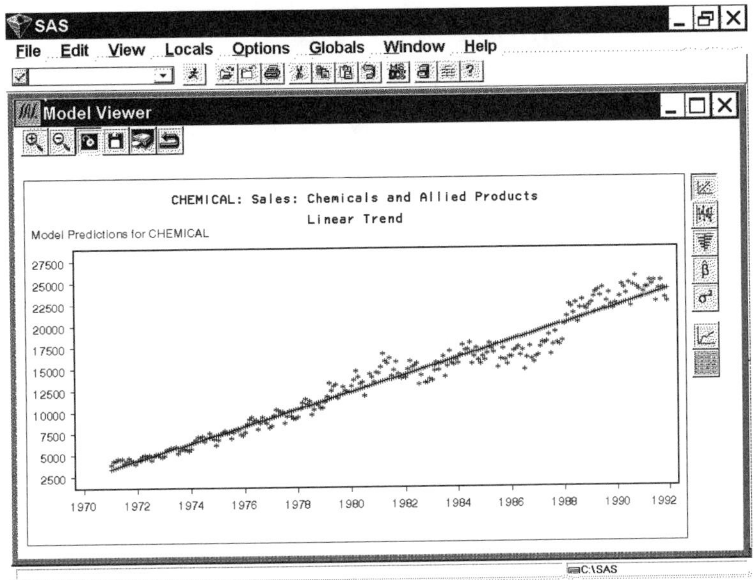

The Model Viewer window displays a plot of model predictions when you first bring it up. The icons in the vertical toolbar on the right side of the Model Viewer window also enable you to view

- □ a plot of prediction errors
- □ plots of residual autocorrelations
- □ a list of parameter estimates
- □ a list of statistics of fit
- □ a plot of forecasts with confidence limits
- □ a listing of the complete forecast data set.

To close the window, select **`End`** from the **`File`** pull-down menu, or select the last button in the horizontal toolbar.

Further Reading

For more information on the Time Series Forecasting System, see *SAS/ETS Software: Time Series Forecasting System, Version 6, First Edition.*

Index

N

S

U

V